THE JOY OF MUSIC IN MATURITY

· Joan Shaw ·

MMB MUSIC, INC.

THE JOY OF MUSIC IN MATURITY
Innovative Programs for Seniors

Joan Shaw, RMT-BC

LIBRARY OF CONGRESS CATOLOGING-IN-PUBLICATION DATA

Shaw, Joan.
  The joy of music in maturity : innovative programs for seniors / Joan Shaw
  488 p. 21.3 x 27.5
  Includes bibliographical references (pp. 485-487)
  ISBN 0-918812-80-1
  1. Music therapy for the aged.
ML3920.S425 1993
362.6--dc20

Editors: Carl Simpson and Elizabeth Susskind
Typesetter: Elizabeth Susskind
Cover design: Linda Brown
Graphics (music menus, visual aids, songsheets, promotional pages, musical games): Linda Brown
Music examples: Randy Scheffel, Inland Sea Music, Green Bay, WI
Printer: Patterson Printing, Benton Harbor, MI
First printing: October 1993
Printed in USA

DEDICATION

*Dedicated to YOU, the activator, because only you can make
these programs come alive for yourself and our older adults.
May the ideas spark your own creativity.*

ABOUT THE AUTHOR

Joan Shaw, a registered music therapist, was a clinician at Delmar Gardens on the Green Nursing Center in St. Louis Missouri for eleven years. She presently teaches on the faculty of Maryville University where she is the Assistant Director of Music Therapy. She is well known for her presentations on geriatric programming at local and national conferences. Her students are already utilizing and adapting these programs throughout the St. Louis area.

This 1955 Senior of the Year at Michigan State University has used her talents with the seniors she loves the most, our elderly population. Joan was an early pioneer in the profession. She completed her internship at Topeka State Hospital and was the first activity therapist at the Champaign County Nursing Home in Urbana, Illinois.

Joan and her husband Roger are actively involved in music in the St. Louis area and delight in entertaining older residents. They both perform with a symphony orchestra, string quartet, jazz band, and a barbershop quartet. Joan plays piano, viola, and sings. Her three children are all musical and enjoy singing four part harmony whenever they get together.

She is the author of the *Color Key Songbook for Children* used nationally by Unity churches. In addition she is in constant demand for her song leadership workshops and ragtime presentations. Her spare moments are with the mountains, the garden, cats and more music. Her book reflects the joy of growing older with music as a close friend.

ACKNOWLEDGEMENTS

This author is grateful to her husband, Roger, for his faith in her, his patience teaching her word processing, and most of his advice. She appreciates all the music in ye olde piano bench that her mother, Ida, nurtured years ago. Thanks also go to Joel Baehr, a Unity minister who sizzles with zeal and inspires many. Her children, Bev, Martha and Gordon deserve applause for their continued singing of these songs. Finally, bouquets of thanks to the residents, staff, volunteers and families of Delmar Gardens on the Green Nursing Center in St. Louis and the music therapy students at Maryville University.

TABLE OF CONTENTS

PART ONE: PURPOSE AND PREPARATION

CHAPTER ONE

Introduction...3
Purpose..3
Rationale and Goals..3
Rationale for Monthly Programming 6
Music Therapy Works...7
Joy of Organization..8
Expanding Your Staff..8
Publicizing Your Theme..9
Cost and Equipment 10
Size of the Group Session 12

CHAPTER TWO

Format of the Program...15
Extensions of the Program...23

PART TWO: MONTHLY PROGRAMS

The following programs for music therapy sessions are listed with a monthly theme and followed by the specific session title of the week. Optional holiday and music programs are also included, to be used if appropriate. All include a related music menu, some include music selections, large print songsheets, and visual aids.

JANUARY THEME – CRUISING THROUGH JANUARY

Promotional Sheet..29
Musical Game...30
Introduction..31

Program 1.   Hawaii Bids You Welcome 32
Program 2.   A Trip to Sunny Italy......................................37
Program 3.   There's Joy in Germany 47
Program 4.   South America Take It Away................................53

Optional: New Year's Day - Everything's Coming Up Roses 59

FEBRUARY THEME – IT'S A LOVE-LY MONTH

Promotional Sheet 65
Musical Game 66
Introduction 67

Program 1.   I Love You and Me 68
Program 2.   It's Valentine Love 73
Program 3.   Love Those Ladies 81
Program 4.   Love Those Stouthearted Men 87
Program 5.   Everyone Loves a Smile 93

Optional: Ground-Hog Day 99
               Presidents' Day - Hail to the Chiefs 105

MARCH THEME – IT'S A COLORFUL WORLD

Promotional Sheet 111
Musical Game 112
Introduction 113

Program 1.   Bye Bye Blues 114
Program 2.   In the Pink 119
Program 3.   It's Not Easy Being Green 127
Program 4.   Hello Yellow 133
Program 5.   Lavender and Old Lace 141

Optional: March into Spring 147

APRIL THEME – IT'S A SENSE-SATIONAL MONTH

Promotional Sheet 149
Musical Game 150
Introduction 151

Program 1.   Hear Ye, Hear Ye 152
Program 2.   How's Your Taste, Bud? 157
Program 3.   Seeing is Believing 163
Program 4.   Reach Out and Touch 169
Program 5.   Stop and Smell the Roses 175

Optional: Easter Parade 180

MAY THEME - WELCOME SWEET SPRINGTIME

      Promotional Sheet 183
      Musical Game 184
      Introduction 185

Program 1.   Spring has Sprung 186
Program 2.   Planting More Than Seeds 191
Program 3.   Let's All Sing Like the Birdies Sing 197
Program 4.   Flower Power 203

Optional: Mother's Day - Universal Mothers Unite 209
           Memorial Day - Memorable Memorial Day 215

JUNE THEME - CELEBRATIONS

      Promotional Sheet 219
      Musical Game 220
      Introduction 221

Program 1.   Graduation Now and Then 222
Program 2.   Dads Are Dandy 227
Program 3.   Here Comes the Groom 233
Program 4.   Take Me Out to the Ball Game 239

Optional: Flag Day - It's a Grand Old Flag 245

JULY THEME - AMERICA, THE BEAUTIFUL

      Promotional Sheet 251
      Musical Game 252
      Introduction 253

Program 1.   Our History in Song 254
Program 2.   They Fought for Freedom 259
Program 3.   North, South, East, West 265
Program 4.   My Hometown 271

Optional: Go Forth On the Fourth of July - In-House Parade 279

AUGUST THEME - IN THE GOOD OLD SUMMER TIME

Promotional Sheet 285
Musical Game 286
Introduction 287

Program 1.   Porches were Precious 288
Program 2.   Ye Olde Fashioned Piano Recital 293
Program 3.   Oh You Beautiful Doll 299
Program 4.   Animal Friends 305
Program 5.   Ice Cream - It's Cool 311

SEPTEMBER THEME - OLD FASHIONED FAVORITES

Promotional Sheet 317
Musical Game 318
Introduction 319

Program 1.   A Labor of Love 320
Program 2.   Dear Old School Days 325
Program 3.   Styles Up to the Ankle 333
Program 4.   Give Me That Old Time Religion 339
Program 5.   You Auto Remember Your Automobile 345

Optional: Ragtime Review 351

OCTOBER THEME - HEALTH IS CONTAGIOUS

Promotional Sheet 357
Musical Game 358
Introduction 359

Program 1.   Healthy Food 360
Program 2.   Healthy Hands 367
Program 3.   Healthy Heart 373
Program 4.   Healthy Bones 379
Program 5.   Healthy Fun 385

Optional: A Healthy Halloween 391

NOVEMBER THEME - A MONTH OF PRAISE

Promotional Sheet 397
Musical Game 398
Introduction 399

Program 1.   Praise for Autumn 400
Program 2.   Praise for the Harvest 405
Program 3.   Praise for Thanksliving 411
Program 4.   Praise for Thanksgiving 417

Optional: Praise for Music 425

DECEMBER THEME - HOLIDAY HAPPINESS

Promotional Sheet 431
Musical Game 432
Extra Holiday Fun Game 433
Introduction 435

Program 1.   The Sights of Christmas 437
Program 2.   The Smells of Christmas 443
Program 3.   The Sounds of Christmas 449
Program 4.   The Spirit of Christmas 455
Program 5.   Chanukah - The Festival of Lights 461

Optional: Celebrate Christmas - Five Possibilities 465
               Goodbye Old Year, Hello New 469

PART THREE: INDEX

General Index 477
Song Title Index 481

PART FOUR: RESOURCES

Music Reference List 485
Book Reference List 486
Recommended Resources 487

PART ONE

PURPOSE AND PREPARATION

CHAPTER ONE

INTRODUCTION

It's a cold, wintry day. You open the door to the nursing home and find a warm, bright atmosphere. Much to your surprise, it is an indoor cruise. Soft music is playing and there are many, many smiles. You notice the colorful decorations and attractive posters of the foreign lands. The menu describes that a Hawaiian dinner is planned and you wonder if you can make a reservation for yourself. The large poster announces the itinerary of the cruises and even mentions that there is no cost involved or long lines at the ticket counter. The staff is involved with the theme and you find there is plenty to talk about, not only with your loved one, but with your new acquaintances too. Could this be a nursing facility? You were reluctant to visit and now you end up staying much longer than you had planned. In fact, you wonder where you can sign up for the next week's cruise to sunny Italy.

PURPOSE

The TOTAL ENVIRONMENT is the emphasis of this book. It is written for everyone involved with the older generation including gerontology specialists, music therapists, activities directors, recreation directors and all those desiring to enhance the environment of the elderly with meaningful programs. The programs presented in this book have application for nursing homes, senior citizen and retirement centers, day care centers, geriatric hospital units and other senior settings. It is intended to involve the complete setting including the residents, staff, friends, family and neighborhood. The contents, including 80 complete programs, have all proven highly successful and most valuable in several Saint Louis, Missouri geriatric centers. The results have inspired the author to share the ideas and organization involved.

RATIONALE AND GOALS

As our earthly years accumulate, they should be surrounded with a fine quality of life in a loving environment. This implies more than just a single activity or the visits of loved ones. Whether we spend our years in the privacy of our own homes or in group housing, the impact of the environment needs to be recognized. High functioning adults as well as people stricken with Alzheimer's disease can benefit from surroundings that are well planned.

> Stimulation in the environment affects the growth and connections of the human brain from its earliest critical periods to its last days—its weight, nutrients, the number of cells. Even in the elderly, the physical brain does not lose a measurable number of cells if the environment is stimulating.[1]

Senior settings are becoming more popular as our population ages and enjoys the benefits of extended years. Sometimes disabilities arise and acute care or day care facilities are

---

[1]   Ferguson, M. (1980) *The Aquarian Conspiracy*, p. 256.

needed. With proper planning and cooperation these years can be the best years of our lives. Going to an organized geriatric center with a positive orientation can be a most pleasant experience and add to the enrichment of life.

In his Pulitzer prize winning book, *Why Survive? Being Old In America*, Dr. Robert Butler shared his vision of the new kind of nursing home that would be a growth-promoting environment for both the residents and community:

> A nursing home should provide a social and intellectual climate that makes it possible for the elderly who can and wish to do so to study, grow and enjoy themselves. Individual identity and dignity can be maintained through social contact, presence of familiar possessions and the exercise of personal freedom and choice.[1]

Dr. Butler's vision and goals have been attained realistically in the St. Louis area especially through the use of theme oriented music therapy. The continuity of a monthly theme has helped the elderly focus their attention around a central idea and has given them an opportunity to respond as individuals.

Music has enriched the lives of this planet since its inception. This book will not be a historical treatise on the effects of music. It will be a practical application of the use of music to benefit people. Today, music therapists are professionally trained in this area. With the accumulated knowledge of music and its affects through the centuries, plus our present understanding of knowledge related to affective behaviors, we can apply the principles to enriching the lives of others.

Music therapists enjoy working with people and are specialists in using music to maintain or change behavior. They receive a thorough education both in psychology and music therapy. In addition, the four year college curriculum includes courses in music, sociology and anatomy. They receive considerable experience at clinical sites applying music to reach specific goals and objectives in various facilities such as geriatrics, psychiatric settings, drug rehabilitation centers, schools for the blind, centers for the orthopedically handicapped and general hospitals. Many have had training specifically with Alzheimer patients including activities which involve the families. Following graduation they complete a six month internship in an approved facility. They are then eligible to apply for national membership in the American Association of Music Therapy or the National Association of Music Therapy. Board certification is received upon passing a national exam. The result is a person who cares deeply about others as well as the application of music.

In a geriatric setting with the frequent physical conditions of hearing loss, poor visibility, physical ailments and disabilities, the music therapist meets the needs of the residents with a variety of approaches and skills. Even more importantly, he or she is trained to meet the emotional needs of residents and their families. With considerable experience and a strong desire to work with the elderly, they bring enthusiasm and energy into any setting.

The programs listed here are best implemented by a qualified music therapist although it is possible to adapt them so that they can be utilized by activity directors or volunteers with a strong musical background. The professional will reach many more goals and objectives that can be charted and documented for state and facility reports. Progress in social,

---

1   Butler, R. (1975) *Why Survive? Being Old In America*, p. 295.

psychological and physical behavior will be charted professionally. The following goals will be set:

Psychological Goals
- Improvement of self concept
- Integration of memory with a common theme
- Heightened memory
- Appropriate expression of emotions
- Ability to overcome depression
- Improvement in attitude
- Encouragement of creativity
- Appreciation of life's experiences

Physical Goals
- Pain relief
- Achievement of deep relaxation
- Stimulation of automatic physical responses to the music
- Increased attention span
- Maintenance of music skills
- Sensory stimulation
- Promotion of gross motor movements to rhythmic stimuli
- Provision of mild exercise

Social Goals
- Aid in adjustment to group living
- Increased socialization with staff, family, others
- Expanded communication
- Stimulation of group interaction
- Increased involvement
- Provision of opportunity for good use of leisure time
- Improvement of social status

Educational Goals
- The learning of recent facts
- The lessening of the generation gap
- The continuation of learning

The theme for the month has proven successful for the entire facility. Everyone involved benefits from the creative planning, participation, and exchange of ideas from the residents, family, friends, staff and even the community. Activity and program directors have a broad, general theme and then choose related activities and entertainment. For example, An Indoor Cruise for the entire month of January is a pleasure to plan and anticipate after the Christmas holidays. It is a theme with variations. Anyone missing the cruise to Hawaii one week can catch the next one to South America. The center is decorated appropriately and the dietician enjoys planning a few meals using foreign foods. Music of the country is played and residents share their experiences and memories of that area. Visitors have more to talk about and find it hard to believe they are in a nursing home.

RATIONALE FOR MONTHLY PROGRAMMING

The Residents – first, we need programs that serve the needs of the residents. The staff is hired not only to serve the physical needs but also the emotional and social needs. Many gerontology books have been written stressing these various factors. The following list of objectives is condensed for your background. All of these objectives are met when using the following programs.

- A feeling of self worth forms as we affirm "any age is a good age."
- The mind is distracted from pain.
- Boredom is relieved.
- Conversation is stimulated.
- The five senses are all implemented at different times.
- Memories are recalled more easily.
- Reality orientation regarding the season is emphasized.
- A variety of activities are inspired by the theme.
- Interest is maintained with a monthly theme.
- Music or activity skills are restored.
- Group participation is anticipated.
- Educational opportunities arise.
- Rhythmic activities give a sense of order to the body.
- Movement activities increase circulation, respiration.
- New friendships arise due to the thematic material.
- Financial insecurity is relieved since there is no cost involved.
- Sharing of treasured possessions is encouraged with the theme.
- Facility is bright, cheerful and meaningful.
- Anticipation is high as staff encourages involvement.
- Loving environment lasts all month long.

The **family** benefits from the monthly theme through:

- Discussing the subject matter with resident;
- Enjoying the atmosphere of the facility;
- Bringing appropriate props or souvenirs;
- Decorating the room with a reminder of the theme;
- Contributing ideas, songs, recipes, pictures;
- Lively conversations that close the generation gap;
- Donating their time when some aspect of the theme appeals to them;
- Sharing an activity with their loved one;
- Observing the Alzheimer patient actively involved.

The **staff** benefits by:

- Sharing their ideas;
- Working in a pleasant, theme related environment;
- Contributing to the bulletin board or decoration;
- Using the theme in conversations with residents as well as the families;
- Deepening friendships with additional conversation;
- Wearing clothing or an accessory related to the theme;

- Lively staff meetings due to increased interest in the facility;
- Taking pride in their place of employment;
- Having numerous opportunities for involvement in various activities that are coordinated;
- Volunteering to assist with the activities that especially interest them;
- Participating in a program that is cost effective;
- Working in a stimulating environment;
- Using new menus related to the theme yet meeting dietary needs;
- Coordinating physical therapy goals within the exercise portion;
- Unifying the activity department with programs and decorations for the entire month;
- Including the maintenance department as part of the entire program as they assist with erecting displays and special arrangements;
- Maintaining an enthusiastic interaction of employees;
- Being associated with an administration that offers a unique well-organized facility.

The **Community** is involved when:

- The generation gap is eased and often disappears;
- Opportunities arise to be of service for short time commitments;
- Nearby neighborhoods are utilized;
- Local talents can contribute to the theme of the month;
- Mayor or local politicians are welcomed for patriotic programming;
- Scout groups can earn badges following a specific, coordinated theme;
- Minor law offenders do social service, enjoy being part of the team;
- Area businessmen contribute with travelogs, ethnic foods, flowers, decorations, other donations and expertise;
- Volunteers enjoy the themes and find it easier to be involved;
- Pride develops within the community regarding the facility.

Public Relations are improved because:

- Facility newsletter carries the theme to residents, family, staff, friends, businessmen, and area newspapers;
- Publicity with a theme makes it easier for the media to promote a specific interest of theirs;
- The facility is ideal for picture taking, television and video taping;
- Promotion of the senior center is heightened;
- The media can use the center as a prime example of the joy of aging and promote the program to other geriatric settings enhancing the lives of residents, their families, and the staff.

MUSIC THERAPY WORKS

Music is very effective and seems to be everyone's friend, especially the resident that is nonverbal. Familiar melodies are always welcome and ease the frustration of the person that can no longer communicate with speech. Often, music is the only bridge for someone with a stroke where the left side of the brain is damaged and the right side of the body is paralyzed.

> Fran, aged 81, could only cry. It was her means of communication. Her husband Harold found his affection for her greater than ever and he would visit daily. There was no way he could converse with her and that made her cry all the more and added to the tension of this wonderful couple. The music therapist knew music was the answer so she started singing the old favorite "Let Me Call You Sweetheart." Fran broke into the biggest smile anyone had seen in months. Fran sang the words of the song along with perfect melody and rhythm. The right side of the brain where much of music is processed was still intact. Not only did Harold sing with her in unison but later they sang for the entire group session of music therapy. There were other songs they could sing together but this was their favorite and Harold always sang it with his arms around her while the staff stood around with tears of joy. Her affliction inspired everyone who saw this example of music therapy. The devotion of this couple will always be a strong, beautiful memory of all who witnessed it.

JOY OF ORGANIZATION

The following 80 programs are to be used with a **theme of the month** decided on by the staff. Depending on your locale, you may choose a theme that is more pertinent to your area at a specific time of year. Each individual program described here is overflowing with thematic activities. Use discretion when applying to your clientele. You know best the potential as well as the limitations of your group. The staff should have a broad outline of the themes they will use for the next six months allowing everyone time for creativity and development. The themes should spark ideas. Set one day a week as your day to focus everyone's attention and celebrate the theme. Residents, staff and families will all be aware that Thursday, for instance, is the target day for the specific theme. Meanwhile other programs can be arranged or music menus designed for dining pleasure. The central theme is a great aid for reality orientation. A word of caution: There is no need to overdo the theme since you want your facility to keep its professional image yet add to the atmosphere with meaningful decor. Bulletin boards, newsletters, programming, food menus, visual aids, entertainers, and announcements are just a few ways to keep the theme alive and in perspective.

EXPANDING YOUR STAFF

Expanding your staff is easy. One must avoid trying to handle the program entirely by oneself. Extra hearts as well as hands are needed to reach residents on a personal basis. The music therapist, or group leader, can meet more of the needs of the residents with the use of volunteers. They are obtained in the following way.

First, the therapist meets with the staff of the facility and families are identified that enjoy helping at the site. Family members are familiar with the facility and enjoy interacting with their loved one. Secondly, a personal invitation is given to the family member to observe the session that is scheduled on a weekly basis involving the theme. Thirdly, the therapist demonstrates how a volunteer can be of assistance and encourages them to come whenever possible. It is not necessary to make a total commitment so that the volunteer has the feeling of freedom. Generally, the volunteer is there regularly but without pressure. Often they arrange for a substitute whenever they know they are unable to attend.

> Mary, aged 85, is in a geriatric chair and shows little response to anything due to her severe stroke. She cannot communicate which frustrates her and the family very much. By attending music therapy celebrations once a week, both Mary and her daughter get involved in an activity they both enjoy. The daughter often initiates the rhythm in her mother's hand and the joy of making music together is apparent in their tearful smiles.

> Grace didn't want to leave her room but once she found out her daughter had volunteered for music every week, she attended regularly. Now Grace is the first one there even if the daughter can't attend.

Volunteers from this source often continue to contribute their time and talents even when their loved one is no longer there. So many good friendships are formed that there is a need to work with others. A monthly newsletter keeps volunteers informed of the program themes, props needed and all announcements.

People with a music background are also great contributors. They want to use their music with others but do not want to perform. With training, they are successful aides. Guidelines are given to them regarding the limitations of the residents as well as suggestions for being useful.

Candy-stripers are a joy to have during the summer. These young teens close the generation gap and add their energy to the program. The Activities Department handles this program with a few assigned to the music therapist. Another source is a person working for the community service credits. Their background need not be musical but it helps.

Services performed by volunteers include inviting the residents individually to attend sessions, humming or singing as they push a wheelchair, distributing song sheets and rhythm instruments, co-leading a round, acting out a song, providing props, distributing visual aids, adding to the group dynamics and most of all giving individual attention. They take the time to initiate responses and their services are priceless.

PUBLICIZING YOUR THEME

Publicizing your theme is first done in-house. A monthly newsletter is ideal to promote the present theme and announce next month's. In addition, announce any details such as the weekly program title, suggestions for clothing, homework to contemplate, invitations to families or friends, songs to recall and a musical game using the theme. "Places to travel" in song titles is an easy one. Publish the answers upside down on the same page for easier access to the solutions. Anyone can contribute to the game section. Announce names of volunteers and welcome them in print.

This book will provide a promotional sheet for each month. It not only announces the monthly theme but provides you with the space to announce the individual sessions and their respective themes. It is visually attractive and can be used as a poster as well as an individual reminder for every resident, staff member, volunteer and family newsletter insert.

Many sites have a daily newssheet. This also keeps the theme current and is helpful on a daily basis as a gentle reminder. Often the daily food menus are printed here and appropriate thematic art work is used.

Use of the intercom speaker system will remind everyone also. Announce the day's activities. Use songs or a brief recording to emphasize the program. Remind everyone of the place, time and theme and offer a genuine welcome. New residents are encouraged to attend and receive a welcome in song.

Local newspapers should be contacted whenever you feel that the program is newsworthy. Television stations will often cover events concerning the elderly enjoying a program that is meaningful. The colorful, decorated backgrounds are very good for interviews and the live music adds an extra good dimension.

COST AND EQUIPMENT

This entire program is possible with a budget under $1000 for the following initial equipment. All of these recommendations should be purchased with quality and longevity in mind. The only future expenditure will be additional equipment as the program gains momentum and more residents, staff, families and volunteers participate. Consider the following:

Piano

If the facility does not already have a fairly good piano, a wise choice is an electronic portable keyboard. These keyboards should have normal size keys. A model that is functional is preferable to the more elaborate models. These instruments never require a professional tuner and have the capability of tuning higher or lower. The rhythm options are a pleasure to use with therapeutic goals and the choice of voices is always a pleasant experience for the residents. By simply pushing a button, you can have a full organ sound for anything from hymn singing to "Here Comes the Bride." The portable keyboards are excellent outdoors, for room visits, to lay on a table or wheelchair, or to share with interested relatives and friends. Consider this as prime, practical equipment.

> Elmer, a new resident, was so impressed that he excused himself from the group to call his relatives to tell them about this new musical wonder, a Casio piano.

Guitar

This is a fine instrument for accompanying large or small groups, for encouraging individual involvement and sustaining old musical skills. It is portable and useful for room visits as well as outdoors.

Autoharp

The autoharp is not essential but a very fine instrument for music therapy. Residents can easily play this instrument with a few simple instructions. The therapist can use it for accompanying groups as well as for room visits. No batteries are needed but it does require tuning and this can be a concern.

Omnichord

The omnichord is the latest electronic portable instrument. It is very satisfying since it is easily played and requires no previous music background. People who have felt inadequate about playing a musical instrument respond readily to the soothing sound and simple instructions. It is always in tune. Many rhythmic effects are possible and there are many fine combinations for making music. The omnichord is essential for a music therapist that delights in positive music experiences that build self esteem easily.

Microphone

The microphone and speaker system will help everyone to hear better especially as the group grows larger. Portable mikes are also effective. A long cord for interviewing is necessary.

Rhythm Band Instruments

The rhythm band instruments need to be of good quality so they are not considered toys. The quality makes a much nicer sound and your equipment will last longer. A good collection of bells, shakers, sticks, castanets, triangles, and finger cymbals are recommended. Also one bass drum head and a snare drum adds a good base to the ensemble.

Tone Bells

One set of good tone bells are valuable and can be used effectively with Alzheimer patients or patients with any disability. Each person holds a rectangular plastic bar (bell) in one hand and strikes the bell with the other while watching the conductor. People with strokes usually put the bell on a chair in front of them or on a side table. A single set of eight bells using the C major scale plus three additional notes, namely F sharp, B flat and high D will give you 3 major keys and minimize the expense. These bells are indestructible and always in tune.

> Gene, aged 84, proudly exclaims, "When I play in the bell band no one notices my stroke, they only hear the music. I never played in a band before and listen to me now."

Fake Books and Sheet Music

Three good fake books will supply most of the music that is suggested in these programs. Actual sheet music is always a pleasure to utilize especially during reminiscence. Generally sheet music, favorite music books and especially ethnic music can be supplied by the families.

Records and Tapes

A record and tape collection that is suitable to your facility will need to be established. Welcome any donations but then use only the tapes that are meaningful to the residents. In the collection should be music of several tempos; lively, calming, energizing, and robust.

Record Player and Tape Player

This equipment need not be elaborate. Purchase a record player, speakers, tape player, or compact disc player combination that can be put on a music cart that can be rolled easily anywhere. Consider a small portable cassette player with earphones for the bedridden or someone who would like to listen to music but does not want to be of interference.

Lectern

A lectern is not essential but is helpful for your notes. In addition it adds dignity for your soloists or poets. Your theme can be posted on the front for all to see.

Music Stand

A portable music stand can be used anywhere in the facility for various programs as well as for individual use. Guest musicians appreciate having the use of one too.

Additional Equipment

In addition this program requires poster board, paper, foam paper plates, plastic bird whistles, crepe paper streamers, construction paper, large marking pens, Scotch tape, bubble pipes, tinsel, live or paper flowers, leaves, greenery, dolls, stuffed animals, silk scarves, colorful fabrics, small flags and one large United States flag. All are mentioned in this book as valuable visual aids.

SIZE OF THE GROUP SESSION

Group size should be limited only to the size of the room. Anyone is welcome to attend from low to high functioning residents, including those in geriatric chairs, wheelchairs, or using oxygen. Family, friends, grandchildren, staff, visitors are all invited. As the group expands in size, divide it into two groups at the discretion of the staff. Separate Alzheimer groups are ideal since more individual attention can be given. However, they function quite well when attending music therapy large group sessions.

Visitors are curious and want to learn more about music therapy when they witness the weekly group session since it is comprised of residents with strokes, multiple sclerosis, cystic fibrosis, terminal cancer, rehabilitation patients, Alzheimer's disease, blind, deaf, and other disabilities. As the group functions as a unit, the medical history is not apparent. Even the confused elderly are attentive and cooperative since the music does the work and reaches them at various levels. The confused elderly are dependent upon external organizers such as music, rhythm, repetitive activities, group rituals and familiar structures in order to maintain themselves.[1] All of these activities are incorporated into every program presented in this book.

If residents are reluctant to attend, invite them to just come and observe for ten minutes or attend with a family member at a later date. Leave a written note or invitation for them as a reminder of their date. Sometimes they prefer to sit outside the inner circle which could be in the hallway. Often you will find them actively participating and in time becoming avid supporters of the program. People sitting in the very back row can be referred to as "the balcony" and enjoy that identity on a regular basis. Encourage people to participate, wherever they sit, but never force them. The environment is stimulating for all attending whether they are active or passive.

Individuals are recognized during the group sessions and a good feeling of camaraderie develops. One popular adage is the response that an elderly person made, "I'm not growing old, I'm getting older and growing." Optimal growth and adaptation can occur throughout the life cycle when an individual's strength and potentials are recognized, reinforced and encouraged by the environment in which he or she lives.[2] The group music session provides this easily.

Charting should be done regularly by someone knowledgeable of those attending. If the music therapist is leading the large group session, another full time staff member should have this assignment. Every name is important. Significant responses to the music should also be recorded. The music therapist should add to the report at the staff meetings.

[1]   Sandell and Johnson. (1987) *Waiting at the Gate: Creativity and Hope in the Nursing Home*, p. 119.
[2]   Butler and Lewis. (1982) *Aging and Mental Health*, p. 26.

CHAPTER TWO

FORMAT OF THE PROGRAM

The following format is designed for a weekly hour long session or celebration of the theme for the month. The order can be re-arranged according to the flow of the material presented or specific needs of the current residents:

- Theme of the Month
- Today's Theme
- Advanced Preparation
- Pre-Session
- Opening
- Guided Imagery
- Greeting
- Exercise
- Reminiscence
- Group Singing
- Education
- Group Discussion
- Song Identification
- Solo Time
- Rhythm Band
- Closing
- Assignment
- Resources

It is not necessary to use all of the components every week or to follow the order as above. The leader must decide what is the most beneficial for the group with regard to the theme.

Advanced Preparation

Visual and musical aids are listed following the general theme for the month and the specific theme for the day. This gives the facility the opportunity to arrange for appropriate decorations, speakers, community involvement, costumes, props, instruments and related music. It also includes publicizing the theme in advance so that everyone is aware of the possibilities that are ahead.

Pre-Session

The time preceding the large group monthly session initiates the spirit of the program. Pre-publicity has been arranged, the session has been announced over the in-house communication system, and volunteers then go to the rooms to escort their elderly friends. Often they will seek the same people every week to establish a rapport with them. A simple "no, thank you" is respected. A genuine invitation to attend for just ten minutes is often accepted and the ten minutes becomes sixty minutes followed by words of gratitude.

The nursing staff and activity staff all contribute to the list of residents who should be approached and those who should not be disturbed that particular day. A warm, friendly invitation should be extended every week even when there has been a negative response previously.

Volunteers and staff can escort residents by singing or humming together, pointing out decorations related to the theme or giving them a *lei* to wear as they board ship for the Hawaiian program, for example.

Upon entering the room, live music is heard on the piano using the theme for the day. Otherwise, recorded music that is appropriate is provided. Friendship, camaraderie and visible reactions to the music are apparent before the official opening.

> Arthur, a professional symphony musician, had no use for this activity. His stroke left him devastated. His oft repeated line to the therapist every week was "It will never work, girlie." He would sit in the hall and listen but refused to join the group or accept a rhythm instrument. He refused to try the drum and be the basis for the band. Then months later he admitted that he saw others that had never participated in any activity, were enjoying themselves and also that the band had sharpened their skills. He quietly sat within the group but only as an observer. One year later, he asked for the bongo drum and now plays regularly.

Opening

This part of the program is extremely important. The group leader greets everyone with a handshake and a warm smile and welcomes each person by name whenever possible. Since the session is designed to meet the needs of various physical and emotional disabilities, it will be a large group attending. Some may appear to be drowsy, asleep or incoherent. They are welcomed too. "Just because a message may never be received does not mean it is not worth sending." according to Segaki.[1] Live music and a friendly environment are to be preferred for the healthy effect it has on the mind and body.

Welcome any new residents, volunteers and guests. Announce the general theme as well as the specific theme for the day. This is also a good time to establish reality orientation with the day of the week, name of the facility and the weather conditions. Mention some of the activities planned for the hour together and encourage everyone to participate and feel the results. Also, suggest that they observe others in the room and learn more about each other.

> Elsie has few friends. Her disposition was best described as grumpy. Years ago she had played a tambourine in a kitchen band and chose that instrument immediately when it came time for rhythmic activity. She played it accurately and beamed. When praised for her fine efforts, her self esteem and body posture improved immensely. In addition, everyone could see that she could be a cheerful person. She reversed many people's negative opinion of her. She still is the tambourine expert and insists on one tambourine as being "hers."

Music can be playing softly in the background during the opening but should not interfere with the effectiveness of hearing clearly.

---

[1]   Segaki, as quoted by R. Bright (1981) in *Practical Planning in Music Therapy for the Aged*, p. 48.

Guided Imagery

Guided imagery and music needs to be led by a professional who has had the proper training. This is a part of a music therapy curriculum at the college level. Its effectiveness in the group is ideal for releasing tensions, attaining a state of relaxation, focusing attention and creating images. The definition given by Lisa Summer, RMT is that "guided imagery is a technique in which the act of listening to classical music is combined with a relaxed state of mind and body in order to evoke imagery for the purpose of self-actualization."[1] It is not programmed on a weekly basis but only used on appropriate occasions. It is ideal following a very active month of holiday happenings when everyone needs to be refreshed before starting a new year. It is also used to help recall those feelings we once had of skills such as ice skating with its free flowing movements.

> Minnie, aged 90, had a limb removed due to a diabetic condition. "With the imagery today I felt so good. I was able to skate again and all the freedom and beauty came back to me. The music made me so happy. I don't regret not being able to skate anymore. After all, I am 90. It is fine to reflect on how good life is to me including now."

Encourage the active use of the imagination and the ability to image, especially with the use of music. The elderly have a huge storehouse of memories to relive and enjoy.

Greeting

Augment your program with the appropriate greeting using the theme. It will establish the theme and get everyone involved immediately. The leader should announce the greeting such as "Aloha" for the Hawaiian program or "Shalom" for Hanukah. Each resident can echo the greeting back and then turn to each other spreading the good word.

Exercise

Music and motion are a regular part of the weekly program. Exercises are seldom popular. However, with the use of the right music, understanding of the possibilities as well as the limitations of the residents, and effective leadership, this is a valuable activity. Everyone needs to increase their circulation and their respiration. It is easier to do this through music and movement activities. Rhythmics, an essential part of the program is designed to reactivate enjoyment of bodily movement, to provide remedial work for the skeleto-muscular problems so frequent in the elderly and to effect reconditioning in motor function. It is also provides an avenue of expression on the nonverbal level.[2]

This is the perfect part of the program to coordinate with the physical therapy department. A physical therapist from the staff or the community should give a talk about the value of movement. They are trained leaders and will know the boundaries for various medical problems. Light exercise is stimulated with props. It is always more interesting to have a visual aid than to just exercise. The use of props will extend the exercise period and makes these activities colorful and more interesting. Props stimulate conversation and divert the mind from the physical

---

[1]   Summer, L. (1988) *Guided Imagery and Music*, p. v.
[2]   *Geriatrics* 1955 10:443. "Personality Changes in an Older Group" by R. Andrus.

involvement. Foam plates are ideal for a variety of themes. Flowers, for example, can be cut during a craft session from pretty flower catalogs. Discussions flow easily as residents recall their favorites, their gardens, their travels, and then anticipate using these props in future sessions. A dash of perfume adds to sensory stimulation. Other series include a variety of fall leaves, animals and birds, yellow smile faces and paper snowflakes with no two alike. Exercises should be well planned with the music using the *iso* principle. Initially use a tempo that reflects the group's mood and then slowly increase or decrease it depending on your therapeutic goal. This approach with props is easily done for those in wheelchairs with pretty plates swinging on the sides, overhead, round and round or dancing on the shoulders, knees and head. The finale is to enjoy throwing this plate at the group leader at the count of three. Residents are reminded of the value of arm extension and should practice before they actually throw it. The group leader gets exercise too picking them all up amidst the laughter. These props are stored for future programs. However, if someone wants to keep theirs, they may do so. The props are often treasured and bring a host of associations that get shared with others.

Alzheimer patients respond well to music and motion especially using a colorful visual aid. Generally, it is their favorite activity since it is based on rhythm and movement and does not require verbalization. Another excellent rhythmic activity is the use of paper streamers or silk scarves. Individual scarves are distributed from a collection you have accumulated or borrowed. An alternative is to use attractive fabric that is cut into appropriate lengths. The colors and fabric add to the visual and tactile stimulation. When coordinated with the theme, participation is increased. Rhythmic movements to music help the limbs flow easily and smoothly. Specific body movements can be exercised with the expertise of the physical therapist.

Well trained volunteers can lead these activities with the music therapist providing the music on the piano. Live music is always preferable for control of the tempo and dynamics, and there is the element of human involvement.

Valerie, aged 91, is afflicted with Alzheimer's disease. She is a famous ballerina who is a permanent resident of the nursing home. Often she will ask "Where am I?" Daily we try to establish her surroundings for her but words are meaningless. The music therapist brought some ballet music for her, Tchaikovsky's *Sleeping Beauty,* and played it on the record player. There was no reaction. The next private session she tried one of Valerie's favorite selections that her family had provided, Gershwin's *Rhapsody in Blue.* Again, no results. The therapist was not discouraged. She knew that a wealth of music and memories were stored inside this wonderful woman. Finally, the therapist asked, "What can I play for you that you will like?" Valerie leaned over from her wheelchair and said, "I only work with live music." That was the answer and also the answer for anyone working with music therapy programs. Live music is always preferred although not always possible. The element of life is present as well as the personality of the therapist combining to make a richer experience. Valerie was wheeled closer to the grand piano and the therapist played the original *Sleeping Beauty* and Valerie's arms danced with incredibly beautiful expression. Entrainment between the two women, the dancer and the pianist, occurred and time lost its meaning.
In later sessions, the physical therapist helped Valerie stand so she could have some use of her legs but weeks later that was not possible due to declining muscular strength and balance. Valerie continued to dance with her arms and head and lovely hands. Others would imitate her. Staff and visitors observed an

unusual sight. They all knew they were in the presence of greatness and witnessing new life in this elderly ballerina. Keep in mind the effect she had on others by living in a nursing home. Elderly, handicapped people were moving their arms and trying ballet for the first time in their lives. Truly Valerie was an inspiration to everyone.

Reminiscence

Reminiscing is an essential part of every program since it allows individual responses that are meaningful to the residents. It also encourages conversation easily as others will often recall similar events that they wish to share. Every program is designed with a topic that is familiar to most people. The elderly have a storehouse of experience to draw from and those who listen become wiser.

In addition the experience of reminiscing can be a source of emotional relief according to Dr. Mary Ellen Wylie of Eastern Montana College. "One can get personal gratification by reminiscing because one can identify with an event or place or past legacy" according to Dr. Wylie.[1]

> Olivia, aged 93, a lovely Greek resident at the nursing home felt estranged due to the language barrier but she would come to music therapy every week and smile. She never entered the conversations nor was she familiar with the songs. She told us that she loved music but didn't know the songs of America. She did not want to hear Greek songs. A music therapy student wisely approached this situation by encouraging her to reminisce about her early days when she supported the family by making shoes. A wealth of information poured out and after several visits and much note taking the sessions were put to poetry and eventually music. Olivia proudly sat before the entire group when "her shoemaker song" was sung. She beamed as she kept the beat by shaking a maraca along with the tempo. She was very proud to share this heritage and the family was elated also.

In a recent study by Mary Ellen Wylie, a reminiscence group revealed the following fact: 35% of the conversation focused on major events in their lives, while everyday happenings accounted for 50%. This is another reason for enriching the present environment.

The role of the therapist is to provide the setting every week to induce memory recall and participation and then to be an active listener. Volunteers can easily write down the essential information that comes forth for further use. Encourage them all to think back and recall their favorite memories of any portion of their life. Include the staff since reminiscing has no age limit.

Group Singing

The whole is equal to more than the sum of its parts. Proper song selection and an enthusiastic leader will bring responses that will please even the nonsinger. Voices that once sang firmly find it easier to sing along with others than to hear themselves and reflect on what used to be. In 1588 William Byrd recognized the value of group singing when he wrote:

---

[1]   Wylie, M.E. (1988) *Reminiscence*. Doctoral thesis, Eastern Montana College.

> The exercise of singing is delightful to nature and good to preserve the health of man. It doth strengthen all the parts of the breast and doth open the pipes. It is a singular good remedy for a stuttering and stammering in the speech.[1]

Singing harmonizes the body as the residents focus their attention on the song and bodily discomfort is eased. The tendency of group singing enhances trust and cooperation due to the influence of music and activity according to the research of Anat Anshel and David Kipper of Barlian University, Israel.[2] The use of visual aids is recommended. Needless to say, songs are filled with memories. However, all the emphasis need not be placed on old songs. It is wise to update to present new ones too.

Song sheets are seldom used since eyesight is often limited and the small print is useless. If song sheets are desired, limit the songs to one or two on the page with large print and add an illustration or border. Residents may keep them afterwards. As the song leader, you want as much eye contact as possible. There is greater group unity with one person conducting and encouraging responses. Trained volunteers are very valuable in encouraging individuals to sing along. If someone takes the time to sing beside another and join hands in rhythm, there is generally a vocal response. Words are not important unless you are using them for a therapeutic goal. Many people simply enjoy humming the melody or using simple syllables. "Because the world of sound cannot be shut out (except for physiological or neurological dysfunctions) …music is a powerful means of communicating with individuals with whom other contact is difficult or impossible."[3]

Group singing is made easier using responsive songs where the leader sings the melody and the residents repeat it back. "Bill Grogan's Goat" is an example of that. Another form that is clear and effective is for the leader to sing the part with the most words and the residents sing the chorus such as "It's a Small World." Songs with actions are highly recommended as well as nonsense songs that are just for fun.

Song writing should always be encouraged either from individuals or using a group technique where everyone contributes. Rewriting "The Twelve Days of Christmas" with a list of gifts the elderly would choose is fun for everyone. Changing words to a familiar song to fit the occasion is a liberty often taken. This technique makes it unnecessary to learn a new melody or rhythm, just the words are new so it is quickly learned.

Rounds are popular if taught first in unison. As the group becomes secure with it, announce that the next version will be a two part round and each section will have a leader so there is no confusion. A resident in a wheelchair with a baton will enjoy this status. Both leaders need to know the key they are using as well as when the second group should enter and also the number of times the round will be sung. Eventually three part rounds are sung.

Songs can be accompanied by piano, organ, electronic piano, guitar, autoharp, omnichord, accordian, rhythm instruments or records. The leader may want to tape an accompaniment so they are free to visibly lead the group. If string bass or drum are available, use them also to add depth.

Group singing can be enhanced with vocal or instrumental solos by the residents and everyone joining in on the repeat. Plan ahead of time so the resident can look forward to this event.

---

1 Byrd, W. (1985) Psalms, Sonnets and Songs. *Dictionary of Musical Quotations*, p. 135.
2 *Journal of Music Thearpy* 1988, 15(3):145. "Influence of Group Singing on Trust and Cooperation" by A. Anshel and D. Kipper.
3 Hodges, D. (1980) *Handbook of Music Psychology*, p. 58.

Education

Education never stops and is a natural part of every group session. Muriel Oberleader claims that "according to intelligence test results there is really only a very slight decline in the mental function of the elderly, and many functions such as vocabulary, practical reasoning and special skills in which the person remains actively engaged, often improve with age."[1] With education we can grow older and better. The programs in this book will implement both old and new facts for everyone attending. References are given for further elaboration or inspiration.

Group Discussion

Group discussion is an important part of this program. In addition It is popular with the high functioning residents and often is a separate activity known as Current Events. When centered around a theme, related thoughts and memories occur more quickly. Volunteers ask leading questions to aid the discussion period. The use of music earlier in the program will also increase memories due to previous associations. The nonverbal aspect of music will stimulate other parts of the brain and more active discussions ensue. This part of the program can be written up in future in-house newspaper articles.

Song Identification

Identifying songs with or without prompting is a popular activity. Often an Alzheimer patient or someone who is very confused will supply the song title after hearing the melody played on the piano. Songs relating to the theme are used, generally about ten of them. Anyone can name the title and with volunteers beside them they are encouraged to hum along until they recall the title or parts of the song. Anyone can submit song titles ahead of time or during the session. It is a good homework assignment that is given weekly. If the song title is not remembered by anyone, the therapist gives a few clues. Discussion is part of this activity since so many memories are evoked. Often they are captured on the microphone to be shared with the group and also written down by the aides for the in-house newspaper. The comments from residents are valuable for they often touch on a bygone era that is quickly being replaced with new technology. These commentaries from our older and wiser residents needs to be preserved now.

> Jenny, who attends the group session regularly, never contributed to the group. She just enjoyed listening. Once a volunteer sat beside her and made her feel that her answer was important she would call out every answer. Not only was Jenny pleased but the staff and her family were elated.

Solo Time

A time for a solo is beneficial for self esteem. Anyone is welcome to sing, play an instrument, dance, recite poetry or a reading.

> Ben, aged 83, loves to play his flute for everyone including every scheduled entertainment. Often it was inappropriate and interfered with community presentations. Solo time gives him the opportunity in a structured way and he performs regularly. His best renditions are repeated publicly on occasion.

---

[1]   Saul, S. (1974) *Aging*, p. 23.

Joanne, aged 82, is dubbed the facility official Songbird. She sings a solo every week. She is proud that she still sings in tune and can hold the last note longer than anyone else.

Ralph, aged 97, writes and recites his poems using the theme. His age and ability inspires younger residents.

Rhythm Band

Rhythmic musical activities are valuable experiences for anyone, anytime. Our entire human body is based on a natural rhythm and order. Disease, disabilities, depression, all affect the body so that one feels disoriented. The Greeks and Romans would remedy these conditions with both music and architecture. Pythagoras believed that if one employed music in daily life according to a proscribed manner, it would make a salutary contribution to one's health.[1] It is this proscribed manner that the music therapist can employ with fine results. Residents generally have an automatic response to music with toe tapping, recognition or some rhythmic body movement. Often this will be the first, nonverbal, visual clue that they are responding to music. A trained therapist will encourage involvement and continuation of the beat. This is especially important when the resident has not had a previous background in music and now a whole new adventure awaits.

Ralph, a wheelchair bound 94-year-old man always wanted to play the drums. Age held little meaning for him and he is now THE drummer of our weekly rhythm band session, at the age of 97! It adds greatly to his status as well as his enjoyment and he inspired everyone to consider making music dreams come true.

During rhythmic involvement the body feels a sense of order. This may be recognized on the conscious level and is praised by the therapist. On the unconscious level, the effect is equally important. The body welcomes order and responds easily with the correct use of music. E. Thayer Gaston, pioneer in music therapy, reminds us of the two great advantages of rhythmic activities.

It is not only the doing, but the doing together that is important and brings so much satisfaction.[2]

Individual sessions with rhythm are very beneficial and then the group process adds to a fuller enjoyment. Attention spans are prolonged, socialization occurs, and bonding occurs within the group. Music is well suited to the treatment of geriatric patients because of the gratification and socialization that may result from creative experiences with it.[3] Being creative means that the resident is still contributing to society plus increasing his own self esteem at any age.

Closing

A feeling of completion and of a job well done is a gratifying feeling for any age, any stage of life. The group session should end with a song beloved by all that indicates closure. The same song can be sung regularly as the final song such as "Bless This House" or "Till We Meet

---

[1]   Shullian, D., Schoen, M. (1948) *Music and Medicine.*, p. 56.
[2]   Gaston, E.T. (1968) *Music in Therapy*, p. 19.
[3]   *Geriatrics* 1955 10:433. "Personality Changes in an Older Group" by R. Andrus.

Again." Residents should be thanked for attending and also participating in a healthy, memorable activity.

Assignment

Your music therapy celebration session is over. However, you can offer the joy of anticipation of next week's program using the same general theme for the month and announcing the specific theme for next week. Residents can dwell up on the topic, confer with relatives, staff, or visitors and start collecting memories, new information, songs, and souvenirs. Most of all, their attention is focused on an event that is stimulating individually as well as collectively.

Resources

Every weekly program will list the major source of music or text used. Piano fake books are ideal and their indexes also give additional musical ideas. More detailed references are given at the end of this book. Try to use the residents for your research on various topics. They enjoy contributing both content and melodies.

EXTENSIONS OF THE PROGRAM

Using Music Selection Menus

Freedom of choice helps us retain our dignity. The ability to make decisions is less frequent in nursing care facilities since so many major choices are no longer options. Investing money, planning trips, arranging social events, even income taxes, are often of the past. A music selection menu may seem like a minor activity but it is the most popular single program. Everyone is familiar with a food menu and it is usually posted somewhere in the facility. A music menu is printed weekly and distributed to each dining room table where residents can make their personal choices.

> Gertrude cannot communicate due to her stroke but she can point on the music menu to exactly the song she wants to hear played on the piano. It is her choice and no one is coaxing her in any way. She beams when she hears "her song." Many times she will hum along with the melody.

There is an old song, "Music With My Meals." Music aids digestion but has many other therapeutic uses. Restoring the memory is made easier both with the written word on the menu or by hearing a few bars of the music suggested. Without the menu, when residents are asked "What can I play for you?" the most frequent response is "anything at all" or "I can't think of anything." By printing a menu using songs that all relate to the theme, the mind is again clarified. Earlier associations with the theme are reinforced and new ideas can emerge. Ten to twelve songs make an interesting menu. The music therapist and an aide go to each person individually at their dining room table and ask for their choice of music. One can also offer to play any other favorite of theirs and research it during the week if it is unfamiliar music. This is "their" song and may produce tears of joy.

Two Greek residents have to hear "Never on Sunday" no matter what the menu suggests. They both quit eating and dance their shoulders much to everyone's pleasure.

Anyone can contribute to the song list since the entire facility is aware of the theme. Every program in this book includes a music selection menu which can be copied directly. Primarily, the music therapist supplies the song titles which can be from various styles of music. This activity is very soothing to a newcomer since they often feel unfamiliar with their new surroundings but music is their friend and gives them a familiar comfortable atmosphere. The song titles and residents' names are announced over the microphone as well as the song most often requested on the Hit Parade. Be aware that one may end up with a singing dining room at times.

Music Games

Music games will extend the theme and can be completed anytime by the individual or with visitors or other residents. The musical game can be printed in the monthly newsletter or circulated during the week. This keeps the theme alive and is easy to complete due to the previous associations. Matching song titles with the picture is a good exercise in recall. Also, one gets extra credit if they can sing or hum the song. This particular game is a good way to ease the generation gap and learn from our elders some of those "good old songs" or discover that the old song has been revived.

> Catherine was having fun working the music game in her room when her granddaughter arrived for a visit. The young girl took in interest in the game and asked Catherine to teach her one of the songs. Catherine did so with pride and told her how meaningful "Don't Sit Under the Apple Tree" (With Anyone Else But Me) was to her since her boyfriend would remind her of that when he went away to war. The girl got interested in the romance as well as the part he played in the war. She learned that her grandmother had knitted khaki stockings for the men. Then Catherine asked if she could learn a song that the younger generation was singing. The generation gap was closed.

Other recommended music games are matching well known songs from the more popular musicals, matching famous musicians with their theme song or the reverse of naming the theme song of the musicians. For example, Kate Smith was famous for singing "God Bless America." Song titles with words removed make a good game and often lead to singing. The entire song can be printed with major words removed and often with prompting, the resident will surprise everyone by completing the song perfectly. Music stimulates recall and is an effective technique with Alzheimer patients.

> Jane and May were both victims of advanced Alzheimer's disease. They were unable to converse rationally, but they could still sing. Words were not always clear but with prompting on the words only, they could sing the entire song with the correct rhythm and melody. Imagine the amazement when they went hand in hand to the administration office and sang "Till We Meet Again" as a duet with May singing perfect harmony. They both beamed as they walked down the hall, again hand in hand, and chatted incoherently.

Bell Band

Organizing a bell band is another effective way to extend the theme since it easily includes various disabilities and no previous talent is needed. This is excellent for stroke victims who are unable to talk but will function perfectly in the band. Those with the use of one hand only can have the bell placed on a chair or small table before them. Eight residents volunteer to play. Anyone can substitute which is an advantage to this activity since the performers may vary week to week.

Each person is given a rectangular tone bar, known as a bell, and one mallet. They represent that one tone only and play when the leader points to them. The tone bar bells are light weight, indestructible and always in tune. They are relatively inexpensive and easily produce a good tone.

Residents should sit in a semi-circle in the order of the scale. It is recommended that the person playing the low note C and the middle G be the same person at every session so that the leader easily identifies the root and fifth of the chord.

Songs are chosen from the theme of the week. Care must be used that the melody lies within the scale and that most people will have an opportunity to play and feel the pride of contributing their tone to the band. Songs recommended in the key of C are Brahms' "Lullaby," "Joy to the World," "Bells of St. Mary's," "Du, Du liegst Mir im Herzen " and "Drink to Me Only With Thine Eyes."

A lot of music can be played in the key of C however, with the purchase of the single tone bars of B flat and F sharp, two more scales are possible. In addition, a high D is very useful. In the key of F, "God Bless America" and "America" (My Country 'Tis of Thee) are favorite songs. The leader must know in advance the key and the starting note.

Anytime a note is missing, it is fun to simply sing it.

> Norma is "Miss G" at every session. "I wouldn't miss this for anything. I never had music in my life before and now I even have a title."

PART TWO

MONTHLY PROGRAMS

Cruising Through January

A Game to Play While You Cruise Through January

What country or nation would you hear the following song? The answers are printed upside down. Example number 1 answer is D=England.

1. God Save the Queen   A. Brazil

2. Hinky Dinky Parlay Voo   B. Australia

3. Waltzing Matilda   C. Italy

4. Aloha Oe (Farewell to Thee) D. England

5. Londonderry Air   E. France

6. Funiculi, Funicula   F. United States

7. Dixie   G. Ireland

8. Kum Ba Ya   H. Hawaii

9. Tico Tico   I. Germany

10. Edelweiss   J. Africa

Answers - 1-D, 2-E, 4-H, 5-G, 6-C, 7-F, 8-J, 9-A, 10-I

CRUISING THROUGH JANUARY

Residents can anticipate a well planned cruise after the busy holidays of last month. This will be an indoor vacation that requires no packing, tickets, luggage or confirmation. Passports are not necessary nor does one need any shots. No lines, no waiting and no lost luggage. The cruise sails every Thursday at 10:30 a.m.

Advertise this program with the microphone, daily newsletter and the monthly newsletter as well as posters and bulletin boards. The entire facility as well as the families should be notified of the schedule with an invitation for anyone to contribute ideas. All are welcome to attend. The invitation on the next page to cruise is sent to every resident as a personal and visual reminder.

Appropriate decorations should be planned by the activities department. The dietary department arranges for a foreign treat of food from the country highlighted each week. A meal or two can also follow the theme with related music. Music menus are provided with this book.

Musical games are included in the monthly newsletter or as an additional handout during the week to continue the theme and stimulate memories and conversation with each other, the staff, families and friends. If anyone misses the boat one week, they can catch the next sailing and cruise through January.

Then set sail with these programs:

Hawaii Bids You Welcome — A lovely way to start the new year with warm, sunny, mini-vacations and lots of bubbles floating everywhere.

A Trip To Sunny Italy — This program features colorful rhythmic activities as well as timeless melodies.

There's Joy In Germany — Enjoy the friendship or Gemütlichkeit of this country with hearty group singing, waltzes and polka music.

South America Take It Away — The rhythms and colors of this area provide the stimulation for a wonderful trip.

OPTIONAL PROGRAM

Everything's Coming Up Roses — This New Year's Day session looks good, sounds good and even smells good. Residents can keep the props as reminders of a rosy year ahead.

ALL ABOARD!

January Theme —   **CRUISING THROUGH JANUARY**

Today's theme —   **Hawaii Bids You Welcome**

Advanced
Preparation:
- Props for this week's session should include:
  - posters, bubble wands and bubble soap,
  - colorful silk scarves,
  - leis, pineapple, souvenirs,
- Organize a Hawaiian dancer to perform for the group.
- Gather together a collection of Hawaiian songs and recorded music.

Pre-Session: Soft Hawaiian records are played or else live music is provided by the pianist. As residents enter or are escorted from their rooms, they are given a lei to wear and a warm welcome to an indoor cruise.

Opening: Introduce yourself as the ship's captain. Give the "ship" a name such as the "SS _____" (name of your facility or one of their choosing). Invite all to cruise for an hour at no cost, no tickets, no baggage, just sheer pleasure.

Guided Imagery: With eyes closed, lead them with a short relaxation technique, and then imagine boarding the ship, being welcomed, and then having a smooth sailing across the ocean to Hawaii where they are warmly welcomed. "Aloha Oe" (Farewell to Thee) is softly played in the background.

Greeting: Suggest all participants greet each other with the word "Aloha." Aides can assist by greeting every person with this expression, which means "hello."

Exercise: To the song "Lovely Hula Hands," exercise with smooth hand motions. If a Hawaiian dance expert is available, discuss hand positions and their meaning such as flower, house, love, man, water.

Reminiscence: Have residents discuss their travels there. Have them recall their favorite memories, the scenery, weather, beaches. Any person who has been there most recently should update them. Any costumes or souvenirs should be acknowledged and displayed.

Education:
- Hawaii is the nickname for the entire chain of islands consisting of Maui, Lanai, Molokai, Kauai, Niihau, Oahu, and Hawaii.
- 80% of the population is in Honolulu.
- In 1770 these islands were discovered by Captain Cook. He named them the Sandwich Islands after an English earl, the Earl of Sandwich.
- In 1820 the missionaries came around the horn of South America and were shocked by the lack of clothes — *mu mus* evolved.
- Years ago newcomers were greeted by rubbing noses, now a lei is hung round the neck.
- It was annexed by the US in 1898.
- It received its statehood in 1959.

Education:
(Cont.)

- The principal industries are sugar cane, pineapple, steamship lines, and tourism. It is a famous defense base.
- Popular food — poi, fish, chicken, bananas, yams.[1]

Song
Identification:

Hawaiian War Chant
Little Grass Shack in Hawaii
Lovely Hula Hands
Now Is the Hour
Our Love and Aloha
Aloha Oe
Tiny Bubbles

Solo Time:

"Tiny Bubbles" sung as a solo and then by the entire group..
    Tiny bubbles in the air, tiny bubbles everywhere.
    Tiny bubbles make me feel so fine
    Give a happy, healthy greeting to these friends of mine.

Bubble wands are passed out or aides assist with this activity as bubbles fill the air.

Finale — several people blow bubbles in front or under a large fan so bubbles fly freely. Everyone sings.

Rhythm Band:

"Lovely Hula Hands" — easy 2 beat.
"My Little Grass Shack" — peppier as a 4 beat rhythm.

Closing:

Chorus of "Aloha Oe" — all gently wave silk scarves or precut silk-like fabric to the music. Wave goodbye as they pretend to board their ship and sail back. Have residents turn to each other and thank the person beside them for their friendship by saying "Mahalo Nui" which means "thank you very much."

Fresh pineapple can be served as a treat.

Assignment:

Everyone is reminded that next week the "SS _____" sails on A TRIP TO SUNNY ITALY. Invite residents to start packing their thoughts or associations with that country and to bring any souvenirs along to the session. Suggest they call their relatives if they need assistance.

Music
Resources:

Ultimate Fake Book (1981)
    "Aloha Oe" p. 9
    "Tiny Bubbles" p. 572
    "Our Love and Aloha" p. 423
    "Pearly Shells" p. 441
Legit Fake Book (1990)
    "Hawaiian War Chant" p. 131
    "My Little Grass Shack" p. 243

---

[1] All information in the Education section from *Information Please Almanac* (1992) pp. 745-746.

Favorite Hawaiian Songs (1989)
   "Hawaiian Wedding Song" p. 21
   "Lovely Hula Hands" p. 32
   "Bali Ha'i" p. 4
   "Now Is the Hour" p. 43
   "Red Sails in the Sunset" p. 60

Music  Menu

Cruise on the "S.S._____"
to Hawaii

1. Cruising Down the River
2. Sailing
3. Our Love and Aloha
4. Pearly Shells
5. Lovely Hula Hands
6. Hawaiian Wedding Song
7. Tiny Bubbles
8. Sweet Leilani
9. On a Slow Boat to "Hawaii"
10. Sunrise, Sunset
11. Red Sails in the Sunset
12. Now Is the Hour

Choose your favorite and I'll
play it just for you!

SAILING

Sailing, Sailing, over the bounding main,

For many a stormy wind shall blow

ere Jack comes home again.

Sailing, Sailing, over the bounding main;

For many a stormy wind shall blow

ere Jack comes home again.

- Godfrey Marks (1880)

January Theme — **CRUISING THROUGH JANUARY**

Today's Theme — **A Trip to Sunny Italy**

Advanced
Preparation:
- Props for this session include:
  - a record of Italian music,
  - a poster of Italy,
  - 2-inch rolls of crepe paper in red, white, and green.
- Prepare and copy responses to "Funiculi, Funicula" song. Response sheets are included at the end of this week's session plan.
- Try to persuade a violinist to come to play a typically Italian piece, such as a tarantella.

Pre-Session:
Italian music on the piano or a tape recording of favorites such as "Oh Marie," "Santa Lucia," and "Ciribiribin" played as residents enter.

Opening:
Pianist plays "By the Beautiful Sea." Instruct residents to close their eyes and imagine their departure by boat. It is a free trip to sunny Italy on a smooth ship. A songsheet is included at the end of this week's session plan.

Greeting:
Upon arrival say "Bon giorno" which is "hello" in Italian. Get residents to turn towards neighbors and greet each other this way.

Exercise:
Distribute red, green and white rolls of 2-inch crepe paper. All hands should be on the paper when possible. These colors of the flag should be unrolled along each row. Using the music, "Oh Marie," have the red streamers all held high in the air and down slowly. Alternate colors. Observe the colorful room. Using a leader vary movements with Italian songs.
> Santa Lucia
> Come Back to Sorrento
> Oh Marie

Reminiscence:
Find out who is of Italian descent or who has traveled there. Interview these people regarding their memories including food festivals, scenery, and customs. Encourage sharing of any souvenirs.

Group Singing:
Response song:"Funiculi, Funicula". (The song was written in 1880 to celebrate the opening of the funicular railway, a cable car, ascending Mount Vesuvius.)

Use the large print responses that are included at the end of this session plan.

Leader	Some think it's time for fun and frolic, and so do I
Response	AND SO DO I
Leader	Some think it's time to be melancholic, to pine and sigh
Response	TO PINE AND SIGH
Leader	But I love to spend my time in singing, some joyous song
Response	SOME JOYOUS SONG

Group Singing: (Cont.)	Leader Response	To set the air with music bravely ringing, is far from wrong IS FAR FROM WRONG
	Chorus:	Listen, listen, music fills the air Listen, listen, music fills the air, funiculi, funiculi, funicula Music fills the air funiculi funicula.

Note: Using three leaders, divide each group into three parts. Sing song using the words ha, ha, ho, ho, he, he, he, he, he. Use a leader for each part.

Education:
- The art of music has its roots in Italy.
- The piano was invented there in the early 1700s.
- Instrumental composers of note are: Scarlatti, Vivaldi, Clementi.
- Opera composers of note are: Verdi, Puccini, Rossini.[1]
- It is the birthplace of much Catholic music and literature.
- The famous violinmaker Stradivari was Italian.

Solo Time: Tarantella — Italian folk dance played on the violin.

Song Identification:

Italian Songs:
Slower beat
    Santa Lucia
    Ciribiribin
Faster beat
    Carnival of Venice
    Tarantella
    Italian street song
Opera Selections
    La Traviata — Verdi (1853)
    Aida — Verdi (1871)
    Pagliacci — Leoncavallo (1892)
    Barber of Seville — Rossini (1810)
    Madam Butterfly — Puccini (1904)
    La Bohème — Puccini (1896)

Solo Time: Residents, staff, volunteers, guest artists have the time to perform any Italian music or poetry or related memories. "O Sole Mio" is a traditional solo.

Rhythm Band: Grand March from *Aida* — very deliberate.
"Oh Marie" — graceful 3 beat.
"Arrivederci, Roma" — quarter note, quarter rest, 2 quarter notes.
"Tarantella" — played rapidly but with a steady beat.

Closing: The cruise ship returns to this great country. All sing "America" (My Country 'Tis of Thee) and loudly stress the words "of thee I sing." Upon end of song, "let freedom ring" all play instruments with vigor, loud and long. (A songsheet of verses 2 and 3 is included at the end of the OUR HISTORY IN SONG [July] weekly session plan.)

---

[1]   Points 3 and 4 in the Education section from *World Book Encyclopedia* (1991) Vol "I"— Italy: Arts, Music, p. 506.

Assignment: Plan on cruising to Germany next week. The assignment is to pack thoughts, memories, and songs of the country and bring along any souvenirs from there.

Music
Resources: *Sunny Italy's Folk Songs and Dances* (1983)
        "O Sole Mio" p. 2
        "Ciribiribin" p. 6
        "Carnival of Venice" p. 8
        "Oh Marie" p. 13
        "Santa Lucia " p. 14
        "Tarantella" p. 20
    Ultimate Fake Book (1981)
        "Funiculi, Funicula" p. 177
        "By the Beautiful Sea" p. 76
        "Come Back to Sorrento" p. 104
        "Arriverderci, Roma" p. 41
    Treasury of Grand Opera (1946)
        Opera music in Song Identification

Songs of Sunny Italy

1. O Sole Mio
2. Come Back to Sorrento
3. Ciribiribin
4. Oh Marie
5. Santa Lucia
6. Carnival of Venice
7. Funiculi, Funicula
8. Tarantella
9. Italian Street Song
10. Arrivederci, Roma

Select your favorite song.
I will play it for you!

BY THE BEAUTIFUL SEA

By the sea, by the sea By the Beautiful Sea
You and I, you and I Oh! how happy we'll be
When each wave comes a-rolling in
We will duck or swim
And we'll float and fool around the water
Over and under and then up for air
Pa is rich, Ma is rich so now what do we care?
I love to be beside your side, Beside the sea,
beside the seaside By the Beautiful Sea.

– Harold Atteridge (1914)

AND SO DO I

TO PINE AND SIGH

SOME JOYOUS SONG

IS FAR FROM WRONG

January Theme — **CRUISING THROUGH JANUARY**

Today's Theme — **There's Joy in Germany**

Advanced
Preparation: Provide:
- violin or tuba for decoration,
- posters of Germany,
- a good recording of a polka band or the "The Blue Danube Waltz" by Johann Strauss.

Pre-Session: A good recording of German songs plays as residents enter the room. All participants should greet each with a handshake and "Guten Morgen" or "Guten Tag" which means "Good morning" or "Good day." Listen especially for responses in German.

Opening: "Gesundheit song." Simply sing "gesundheit, gesundheit, gesundheit, gesund." Repeat. It means good health to you. (Music is included on page 50.) Aides circulate with singing and shaking hands passing along their good health. All should be encouraged to do the same. Continue singing and sharing healthy friendships as long as possible.

Exercise: Song with actions "Ich bin der Musikant" — Music is included on page 50. Ask German resident for help with pronunciation.[1]

Verse 1:
Leader	Ich bin ein Musikant (I am a musician)
	Ich komm von _____ (Name of your town)
	Ich kann spielen (I can play)
Response	DU KANNST SPIELEN? (You can play?)
Leader	Auf der Violine
Response	AUF DER VIOLINE
All	VIO, VIO, VIOLIN, VIOLIN, VIOLIN
	VIO, VIO, VIOLIN, VIO, VIOLIN. HEH!

(Add a loud HEH to the end of every verse)
Actions: sing and play violin using both arms correctly

Verse 2
Leader	Ich bin ein Musikant (I am a musician)
	Ich komm von _____ (Name of your town)
	Ich kann spielen (I can play)
Response	DU KANNST SPIELEN? (You can play?)
Leader	Auf der Bass viol
Response	AUF DER BASS VIOL

---

[1] There are variations in the words since the German language has feminine and masculine nouns; so one uses *der violine, dem piano, ein conductor, dem bagpipe*. Source is Frederick Herzer, German specialist in Webster Groves, MO in a private communication, October 17, 1992.

Exercise: All   ZUMBA, ZUMBA, ZUMBA, ZUM, ZUMBA, ZUM, ZUMBA, ZUM.
(Cont.)   ZUMBA, ZUMBA, ZUMBA, ZUM ZUMBA, ZUMBA, ZUM HEH!
                   Action: pretend to use bass bow by moving arm back and forth at waist level.

Verse 3
Same format. Use "auf dem Piano" for the instrument line and "plink plink, plink, plink...HEH!" for the last two lines.
Action: play pianistically either chords, scales, or one finger.

Verse 4
Same format. Use "Wie ein Conductor" for the instrument line. For the two lines at the end, all should imagine the melody and conduct silently in the air with 4 beats to a measure. End with a HEH!
Action: follow the conductor and direct the music with one arm.

Verse 5
Same format. Use "auf dem Bagpipe" (or dudelsack) for the instrument line and "wah, wah, wah, wah...HEH!" for the last two lines.
Action: hold nose for nasal sound while squeezing right arm into and out from the body.

Reminiscence: Find out who has German heritage. Encourage them with interviews. Tell travel tales, share souvenirs. Talk about the Danube River or the Rhein River, famous festivals, beer gardens, flowers, restaurants, castles, village bands, tubas, accordians, and violins.

Education: • 1961 — Berlin wall built to divide the city due to rising tension and to shut off the flow of refugees into West Germany.
                   • 1989 — Communists relaxed travel restrictions to the West and the wall was demolished.[1]
                   • Slogan of Chancellor Helmut Kohl in 1990 was "we are somebody again" as Germany unites.
                   • 80 million people combine to make a new superpower.[2]
                   • Germans swore off nuclear weapons long ago.
                   • Industries include Volkswagen cars, chemicals, tools.
                   • Some favorite foods are sauerbraten, beer, schnitzel, noodles.
                   • Famous Germans include Beethoven, Luther, Nietzsche.
                   • Love of family is still strong as is the love of music.[3]

Song
Identification:

Brahms' Lullaby	O Du lieber Augustin
The Blue Danube Waltz	Du, Du, liegst Mir im Herzen
Lili Marlene	Edelweiss
Stille Nacht — Silent Night	Lorelei
O Tannenbaum — O Christmas Tree *	

* A songsheet is included at the end of this week's session plan.

---

[1] Points 1 and 2 in Education section from *Information Please Almanac* (1992) "Countries of the World" — Germany, pp. 190-193.
[2] Points 3 and 4 from *Newsweek* Feb 26, 1990:16-18. "Special Report - A United Germany. The New Superpower" by Watson, R., M. Megeis, D. Pedersen, *et al.*
[3] Points 5-9 from *World Book Encyclopedia* (1991) Vol "G"— Germany, pp. 144-161.

Solo Time: Assemble your German residents up front and have them sing "Du, Du, liegst Mir im Herzen." Audience can join in the famous chorus of "Ja, Ja, Ja, Ja, " Encourage any German solos.

Rhythm Band: "O Du lieber Augustin" — 3/4 time. Use bass drum on the first beat with residents playing on the second and third beats.
                "Du, Du, liegst Mir im Herzen" — all play especially on the famous "Ja" chorus part.
                "Happy Wanderer" — all join in — play deliberately, the second time faster.
                "The Blue Danube Waltz" — as a response song — pianist plays the first part and the residents respond on the second and third beats.
                Piano: Danube so blue
                Residents: SHAKE, SHAKE, (rest) SHAKE, SHAKE.
                Continue on until ending when all play together in 3/4 time.
                "The Beer Barrel Polka" — merrily.

Closing: Song — tune of "O Du lieber Augustin"

                The more we get together, together, together,
                The more we get together, the happier we'll be
                For your friends are my friends
                And my friends are your friends
                The more we get together the happier we'll be

                Turn to each other and say "Auf Wiedersehn" which does not mean "goodbye," but "until we meet again."

Assignment: Encourage residents to enjoy memories of Germany and also appreciate German friends or heritage. Next week the ship will be cruising to Mexico and South America where it is sunny and warm. Invite them to bring along any memories of that area or any souvenirs. They should plan to dress lightly and expect a sunny time. SOUTH AMERICA TAKE IT AWAY.

Music
Resources: *Ultimate Fake Book* (1981)
                    "Lili Marlene" p. 343
                    "Edelweiss" p. 146
                    "Happy Wanderer" p. 204
                    "The Beer Barrel Polka" p. 52
                Legal Fake Book (1979)
                    "Lorelei" p. 178
                Germania Album (1934)
                    "O Du lieber Augustin" p. 29
                    "Du, Du, liegst Mir im Herzen" p. 3
                    "O Tannenbaum" p. 31
                Wee Sing Children's Songs and Fingerplays (1986)
                    "John Jacob Jingleheimer Schmidt" p. 26
                Songs for Swinging Housemothers (1961)
                    "Ich bin der Musikant" p. 406

GESUNDHEIT

Words & Music: J. Shaw

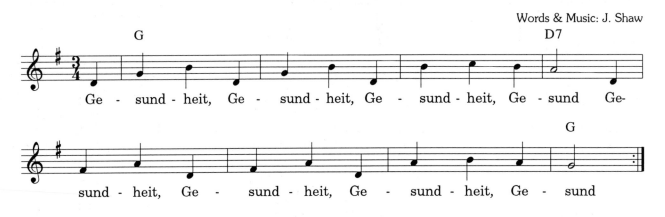

Ge - sund - heit, Ge - sund - heit, Ge - sund - heit, Ge - sund Ge-

sund - heit, Ge - sund - heit, Ge - sund - heit, Ge - sund

ICH BIN DER MUSIKANT

German Folk Song

Ich bin der Mus - i - kant, Deutsch - es Vat - er - lan - de. Ich kann es

spiel - en. Was kannst du spiel - en? Spiel - en on my vi - o - lin,

vi - o, vi - o, vi - o - la, vi - o, vi - o, vi - o - la, vi - o, vi - o, vi - o - la.

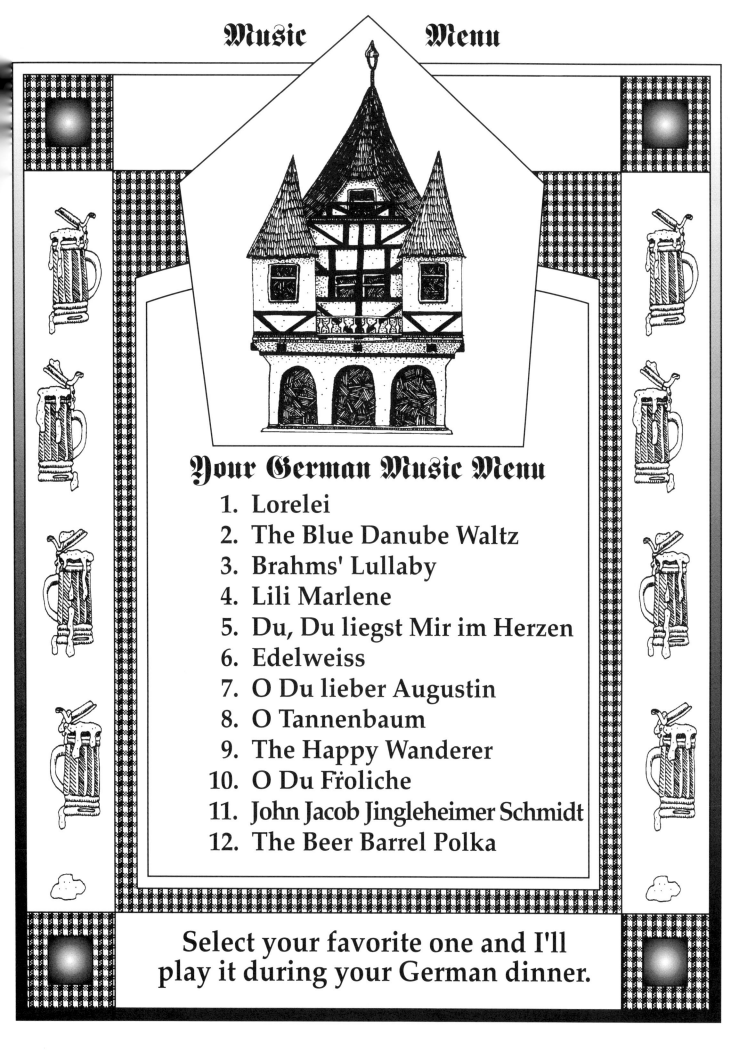

Your German Music Menu

1. Lorelei
2. The Blue Danube Waltz
3. Brahms' Lullaby
4. Lili Marlene
5. Du, Du liegst Mir im Herzen
6. Edelweiss
7. O Du lieber Augustin
8. O Tannenbaum
9. The Happy Wanderer
10. O Du Fröliche
11. John Jacob Jingleheimer Schmidt
12. The Beer Barrel Polka

Select your favorite one and I'll
play it during your German dinner.

O Tannenbaum

O Tannenbaum, O Tannenbaum, wie treu sind deine Blätter.

O Tannenbaum, O Tannenbaum, wie treu sind deine Blätter.

Du grunst nicht nur zur Sommerzeit,

Nein auch im Winter wenn es schneit.

O Tannenbaum, O Tannenbaum, wie treu sind deine Blätter.

– German Traditional

O Christmas Tree

O Christmas Tree, O Christmas Tree, thy leaves are so unchanging.

O Christmas Tree, O Christmas Tree, thy leaves are so unchanging

Not only green when summer's here,

But also when 'tis cold and drear.

O Christmas Tree, O Christmas Tree, thy leaves are so unchanging.

– English verse by James Ryder Randall (1861)

January Theme — **CRUISING THROUGH JANUARY**

Today's Theme — **South America Take It Away**

Advanced
Preparation:
- Collect the following props:
  - Mexican hat,
  - marachas,
  - record of Latin American music,
  - decorations/posters,
  - lots of plants,
  - serapes,
  - Mexican blankets.

Pre-Session: Latin American records play as residents enter the room that has been colorfully decorated with sombreros, Mexican hats, bongo drums, and plants.

Opening: Welcome everybody aboard the cruise ship as it sails to South America. Suggest residents close their eyes while pianist plays "Sailing." Imagine a smooth cruise southward. They can then open eyes and experience the warm sunshine that greets everyone. Using the scale on the piano, have residents say "ahhhhhhhhhh" as they raise their voices and warm up to the climate. Then descend using the scale and soft ending.

Exercise: Using the song "La Cucaracha," teach the following words so all can sing easily

    La cucaracha, la cucaracha, it's a lively latin dance
    La cucaracha, la cucaracha, it's the rumba of romance.

Exercise: Clap hands, lift shoulders, clasp hands and sway from side to side, slight body twist.

Wheelchair
Dance: Place large Mexican hat in center of room. Four aides assist four wheelchair residents with the dance. Music is the "Mexican Hat Dance." Circle around the hat to eight bars of music. Reverse direction next eight bars. All four pull backwards eight bars, to the center eight bars, reverse eight bars, center eight bars, repeat the circle. Everyone else clapping at the same time. Invite another set of dancers.

Reminiscence: Share any memories of this area including the South American countries as well as Mexico. Talk about the landscapes, the people, the weather, flowers, piñatas, food, music, instruments used. Share any souvenirs or note clothing that they are wearing.

Education: **Mexico**
                    • The capital of Mexico is Mexico City where they use the peso for currency.
                    • There is a 88% literacy rate.
                    • They grow corn, sugar, cotton.
                    • It is one fifth the size of the US.
                    • Spanish is the language spoken.[1]
                    Brazil
                    • This country occupies half of South America.
                    • They grow coffee, sugar, oranges, cocoa, soybeans, tobacco, and raise cattle.
                    • There are steel and chemical plants.
                    • There is a 76% literacy rate.
                    • It is the 5th largest country in the world behind USSR, Canada, China and the US.[2]
                    • Portugese is the language spoken.

Song
Identification: All Spanish songs:
                        South America Take it Away
                        The Dove — La Paloma
                        Mexican Hat Dance — Jarabe Tapatio
                        Beautiful Heaven — Cielito Lindo
                        Clap Hands Dance — Chiapanecas
                        Goodbye Boys — Adios Muchachos
                        In a Little Spanish Town
                        Tico Tico
                        Take Back Your Rumba

Rhythm Band: "Toreador Song" — 2 strong beats
                    "Tico Tico" — lilting 2 beat
                    "In a Little Spanish Town" — shakers or maracas only.
                    "Take Back Your Rumba" — demonstrate tempo first.
                    "La Cucaracha" — strong beats.
                    "El Relicario" — swinging 3 beat.
                    "Chiapanecas" — start familiar part first with piano solo. Indicate when
                        residents should respond with instruments. 3/4 section everyone plays
                        together.
                    "Tarantella" — lively finale.

Closing: This ends the January cruise. Recall all the places they have been and that
                    there is no place like home. Board the ship and with joyful voices conclude
                    with singing "America" (My Country, 'Tis of Thee) or "God Bless America."
                    (A songsheet with verses 2 and 3 of "America" is included at the end of the
                    OUR HISTORY IN SONG [July] weekly session plan.)

---

[1] Information from *Information Please Almanac* (1992) "Countries of the World" — Mexico, pp. 224-225.
[2] Ibid. "Countries of the World" — Brazil, pp. 158-159.

Assignment: Ask that residents appreciate the United States. They can enjoy recalling some of the trips they took years ago not only to foreign lands but also in the US. Encourage them to get out their scrapbooks and reminisce. Then give thanks for the privilege of living in this great country. Suggest they think of some of their favorite songs about America.

Music
Resources: *Latin American Music for Piano or Organ* (1969)
        "La Paloma" (The Dove) p. 19
        "Cielito Lindo" (Beautiful Heaven) p. 3
        "Chiapanecas" (Clap Hands Dance) p. 4
        "Adios Muchachos" (Goodbye Boys) p. 14
        "El Relicario" (Rendezvous) p. 12
    Ultimate Fake Book (1981)
        "Mañana" p. 363
        "Toreador Song" p. 599
    Great Latin American Song Book (1985)
        "Mexican Hat Dance" p. 226
        "South America Take it Away" p. 289
        "Tico Tico" p. 322
    Song Session Community Song Book (1953)
        "Sailing" p. 77
    Sixty Progressive Piano Pieces (1938)
        "Tarantella" p. 104

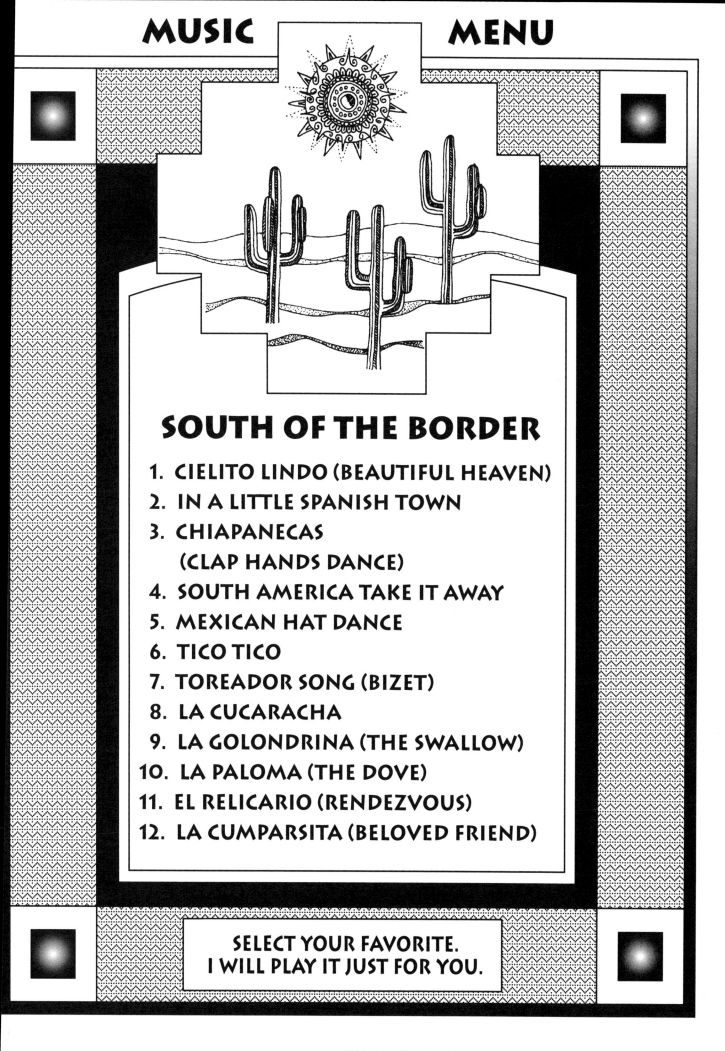

SOUTH OF THE BORDER

1. **CIELITO LINDO (BEAUTIFUL HEAVEN)**
2. **IN A LITTLE SPANISH TOWN**
3. **CHIAPANECAS (CLAP HANDS DANCE)**
4. **SOUTH AMERICA TAKE IT AWAY**
5. **MEXICAN HAT DANCE**
6. **TICO TICO**
7. **TOREADOR SONG (BIZET)**
8. **LA CUCARACHA**
9. **LA GOLONDRINA (THE SWALLOW)**
10. **LA PALOMA (THE DOVE)**
11. **EL RELICARIO (RENDEZVOUS)**
12. **LA CUMPARSITA (BELOVED FRIEND)**

**SELECT YOUR FAVORITE.
I WILL PLAY IT JUST FOR YOU.**

January Theme — **CRUISING THROUGH JANUARY**

Today's Theme — **Everything's Coming Up Roses**
(Optional)

Advanced
Preparation:
- Prepare some foam or paper plates with pictures of roses pasted on them. Rose catalogs are very useful here! Lightly spray rose perfume on them.
- Decorate the room with paper or silk roses in a vase.
- Have ready a collection of songs about roses.
- Organize a vocalist to sing "Everything's Coming Up Roses."

Pre-Session: Live piano music or taped songs about roses can be played as residents enter.

Opening: Announce the theme of this being a brand new year and with a positive attitude we can experience the expression that EVERYTHING'S COMING UP ROSES.

Opening song — "Make New Friends" — discuss the significance.
Review the song as follows. Sing in unison, then as a round. Practice first as a chant:

> Make new friends but keep the old.
> One is silver and the other is gold.

Exercise: Use the prepared paper plates. Share flowers with others by raising all the red roses in the air for all to see. Then the other colors.

"Sweet Rosie O'Grady" — Circle with one arm. Change arms. Note the scent of the air
"Yellow Rose of Texas" — Swing arm beside chair in tempo.
"Second Hand Rose" — Tap plate on lap to the music, change to other body parts keeping the tempo.
Finale — Good arm extension. At the count of three, throw the roses right at your leader. Watch her pick them all up.

Reminiscence: Talk about New Year celebrations in the past. Tie it in with the subject of old friends and new friends and the joy of each. Ask the question "how important is it to keep on making new friends?" Friends are just like the roses, very precious.

Education:
- New Year's Day is the first day of the Gregorian calendar year. 1990 was the 6703rd year of the Julian period, a time frame consisting of 7980 years which began on January 1st, 4713 B.C.
- It is a public holiday in many countries, a time for stocktaking, closing the past year's business log and starting a new financial period.
- The new year will have us all traveling 583,416,000 miles in orbit around the sun in 365 days.

Education (Cont.)	• Sometimes it is called "everyone's birthday" since some countries observe this day as the day your age changes not the actual anniversary of your birth.[1]
Song Identification:	All of the following songs have the word rose in the title. Be the first to identify it as the pianist plays them.

The ROSE of No Man's Land
The ROSE of Tralee
My Wild Irish ROSE *
ROSES of Picardy
Red ROSES for a Blue Lady
Love Sends a Little Gift of ROSES
Yellow ROSE of Texas
Mexicali ROSE
Second Hand ROSE
Moonlight and ROSES
ROSE of Washington Square
ROSE of Mandalay

* A songsheet is included at the end of this week's session plan.

Solo Time:	"Everything's Coming Up Roses" — guest artist or resident. Any song about roses or group singing
Rhythm Band:	Welcome the New Year with rhythm instruments. "Yellow Rose of Texas" — all play merrily. "Second Hand Rose" — play with instruments swaying side to side. "The Rose of Tralee" — waltz tempo. "Ramblin' Rose" — all together with a deliberate beat. "America" — all sing and play. At the end "let freedom ring" play with vigor for as long as possible. (A songsheet of verses 2 and 3 is included at the end of the OUR HISTORY IN SONG [July] weekly session plan.)
Closing:	All sing to the tune of "Happy Birthday" ("Good Morning"). Music is included on page 61. Verse: 1. Happy New Year to you. (pointing to each other as they sing) 2. Happy New Year to me. (point to self) 3. Happy New Year to us. (arms up high)
Assignment:	Invite residents to make a resolution right now to contact an old friend with a phone call, a note, or a good thought and tell them they are appreciated. Then resolve to make a new friend today. Get ready for the New Year by CRUISING THROUGH JANUARY—the theme for the month.

---

[1] All information in the Education section from *Chases Annual Events* (1992) "Christian Calendar" p. 2.

Music
Resources: *Ultimate Fake Book* (1981)
                    "Everything's Coming Up Roses" p. 148
                    "Red Roses for a Blue Lady" p. 468
                    "The Rose of Tralee" p. 472
                    "Rose of Washington Square" p. 475
                    "Roses of Picardy" p. 476
             Greatest Legal Fake Book of All Times (1981)
                    "Yellow Rose of Texas" p. 616
                    "My Wild Irish Rose" p. 338

GOOD-MORNING TO YOU

Words: Mildred J. Hill

Music: Patty S. Hill

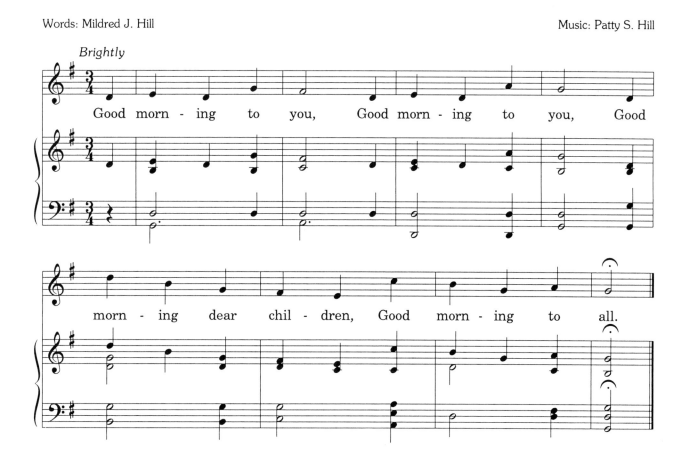

Everything's Coming Up Roses

1. Roses of Picardy
2. My Wild Irish Rose
3. Yellow Rose of Texas
4. Red Roses for a Blue Lady
5. Ramblin' Rose
6. Moonlight and Roses
7. Rose of Washington Square
8. To a Wild Rose
9. Lida Rose
10. 'Tis the Last Rose of Summer
11. Mighty Lak' a Rose

Choose your favorite.
I'll play it just for you.

MY WILD IRISH ROSE

My wild Irish Rose,
the sweetest flow'r that grows,
You may search ev'rywhere
but none can compare
with my wild Irish Rose.
My wild Irish Rose,
the dearest flow'r that grows,
and some day for my sake,
she may let me take
the bloom from my wild Irish Rose.

– Chauncey Olcott (1899)

February

It's a
Love-ly
Month

Musical Game
— for —
February

February is famous for being a month full of love. Here are some of the artists you have loved through the years. Match the song that made them beloved to our hearts. Here is an example: The answer to number one, Kate Smith, is letter B or God Bless America. Ask the younger generation if they know any of these famous songs.

1. Kate Smith

2. Maurice Chevalier

3. Jack Benny

4. Ethel Merman

5. Jimmy Durante

6. Marlene Dietrich

7. Nelson Eddy

8. Bing Crosby

9. Bob Hope

10. Judy Garland

A. White Christmas

B. God Bless America

C. Sweethearts

D. Thanks for the Memory

E. There's No Business Like Show Business

F. Love in Bloom

G. Lili Marlene

H. Over the Rainbow

I. Thank Heaven for Little Girls

J. Inka Dinka Doo

The answers are upside down.

1. B, 2. I, 3. F, 4. E, 5. J, 6. G, 7. C, 8. A, 9. D, 10. H

Now for extra points, see if you can sing or hum these songs. You get 10 points for each one. You'll be a sweetheart if you get seventy. If you get all of them, then you get to make up the next puzzle.

IT'S A LOVELY MONTH
FEBRUARY

Traditionally Valentine's Day is the highlight of the month with love being the theme. Decorations are easy and the environment is a loving one throughout the month. Schedule Ground-Hog Day and Valentine's Day first and then arrange the programs to best meet the needs of your residents. The final order of programs should be publicized with a huge poster and also announced in the daily news and monthly newsletter.

The following programs keep the love theme alive with many opportunities for reflection and appreciation.

I Love You and Me — Friendships are necessary to human growth and development. No man is an island. It starts with loving oneself and then extending outward to others. This program makes it easy to do.

It's Valentine Love — Time for celebrating this holiday with red hearts, love songs galore and then wearing a heart that tells the world who you love.

Love Those Ladies — This is a very popular activity so extra hands are needed. Staff, residents, and family all are curious as to the meaning of their name. Wearing that information as a badge takes extra time so volunteers are needed to research and write the information on large paper hearts and then scotch tape them to each person. Several resource books should be on hand. It is advisable to write several name tags ahead of time. Example: on a large paper heart write person's name and the meaning.

Love Those Stouthearted Men — Everyone has had a meaningful man in their life and it's time to honor them. This program is similar to the "Ladies" session. It investigates men's names and instigates many a song.

Everyone Loves a Smile — You get to pack up all your troubles in an old kit bag for one hour. Results guaranteed and no one wants their troubles back so smile, smile, smile.

OPTIONAL PROGRAMS

Ground-Hog Day — Be prepared for lots of conversation no matter what the weather is that day. There are lots of appropriate songs and you will end up looking for the silver lining.

Presidents' Day — Hail to the Chiefs — Programs designed to honor all our great leaders. Presidents Lincoln and Washington are highlighted since many recall honoring them years ago specifically on their respective birthdays in February.

LOVE LIFTED ME

February Theme — **IT'S A LOVELY MONTH**

Today's Theme — **I Love You and Me**

Advanced
Preparation:
- Prepare some paper plates with roses pasted on them and scented lightly with rose perfume.
- Prepare a collection of songs about "you and me."
- Prepare music for "Tea for Two" and "Make New Friends." You will also need music to "It's Love That Makes the World Go 'Round" which is included at the end of this week's session plan.

Pre-Session: Love songs are played on the piano or tape recorder as residents enter room.

Opening: Song: "Make New Friends"
                  Make new friends but keep the old
                  One is silver, and the other gold.
                  Teach in unison, and then sing as a 2-part round with each part being led by a strong singer, one of whom should be a resident.

Exercise: Use paper plates with roses pasted on them. Identify colors first, all those with red roses should display theirs for all to see. Continue with yellow, white, pink. Exercise with these YOU songs.
                  YOU songs:
                  "When YOU Wore a Tulip and I Wore a Big Red Rose"— exercise leader important.
                  "YOU Are My Sunshine" — roses overhead, circular movements.

                  ME songs:
                  "For ME and My Gal" — sideways
                  "ME and My Shadow" — lead with 8 counts on various parts of the body.
                  Finale — On the count of 3, enjoy tossing the plate right at the therapist. She needs the exercise too.

Reminiscence: Get residents to talk about an old friendship that has stood the test of time. Ask them what makes it precious? Describe one person that is still very important in their life. The YOU and ME relationship is a treasure. The song "Make New Friends but Keep the Old" has extra meaning as we all value the years of friendship we have known, but the song reminds everyone to make new friendships.

Education: Famous quotations to be read by residents.

                  - "The only way to have a friend is to be one." — Ralph Waldo Emerson.[1]
                  - "Be courteous to all, but intimate with few, and let those few be well tried before you give them your confidence. True friendship is a plant of slow growth." — George Washington.[2]

---

[1] Safire and Safir (1982) *Good Advice,* p. 131.
[2] Ibid. p. 130.

Education: (Cont.)

- "Heaven's eternal wisdom has decreed that man should *ever* stand in need of man." — Theocritus.[1]
- "It is great to have friends when one is young, but indeed it is still more so when you are getting old. When we are young, friends are like everything else, a matter of course. In the old days we know what it means to have them." — Edvard Grieg.[2]
- Friendship poem:
    Whenever I am plunged in woe
    My true friends rally round
    So trouble is a friendship test
    If nothing else, I've found.[3]

Song Identification:

Songs with You and/or Me in the title

YOU Made Me Love YOU
YOU Are My Sunshine
YOU Light up my Life
When YOU Were Sweet Sixteen
When YOU Wore a Tulip and I Wore a Big Red Rose
Have I Told YOU Lately That I love YOU
Meet ME in St. Louis, Louis
For ME and My Gal
ME and My Shadow
Drink to ME Only With Thine Eyes *
YOU Were Meant for ME
YOU Tell ME Your Dream

* A songsheet is included at the end of the SEEING IS BELIEVING [April] weekly session plan.

Rhythm Band:

"For Me and My Gal" — bells only.
"Me and My Shadow" — sticks only.
"You are My Sunshine" — all the other instruments.
"All of Me" — everybody join in.
"Tea for Two" — Divide the group into two sections. One part plays only on the YOU, the other on the word ME.
    Picture YOU upon my knee, just tea for two and two for tea
    Just YOU and ME and YOU for ME alone.
    Nobody near us to see us to hear us,
    No friends or relations on weekend vacations,
    We won't have it known, dear, that we own a telephone, dear.
    Day will break and YOU'll awake and start to bake a sugar cake
    For ME to take for all the boys to see
    WE will raise a family, a boy for YOU, a girl for ME
    Oh, can't YOU see how happy we would be.
End with a march that includes you, me, and everybody.

---

[1] Edwards, T. (1936) *New Dictionary of Thoughts*, p, 125.
[2] Ibid. p. 207.
[3] McCann, R. (1932) *Complete Cheerful Cherub*, p. 176.

Closing: Group singing: (the music is included below.)
                      Verse:
                      1. It's love it's love, it's love that makes the world go 'round. (sung three
                         times)
                         It's love that makes the world go 'round.
                      2. It's YOU that makes the world go 'round (point to each other, aides,
                         circulating rapidly around room pointing)
                      3. It's ME that makes the world go 'round (point to self)
                      4. It's US that makes the world go 'round (all arms up)

Assignment: Encourage residents to name three good friends and analyze what makes them
                      so special. They could write, phone, or tell them personally of the value of the
                      friendship.

Music
Resources: *We Sing Around the Campfire* (1984)
                              "Make New Friends" p. 45
                      Legal Fake Book (1979)
                              "Tea for Two" p. 283
                      Wings of Song (1984)
                              "It's Love that Makes the World Go 'Round" page 354
                      All American Song Book (1984)
                              "When you Wore a Tulip" p. 35
                              "Drink to Me Only with Thine Eyes" p. 45
                      Treasury of Best Loved Songs (1981)
                              "For Me and My Gal" p. 178
                      Ultimate Fake Book (1981)
                              "Me and My Shadow" p. 375

IT'S LOVE THAT MAKES THE WORLD GO 'ROUND

Traditional

It's love, it's love, it's love that makes the world go 'round. It's love, it's
love, it's love that makes the world go 'round. It's love, it's love, it's
love that makes the world go 'round. It's love that makes the world go 'round.

MUSIC MENU

Songs about YOU and ME

1. *YOU* Made Me Love *YOU*
2. I Love *YOU* Truly
3. *YOU* are My Sunshine
4. When *YOU* were Sweet Sixteen
5. When *YOU* Wore a Tulip
   and I Wore a Big Red Rose
6. Have I Told *YOU* Lately
   that I Love *YOU*
7. Meet *ME* in St. Louis, Louis
8. For *ME* and My Gal
9. *ME* and My Shadow
10. Drink to *ME* Only With Thine Eyes
11. *YOU* were Meant for *ME*
12. *YOU* Tell *ME* Your Dream

_____

Let ME play your choice for YOU.

I Love You Truly

I Love You Truly, truly dear!
Life with its sorrow,
Life with its tear,
Fades into dreams
When I feel you are near,
For I love you Truly,
truly dear!

– Carrie Jacobs Bond (1901)

February Theme — **IT'S A LOVELY MONTH**

Today's Theme— **It's Valentine Love**

Advanced
Preparation:

- Props will include:
  - a collection of love songs,
  - paper and pen for reporters and scotch tape
  - 4-inch red paper hearts for everyone using the templates at the end of this session plan,
  - old sheet music.
- Suggest that everyone wear something red or white or use a red accessory.
- Make enough copies of the large print songsheet of "Love's Old Sweet Song" for everyone, included at the end of this week's session plan.
- See if you can get a violinist to play for Solo Time.

Pre-Session: Love songs being played on the piano as residents enter the room could include "Love's Old Sweet Song," "I Love You Truly," "Indian Love Call," "Liebestraum" (Dream of Love). (A songsheet to "I Love You Truly" is included at the end of the I LOVE YOU AND ME [February] weekly session plan.)

Opening: Group singing **and** exercise. The music is included on page 70.
Verse:
1. It's love it's love, it's love that makes the world go 'round. (sung three times)
   It's love that makes the world go 'round.
2. It's peace......
3. It's faith ......
4. It's you... (point directly to people all around the room)
5. It's me... (point to self and realize this truth)
6. It's us... (all arms up)

Group Singing: "Love's Old Sweet Song" — use large print songsheets.
"Let Me Call You Sweetheart" — a great favorite.

Education:
- This is a celebration of 2 Christian martyrs, a priest and a physician.
- The tradition of choosing one's valentine may be traced to the Roman feast of Lupercalia, which began on Feb. 15. The selection was random. Roman maidens would place their names in an urn. A 12-month courting period would ensue, including the writing of love notes.
- The first known Valentine card was sent from the Tower of London by a French prisoner to his wife in 1415.
- In 1988, 900 million Valentines were sent in the US.
- It is the most widely observed unofficial holiday.[1]

Solo Time: Violin solo of "Beautiful Thoughts of Love" or piano solo of "Liebestraum" (Dream of Love) by Lizst.

---

[1] All information in the Education section from *Chases Annual Events* (1992) "Chronological Calendar" p. 50.

Group
Discussion: Ask the residents: "Who do you love or have you loved?" Volunteer writes
                       response on paper red heart that says "I love _____. It can be an
                       employee, relative, pet or politician. Attach with scotch tape that has been
                       pre-cut for efficiency.

Song
Identification: All the following songs have LOVE in the title. Pass around old sheet music
                       with the nostalgic covers for stimulation.

                              I LOVE You Truly
                              The LOVE Nest
                              I'm Falling in LOVE with Someone
                              LOVE in Bloom
                              I LOVE You
                              What is this Thing Called LOVE?
                              I'll Be LOVING You Always
                              If I LOVED You
                              Indian LOVE Call
                              I LOVE Coffee *

                       *   Music is included on page 160.

Guided Imagery: In this exercise, residents can send a Valentine to their loved one. Group
                       closes their eyes and listens to soft music played as they recall someone they
                       love. They mentally picture them in their minds and send them a loving
                       message silently, knowing that they will receive it. Encourage residents to send
                       several this way later on. This eases frustration of mailing, postage, and
                       selection and makes the holiday meaningful.

Rhythm Band: "The Love Nest" — simple 2 beat.
                       "True Love" — waltz tempo.
                       "Will You Remember" (Sweetheart) — same.
                       "Peg o' My Heart" — lively 2. (A songsheet is included at the end of the
                           HEALTHY HEARTS [October] weekly session plan.)
                       "Dear Hearts and Gentle People" — livelier tempo. (A songsheet is included at
                           the end of the MY HOMETOWN [July] weekly session plan.)

Closing: Closing song to the tune of "I've Got Music in My Hands." (The music is
                       included on page 75.)
                       1. I've got love in my hands and its keeping me alive, keeping me alive,
                          keeping me alive. (repeat)
                       2. Love in my hands (clap hands)
                       3. Love in my feet (wiggle feet)
                       4. Love in my shoulder (lift shoulders)
                       5. Love everywhere (arms out with smiles)

Assignment: Next week's theme is LOVE THOSE LADIES. Get the residents to start thinking about some of their favorite ladies' names including their own. Ask them to think of a song about them. Do the know the meaning of their names?

Music
Resources:
Golden Book of Favorite Songs (1946)
  "Love's Old Sweet Song" p. 45
Wings of Song (1984)
  "It's Love that Makes the World Go 'Round" p. 354"
Great Music's Greatest Hits (1982)
  "Liebestraum" p. 173
Family Song Book of Faith and Joy (1981)
  "Dear Hearts and Gentle People" p. 8
Legal Fake Book (1979)
  The Love Nest" p. 181
Ultimate Fake Book (1981)
  "I Love You Truly" p. 238

I'VE GOT MUSIC IN MY HANDS

Words by Joan Shaw   Music: African-American Spiritual

Music Menu

LOVE

1. I **LOVE** You Truly
2. The **LOVE** Nest
3. **LOVE** in Bloom
4. Beautiful Thoughts of **LOVE**
5. Pagan **LOVE** Song
6. What is this Thing Called **LOVE**
7. **LOVE** and the Weather
8. **LOVE** Sends a Little Gift of Roses
9. **LOVE'S** Old Sweet Song
10. If I **LOVED** You
11. I'm Falling in **LOVE** with Someone
12. It's **LOVE** that Makes the World Go 'Round

Select your favorite LOVE music.
Cupid will play it just for you!

LOVE'S
OLD SWEET
SONG

Just a song at twilight
When the lights are low
And the flickering shadows
Softly come and go.

Tho the heart be weary
Sad the day and long
Still to us at twilight
Comes love's old song -
        Comes
Love's old sweet song.

*– G. Clifton Bingham &
James L. Molloy (1884)*

I LOVE
_____

I LOVE
_____

I LOVE
_____

I LOVE
_____

February Theme — **IT'S A LOVELY MONTH**

Today's Theme — **Love Those Ladies**

Advanced
Preparation:

- Make yellow star-shaped nametags using the templates at the end of this week's session plan.
- Provide:
    - black magic markers, scotch tape,
    - songs with ladies' names in the title.
- Find some books containing the meaning of names and make a list of those most commonly used in your facility.[1]
- This program will need aides.
- As set out in the Reminiscence section, it might be a good idea to find out the meaning of some of the residents' names before the session.

Pre-Session: Live piano music using songs with ladies' names in them playing as residents enter the room. Announce the theme of LOVE and that the ladies will be honored today. Next week it will be the men's turn.

Opening: Song sung by music therapist and aides as they shake hands with everyone. Repeat till all hands are shaken. Sing to the tune of "Goodnight Ladies."
                 Hello ladies, hello ladies, hello ladies
                 It's time to greet you now.
                 Merrily we sing along, sing along, sing along
                 Merrily we sing along, sing along to you.

                 As familiarity increases, residents join in singing and sing to person beside them.

Exercise: Sing to the tune of "He's Got The Whole World in His Hands"
                 Verse:
                 1. He's got all the ladies in His hands (clap hands)
                    He's got all the ladies in His hands
                    He's got all the ladies in His hands
                    He's got the ladies in His hands.
                 2. He's got all the ladies in His arms (cross arms over chest and move out and in)
                 3. He's got all the men in His hands (clasp hands, sway side to side)
                 4. He's got [use one person's name] in His hands (clap hands)
                 5. He's got everybody in His hands (arms overhead and down)

Reminiscence: Ask some of the following questions to stimulate recall and discussion:
                 - Who named you?
                 - Do you like your name?
                 - Do you know what it means?
                 Use the volunteers to look up the meaning using library books. This can be done earlier using list of residents. If the name is not listed or is negative in

---

[1]   Kolatch, A. (1986) *Name Dictionary.*

| Reminiscence: (Cont.) | meaning, let the group decide on a new meaning. Use pre-cut large yellow paper stars with person's name and meaning on them and scotch tape to blouses/shirts for all to see and comment on. |

Education:

- Ask if anyone has ever wondered if their name was popular. Read the popular names of 1906 — Mary (3,720,000) was the number one name followed by Elizabeth, Barbara and Dorothy.[1] Now they are Jessica, Amanda, Ashley, Jennifer, Sarah, Nicole, and Megan.[2] Find out from residents some of the modern names of their grandchildren.[3]
- Ask the residents if they like their names. Ask if anyone has ever wanted to change their name. See if they know the stage names of the following:[4]

Diane Belmont — Lucille Ball   Frances Gumm — Judy Garland
Lucille Lesuer — Joan Crawford   Gretchen Young — Loretta Young
Doris Kappelhoff — Doris Day
Esther "Eppi" Pauline Freidman Lederer — Ann Landers

Song Identification:

Read the ladies' names and remember a song about them. Sing part of it. If popular, everyone can sing it:

Adeline — Sweet Adeline   **Lucille** — In My Merry Oldsmobile *
Alice — Alice Blue Gown   **Katy** — K-K-K-Katy §
Amy — Once in Love with Amy   **Linda** — same
Annie — Annie Laurie,   **Maggie** — When You and I Were
         Little Annie Rooney   Young
Bonnie — My Bonnie Lies Over the   **Maria** — Ave Maria
         Ocean   **Marie** — Oh Marie
Mary Lou — Mary Lou I Love You   **Mame** — same
Cecelia — same   **Margie** — same
Daisy — Daisy, Daisy   **Mona Lisa** — same
Dinah — Aunt Dinah's Quilting   **Mary** — Mary's a Grand Old Name
         Party   **Nellie** — Seeing Nellie Home
Grace — Amazing Grace   **Peg** — Peg o' My Heart †
Genevieve — Sweet Genevieve   **Peggy** — Peggy O'Neil
Georgia — Sweet Georgia Brown   **Polly** — Polly, Wolly Doodle
Ida — Ida, Sweet as Apple Cider   **Susie** — If You Knew Susie
Jeannie — I Dream of Jeannie   **Sally** — I Wonder What's Become of
Jeannine — Jeannine I Dream   Sally

*   A songsheet is included at the end of the YOU AUTO REMEMBER YOUR AUTOMBILE [September] weekly session plan.
§ A songsheet is included at the end of the THEY FOUGHT FOR FREEDOM [July] weekly session plan.
† A songsheet is included at the end of the HEALTHY HEARTS [October] weekly session plan.

1 *Modern American Encyclopedia of Names for Your Baby.* "Names 25 Years Ago" pp. 17-22.
2 Rosenkrantz and Satran (1988) *Beyond Jennifer and Jason* p. 40.
3 For further reference on names, recommended books include: Stewart, G. (1979) *American Given Names;* Bailey, S. (1982) *Big Book of Baby Names;* Train, J. (1977) *Remarkable Names of Real People.*
4 Lansky and Lansky (1984) *Best Baby Name Book.* "The Name Exchange" pp. 25-28.

Song
Identification:
(Cont.)
	Josephine — Come, Josephine,
	      in my Flying Machine
	Juanita — same
	Kathleen — I'll Take You Home
	      Again, Kathleen
		Tootsie — Toot Toot Tootsie
		Violet — Sweet Violets
		Virginia — Carry Me Back
		Liza Jane — same

Rhythm Band:
    "Alice Blue Gown" — nice 3.
    "Peggy O'Neil" — faster 3.
    "Cecelia" — in 4 deliberately.
    "Aunt Dinah's Quilting Party" — faster 4.
    "Georgia Brown" — fast 2.
    "Peg o' My Heart" — in 2 for first part, strong 1 beat in middle section. (A songsheet in included at the end of the HEALTHY HEARTS [October] weekly session plan.
    "Cleopha's March" — Scott Joplin — strong 2.

Closing:
    Sing to the tune of "Goodnight Ladies":
        So long ladies, so long ladies, so long ladies until we meet again.
    Turn to each other and sing. Include a men's verse.

Assignment:
    Next week the STOUTHEARTED MEN are honored. The assignment is to start thinking about favorite men in their life, their names and any songs that include their names.

Music
Resources:
    Golden Book of Favorite Songs (1946)
        "Good Night Ladies" p. 116
        "Aunt Dinah's Quilting Party" p. 125
    All American Song Book (1984)
        "Peggy O'Neil" p. 39
        "Peg o' My Heart" p. 33
    Treasury of Best Loved Songs (1981)
        "Alice Blue Gown" p. 204
    Collected Piano Works of Scott Joplin (1972)
        "Cleopha's March" p. 47

Can you name a song about these LADIES?

Nola Annie Marie Ida

Peg Katy Alice Rose

Susie Margie Georgia Adeline

Genevieve Josephine Caroline

I will play it for you!

Music Menu

Yellow

February Theme –   **IT'S A LOVELY MONTH**

Today's Theme –   **Stouthearted Men**

Advanced
Preparation:
- Cut out the yellow star-shaped nametags as done for LOVE THOSE LADIES.
- Provide:
    - black magic markers, scotch tape,
    - songs with men's names in the title.
- Find some books containing the meaning of names and make a list of the most commonly used names in your facility.[1]
- This program will need aides.
- As set out in the Reminiscence section, it might be a good idea to find out the meaning of some of the residents' names before the session.

Pre-Session: Live piano music using songs with men's names in them should be played as they enter, such as "Bill Bailey, Won't You Please Come Home," "Oh Johnny, Oh Johnny, Oh!" "Oh Jimmy Crack Corn," "Peter Cottontail." Last song should be "Stouthearted Men." Announce the theme of LOVE THOSE STOUTHEARTED MEN.

Opening: Song sung by music therapist and aides as they shake hands with everyone. Repeat till all hands are shaken. Sing to the tune of "Goodnight Ladies."
Hello gentlemen, hello gentlemen, hello gentlemen
It's time to greet you now.
Merrily we sing along, sing along, sing along
Merrily we sing along, sing along to you.

As familiarity increases, residents join in singing and sing to the men in the room, pointing to them.

Exercise: Sing to the tune of "He's Got The Whole World in His Hands"
Verses:
1. He's got all the gentlemen in His hands (clap hands)
2. He's got all the gentlemen in His arms (cross arms over chest and move out and in)
3. He's got all the grandfathers in His hands (clasp hands, sway side to side)
4. He's got [use one person's name] in His hands (clap hands)
5. He's got everybody in His hands (arms overhead and down)

Reminiscence: Ask some of the following questions to stimulate recall and discussion:
- Who named you?
- Do you like your name?
- Do you know what it means?
Use the volunteers to look up the meaning using library books. This can be done earlier using a list of the residents. If the name is not listed or is negative in meaning, let the group decide on a new meaning. Use pre-cut large yellow paper stars with person's name and meaning on them and scotch tape to blouses/shirts for all to see and comment on.

---

[1]   Kolatch, A. (1986) *Name Dictionary.*

Education: • Ask if anyone has ever wondered if their name was popular. Read the popular names of 1906 — John (5,837,000) then William, George, Robert, Thomas, Henry and Joseph.[1] In 1992 they were Michael, Christopher, Matthew, Andrew, Daniel, Joshua, David and Joseph.[2] Find out from residents some of the modern names of their grandchildren.[3]
                    • Ask the residents if they like their names. Ask if anyone has ever wanted to change their name. See if they know the stage name of the following:[4]
                         Joe Yule, Jr.— Mickey Rooney
                         Leslie Towns Hope — Bob Hope
                         William Sidney Porter — O. Henry
                         Archibald Leach — Cary Grant
                         William Claude Dirkenfield — W.C. Fields
                         Frederick Austerlitz — Fred Astaire
                         Joseph Kubelsky — Jack Benny
                         Nathan Birnbaum — George Burns
                         Israel Baline — Irving Berlin

Song
Identification: All names of men are in the title.

ALEXANDER'S Ragtime Band   JOHN JACOB Jingleheimer Schmidt
BILL Bailey, Won't You Please   Oh JOHNNY, Oh JOHNNY, Oh!
          Come Home   Meet Me in St. LOUIS, LOUIS
Red, Red ROBIN Comes   MICHAEL Row the Boat Ashore
          BOB-BOB-BOBbin' Along   PETER Cottontail
DANNY Boy   Waiting for the ROBERT E. Lee
JACK and Jill   Ragtime Cowboy JOE
JESUS Loves Me   WILLIAM Tell Overture

Rhythmic
Activity: CHANT: occupations of men
                         Rich man, poor man, beggar man, thief,
                         Doctor, lawyer, merchant, thief,
                         Butcher, tailor, tinker sailor

                    Today's chant — read by volunteer — discussion follows.
                         T.V. repairman, pilot, plumber
                         Announcer, sportscaster, long distance runner.

                         Weatherman, mailman, supermarket clerk,
                         Whatever happened to the soda jerk?

                         Stockbroker, chemist, sanitary engineer,
                         No matter what profession, let's give a cheer.

[1] *Modern American Encyclopedia of Names for Your Baby.* "Names 25 Years Ago" p. 21.
[2] Rosenkrantz and Satran (1988) *Beyond Jennifer and Jason* p. 41.
[3] For further reference on names, recommended books include: Stewart, G. (1979) *American Given Names;* Bailey, S. (1982) *Big Book of Baby Names;* Train, J. (1977) *Remarkable Names of Real People.*
[4] Lansky and Lansky (1984) *Best Baby Name Book.* "The Name Exchange" pp. 25-28.

Rhythm Band: Celebrate men's professions with instruments all playing after establishing the beat.
"Stouthearted Men" — strong 2.
"Alexander's Ragtime Band" — lighter, faster 2.
"When Johnny Comes Marching Home Again" — no piano on the "hurrah" part. Sing and play it.

When Johnny comes marching home again
        hurrah, hurrah
We'll give him a hearty welcome then,
        hurrah, hurrah.
The men will cheer, the boys will shout,
The ladies they will all turn out
And we'll all feel gay when Johnny comes marching home.

"MacNamara's Band" — strong joyous march.

Closing: Sing to the tune of "Goodnight Ladies":
So long gentlemen, so long gentlemen, so long gentlemen, until we meet again.
Turn to each other and sing. Include a ladies' verse.

Assignment: Encourage residents to continue thinking about the favorite men in their lives. Next time they see them, residents should tell them about today's program and express their gratitude. Even if they are not going to see them for a while, suggest residents send them thanks silently.

Music
Resources: *Golden Book of Favorite Songs* (1946)
        "Good Night Ladies" p. 116
        "Aunt Dinah's Quilting Party" p. 125
Family Song Book of Faith and Joy (1981)
        "Stouthearted Men" p. 168
        "When Johnny Comes Marching Home" p. 248
Great Music's Greatest Hits (1982)
        "William Tell Overture" p. 75
Greatest Songs of 1890-1920 (1990)
        "Alexander's Ragtime Band" p. 10
Best of Irish Music (1992)
        "MacNamara's Band" p. 154

MEN in MUSIC

1. **Billy** Boy
2. **Danny** Boy
3. Stouthearted **Men**
4. Over Hill, Over **Dale**
   (U.S. Field Artillery March)
5. **Ezekiel** Saw de Wheel
6. **William** Tell Overture
7. Oh **Johnny**, Oh Johnny Oh!
8. **Alexander's** Ragtime Band
9. Meet Me in St. Louis, **Louis**
10. Waiting for the **Robert** E. Lee
11. Bill Bailey, Won't You Please
    Come Home

Select your favorite and I'll play it for you.

Music Menu

Yellow

February Theme –   **IT'S A LOVELY MONTH**

Today's Theme –   **Everyone Loves a Smile**

Advanced
Preparation:
- Prepare aides as reporters with paper and pencil to take down responses.
- Provide a kit bag to put the responses in.
- Prepare yellow paper plates with smiling faces already drawn on them with black marker.
- Collect the following songs together: "Pack Up Your Trouble," "Till We Meet Again," "Battle Hymn of the Republic."

Pre-Session: Smile songs on the piano or tape recorded ones such as "Smiles," "When Irish Eyes Are Smiling," "When You're Smiling," are played as resident enter.

Opening: Sing the song: "Pack Up Your Trouble." (A songsheet is included at the end of the THEY FOUGHT FOR FREEDOM [July] weekly session plan.)

> Pack up your trouble in your old kit bag and smile, smile, smile.
> While you've a lucifer to light your fag
> Smile boys that's the style.
> What's the use of worrying
> It never was worthwhile so
> Pack up your trouble in your old kit bag and smile, smile, smile.

Have aides find out who has any troubles and write them down on paper. Place troubles in a kit bag of any kind. Sing the song together. At end of the session, ask if anyone wants their troubles back.

Exercise: 1. Moderate exercise to the tune of "Till We Meet Again" all should follow directions as you sing slowly. (A songsheet is included at the end of the THEY FOUGHT FOR FREEDOM [July] weekly session plan.)

> Smile a while and give your face a rest.
> Sit up straight and elevate your chest.
> Reach your hands up towards the sky
> While you watch them with your eye
> Twist a while and shake a leg there sir,
> Now lean forward, backward as you were
> Then reach out to someone near
> Shake his hand and smile.

2. Stronger exercises with yellow paper plates that have smile faces on them. Residents should place in front of their face to get everyone in the mood. Do consistent rhythmic movements to "Smiles," "Sunny Side Up," and "When You're Smiling."

3. At the count of 3, all fling their smiling plates up front.

Group Singing: Sing the following to the tune of the "Battle Hymn of the Republic."
                  1. It isn't any trouble just to s-m-i-l-e
                      It isn't any trouble just to s-m-i-l-e
                      It isn't any trouble, troubles vanish like a bubble
                      It isn't any trouble just to s-m-i-l-e.
                  2. G-r-i-n, grin
                  3. L-a-u-g-h

                  Bubble pipes are very effective here.

Education: • It takes 202 muscles to frown, only 187 to smile.
                  • A smile is the shortest distance between two points.

Song
Identification: Blue Skies (Smiling at Me)
                  Let a Smile Be Your Umbrella on a Rainy Day
                  When Irish Eyes Are Smiling *
                  When You're Smiling
                  Pack Up Your Trouble
                  Put on a Happy Face
                  Sunny Side Up

                  *   A songsheet is included at the end of the IT'S NOT EASY BEING GREEN [March] weekly
                      session plan

Rhythm Band: Cheer — Residents respond with the letter name and musical sound with their
                  rhythm instrument.

                          Give me an S
                          Give me an M
                          Give me an I
                          Give me an L
                          Give me an E
                          What does that spell?
                          Show me how you feel.

                  "Smiles" — peppy 2 beat. (A songsheet is included at the end of this week's
                      session plan.)
                  "When You're Smiling" — slower 2 beat with a smile.
                  "Pack Up Your Trouble" — faster 2 beat with a big smile.

                  Ask if anyone wants their troubles back out of the old kit bag.

Closing: Sing a closing song, several times, to the tune of "Love Is Something"
                          A smile is something when you give it away,
                                  give it away, give it away,
                          A smile is something when you give it away,
                                  and you end up having more.

                  Smile at the person next to you and pass this smile around the room. Some
                  may need prompting to keep it continuous.

Assignment: If you see someone without a smile, give him one of yours!

Music
Resources: *Ultimate Fake Book* (1981)
                        "Pack Up Your Trouble" p. 439
                        "Battle Hymn" p. 41
                Legal Fake Book (1979)
                        "Till We Meet Again" p. 294
                Greatest Legal Fake Book of all Times (1985)
                        "When You're Smiling" p. 589
                Tune Book Songs (1982)
                        "Love is Something" p. 141, adapted from "The Magic Penny"

Smile Songs

Music Menu

1. Smiles
2. When You're Smiling
3. Till We Meet Again (Smile Awhile)
4. Sunny Side Up
5. It Isn't Any Trouble Just to S-M-I-L-E
6. Pack Up Your Trouble
7. Blue Skies (Smiling At Me)
8. When Irish Eyes Are Smiling
9. Let a Smile Be Your Umbrella
   on a Rainy Day
10. A Smile Is Something When You
    Give It Away

———————

Request these or others
for your noontime pleasure!

Smiles

There are smiles that make us happy,

there are smiles that make us blue;

There are smiles that steal away the teardrops

as the sunbeams steal away the dew;

There are smiles that have a tender meaning

that the eyes of love alone may see,

and the smiles that fill my life with sunshine

are the smiles that you give to me.

– J. Will Callahan (1917)

February Theme — **IT'S A LOVELY MONTH**

Today's Theme— **Ground-Hog Day February 2**
(Optional)

Advanced
Preparation:
- Prepare some foam paper plates with pictures of animals pre-pasted on them. Make sure that one of them has a ground-hog on it! (See Exercise section.)
- Organize a special chair for the Queen/King, and provide a sash and cape for her/him.
- Make enough copies of the large print songsheet of "Look for the Silver Lining." Use the verses set out in Group Singing section. Also see that there are enough copies of the songsheet "Bless This House" which is included at the end of this session plan.

Pre-Session: Pianist plays songs that will be used later in the program as residents enter the room. Examples: "I Got the Sun in the Morning," "Me and My Shadow," "Asleep in the Deep."

Opening: "Hail, Hail the Gang's all Here" — group singing.
   Hail, hail the gang's all here
   never mind the weather
   here we are together.
   Hail, hail the gang's all here
   let the music start RIGHT NOW.

Exercise:
1. Pass out paper plates with animals on them. The one who receives the plate with the ground-hog on it is Queen/King for the Day.
2. Have Queen/King sit up front and crown with a fur cape.
3. Light exercises to piano music of
   "Me and My Shadow" — plates swung side to side.
   "Rise and Shine" — plates held overhead.
   "I'm Looking Over a Four Leaf Clover" — tap plates on body.
   "Pop goes the Weasel" — toss plates on "pop."

Education (I): Residents learn a new poem called "Whether" - source unknown.

   Whether the weather be cold, whether the weather be hot
   Whether the weather be fair, or whether the weather be not
   We'll weather the weather, whatever the weather
   Whether we like it or not.

Group Singing: "Look for the Silver Lining" — Use a large print songsheet with an attractive border suitable for hanging as a visible reminder of the philosophy. (A songsheet is included at the end of the BYE BYE BLUES [March] weekly session plan.)

Group Singing: Look for the silver lining,
(Cont.)   When-e'er a cloud appears in the blue.
                       Remember somewhere the sun is shining
                       And so the right thing to do
                       Is make it shine for you.

                       A heart full of joy and gladness
                       Will always banish sadness and strife
                       So always look for the silver lining
                       And try to find the sunny side of life.

                       1. Discuss the concept of finding the good in situations. Often a situation may
                          not appear to be good at the time. As time passes, we see it in
                          perspective.
                       2. Mention the fact that the sun is always shining above the clouds. Ask who
                          has experienced that in a plane. Relate it to the song's message.

Education (II):   • It is an old belief that if the sun shines on Candlemas day or if the ground-
                         hog sees his shadow when he emerges on this day, February 2nd, 6 more
                         weeks of winter will ensue.
                       • Punsxutawney Phil, a ground-hog in Punsxutawney, Pennsylvania is the
                         king of the weather prophets. Other cities have their own traditions
                         regarding ground-hogs from their zoo or animal shelter.[1]

Group
Discussion: To stimulate discussion, ask if anyone ever believed this myth or have in fact
                       seen a ground-hog on February 2. Ask where it was.

Song
Identification: Identify the songs that are woven into this story:

                       Once upon a time there was a ground-hog named ["I'm Just Wild About
                       Harry"] who was ["Asleep in the Deep"]. I wonder what I will find, he thought,
                       as he awoke from his long, winter sleep. Will it be a ["Winter Wonderland"]
                       out there? Aw, guess I will go back to sleep and ["Let It Snow, Let It Snow,
                       Let It Snow"]. But nature called and said ["Rise and Shine"]. OK, he said, and
                       stretched and yawned. Here goes just ["Me and My Shadow"]. He looked out
                       of his hole in the ground and yelled ["I Got The Sun in the Morning"] and saw
                       his shadow even in the partial ["Shade of the Old Apple Tree"]. Well, when he
                       saw that he knew there would be 6 more weeks of winter but he was looking
                       over a ["I'm Looking Over a Four Leaf Clover"] and burst into song singing
                       ["Look for the Silver Lining."]

Rhythm Band: Songs about weather.
                       "Oh What a Beautiful Mornin'" — waltz tempo.
                       "Winter Wonderland" — bells only.
                       "On the Sunny Side of the Street" — peppy 2 beat.
                       "The Rain in Spain" — tango beat.

---

[1] Education facts from *Chases Annual Events* (1992) p. 36.

Closing:
- "Bless This House" — group singing. Hand out copies of songsheet. Those unable to sing should add their good thoughts at this time for their facility.
- Thank the King or Queen of Ground-Hog Day for reigning.
- Ask for their reaction to today's program.

Assignment: Encourage residents to give thanks no matter what the weather happens to be, and to appreciate the change and reflect on the various experiences that are due to the change of seasons.

Music
Resources:

Family Song Book of Faith and Joy (1981)
"Look for the Silver Lining" p. 54
"Oh What a Beautiful Mornin'" p. 52
Bill Hardey's Songs of the Gay Nineties (1942)
"Hail, Hail, the Gang's all Here" p. 83
Treasury of Best Loved Songs (1981)
"On the Sunny Side of the Street" p. 25
Ultimate Fake Book (1981)
"The Rain in Spain" p. 469
Wee Sing Bible Songs (1986)
"Rise and Shine" p. 59

Ground-Hog Music

1. Me and My Shadow
2. Oh What a Beautiful Mornin'
3. Asleep in the Deep
4. I Got the Sun in the Morning
5. On the Sunny Side of the Street
6. Blue Skies
7. The Rain in Spain
8. Stormy Weather
9. I'm Looking Over a Four Leaf Clover
10. Look for the Silver Lining
11. God Bless America

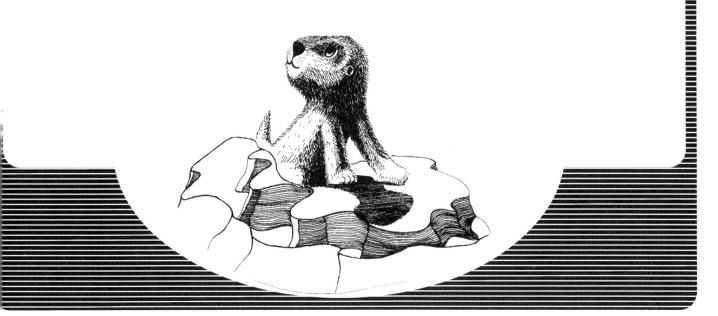

Bless This House

Bless this house, oh Lord, we pray.
Make it safe by night and day.

Bless these walls, so firm and stout,
Keeping want and trouble out.

Bless the roof and chimney tall.
Let thy peace lie over all.

Bless this door that it may prove
ever open to joy and love.

Bless these windows shining bright
Letting in God's heavenly light.

Bless this home that's filled with caring,
Loving, laughing, praying, sharing.

Bless the folk who all live here.
Keep them kind and free from fear.

Bless us all that we may be
Fit, oh Lord, to dwell with thee.

Bless us all that one day we
May dwell, oh Lord, with thee.

February Theme — **IT'S A LOVELY MONTH**

Today's Theme — **Presidents' Day — Hail to the Chiefs**
(Optional)

Advanced
Preparation:
- Cut some red, white, and blue streamers into 15-inch lengths,
- Print the individual letters of L-I-N-C-O-L-N on a poster board,
- Decorate the room with a large flag, and pictures of US Presidents.
- Organize a soloist to sing the official presidential song "Hail to the Chief." The music is included on page 108.

Pre-Session: March music played on the piano or tape recorder as residents enter.

Opening: Announce that all US Presidents will be honored with the theme HAIL TO THE CHIEFS. The first to be honored will be spelled out by the group. Hint — He is the most beloved. Use flash cards held by 8 residents. You lead with

Leader	Give me an L
Response	L
Leader	Give me an I
Response	I
[Continue for N-C-O-L-N]	
Then:	
Leader	What does that spell?
Response	LINCOLN
Leader	Who is the most beloved President?
Response	LINCOLN
Leader	Who is our first president?
Response	WASHINGTON

Exercise: Use individual patriotic streamers of crepe paper exercising to the tune of "He's a Jolly Good Fellow." (A songhseet is included at the end of this week's session plan.)
1. Exercise arms like a window washer by accenting "He's" with streamer on left and "Fellow" on right.
2. Using the same song make broad circles — change hands.
3. Hold both ends of streamer using a push/pull motion.

Music — "Hail to the Chief" — official Presidential music.
1. Use one hand — raise and lower streamer to slow beat of music.
2. Stretch arm and streamer up high and shake wildly to the music while giving thanks for each President that has led our country. Change hands.

Memory
Association: Allow time for conversations by asking some of the following questions:
- Who is associated with chopping a cherry tree? (Washington)
- Who lived in a log cabin? (Lincoln)
- Which two signed the Declaration of Independence? (Adams, Jefferson)

Education: • Which first lady is associated with ice cream? (Dolly Madison)
(Cont.)   • Who was our first Catholic President? (Kennedy)
                    • Who was the tallest President? (Lincoln at 6'4")
                    • Who was the shortest? (Madison at 5'4")
                    • Who was the heaviest? (Taft at 332 pounds)
                    • Who was the slightest? (Madison at 100 pounds)
                    • Name those in office during a depression (Van Buren, Buchanan, Grant, Cleveland, T. Roosevelt, Wilson, Hoover)
                    • Who was assassinated while in office? (Lincoln, Garfield, McKinley, Kennedy)
                    • Who died on July 4th? (Adams, Jefferson, Monroe)[1]

Reminiscence: The following questions will stimulate recall:
                    • Have you ever attended a political rally?
                    • Did the train stop in your town as a whistle stop?
                    • Did you ever meet a President?
                    • Did you ever run for political office? What happened?
                    • Do you recall your early voting days in a voting booth?
                    • Have you ever felt the country was doomed when your candidate lost?
                    • Who was your favorite president? Take a poll of the group.

Special Honorees   George Washington
                    • The first president, 1732-1799.
                    • He presided 1789-1797.
                    • He is known as the "father of our country" and is one of the most honored Presidents.[2, 3]
                    • Abraham Lincoln said "to add brightness to the sun a glory to the name of Washington is alike impossible. Let none attempt it. In solemn awe we pronounce the name and in its naked deathless splendor leave it shining on."

Group Singing: "He's a Jolly Good Fellow." Using the present tense is still plausible after hearing the tribute given by Lincoln.

Special Honoree: Abraham Lincoln
                    • He was born in Kentucky in 1809.
                    • He moved to Indiana and at age 21 to Illinois.
                    • He read the Bible, Shakespeare and Aesops fables which added to his education and forming of the immortal Gettysburg address. "This nation, under God, shall have a new birth of freedom: the government of people, by the people and for the people, shall not perish from the earth."
                    • The Lincoln Memorial in Washington DC is one of many tributes to this leader of our country.[2, 4]

---

[1] All information in Education section from Taylor, T. (1972) *Book of Presidents* "Statistical Summary" pp. 657-683.
[2] Myers, R. (1972) *Celebrations*, "Widely Observed Holidays" pp. 63-70.
[3] Taylor T. (1972) *Book of Presidents* "George Washington" pp. 1-25
[4] Ibid, "Abraham Lincoln" pp. 174-192.

Group Singing:	"Old Abe Lincoln" — to the tune of "Old Grey Mare" Verses: 1. Old Abe Lincoln came out of the wilderness, (sung 3 times) Old Abe Lincoln came of the wilderness, down in Illinois. 2. Old Abe Lincoln was our sixteenth President ......many long years ago 3. Old Abe Lincoln freed our nation from slavery........many long years ago.
Education:	55 historians ranked our Presidents as being great or a failure according to Harvard's Dr. Schlesinger.[1] The greatest were ranked in this order: Lincoln, Washington, F.D, Roosevelt, Wilson, Jefferson, Jackson.
Solo Time:	"Hail to the Chief" — official Presidential song. The music is heard frequently however there are words by Sir Walter Scott in *The Golden Song Book* that do not apply to the office of President.
Rhythm Band:	Using rhythmic instruments and small flags. "Over There" — Pres. Wilson's favorite in 1916 — enjoy peppy 2 beat. "K-K-K-Katy" — sung by soldiers in 1918 as a stammering song. Stress the upbeat of 1.2.3. (K-K-K-Katy). (A songsheet is included at the end of the THEY FOUGHT FOR FREEDOM [July] weekly session plan.) "Missouri Waltz" — Truman's favorite — all play with a strong downbeat. Add the afterbeats of 2 and 3. "Washington Post March" — joyous march honoring our leaders. "Stouthearted Men" — song represents a presidential quality. "Hail to the Chief" — deliberate, slow march played with dignity.
Assignment:	After this session encourage everyone to think about their chief concern for our country today that would be their plank of their platform if they ran for a political office. They can share it with each other and celebrate the freedom of speech especially during Presidents' Day.

Music
Resources:
	Wee Sing America (1988)
	   "Old Abe Lincoln" p. 23
	Golden Book of Favorite Songs (1946)
	   "Hail to the Chief" p. 40
	All American Song Book (1984)
	   "He's a Jolly Good Fellow" p. 145
	Legit Fake Book (1990)
	   "K-K-K-Katy" p. 199
	   "Over There" p. 272
	Festival of Popular Songs (1977)
	   "Missouri Waltz" p. 108

---

[1] Neele, M.E., Jr. (1982) *Abraham Lincoln Encyclopedia* "P — Powers of the Presidency" p. 246.88

HAIL TO THE CHIEF

Sir Walter Scott   James Sanderson

Majestically

HAIL to the CHIEFS

Music Menu

1. Washington Post March
2. Stouthearted Men
3. This is My Country
4. America
5. This Land is Your Land
6. God Bless America
7. The Star Spangled Banner
8. America, the Beautiful
9. Hail to the Chief
10. For He's a Jolly Good Fellow

Exercise your precious right - vote for your favorite.

FOR HE'S A JOLLY GOOD FELLOW

For he's a jolly good fellow,
For he's a jolly good fellow,
For he's a jolly good fellow,
Which nobody can deny.
Which nobody can deny,
Which nobody can deny,
For he's a jolly good fellow,
Which nobody can deny.

We won't go home until morning,
We won't go home until morning,
We won't go home until morning,
Till daylight doth appear!
Till daylight doth appear!
Till daylight doth appear!
We won't go home until morning,
Till daylight doth appear.

MARCH

IT'S A
COLORFUL
WORLD

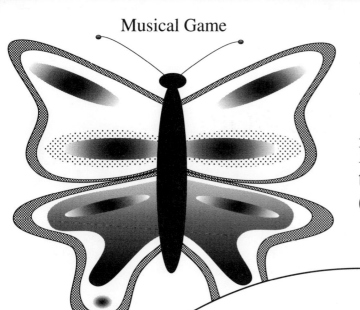

Musical Game

It's a Colorful World

All of these songs have a color in the title. If you are over 65 you will easily guess the answers.
(Answers are upside down.)

1. Bye Bye _____

2. _____ Sails in the Sunset

3. _____ Christmas

4. When the _____, _____ Robin Comes

Bob, Bob, Bobbin' Along

5. A Tisket, a Tasket, a _____ & _____ Basket

6. _____ Threads Among the _____

7. _____ You Glad You're You (A Pun)

8. The Little _____ Church

9. Little _____ Jug

10. Old _____ Joe

IT'S A COLORFUL WORLD
MARCH

Awareness of the changes and colors of nature at this time of the year is the purpose of these programs. Residents in senior settings often need encouragement to activate this realization. The following programs will stimulate interest in both the indoor and outdoor environment. The philosophy is to make it a more colorful world even if nature is a bit slow.

This month is color coordinated as all staff, residents, and volunteers are encouraged to wear the color of the week and enjoy the theme association. Anticipation is high as everyone finds something to wear no matter how humorous. Bulletin boards are colorful and the entire facility appears to be blooming with the joy of color. Try to have coordinated colored paper for the music menus.

Announce the themes early in newsletters and bulletin boards. Families then have time to find appropriate colors that can be included in the programming. Watch the affect on newcomers when they enter the door into a colorful world.

Bye Bye Blues — All depression, aches and pains are alleviated as we bid bye, bye to the blues and welcome "blue sky" thinking.

In The Pink — Health is emphasized. Praise is given to all the body functions that still work plus reflection on all those active years that allowed longevity.

It's Not Easy Being Green — King and Queen are honored but also all the other nationalities that don't have a special day.

Hello Yellow — Sunshine and smiles are beaming everywhere. The effect of the color and theme is contagious.

Lavender and Old Lace — Old things have special value. This includes old friendships, antiques and a favorite pair of old shoes. Lavender scent recalls old fashioned memories.

OPTIONAL PROGRAM

March Into Spring — Plan an indoor march anytime of the month. Extra volunteers will be needed. Goals should be set and plenty of time for publicity to increase anticipation. After the winter months, this march is a festive, heartwarming event. Spring colors recommended.

IT'S A COLORFUL WORLD — WE MAKE IT

March Theme —   **IT'S A COLORFUL WORLD**

Today's Theme —   **Bye Bye Blues**

Advanced
Preparation: • Provide
                       - paper and pencils for reporters,
                       - blue bag.
                   • Cut blue lace streamers or crepe paper into 18-inch lengths.
                   • Make enough copies of the large print songsheet of "Look For The Silver
                     Lining," included at the end of this session plan.
                   • Publicize the week's theme and encourage people to wear something blue.
                   • Print the music menu on blue paper.

Pre-Session: Piano music or taped music with blues in the title such as "Alice Blue Gown,"
                   "My Blue Heaven," "Bye Bye Blues," "The Blue Danube Waltz," playing as
                   participants enter.

Opening: Song: "Little Sir Echo" — therapist doing leading part, residents respond with
                   echo in large letters, no songsheet.

                   Verse 1:
                   Leader   Little Sir Echo, how do you do. Hello,
                   Response   HELLO
                   Leader   Hello
                   Response   HELLO.
                   Leader   Little Sir Echo is very blue, Hello
                   Response   HELLO
                   Leader   Hello
                   Response   HELLO.
                   Leader   Hello
                   Response   HELLO.
                   Leader   Hello
                   Response   HELLO.
                   Leader   Won't you come over and play?
                   Response   AND PLAY?
                   Leader   You're a nice little fellow, I know by your voice
                                   But you're always so far away
                   Response   AWAY.

                   Verse 2
                   Leader   Little Sir Echo, how do you do. Hello,
                   Response   HELLO
                   Leader   Hello
                   Response   HELLO.
                   Leader   Little Sir Echo will answer you. Hello
                   Response   HELLO........
                   [Continue as format in Verse 1.]

Reminiscence:	"Little Sir Echo" is blue until there is an answer. Talk about feeling blue and now is the time to talk about it. After a few people share their blues, have aides go up to them individually and write down one of their concerns on a piece of paper and place them all in a blue bag. These cares have been set aside for one hour.
Exercise:	After putting the cares aside, it is time for some light exercise with blue lace streamers: "Dream When You're Feeling Blue" — wave gently up high. "Alice Blue Gown" — left to right in waltz tempo. "My Blue Heaven" — two beat, sing along and wave.
Group Singing:	"Gonna Lay Down My Blues Awhile" to tune of "Down By The Riverside."

Gonna lay down my blues awhile (clap, clap)
Right on the brighter side, (clap,clap)
Right on the brighter side.
Gonna lay down my blues awhile (clap,clap)
Right on the brighter side, (clap (rest), clap)

Conclude with bump, diddy, bump, bump (rest), bump, bump.

Education:	Discuss how to handle the blues. The first step is to admit feeling blue. It does not help to "hide it under the rug," it will only resurface. Suggest residents talk to someone they trust. Gently hint that it's better not to tell everyone your problems, they probably don't want to hear them. Encourage residents to plan a course of action that will lighten the situation.
Solo Time:	"Look For The Silver Lining" — followed by group singing. Discuss the meaning of the song.
Song Identification:	All the following songs have "Blue" in the title. As soon as the melody is recognizable, residents should call it out.

Alice BLUE Gown
The BLUE Bell of Scotland
The BLUEtail Fly
Rhapsody in BLUE
Birth of the BLUES
Five Foot Two, Eyes of BLUE
Lavender's BLUE
St. Louis BLUES
BLUE Tango
BLUE Suede Shoes
BLUE Birds Over the White Cliffs of Dover
BLUE Hawaii

Rhythm Band: "The Blue Bell of Scotland" — bells only.
                 "The Blue Danube Waltz" — echo response song, piano plays "Danube so
                      blue" and band responds in sound (ding dong, ding dong).
                 "Five Foot Two, Eyes of Blue" — all play merrily. (A songsheet is included at
                      the end of the STYLES UP TO THE ANKLE [September] weekly session plan.)
                 "Columbia, the Gem of the Ocean" (Three Cheers for the Red, White and
                      BLUE) — with gusto. (A songsheet is included at the end of the IT'S A
                      GRAND OLD FLAG [June], and GO FORTH ON THE FOURTH OF JULY [July]
                      weekly session plans.)

Closing: Ask if anyone wants their blues back from the blue bag. Ask if they want
                 someone else's blues. The feeling of blues can always be lightened with music
                 especially a song that is personally meaningful.

                 All sing the closing song: "Bye Bye Blues" — shortening the words to:

                      Bye, bye blues, bye, bye blues, bells ring, birds sing
                      Sun is shining no more pining,
                      Bye, bye blues, bye bye blues, bells ring, birds sing
                      Bye, bye blues.

Assignment: Suggest that it is better not to dwell on the blues, but to accentuate the
                 positive, find the bright side of life, learn to laugh and look for the silver lining.
                 The silver lining is always there only sometimes it takes longer to find it. The
                 assignment is to look for the silver lining in a personal problem. Encourage
                 residents to enjoy chasing the blues.

                 Next week's theme is IN THE PINK and the program is guaranteed to improve
                 everyone's health. Everyone can bring any aches or pains and leave the blues
                 behind. Encourage all staff, residents and family to wear something pink, even
                 a ribbon will do. It's a colorful month and the color blue should act as a
                 reminder to say BYE BYE BLUES.

Music
Resources: *Family Song Book of Faith and Joy* (1981)
                      "Look for the Silver Lining" p. 54
                 Mitch Miller Community Song Book (1962)
                      "Down by the Riverside" p. 19
                 Ultimate Fake Book (1981)
                      "Bye Bye Blues" p. 76
                 Greatest Legal Fake Book of All Times (1985)
                      "Little Sir Echo" p. 307
                      "My Blue Heaven" p. 366
                      "Dream" p. 119
                 Wee Sing America (1989)
                      "Columia the Gem of the Ocean" (Three Cheers for the Red, White and
                      Blue) p. 11
                 Great Music's Greatest Hits (1982)
                      "The Blue Danube Waltz" p. 50

Blue Music Menu

1. The Blue Danube Waltz
2. My Blue Heaven
3. Bye Bye Blues
4. The Blue Bell of Scotland
5. Red Roses for a Blue Lady
6. Alice Blue Gown
7. Five Foot Two, Eyes of Blue
8. The Blue Tail Fly
9. Blue Skies
10. Blue Hawaii
11. Rhapsody in Blue
12. Saint Louis Blues

Choose Your Favorite

Look for the Silver Lining

Look for the silver lining

When e'er a cloud appears in the blue.

Remember somewhere the sun is shining

And so the right thing to do

is make it shine for you.

A heartful of joy and gladness

will always banish sadness and strife.

So always look for the silver lining

And try to find the sunny side of life.

– B. G. DeSylva

March Theme —   **IT'S A COLORFUL WORLD**

Today's Theme —   **In The Pink**

Advanced
Preparation:
- Invite everyone to wear pink or a bit of it somewhere. Announce the color theme on the microphone and in the newsletter.
- Prepare foam paper plates with various colors of roses pasted on them.
- Make pink roses lightly scented with perfume
- Make enough copies of the large print songsheet of "Ac-cent-tchu-ate the Positive," which is included at the end of this session plan.
- Cut out tulip shapes from pink paper with "I am in the pink" boldly written on them using the templates at the end of this session plan.
- Provide:
     - scotch tape,
     - paper and pencils for reporters.
- Print music menu on pink paper.

Pre-Session: As residents leave their room, remind them to wear something pink. Piano music as residents enter the room. "Ac-cent-tchu-ate the Positive," "Get Happy," "Look for the Silver Lining," and "Oh What a Beautiful Mornin'," are songs that get us IN THE PINK.

Opening: Talk about feeling IN THE PINK. Even though some body parts may not be functioning perfectly, other parts still do. The purpose is to maintain and improve one's health with positive thinking.

Song:
1. I've got that joy, joy, joy, joy down in my heart (sung 3 times ending with "down in my heart today.")
2. I've got gooood health, gooood health inside of me (sung 3 times ending with "and it is growing today.")
3. You've got gooood health, gooood health....etc.
4. We've got gooood health, gooood health...etc.

Exercise: Use the foam plates with roses pasted on them. All those who have pink roses on theirs should hold them up. Next the red ones should be identified and then other colors. Lead light exercises to these songs.
"Country Gardens" — light tapping of plates on head, shoulders, thighs. (Music in included on page 206.)
"TipToe Through the Tulips " — wave from side to side.
"Ac-cent-tchu-ate the Positive" — up, up, up in three steps.
Finale — toss "roses" at the leader.

Reminiscence: Encourage the sharing of ideas of health tips that have worked, including folk lore, wives' tales. Note the changes; modern medicine, holistic thinking and most of all, attitude. Reporters or assistants should write down responses for the facility newsletter or separate flyer to preserve the wisdom of the ages.

Group Singing	To increase the memory, keep the mind active, healthy!
	To the tune of: "My Bonnie Lies Over the Ocean" words by Charles King.

> I have such a wonderful memory, I have such a wonderful mind
> I have such a wonderful memory, I have such a wonderful mind.
> Praise God, Praise God, I have such a wonderful memory
> Praise God, Praise God, I have such a wonderful mind.

Using the large print songsheet already copied, sing the following:

> You've got to ac-cent-tchu-ate the positive
> Eliminate the negative,
> Latch on to the affirmative
> Don's mess with mister in-between.

Residents may keep the songsheets to remind them to AC-CENT-TCHU-ATE THE POSITIVE!

Recognition: All who participate have a pink tulip taped on them that says in bold letters, "I am in the pink." Suggest they wear them all day and that they watch the reaction from others as well as their own. Accent the positive.

Education:
- "Remember, love heals. I do not claim love cures everything but it can heal and in the process of healing cures occur also."[1]
- "When you were born, you cried and the world rejoiced. Live your life in such a manner that when you die the world cries and you rejoice.' Traditional Indian saying."[2]

Solo time: A pianist and vocalist could sing "Pink Panther" which is a modern song. A more traditional song is "Cherry Pink and Apple Blossom White."

Song Identification: The following songs all contain healthy ideas. Name the concept as quickly as you can.

> Smiles (humor is important)
> For Health and Strength and Daily Bread (thanks for food) *
> I'm Gonna Sit Right Down and Write Myself a Letter (write to a friend)
> Let's All Sing Like the Birdies Sing (singing is healthy)
> Button up your Overcoat (dress properly)
> Praise God From Whom All Blessings Flow (praising God)
> Brahms' Lullaby (getting a good night's sleep or a good nap in the day)
> All Alone (By the Telephone) (phone a friend)
> Ac-cent-tchu-ate the Positive (positive thinking)

> * Music is included on page 364.

---

1   Siegel, B. (1988) *Love, Medicine and Miracles*, p. xii.
2   Ibid. p. 224.

Rhythm Band: "Smiles" — play with a smile and a peppy 2 beat. (A songsheet is included at the end of the EVERYONE LOVES A SMILE [February] weekly session plan.)

"Button up Your Overcoat" — play with instruments, all sing the line "take good care of yourself."

"Let's All Sing Like the Birdies Sing" — piano plays the main refrain, residents respond with instruments on the "tweet" parts:

Let's all sing like the birdies sing — tweet 5 times (repeat)

Let's all warble like nightingales give your throat a treat.

Take your tune from the birds, now you all know the words

Tweet, tweet, tweet, tweet, tweet.

[Vary with specific instrument groups.]

(Music is included on page 200.)

"Enjoy Yourself, It's Later Than You Think" — rousing finale with energy.

Closing: Closing song:

Enjoy yourself, it's later than you think

Enjoy yourself, while you're still IN THE PINK

The years go by and quickly as a wink,

Enjoy yourself, enjoy yourself, it's later than you think.

Conclude with singing "Bless This House." Use the large print songsheet found at the end of the GROUND-HOG DAY [February] session plan.

Assignment: Encourage everyone to wear the pink tulip telling everyone that you are IN THE PINK or at least parts of the body are perfect. Better health is the aim. Release doubt and gloom and use positive thinking and acting from now on.

Music
Resources: *Children's Song Book* (1988)
     "Pink Panther" p. 46
Family Song Book of Faith and Joy
     "Bless This House" p. 268
Greatest Legal Fake Book of All Times (1985)
     "Enjoy Yourself, It's Later Than You Think" p. 130
     "Smiles" p. 474
     "Tip Toe Through the Tulips" p. 158
Festival of Popular Songs (1977)
     "Button up Your Overcoat"
Wings of Song (1984)
     "I've Got the Joy" p. 340.
Remembering Yesterday's Hits (1986)
     "Ac-cent-tchu-ate the Positive" p. 60
Best Fake Book Ever (1990)
     "Let's All Sing Like the Birdies Sing" p. 367
One Thousand and One Jumbo (1985)
     "Country Gardens" p. 386

"In the Pink"

How to be Healthy

1. **Enjoy** Yourself, It's Later Than You Think
2. Let's All **Sing** Like the Birdies Sing
3. Just a Closer **Walk** with Thee
4. There are **Smiles** That Make Us Happy
5. **Music** Music Music
6. **Praise** God From Whom All Blessings Flow
7. All Alone (by the **Telephone**)
8. Brahms' Lullaby (**Sleep** Well)
9. Ac-cent-tchu-ate the Positive (**Attitude**)
10. Button Up Your Overcoat (**Dress** Right)
11. I Have Such a Wonderful Memory
    (**Use Your Mind**)

Choose Your Favorite

AC-CENT-TCHU-ATE THE POSITIVE

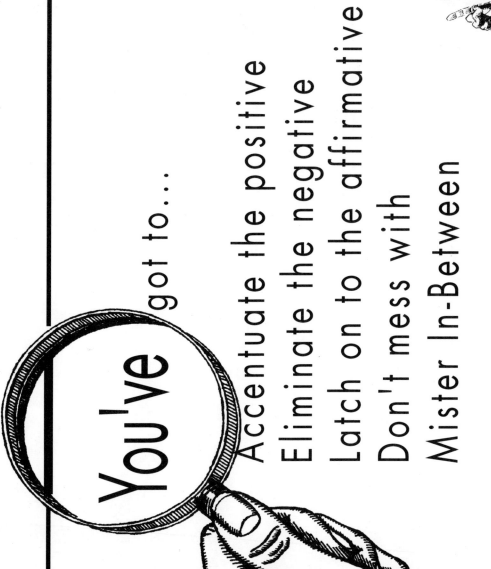

You've got to....

Accentuate the positive
Eliminate the negative
Latch on to the affirmative
Don't mess with
Mister In-Between

—Johnny Mercer

Pink

I Am In The Pink

I Am In The Pink

I Am In The Pink

I Am In The Pink

March Theme — **IT'S A COLORFUL WORLD**

Today's Theme — **It's Not Easy Being Green**

Advanced
Preparation:
- Invite everyone to wear something green.
- Prepare a throne for the King and Queen of Green and a satin sash.
- Cut out green crepe paper streamers.
- Provide:
    - collection of Irish songs,
    - soloist for "It's Not Easy Being Green."
    - Kermit the frog green stuffed animal or puppet,
    - plan for naming the king and queen.
- Make enough copies of the songsheet "When Irish Eyes are Smiling" which is provided at the end of this session plan.
- Print music on green paper.

Pre-Session: Irish songs can be played on the tape recorder or turntable, or a pianist can play such songs as "Peggy O'Neil," "Sweet Rose O'Grady," "Mary's a Grand Old Name," and "Danny Boy."

Opening: Song to the tune of "Happy Birthday." (Music is included as "Good Morning to You" on page 61.)

> Top of the morning to you,
> Top of the morning to you,
> Top of the morning, dear neighbor,
> Top of the morning to you.

Greet each other in song and in spirit.

Announcement of the King and Queen of Green. Have them sit up front on their decorated throne and witness the entire session during their reign. Interview them.

Exercise: With green and white streamers or two shades of green. 18 inch length given to each person for mild exercise as follows:
"When Irish Eyes are Smiling" — float streamers in the air.
"My Wild Irish Rose" — make figure eights. (A songsheet is included at the end of the EVERYTHING'S SOMING UP ROSES [January] weekly session plan.)
"I'm Looking Over a Four Leaf Clover" — tap shoulder, knees, arms 8 beats. Good leader necessary.
"Wearing of the Green" — alternate greens up and down.

Reminiscence: After a greeting, single out all of Irish descent. Discuss Irish heritage, pros an cons. Recall former celebrations including favorite Irish songs. Play these favorites during the Irish meal.

Wheelchair
Dance: Four aides assist four in wheelchairs to dance around the King and Queen using an Irish jig or the "Irish Washerwoman" for music. Circle one way, then the other, pull back, go forward, circle.

Group Singing: Using large print songsheets, sing "When Irish Eyes Are Smiling."

Education: • March 17 celebrates the patron saint of Ireland, Bishop Patrick, A.D. 369-461. He left his home in the Severn valley, England, to introduce Christianity into Ireland. At age 16, he was captured by the Gaels and was captive for 6 years in Ireland. His destiny appeared in a dream and he escaped and traveled 200 miles to reach a ship that he dreamt would be waiting for him. As Bishop, he freed the slaves.
                    • March 17 is a national holiday in Ireland and Northern Ireland, a feast day in the Catholic church and honored by a large parade on 5th Avenue in New York.[1]
                    • Famous Irish Americans: Andrew Jackson, Ronald Reagan, Woodrow Wilson, JFK, James Cagney, William Buckley, Maureen O'Hara, V. Herbert.

Solo Time: "It's Not Easy Being Green" — use the green puppet Kermit the frog which is familiar to all their grandchildren. Not everyone is Irish so celebrate the other nationalities as well since most do not have a specific day for festivity.

Song
Identification: Name the following non-Irish countries that these melodies recall.

                    Du, Du, liegst Mir im Herzen (Germany)
                    Never on Sunday (Greece)
                    Song of India (India)
                    O Sole Mio (Italy)
                    Volga Boat Song (Russia)
                    Marseillaise (France)
                    America (United States) *
                    God Save the Queen (United Kingdom)

                    *   A songsheet for verses 2 and 3 is included at the end of the OUR HISTORY IN SONG [July] weekly session plan.

Musical Game: Fill in the blanks with the song titles heard as the pianist plays them and reads the script:

                    Once there was ["My Wild Irish Rose"]. It was the ["Last Rose of Summer"]. It could be found in [state song]. Along came ["Winter Wonderland"] and the rose was soon ["Lullaby and Good Night"] and frozen in the ["Massa's in the Cold, Cold Ground"].

---

[1] Points 1 and 2 in the Education section from *Chases Annual Events* (1992) p. 88

Musical Game: (Cont.)	Well, the weather continued with ["Let it Snow"] so it was time to build ["Frosty, the Snowman"]. He enjoyed a wonderful season until it was time for the ["Easter Parade"]. Then he said ["Nobody Knows the Trouble I've Seen"] because he was exposed to ["You Are My Sunshine"]. You know what happened to the snowman ["After You've Gone"]. He melted ["With a Song in My Heart"] right on top of the ["Yellow Rose of Texas"].
	The rose was nurtured by the liquid snow and sang ["My Faith Looks Up to Thee"] and pushed through the ground to begin a new season. The plant then told the world our theme today ["It's Not Easy Being Green"].
Rhythm Band:	Rose medley: "The Rose of Tralee," "My Wild Irish Rose" — 3/4 time. "Wearing of the Green" — only the Irish play. "MacNamara's Band" — all celebrating the festive season. "Irish Washerwoman" — spirited finale.
Closing:	Song celebrating all nationalities — "God Bless America."
Assignment:	All give thanks for the Irish and everyone else. Encourage residents to enjoy all the green symbols and objects they see and know that it also represents the green growth of spring, a time of renewal. Announce next week's theme of HELLO YELLOW and the assignment is to recall all the songs they can about sunshine.
Music Resources:	*Legit Fake Book* (1990) "Never on Sunday" p. 249 "Volga Boat Song" p. 461 "O Sole Mio" p. 257 *Mitch Miller Community Song Book* (1962) "I'm Looking Over a Four Leaf Clover" p. 90 "When Irish Eyes are Smiling" p. 84 *Song Session Community Song Book* (1953) "Wearing of the Green" p. 106 "My Wild Irish Rose" p. 18 *Ultimate Fake Book* (1981) "Irish Washerwoman" p. 298 "The Rose of Tralee" p. 472 *Children's Song Book* (1988) "It's Not Easy Being Green"[1] p. 10

---

[1] Although the actual song title is "Green (Being Green)", this more familiar title has been used throughout.

THE GREEN SCENE

1. MacNamara's Band
2. How are Things in Glocca Morra
3. Danny Boy
4. The Rose of Tralee
5. I'm Looking Over a Four Leaf Clover
6. Peggy O'Neil
7. When Irish Eyes are Smiling
8. Irish Washerwoman
9. My Wild Irish Rose
10. Harrigan
11. Galway Bay
12. It's Not Easy Being Green

Select your favorite sure, and I'll play it for you.

When Irish Eyes Are Smiling

When Irish eyes are smiling
Sure it's like a morn in spring.

A bit of Irish laughter
You can hear the angels sing.

When Irish hearts are happy
All the world seems bright
and gay.

And when Irish eyes
are smiling
Sure they steal your heart away.

– Chauncey Olcott

March Theme —   **IT'S A COLORFUL WORLD**

Today's Theme —   **Hello Yellow**

Advanced
Preparation:
- Using the template at the end of this session plan, make "I am sunny" badges for everyone on bright yellow paper.
- Prepare some yellow plastic plates with smiley faces drawn on them with thick black lines.
- Organize aides to act as reporters and supply them with a pad and pencil.
- Make copies of the large print songsheet of "Open Up Your Heart" (and Let the Sunshine In), which is included at the end of this session plan.
- Publicize the theme so that people come wearing something yellow..
- Provide:
    - smile face scratch and sniff stickers,
    - a collection of "yellow" songs.
- Print the music menu on yellow paper.

Pre-Session:
Piano music featuring yellow songs such as "Yellow Rose of Texas," "Follow the Yellow Brick Road," "Tie a Yellow Ribbon Round the Ole Oak Tree," all played as participants enter.

Opening:
Sing the opening song to the tune of "On Top of Old Smokey."

> Thank God for the sunshine, thank God for the dew
> Thank God for your friendship and blessings on you.

Sing while shaking hands and greeting each other with smiles.

Exercise:
Pass out yellow paper plates with smile faces on them. All hold up plates in front of their face, especially frowners. Suggest they observe the effect all around the room.
"You Are My Sunshine" — Intro — tap knees 7 times with plate, count off, then sing song. Tap shoulders, knees, head, chest — 8 or 16 beats for each part.
"Sunny Side Up" — plate on lap raise slowly on the words "Up, Up," sway above head, lower slowly, repeat.
"Put On Your Old Grey Bonnet" — follow the leader. (A songsheet is included at the end of the REACH OUT AND TOUCH [April] weekly session plan.)
Closing exercise — toss plates at therapist on count of three.

Reminiscence:
Ask everyone to recall someone who has brought sunshine into their life. The person need not be presently living. Allow time for a well thought out response. Reporters should write these down for the facility newspaper. Encourage residents to share if they wish. Follow through by telling the person named or writing them of their positive influence.

Group Singing: Song: "Open Up Your Heart" (and Let the Sunshine In)

Let the sunshine in, and face it with a grin
Smilers never lose and frowners never win
So, let the sunshine in, face it with a grin
Open up your heart and let the sunshine in.

Distribute smile face scratch and sniff stickers to all who sang or listened.

Education: • Discuss the effects of sunshine on the body as well as the planet. Then discuss the effect of a "sunny" disposition.
                 • An article in the St. Louis *Post Dispatch*, "Can Optimism Pay Off?" found that pessimists had a weakened immune system and were more susceptible to disease. Optimists were more careful with their health. Optimists were more likely to get a job. If you were an optimist as a teenager you are most likely to be one at age 80.[1]
                 • Knowing that optimism does payoff, discuss if it is too late to be one.

Solo Time: Any song about sunshine — "Wait 'Til the Sun Shines, Nellie" or "Sunshine in My Soul."

Song
Identification: Name the songs played that have either yellow in the title or the first line.

YELLOW Rose of Texas
Round Her Neck She Wore a YELLOW Ribbon
YELLOW Submarine
Itsy Bitsy Teenie Weenie YELLOW Polka Dot Bikini
Tie a YELLOW Ribbon Round the Ole Oak Tree
A Tisket, a Tasket, a Green and YELLOW Basket
Follow the YELLOW Brick Road
YELLOW Bird
When You Wore a Tulip and I Wore a Big Red Rose

Sunshine Songs:
Wait 'Til the SUN Shines, Nellie
That Lucky Old SUN
Powder Your Face With SUNSHINE
Softly as in a Morning SUNrise
I Don't Care If the SUN Don't Shine
SUNSHINE (Irving Berlin)
World Is Waiting for the SUNrise
Zip-a-dee-doo-dah (plenty of SUNSHINE)

Rhythm Band: "Yellow Brick Road" — 2/4 time.
                 "Yellow Rose of Texas" — faster 2 beat.
                 "Softly as the Morning Sunrise" — beat one, rest, beat three and four.
                 "Sunshine in My Soul Today" — play and sing.

[1]   *St. Louis Post Dispatch*, March 7, 1987, p. D3 - "Can Optimism Pay Off? by D. Coleman.

Assignment: All who attended receive a yellow sun to wear that proclaims to all the world "I am sunny." They can observe the effect it has all day long.

Closing: Conclude with opening song of "Thank God for the Sunshine." Stress that they are the sunshine.

Music
Resources:
Legal Fake Book (1979)
    "Softly, as in a Morning Sunrise" p. 269
Legit Fake Book (1990)
    "Wait 'Til the Sun Shines, Nellie" p. 359
    "The Yellow Rose of Texas" p. 384
    "Zip-a-Dee-Doo-Dah" p. 385.
Mitch Miller Community Song Book (1962)
    "On Top of Old Smokey" p. 5
    "Put on Your Old Grey Bonnet" p. 89
Sheet music: Stuart Hamblen, Shawnee Press, Delaware Water Gap PA 18327 (1955)
    "Open Up Your Heart"
Sheet music: Hewitt and Sweney, Shawnee Press, Delaware Water Gap PA (1970)
    "Sunshine in My Soul"

Your YELLOW Music Menu

1. Yellow Rose of Texas
2. When You Wore a Tulip and I Wore a Big Red Rose
3. Round Her Neck She Wore a Yellow Ribbon
4. Yellow Submarine
5. Itsy Bitsy Teenie Weenie Yellow Polkadot Bikini
6. You are My Sunshine
7. Tie a Yellow Ribbon Round the Ole Oak Tree
8. Sunshine in My Soul Today
9. Wait 'til the Sun Shines, Nellie
10. Sunny Side Up
11. I Got the Sun in the Morning
12. Sunshine (Irving Berlin)

Request your favorite song. I'll announce it and play it for YOU.

Open Up Your Heart and Let the SUNSHINE In

Let the sunshine in and
Face it with a grin
Smilers never lose and
Frowners never win.

So let the sunshine in
Face it with a grin
Open up your heart and
Let the sunshine in.

– Stuart Hamblen

Yellow

I AM
SUNNY

March Theme —   **IT'S A COLORFUL WORLD**

Today's Theme —   **Lavender and Old Lace**

Advanced
Preparation:
- Invite everyone to wear something lavender, purple or with some lace, and to bring something old.
- You might be able to obtain some lavender sachets pre-made by the craft group of dried lavender tied in a bit of lace with purple ribbon.
- Props will include:
    - antiques such as a lantern,
    - photo album,
    - lace doilies,
    - song collection with "old" in the title.
- Print music menu on purple paper.

Pre-Session: Songs such as "Mary's a Grand Old Name," "Old Grey Mare," "Old Refrain," "Dear Old Girl," "We're Old and We're Proud of It" are played on the piano or on a tape recorder as people enter.

Opening and
Reminiscence: Announce the theme of LAVENDER AND OLD LACE and the value of things as they age such as antiques, wine, and people. Interview them and write down their response to "What do you consider old and why is it beloved?" Use the song "My Favorite Things" preceding the interview. Discuss props or old items they brought.

Exercise: Distribute lavender sachets and exercise with them to get the scents in the air and to distract them from exercising.
"Old Grey Mare" (She ain't what she used to be) — at end of the song shout "She's better." Wave sachet to the music while singing.
"Dear Old Girl" — slowly wave sachet over head to the music.

Group Singing: First relate the story of the mares trying to plough a field and they don't plow it with any regularity. It was the old grey mare who ploughed it in a straight line from experience.
Sing the following song to the tune of "If You're Happy and You Know It Clap Your Hands." (Music is included on page 322.)
Verses:
1. If you're happy and you know it clap your hands
2. If you're living and you know it shout hoorah
3. If you're growing and you know it shout amen.

"We're Old and We're Proud of It" by Darrell Faires (excerpt). The music is
    included on page 144.
    We're old and we're proud of it
    We're old but not out of it
    We're old and we're glad to be alive.
Repeat entire song.

Education:
- An older person should be seen as a human being who escaped becoming an infant mortality statistic, victim of fatal childhood disease, accident in midlife, or disorder in later life according to Hugh Downs.[1] This must be celebrated.
- An older person is simply one who has lived a long time.[2]
- An older person may appear slower in thought process due to sifting through a large store of experience and data before giving you the best answer.[3]
- Many are smarter in their vintage years due to experience and accumulated knowledge. You think, speak, and write better than a youngster.[4]
- Memory is affected by overload and/or lack of interest.[5]
- The best way of improving memory is by using your brain with continued activity, learning and by enriching the environment.[6]
- Elderly take a broad view of life across the generations and feel a sense of comradeship with all humankind.[7]

Solo Time: Poem by Darrell Faires in the song "Growing Old Is a Gentle Art" (excerpt).

Life just gets more precious as we travel through the years.
Life will surely bless us with more laughter, joys and tears.
Growing old is a gentle art, a gentle art of living.
We've been told we've got a good start, so we'll just keep on giving.
Growing old is a gentle art a time for graceful sharing.
As life unfolds we'll play our part and we'll just keep on caring.

Song
Identification: Beloved songs with "Old" in the title.

Put On Your OLD Grey Bonnet	OLD MacDonald Had a Farm
When I Grow Too OLD to Dream	OL' Man River
Little OLD Lady	The OLD Oaken Bucket
Pack up Your Trouble *	The OLD Rugged Cross
On Top of OLD Smokey	In the Shade of the OLD Apple Tree
Shanty in OLD Shanty Town	That Lucky OLD Sun
Cheer, Cheer for OLD Notre Dame	In the Good OLD Summer Time §
Dear OLD Girl	

*   A songsheet is included at the end of the THEY
FOUGHT FOR FREEDOM [July] weekly   session plan.
§ A songsheet is included at the end of the TAKE ME OUT TO THE BALL GAME [June] weekly session plan.

---

1   Downs, H. (1975) *Thirty Dirty Lies About Old* Lie #29: "Old People Die Because They're Old" p. 155
2   Ibid. Lie #1: "An Old Person is an Old Person" p. 13.
3   Ibid. Lie # 14: "Thinking Slows Up as You Age" p. 85.
4   Comfort, A. (1976) *A Good Age,* p. 120.
5   Cosby, B. (1987) *Time Flies*, p. 8 in Introduction by Dr. A. Poussiant.
6   Comfort, A. (1976) *A Good Age* ,p. 120
7   Cosby, B. (1987) *Time Flies*, p. 18 in Introduction by Dr. A. Poussiant.

Rhythm Band: "Old MacDonald Had a Farm" with separate parts.

> Leader sings Old MacDonald had a band, 1, 2, 3, 4, 5
> And in his band he had some bells, 1, 2, 3, 4, 5
> With a ring-a-ling here, and a ring-a-ling there
> Here a ring, there a ring, everywhere a ring-a-ling.
> Old MacDonald had a band, 1, 2, 3, 4, 5.

Additional verses feature shakers, drums, sticks, end with all playing.

"Down by the Old Mill Stream" — sing and play at the same time. Sing words, at end of phrase play instrument with vigor. Band plays as long as you direct.

Closing: Repeat song "We're Old and We're Proud of it."

Assignment: Get residents thinking about the old things that are treasured including smells like lavender, and sights like fancy laces and doilies. They can write them down and share with others, especially the relatives.

Music
Resources:

Mitch Miller Community Song Book (1962)
> "Mary's a Grand Old Name" p. 13
> "The Old Refrain" p. 50
> "Dear Old Girl" p. 6

Festival of Popular Songs (1977)
> "Down by the Old Mill Stream" p. 106

Merry Christmas Song Book (1987)
> My Favorite Things" p. 114

Tune Book Songs (1982)
> "If You're Happy and You Know It" p. 212

Sheet music: Darrell Faires, Shalom Publications, Hazlewood, MO. Used by permission.
> "We're Old and We're Proud of It"
> "Growing Old is a Gentle Art"

From: *Older is Beautiful, Too* (1987)

WE'RE OLD AND WE'RE PROUD OF IT!

Darrell Faires, Sr.

Lavender and Old Lace

Old is Beautiful

1. We're **Old** and We're Proud of It
2. In an **Old** Dutch Garden
3. **Ol'** Man River
4. The **Old** Refrain
5. Give Me That **Old** Time Religion
6. The **Old** Rugged Cross
7. Mary's a Grand **Old** Name
8. Cheer, Cheer for **Old** Notre Dame
9. (In) A Shanty in **Old** Shanty Town
10. You're an **Old** Smoothie

Request your favorite old song. I'll be glad to play it.

MARCH INTO ......

SPRING

Spring Theme — **AN INDOOR PARADE**
                AN ANNUAL CELEBRATION

Today's Theme — **March Into Spring**
(Optional)

Purpose:
        The purpose is to provide an opportunity to establish a ritual of welcoming the season of Spring, a time of new life and renewal; to increase awareness of the new season, use mobility as a goal, establish friendships and tour the facility during the parade.

Advanced
Preparation:

- Plan with staff an appropriate date and time.
- Publicize the date early for anticipation. Countdown posters "Only 5 days until…" "4 days until…" should be put up around facility.
- Encourage staff, residents, aides, and families to wear pastel colors.
- Have ready pre-taped music—2 or 3 copies so that the same music can be played on tape players at 2 or 3 places or the facility intercom.
- Decorate chairs, canes, and, walkers, etc. with flowers, pastel streamers. This can be easily done by a scouting group the day before.
- Contact volunteers to assist with wheelchairs, and who will provide extra support. This is another chance for the community to serve.
- Provide a fresh or paper flower for every marcher and room stop-over.

Decorations:

- Activity Department or community service group can help residents make colorful Spring hats by remodeling old hats or creating new inexpensive ones that can be used for room decors or decorations.
- Fill helium balloons and attach them to wheelchairs, canes, or wrists.
- Decorate the bulletin boards with things that have a spring theme to them.

Music:
        Pre-tape the following music:
           In Your Easter Bonnet
           Tip Toe Through the Tulips
           Glory, Glory Hallelujah
           When You Wore a Tulip and I Wore a Big Red Rose
           When It's Springtime in the Rockies
           Let Me Call You Sweetheart
           I'm Looking Over a Four Leaf Clover
           God Bless America

Planning
Parade:

- Invite residents to help with the planning. Encourage them to help someone else decorate.
- Send a letter of invitation to families. No observers allowed, all will participate.
- Plan with staff who is eligible to march and who must be escorted.
- Put a symbol on the doors of residents who are not to be disturbed for a visit by the marchers, or to be included in parade.

Day of Parade:
- Announce over the intercom the place and time to meet.
- Escort anyone to a general meeting place that has been pre-arranged. Taped music or piano music should be playing.
- Add any additional decorations.

March Into Spring:

Opening
Program:

Welcome everyone to the annual event. Open with the following song of introduction to the tune of "Frère Jacques?"

Leader	Where are the volunteers, where are the volunteers?
Response	HERE WE ARE, HERE WE ARE.
Leader	How are you today, friends?
Response	VERY WELL WE THANK YOU,
Leader	God bless you,
Response	GOD BLESS YOU.

Continue song by identifying residents, staff, families, scouts. Last verse should be "Where are the marchers?"

Parade
Warm-up:•

Pass out rhythm instruments — warm up with a march.
- Choose several parade leaders depending on group size and number of wheelchairs. Give each group a name. Example — "Tulip" group goes first to the nearest area where they will march. Give group leader a tall paper flower—relevant to the group name—to hold high.
- Assign areas for each group of marchers. Size of groups determines area to be covered. Do not attempt to involve everyone to cover the entire facility. Area assigned should be fairly short. This is both an exhilarating and a tiring activity for many.

Marching Into
Spring Parade:
- Music begins on various tape players, one in meeting place, another in hall farther away or else all on the intercom.
- March units are called by groupings and begin. Everyone is encouraged to sing along with the tape and let their voices welcome springtime.
- Marchers leave a fresh or paper flower in every room where they pass by. Do not stay, continue with march but offer to come back.
- Return to general meeting area for light refreshments.
- Collect rhythm instruments.
- Have volunteers with reporter sign on their lapel interview some of the happy marchers.
- Print event in local newspaper.

Closing:
- Participants can stay and visit.
- Escort residents back to their rooms.
- Put hats or some other decoration on their doors.
- Collect unwanted hats, decorations.
- Thank everyone for the official WELCOME TO SPRING.

APRIL

Music Menu

The EYES
Have It

1. Five Foot Two, *Eyes* of Blue
2. Beautiful, Beautiful Brown *Eyes*
3. Smoke Gets in Your *Eyes*
4. Drink to Me Only with Thine *Eyes*
5. Ma! He's Making *Eyes* at Me
6. There's Yes, Yes in Your *Eyes*
7. When Irish *Eyes* are Smiling
8. Dark *Eyes*
9. Chiapanecas - *Eye, Eye*
10. *Eye* Love You Truly

Choose your favorite song. Eye'll play it for you!

IT'S A SENSE-SATIONAL MONTH
APRIL

Learning more about the five senses is fascinating for every age. The educational part of these five programs will update everyone on not only the changes that take place but also give positive advice on coping with these changes. For example, the loss of taste buds can all be enhanced with serving attractive foods, appreciating the various textures of foods and enjoying the ability of the nose to smell. In addition, there is the power of the mind to associate and recall numerous tastes. Many of the programs overlap with this particular theme since the five senses are interrelated. The main emphasis should be on appreciation of the past usage and the possibilities and expansion of the present senses.

If the month you choose for this theme has only four sessions for presentation, the fifth program "Stop and Smell the Roses" on the olfactory sense, can easily be adapted into "Flower Power" the first session of the next month.

Hear Ye, Hear Ye — Everyone can hear the tape of bells pealing as they enter the room Later they enjoy identifying many other sounds. Stress that change is normal as one ages and one can accommodate for hearing loss.

How's Your Taste, Bud? — Try a taste test. Learn what affects our taste and why hospital food might not taste so good. Then sing about it.

Seeing is Believing — Seeing *is* believing or can we see in other ways? This session lets you experience guided imagery and seeing with new eyes and meaning.

Reach out and Touch — It is fun to collect bags full of touchables that provide many memory associations especially for the elderly. Test their ability to feel and verify the fact that this sense often changes with the passage of time.

Stop and Smell the Roses — There is lots to sniff and smell. This sense appeals to all ages and stages of life. Volunteers can help contribute to the Smell Collection. Be prepared to laugh a lot.

OPTIONAL PROGRAM

Easter Parade — Preplanning is a necessity and well worth the time. Make this an intergenerational activity and it wil be a highlight of the year. It can also be adapted into a Welcome Springtime Parade.

IT ALL MAKES SENSE

April Theme —   **IT'S A SENSE-SATIONAL MONTH**

Today's Theme —   **Hear Ye, Hear Ye**

Advanced
Preparation:
- Obtain or make a record/tape of various sounds, e.g. animal sounds, throwing dice, baby crying.
- Provide:
  - large sheet,
  - egg beater,
  - hammer, nails, board,
  - drum, cow bell and other loud instruments.
- Arrange for a soloist to sing "Aren't You Glad You're You."

Pre-Session: Tape or record of joyous bells ringing out as people enter[1].

Opening: Announce the theme HEAR YE, HEAR YE, and that the emphasis today is on the ability to hear. Stress that changes are normal as we all age. Ask if bells were heard as they entered today's session. If so, they have passed the hearing test.

Opening Song "I've Got Music in My Hands" (Music is included on page 75.).Move the relevant body parts to the music.
Verse:
1. I've got music in my hands and it's keeping me alive.
2. I've got music in my ears......
3. I've got music in my shoulders.....
Continue with neck, fingers, feet, and body.

Reminiscence:
- Get residents to identify the sounds they hear on these tapes[2][3] — sea lions, chicken coop, turkeys, rooster, geese and ducks, sheep, goats, pigs, guinea pigs, puppies, skipping, walking in the snow, children at a playground, baby crying, baby sneezing, baby laughing, shuffling and dealing cards, throwing dice.
- They can try and identify the sounds coming from behind the screen or sheet. Volunteers hold up a sheet and activate an egg beater, drum, cow bell, hammer, music box.
- To stimulate a group discussion, suggest residents recall some of their favorite sounds.

Education:
- Hearing involves detecting pitch, intensity or loudness, and duration.
- Hearing loss is more common in men. This could stem from jobs which cause the eardrums to thicken.[4]
- Hearing loss is a normal aging process— we all lose the higher pitches no matter how loud they are.[5]

---

1   "Let Fredom Ring" Colpix Records, CP 515, Columbia Pictures Corp. New York.
2   *Documentary Sounds* Vol. 1. Folkways Records.
3   *Sounds of Animals* Science Series. Folkways Records.
4   Points 1 and 2 in Education section from Ciolfi, Dearing, Summers, and Wasserman (1987) *Sense Up*, p. 12.
5   Hendricks, J. (1981) *Aging in Mass Society*, p. 152.

Education: (Cont.)	**Solutions**: • Don't withdraw but compensate by lip reading, body language, touch, voice intonation. • Ask people to stand in front of you when they talk. • Ask them to talk slowly. • Try to eliminate background noises. • Get an examination, ears do change.
Solo Time:	Encourage sounds they can make. Everyone has a chance to be a soloist. Try whistling, whispering, meowing, clucking with the tongue, snapping fingers, coughing.

Soloist sings "Aren't You Glad You're You" which contains all five senses.

> Every time you're near a rose, aren't you glad you've got a NOSE,
> And if the day is fresh with dew, aren't you glad you're you.
> When a meadowlark appears, aren't you glad you've got two EARS,
> And if your heart is singing too, aren't you glad you're you.
> You can SEE a summer sky or TOUCH a friendly hand,
> Or TASTE an apple pie.
> Pardon the grammar, but ain't life grand,
> And when you wake up each morn, aren't you glad that you were born,
> Think what you've got the whole day through, aren't you glad you're you.

Song Identification:	The following songs test both hearing and memory. Name the sounds in the song titles.

> MacNamara's BAND
> Let's all Sing Like the BIRDIES Sing *
> Little Sir ECHO
> Flight of the BUMBLEBEE
> WOODPECKER Song
> Let It SNOW, Let It SNOW, Let It SNOW
> Silver BELLS
> All Alone (By the TELEPHONE)

* Music is included on page 200.

Rhythm Band:	Emphasize auditory discrimination by using instruments in various groups such as the bells only, shakers, drums, sticks.
	"Old MacDonald Had a Farm"
	    Sing the name of your facility followed by "had a band, e-i, e-i, o
	        And in this band he had some bells, e-i, e-i, o
	        with a ring-a-ling here and a ring-a-ling there,
	        here a ring, there a ring, everywhere a ring-a-ling..."
	Continue with other instruments, ending with "and they all joined in."
	"Silver Bells" — bells only.
	"Chopsticks" - sticks only.

Rhythm Band: (Cont.)	Any march - drums only. "La Cucaracha" — shakers only. "Toreador Song" — tambourines. "MacNamara's Band" — everybody.
Closing:	Closing song: "We're Old and We're Proud of It." (Music is included on page 144.)

<blockquote>
We're old and we're proud of it
We're old and not out of it
We're old and we're glad to be alive.

Repeat.
</blockquote>

Assignment:	We should all give thanks for two ears and years of years of hearing. Encourage residents to appreciate what they can hear and also what they can't hear, like closing their ears to gossip or the sound of their internal organs. Get residents thinking about that this week.

Announce that next week is sense-sational too. The group session of celebration will include discussion and music about the gastatory sense, our sense of taste. Encourage everyone to start recalling their favorite tastes. The title of next week's session is HOW'S YOUR TASTE, BUD?

Music Resources:	*Ultimate Fake Book* (1981)
	     "Aren't You Glad You're You" p. 38
	     "La Cucaracha" p. 325
	     "Toreador Song" p. 599
	 One Thousand and One Jumbo (1985)
	     "Flight of the Bumblebee" p. 263
	     "Let It Snow, Let It Snow, Let It Snow" p. 83
	 Greatest Legal Fake Book of All Times (1985)
	     "Little Sir Echo" p. 307
	 Sheet music: Darrell Faires, Shalom Publications, Hazlewood, MO. Used by permission.
	     "We're Old and We're Proud of It"
	 From: *Older is Beautiful, Too* (1987)

Music Menu

1. Schubert: *Ave Maria*
2. Chopin: *Polonaise*
3. Dvořák: *Humoresque*
4. Beethoven: *Ode to Joy*
5. Offenbach: *Barcarolle*
6. Rossini: *William Tell Overture*
7. Beethoven: *Minuet in G*
8. Tschaikowsky: *Violin Concerto*
9. Rachmaninoff: *Piano Concerto #2*
10 Liszt: *Liebestraum*

Select your classical favorite or name another.

April Theme — **IT'S A SENSE-SATIONAL MONTH**

Today's Theme — **How's Your Taste, Bud?**

Advanced
Preparation:
- Prepare a platter of fresh fruit for everyone,
- Provide samples of fruit, olives ,sour cherry, and pickle for four people.
- Make enough copies of the large print songsheet of "Yes! We Have No Bananas," which is provided at the end of this week's session plan.
- You will need the music to the "Hokey-Pokey," and "On Top of Spaghetti."

Pre-Session:
Play songs on the piano or tape recorder with food associations such as "Billy Boy" (Can She Bake a Cherry Pie?), "Yes! We Have No Bananas," "Tea for Two," and "Big Rock Candy Mountain."

Opening:
Announce the theme of HOW'S YOUR TASTE, BUD? Use the following opening song to the tune of "I Love Coffee." (Music is included on page 160.)
> I love coffee, I love tea
> I love feeling neighborly.

Greet person beside you, continue singing till aides have shaken every hand.

Exercise:
To the tune of "Hokey-Pokey"
Verse:
1. You put your right hand in, you take you right hand out,
   You put your right hand in and you shake it all about.
   You do the hokey pokey now way up high (hands overhead)
   You bring them down and give a sigh.
2. You put your left hand in........
3. You put your right foot in........
4. You pur your left foot in......
5. You put your shoulders in.......

Reminiscence:
All sing the commercial "Ummmm good."
> Umm good, Umm good
> Tell us what you think is ummmmm good.[1]

Recall favorite tastes but sing the verse between each recollection.

Education:
- The tongue is one of the extremely sensitive sensory organs for tasting and also the producer of stimuli that excite another sense with the ability to talk. Which is more important? The taste bud is 30-80 non-nerve cells. It survives only 10 days, yet is constantly renewing. Taste changes when you have a cold with increased mucus and no smell. It also changes with medications.[2]
- Taste perception is regarded as a chord of the chemical senses playable on 4 notes: sweet, salt, sour, bitter.[3]

---

[1] Bitcon, C. (1976) *Alike and Different*, p. 86.
[2] Whitfield, P. (1984) *Hearing, Taste and Smell*, pp. 64-85.
[3] Ibid. pp. 85-101.

Education: • With aging, receptors are replaced at a slower rate, so one needs to
(Cont.)   increase sensation — more salt is dangerous but one can make it more
                   attractive, and enjoy texture of foods.[1]
                 • Two thirds of taste sensations depend on the ability to smell.[2]
                 • A child has more taste buds than an adult, and prefers sweet things.[3]
                 • One can accent flavors with nitrogen: for example — milk on apple pie,
                   radish with beer in Germany.
                 • Flavors depend on external smell (nose), internal smell (taste buds), texture
                   of food, sound of food (crunch) and eye-appeal (color).

Sensory
Stimulation: Invite 4 people up front to take a taste test, blindfolded or with closed eyes.
                 Let them taste a pickle, olive, sour cherry, and sweet candy. Ask others if they
                 could "almost taste it."

                 Serve a very attractive platter of fresh fruits or some good chocolate (diabetic
                 necessary) to everyone. Review the above suggestions for increasing the
                 satisfaction of taste.

Song
Identification: What can you taste in the following songs? Play the tunes and see if the
                 food/drink contained in the song is recognized.[4]

                         Yes! We Have No BANANAS
                         Billy Boy (Can She Bake a Cherry Pie?)
                         Yankee Doodle (... and called it MACARONI)
                         TEA for Two
                         Take Me Out to the Ball Game (buy me some PEANUTS and CRACKER
                                 JACK)
                         Hot Cross BUNS
                         Big Rock CANDY Mountain
                         Don't Sit Under the APPLE Tree
                         Goober PEAS
                         MEAT me in St. Louis, Louis (pun)

Solo Time: Resident to sing "On Top of Spaghetti" to the tune of "On top of Old
                 Smokey."

                 On top of spaghetti all covered with cheese
                 I lost my poor meatball when somebody sneezed.

                 It rolled off the table and onto the floor
                 And then my poor meatball rolled right out the door.

---

[1] Ciolfi, Dearing, *et. al* (1988) *Sense Up*, p. 33.
[2] Butler, R. *Aging and Mental Health*, p. 47.
[3] Erb. R. (1968) *Common Sense of Smell*, p. 33.
[4] Karras, B. (1988) *With a Smile and a Song,* p. 32.

Solo Time: (Cont.)	It rolled into the garden and under a bush And then my poor meatball was nothing but mush.
Group Singing:	All sing "Yes! We Have No Bananas," from the songsheet provided. Yes! we have no bananas, we have no bananas today. We've got string beans and onions, cabbages and scallions And all kinds of fruit and say We have an old fashioned tomato, long island potato, But, yes! we have no bananas, we have no bananas today.
Rhythm Band:	"Chopsticks" — sticks only. "Turkey in the Straw" — everyone. (A songsheet is included at the end of the LET'S ALL SING LIKE THE BIRDIES SING [May] weekly session pan.) "Tea for Two" — be creative with extra beats. "Shortnin' Bread" — play softly and then louder on word "shortnin' bread." "The Beer Barrel Polka" — every plays merrily.
Closing:	All sing to the tune of "It's Love that Makes the World Go 'Round." This music is included on page 70. Verse: 1. It's love that makes the world go 'round; 2. It's you that makes the world go 'round (point to each other) 3. It's me... (point to self) 4. It's us... (lift arms up high) 5. It's taste that makes the food so good.
Assignment:	Remind residents to taste food with a deeper appreciation now that the facts are known. They can now realize that other associations are important such as the smell and appearance. Encourage them to enjoy the fact that the tongue still works. Next week's theme is SEEING IS BELIEVING or THE EYES HAVE IT.

Music Resources:	*Mitch Miller Community Song Book* (1962)
	      "On Top of Old Smokey" p. 5
	Ultimate Fake Book (1981)
	      "Yes! We Have No Bananas" p. 658
	      "Turkey in the Straw" p. 594
	      "The Beer Barrel Polka" p.52
	Children's Song Book (1988)
	      "On Top of Spaghetti" p. 128
	Legal Fake Book (1979)
	      "Tea for Two" p. 283
	Wings of Song (1984)
	      "It's Love that Makes the World Go 'Round" p. 354

I LOVE COFFEE, I LOVE TEA

Traditional

I love cof - fee,   I love tea.   I love feel - ing   neigh - bor - ly.

Music Menu

What can you almost **TASTE** in these songs?

1. Yes! We Have No Bananas
2. Tea for Two
3. Hot Cross Buns
4. Take Me Out to the Ball Game
5. Turkey in the Straw
6. Shortnin' Bread
7. Big Rock Candy Mountain
8. Yankee Doodle
9. Meat Me in St. Louis, Louis
10. Never on Sundae!
11. Name One of Your Flavorites

I'll play it tastefully for you!

YES! WE HAVE NO BANANAS
WE HAVE NO BANANAS TODAY
WE'VE STRING BEANS & ONIONS
CABBAGES & SCALLIONS
AND ALL KINDS OF FRUIT
AND SAY -
WE HAVE AN OLD FASHIONED
TOMAHTO,
LONG ISLAND POTAHTO BUT,
YES,
WE HAVE NO BANANAS
WE HAVE NO BANANAS TODAY.

– *Frank Silver*

April Theme —   **IT'S A SENSE-SATIONAL MONTH**

Today's Theme —   **Seeing is Believing**

Advanced
Preparation:
- Place enough silk scarves in a basket for everyone.
- Prepare a song collection referring to the *eyes*.

Pre-Session: Play songs on the piano or with the tape recorder music that has a relationship to *eyes*. For example, "The Eyes of Texas," "Ma! He's Makin' Eyes at Me" "Dark Eyes," "When Irish Eyes Are Smiling."

Opening: Announce continuation of the theme, IT'S A SENSE-SATIONAL MONTH and NOW THE EYES HAVE IT. Seeing is believing, or can we see in other ways?

An easy exercise, simply follow the directions of the song to the tune of "Till We Meet Again."
> Smile a while and give your face a rest (smile)
> Stretch a while and ease you weary chest (stretch)
> Reach your hands up toward the sky (reach overhead)
> While you watch them with your EYE.
> Give a nod and shake a leg there, Sir (nod then shake leg)
> Now stretch forward, backward as you were (out then back)
> Then reach out to someone near (reach)
> Shake his hand and smile. (smile)

Exercise: Distribute colorful pieces of silk or silk scarves to each person for motion and movement activity.
> "When Irish Eyes Are Smiling" — float in 3/4 time. (A songsheet is included at the end of the IT'S NOT EASY BEING GREEN [March] weekly session plan.)
> "Five Foot Two, Eyes of Blue" — dance scarves — 2 beat. (A songsheet is included at the end of the STYLES UP OT THE ANKLE [September] weekly session plan.)
> "Drink to Me Only with Thine Eyes" — create your own. (A songsheet is included at the end of this week's session plan.)

Reminiscence: Use your imaging powers. With eyes closed have residents conjure up images from their past as you play piano and announce the scenario. Use some of the following descriptive songs:
> Alice Blue Gown
> Wedding Chorus (Here Comes the Bride) (from *Lohengrin*)
> The Little Brown Church
> I Say Mommy Kissing Santa Claus
> Let There Be Peace on Earth

Discuss.

Education: • The ability of the eye to change shape decreases with age.
                  • Loss of focusing power due to reduced elasticity of the lens of the eye called presbyopia or lens change.
                  • It becomes harder to focus on near objects.
                  • Color discrimination weakens — lens becomes yellow.[1]
                  • There can be a slower adaptation to darkness.
                  • A temporary loss of sight occurs due to slower circulation to the retina.[2]
                  • 25% of those over 70 have cataracts (clouding of the lens).[3,4]

                  Solutions:
                  • Get an eye exam, especially when you've experienced a change in medication or stress.
                  • Use extra good lighting, be kind to your eyes.
                  • Use bold and dark contrasts in your environment.
                  • See outlines.
                  • Accommodate by hearing better, listen closely to a bird that you can't see well.
                  • Use large print editions of books, papers.
                  • See deeply — beauty from the inside that shows through.
                  • Use you imaging powers more.

Solo or Group
Singing: Sing to the tune of "The Battle Hymn of the Republic."

                  Mine eyes have seen the glory of the coming of this spring....
                  As time goes marching on.

                  Chorus: Glory, Glory, Hallelujah.

Song
Identification: The songs to be played are all about the eyes. Name them out loud as quickly as you can remember them or sing it.

                      Smoke Gets in Your EYES
                      Drink To Me Only with Thine EYES
                      When Irish EYES Are Smiling
                      Don't Let the Stars Get in Your EYES
                      Ma! He's Making EYES at Me
                      The EYES of Texas
                      Five Foot Two, EYES of Blue
                      Dark EYES
                      There's Yes, Yes, in Your EYES
                      EYE Love You Truly (pun)

---

[1] Ciolfi, Dearing, *et. al* (1988) *Sense Up*, p.45.
[2] Coni, Davison and Webster (1984) *Ageing [sic] The Facts.*, p. 113.
[3] Ciolfi, Dearing, *et. al* (1988) *Sense Up*, p p.45 and 46.
[4] Recommended reading: Hendricks, J. (1981) *Aging in a Mass Society.*

Rhythm Band: "When Irish Eyes Are Smiling" — 3/4 time.
                 "Five Foot Two, Eyes of Blue" — peppy 2 beat.
                 "Chiapanecas" — piano solo with band response on "Ei Ei" (pun!). All
                     together on chorus.
                 "MacNamara's Band" — play with eyes closed, realize the joy of playing in a
                     band even without sight. Open eyes for finale.

Closing: Group singing of "Bless This House." (A songsheet is included at the end of
                 the GROUND-HOG DAY [February] weekly session plan.)

Assignment: We should all give thanks for years of seeing many sights. Realize they have
                 been cataloged in the brain. Affirm together "I am older and wiser." Next
                 week's theme that is sense-sational is REACH OUT AND TOUCH.

Music
Resources: *Latin American Music* (1969)
                        "Chiapanecas" p. 4
                 Ultimate Fake Book (1981)
                        "Dark Eyes" p. 125
                        "Battle Hymn of the Republic" p. 41
                        "When Irish Eyes are Smiling" p. 628
                        "Smoke Gets in Your Eyes" p. 490
                        "I Love You Truly" p. 238
                 Song Session Community Song Book (1953)
                        "Till We Meet Again" p. 35
                        "Drink to me Only with Thine Eyes" p. 105
                 One Thousand and One Jumbo (1985)
                        "The Eyes of Texas" p. 410

Music Menu

The EYES Have It

1. Five Foot Two, *Eyes* of Blue
2. Beautiful, Beautiful Brown *Eyes*
3. Smoke Gets in Your *Eyes*
4. Drink to Me Only with Thine *Eyes*
5. Ma! He's Making *Eyes* at Me
6. There's Yes, Yes in Your *Eyes*
7. When Irish *Eyes* are Smiling
8. Dark *Eyes*
9. Chiapanecas - *Eye, Eye*
10. *Eye* Love You Truly

Choose your favorite song. Eye'll play it for you!

Drink to Me
Only with Thine Eyes

Drink to me only with thine eyes,

and I will pledge with mine.

Or leave a kiss within the cup,

and I'll not ask for wine:

The thirst that from the soul doth rise,

Doth ask a drink divine;

But might I of Jove's nectar sup

I would not change for thine.

– Ben Jonson (1780)

April Theme —   **IT'S A SENSE-SATIONAL MONTH**

Today's Theme —   **Reach Out and Touch**

Advanced
Preparation:
- Prepare some shiny bags containing objects they can feel, such as cotton, coal, soap, sugar cube, brush, ice cubes in plastic bag, banana, potato with eyes, silk, fur, sand, or money.
- Gather a collection of songs as suggested by this theme.
- You will need a soloist for Solo Time to sing "The Best Things In Life are Free." A songsheet is included at the end of the SPRING HAS SPRUNG [May] weekly session plan.
- Pre-tape "Reach Out and Touch." This music is included on page 172.
- Practice "My Hand on My Head" with music that is included on page 172.

Pre-Session: Play the theme "Reach Out and Touch" several times on the piano or a recording. Also play songs that have 'touched the heart strings' through the years such as "Danny Boy," "Drink To Me Only with Thine Eyes," "Old Refrain," "There's a Long, Long Trail" and several familiar waltzes as residents enter the room.

Opening: Announce the theme and introduce the theme song.
> Reach out and touch somebody's hand
> Make this a better place and you can.

As you sing, shake every hand, encourage them to shake their neighbor's hand or at least touch them.

Exercise: Teach the song "My Hand on My Head" including motions emphasizing the texture of each verse of the song. Do this exercise slowly to stimulate the sense of touch as well as exercise.
1. My hand on my head, what have I here?
   This is my top-notcher, my mama dear.
   Top-notcher, top-notcher, dickey, dickey doo.
   That's what I learned in the school. Oh-kay. (slap thighs)
2. My hand on my brow, what have I here?
   This is my sweat boxer, my mama dear.
   Sweat boxer, top-notcher, dickey, dickey doo.
   That's what I learned in the school. Oh-kay.
3. Eye........eye blinker, sweat boxer, top-notcher.
4. Nose.... smell sniffer... etc.
5. Mouth..... food grinder.... etc.
6. Hands...bug smasher... etc.
7. Stomach..... bread basket... etc.

Reminiscence: Discuss some of the things that are enjoyable to touch. Then pass around colorful bags with shiny surfaces that have touchable contents. Guess the contents by placing the hand inside the bag. See suggestions in the Advanced Preparations section.

Education:
- The skin is the largest living sense organ of the body. It covers the entire surface and is capable of receiving sensory stimuli from the environment. [1]
- With aging comes a change in the sense of touch and also in being touched. Changes in the skin make it more fragile, less sensitive.[2]
- The cells do regenerate but more slowly.[3]
- Touch includes pressure, temperature, and pain. Pain is felt less as one ages.[1]
- Extreme hot/cold temperatures not felt in the hand can be the brain's inability to register the temperature, not a function of touch.[3]

Solutions:
- Increase the stimulation by using more texture.
- Take more time to enjoy touching with greater thought.
- Allow more time for the brain to receive message.
- Enjoy human touch, the best one of all.

Song
Identification: Name things you can touch in these song titles.

I'm Forever Blowing BUBBLES
Baby FACE
I'm Looking Over a FOUR LEAF CLOVER
You're a Grand Old FLAG *
Keep the Home FIRES Burning
Last ROSE of Summer
Three Blind MICE
Aunt Dinah's QUILTING Party
Shortnin' BREAD
Put on Your Old Grey BONNET §
Singin' in the RAIN
ANVIL Chorus

* A songsheet is included at the end of the MEMORABLE MEMORIAL DAY [May] weekly session plan.
§ A songsheet is included at the end of this week's session plan.

Solo Time: "The Best Things in Life are Free" — pre-arrange as a vocal solo.

Rhythm Band: All songs regarding touchables.
"Baby Face" — everyone play.
"Shortnin' Bread" — played softly except on word "shortnin' bread' — loud.
"Anvil Chorus" — divide band in half, each side alternates one note.
"Turkey in the Straw" — everyone play. (A songsheet is included at the end of the LET'S ALL SING LIKE THE BIRDIES SING [May] weekly session plan.)
"Anchors Aweigh" — spirited march.

1 Ciolfi, Dearing, *et. al* (1988) *Sense Up,* p. 1.
2 *St. Louis Post Dispatch,* Oct. 15, 1988, p. D1. "Making Sense of the Senses" by S. Rovner.
3 Ibid.p. D8.

Closing: All sing "Reach Out and Touch" joining all hands and swaying as the words and melody take effect. Aides needed.

Assignment: Encourage residents to share their knowledge of touch with others, to enjoy the sense of touch by touching with greater feeling and allowing the brain to process it. Let various stimuli bring back memories and share these with others. Suggest that they report back any experiences.

                     Announce next week's theme is also sense-sational — STOP AND SMELL THE ROSES — the olfactory sense.

Music
Resources:

Family Song Book of Faith and Joy (1981)
       "The Best Things in Life are Free" p. 66
Wee Sing Silly Songs (1984)
       "My Hand on My Head" p. 23
Song Session Community Song Book (1953)
       "Drink to Me Only with Thine Eyes" p. 105
       "There's a Long, Long Trail" p. 37
       "Baby Face" p. 34
       "I'm Looking Over a Four Leaf Clover" p. 39
       "Aunt Dinah's Quilting Party" p. 99
Sheet Music: Charles Brown, Ashford, and Simpson, Jobete Music Co. Hollywood, CA. (1970)
       "Reach Out and Touch"

REACH OUT AND TOUCH

Charles F. Brown

Reach out and touch some-bod-y's hand. Make this a bet-ter place— and you can.

© Copyright C.F. Brown
Used by permission

MY HAND ON MY HEAD

Traditional

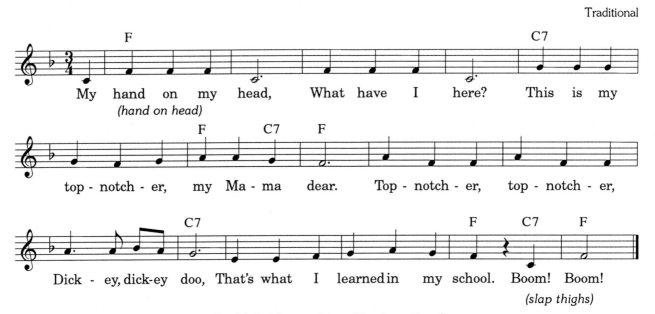

My hand on my head, What have I here? This is my
(hand on head)
top - notch - er, my Ma - ma dear. Top - notch - er, top - notch - er,
Dick - ey, dick-ey doo, That's what I learned in my school. Boom! Boom!
(slap thighs)

2. My hand on my brow, What have I here?
   This is my sweat boxer, my Mama dear.
   Sweat boxer, top-notcher, Dickey, dickey doo,
   That's what I learned in my school.
   Boom! Boom!
3. eye. . . eye blinker, sweat boxer, top-notcher. . .
4. nose. . . smell sniffer. . .
5. mustache. . . soup strainer. . .
6. mouth. . . food grinder. . .
7. chin. . . chin chopper. . .
8. chest. . . air blower. . .
9. stomach. . . bread basket. . .
10. lap. . . lap sitter. . .
11. knee. . . knee bender. . .
12. foot. . . foot stomper. . .

Music Menu

Things We Can TOUCH

1. Put Your Hand in the <u>Hand</u>
2. <u>Maple Leaf</u> Rag
3. The March of the <u>Toys</u>
4. <u>Baby Face</u>
5. <u>Sheep</u> May Safely Graze
6. <u>Peacherine</u> Rag
7. Parade of the <u>Wooden Soldiers</u>
8. Three Blind <u>Mice</u> Variations
9. <u>Stars and Stripes</u> Forever
10. To a Wild <u>Rose</u>
11. Reach Out and Touch (<u>Somebody's Hand</u>)

Choose your favorite I'll tickle the ivories!

Put on Your Old Grey Bonnet

Put on your old grey bonnet

with the blue ribbons on it,

While I hitch old Dobbin to the shay,

And through fields of clover,

We'll drive up to Dover

on our golden wedding day.

– Stanley Murphy (1909)

April Theme —   **IT'S A SENSE-SATIONAL MONTH**

Today's Theme —   **Stop and Smell the Roses**

Advanced
Preparation:

- Prepare individual foam paper plates with pictures of roses from flower catalogs pasted on them.
- Obtain some rose perfume.
- Make bags with holes punched in them. Fill bags with strong scents such as lemon, onions, popcorn, Vicks Vaporub, cloves, even an old shoe!
- Arrange for a resident to read the poem in Solo Time.

Pre-Session: Tapes or live music using song titles about roses plays as participants enter. For example, "My Wild Irish Rose," "Yellow Rose of Texas," "Roses of Picardy," "The Rose of No Man's Land," "Red Roses for a Blue Lady."

Opening: Song:
    The more we get together, together, together,
    The more we get together, the happier we'll be.
    For your friends are my friends,
    And my friends are your friends.
    The more we get together, the happier we'll be.

Exercise: Use the rose foam plates for light exercise, one for each person. Follow leader's directions. Note scent on plate and in the air.
    "My Wild Irish Rose" — circle plate overhead to a slow waltz tempo. (A songsheet is included at the end of the EVERYTHING'S COMING UP ROSES [January] weekly session plan.)
    "Yellow Rose of Texas" — swing plate along side back and forth.
    "Second Hand Rose" — fan in front of face and smell perfume.
    Finale — at the count of three, toss plates at song leader. Call it a flower shower. Remind everyone that it's harmless and good exercise.

Reminiscence: Talk about favorite smells starting with a discussion on roses as well as other flowers. How about the smell of fresh laundry, baked bread, cedar closet, fresh lumber, mothballs, peppermint, coffee, citronella, Vicks Vaporub, chocolate cake, popcorn, lemons?

Education:

- This is the most primitive, least studied of the 5 senses. The study of smell is called osmics. An anosmic person is one who cannot detect odor.[1]
- Non-smokers and women smell most easily. Every second some odor influences you. The average person smells 2000 odors, and can smell 4000 odors if trained.[2]
- One smells externally through the nose and internally with taste buds.[3]

---

[1] Erb. R. (1968) *Common Sense of Smell* "Osmics" p. 13.
[2] Ibid. "Osmics" p. 15.
[3] Ibid. "The Smell of Food and Beverages" p. 27.

Education:
(Cont.)
- There is little change as we age but as the nerve endings weaken, all scents smell the same.[1]
- In the Bible, Ruth used ointments while bathing to enhance herself and mask body odor.[2]
- Bing Crosby used heliotrope to stimulate his love making when making movies. Martha Raye used geraniums to stimulate comedy. On a movie set, mint vapors were used at 4 p.m. to stimulate lagging energy.[3]
- Odor helps us detect danger.[4]
- Of the five senses, smell and taste sensations last the longest in the human body.[5]
- Take frequent short sniffs. It forces more air into the olfactory clefts. Use one nostril and then the other.[6]

Guided Imagery: Using relaxation techniques, gently lead residents to a relaxed state and then have them recall a scene which smelled very good to them. Play gentle music in the background during imagery.

Sensory
Stimulation: Pass around small paper bags with holes punched in them for all to smell. Include lemons, onions, popcorn, Vicks Vaporub, cloves, strong chocolate, even an old shoe. Aides need to circulate the bags so more smells can be enjoyed by more people. Allow time for processing.

Song
Identification: What smells are in these songs?

> Old MacDonald Had a Farm
> How Much is that Doggie in the Window
> Smoke Gets in Your Eyes
> When the Roll is Called Up Yonder *
> O Christmas Tree §
> Rock-a-Bye Baby
> I Love Coffee †
> School Days

Discuss.

* A songsheet is included at the end of the THE SMELLS OF CHRISTMAS [December] weekly session plan.
§ A songsheet is included at the end of the THE SIGHTS OF CHRISTMAS [December] weekly session plan under the title "O Tannenbaum."
† Music is included on page 160.

---

1 Ciolfi, Dearing, *et. al* (1988) *Sense Up* "Olfactory" p. 24.
2 Erb. R. (1968) *Common Sense of Smell* "The Smell of Society" p. 53.
3 Ibid. "Classification of Smells" p. 20.
4 Ibid. "The Smell of Danger" p. 116.
5 *St. Louis Post Dispatch,* Oct. 15, 1988, p. D1. "Making Sense of the Senses" by S. Rovner.
6 Whitfield, P. (1984) *Hearing, Taste and Smell,* p. 110.

Solo Time: Poem "Honey Dripping from the Comb" by James Whitcomb Riley read by a
                    resident.[1]

> How slight a thing may let one's fancy drifting
> Upon the dead sea of the Past!—A view —
> Sometimes an odor—or a rooster lifting
> A far off "Ooh! Ooh-ooh!"
> And suddenly we find ourselves astray
> In some wood's pasture of the Long Ago—
> Or idly dream again upon a day
> Of rest we used to know.

Rhythm Band: "Stop and Smell the Roses" — control group on STOP.
                    "School Days" — as you play, recall those familiar smells. (A songsheet is
                        included at the end of the DEAR OLD SCHOOL DAYS [September] weekly
                        session plan.)
                    "Rock-a-Bye Baby" — play very softly.
                    "Old MacDonald Had a Farm" — do various instrumental groups separately.
                    "Shortnin' Bread" — play softly until the word "shortnin' bread" — loud.
                    March — of your choosing.

Closing: Group singing of "Stop and Smell the Roses."

Assignment: Suggest that residents give thanks for their noses and all the wonderful smells
                    it has enjoyed through the years. Remind them that sight and appearance of
                    something also enhances their sense of smell and that recalling smells with
                    their memory is a valuable link. Enjoy it.

                    Next week is a brand new series called WELCOME SWEET SPRINGTIME. Everyone
                    is invited to join in the welcoming.

Music
Resources: *Family Song Book of Faith and Joy* (1981)
                        "Stop and Smell the Roses" p. 85
                        "When the Roll is Called Up Yonder" p. 144
                    One Thousand and One Jumbo (1985)
                        "Yellow Rose of Texas" p. 591
                    Legit Fake Book (1990)
                        "My Wild Irish Rose" p. 230
                    Festival of Popular Songs (1977)
                        "Second Hand Rose" p. 138
                    Ultimate Fake Book (1981)
                        "Roses of Picardy" p. 476
                    Mitch Miller Community Song Book (1962)
                        "Shortnin' Bread" p. 20

---

[1] *Complete Works of James Whitcomb Riley* (1937) p. 55.

Your Gift of Smell

What do you smell?

1. *Pine Apple Rag*
2. *Ol' Man River*
3. *Singin' in the Rain*
4. *Lida Rose*
5. *I Love Coffee, I Love Tea*
6. *The Trail of the Lonesome Pine*
7. *Old MacDonald Had a Farm*
8. *April Showers*
9. *Yes Sir, That's My Baby*
10. *How Much is that Doggie in the Window*
11. *Apple in the William Tell Overture*
12. *I'm a Lonely Little Petunia in the Onion Patch*

Select your favorite, I'll play it for you.

EASTER PARADE

Theme — (Optional)	**EASTER PARADE**
Purpose —	**Intergenerational Activity**

Rationale: Often an Easter parade is limited to residents of the Christian religion. Consider having a March Into Spring parade with similar arrangements. The Spring Parade involves the concept of renewal and new life which is a part of all religions. See March section of the book for the details. The following adaptation could be made for a specific Easter parade.

Pre-Planning: Plan the parade months in advance so that the community and families are involved. An intergenerational activity is always a highlight of any activity department and welcomed by the residents. Choose the group that is best for your facility.

> Scout group
> Adopt a grandparent project
> Christian church group
> College students
> Candystriper program
> Especially families and grandchildren

Send invitations early to all concerned since half the fun is in anticipation and planning. Use promotional aid in this book for publicity purposes.

Advanced
Preparation: Decide on Easter bonnets. These can be made with old hats and trimmings earlier in the year or families can bring or borrow some hats. Hats of any kind can be useful or purchase baseball style caps and decorate over them. Women's and men's hats can reflect their careers. For example, money around the hatband for bankers; dried wheat, grasses, fake vegetables for farmers; or chef hats for barbecue experts. Extra hats needed for emergencies or newcomers.

Official photographer, special photography area, rented bunny suit, taped march music, refreshments.

Opening: Meet in one general area for a short group session and parade instructions. Welcome everyone. Easter bunny should lead the group with a song to the tune of "Where is Thumbkin?"

Bunny	Where are the ladies, where are the ladies?
Ladies	HERE WE ARE, HERE WE ARE.
Bunny	How are you today, friends?
Ladies	VERY WELL, WE THANK YOU.
Bunny	God bless you.
Ladies	GOD BLESS YOU.

Continue with verses that will include everyone such as: where are the families, grandchildren, volunteers, parade lovers, college kids, etc.

To the tune of "Goodnight Ladies":

> Hello marchers, hello marchers, hello marchers,
> It's time for our parade.
> Merrily we march along, march along, march along,
> Merrily we march along to honor Easter Day.

Education:
- Easter is observed in all Christian churches to commemorate the Resurrection of Jesus.
- It is celebrated on the first Sunday after the full moon which occurs after March 20 and is therefore celebrated between March 22 and April 25 inclusive.
- The date was fixed by the council of Nicea in A.D. 325.[1]

Parade Music: Pre-tape music of well known marches, "Easter Parade," "Battle Hymn of the Republic," "Seventy-six Trombones," "Marching Through Georgia" "MacNamara's Band," and other favorites with a 2/4 beat. If parade route is long, plan on several tapes in various sites or else broadcast one over the intercom system.

Parade Procedure: Indoors or outdoors.
1. Easter hat parade - Parade in a circle or by rows so everyone can see the hat creations. Everyone is a winner, there is no contest.
2. Easter bunny leads parade marchers on designated routes. Plan ahead how many people go to one area, the number to another area. There must be plenty of escorts that have all been pre-arranged.
3. Those not parading can have their picture taken by the official photographer in a decorated area or just a snapshot.
4. Keep the parade fairly short. They are tiring partially due to the excitement and anticipation.
5. Paraders that return from marching should be invited to be photographed. Best photographs should be made into poster size for the walls. These are joyous pictures that enhance the environment.
6. Refreshments are served.
7. Hats are returned or saved till next year.
8. Easter bunny shakes every paw.

---

[1] *Information Please Almanac* (1992) "Holidays, Religious and Secular — Easter Sunday," p. 586.

May

Welcome, Sweet Springtime

Welcome Sweet Springtime

A musical game for the month of May

YOU DESERVE A BOUQUET TODAY, you made it thru the winter time and now you are filled with new life, new energy. Yes, you deserve a bouquet of flowers but you have to figure out which flowers are in it. The following song titles will tell you. The answers are upside down.

1. My Wild Irish _____
2. _____ , _____ Give Me Your Answer True
3. I'm a Lonely Little _____ in an Onion Patch
4. When You Wore a _____ and I Wore a Big Red Rose
5. I'll Be With You in _____ _____ Time
6. Jeannine, I Dream of _____ Time
7. E_____ , E_____ Bless My Homeland Forever
8. Hi_____ Hi-Lo

With your flowers you also get:

9. Down Among the Sheltering _____
10. Tie a Yellow_____ Round the Ole Oak Tree

10 points for every melody you can sing. If you get 100 points for all 10 you deserve 2 bouquets, if you get 90 points, you deserve a ribbon, 80 points gets a vase, 70 points gets some water, 60 points gets some flower seeds and 50 points gets a flower catalog.

ANSWERS: 1. Rose 2. Daisy 3. Petunia 4. Tulip 5. Apple Blossom 6. Lilac 7. Edelweiss 8. Lily 9. Palms 10. Ribbon

WELCOME SWEET SPRINGTIME
MAY

Is there anyone who doesn't welcome springtime? This series of programs is one of the most joyous and thought provoking. It appeals to the five senses with nature providing many objects to touch, smell, see, taste, and hear. In addition, these programs are designed to appeal to the the intellect so both high and low functioning adults can enjoy each session.

The purpose of the programs is to appreciate the fact that each life has been given the opportunity to welcome and experience another spring. Awareness of nature and its effects is the secondary goal and it is attained indoors with the proper use of nature's sensory stimulators. Decorations are easy and the community can bring the outside in to increase awareness for residents as well as the staff.

Spring Has Sprung — Welcome springtime with song, flowers, color, movement, memories, and scent. There's lots to sing about.

Planting More Than Seeds — The theme of PLANTING is filled with memories. However, actually planting outdoors is often impractical. Planting "seed thoughts" is an excellent use of the mind. Encourage everyone to think thoughts that are worth repeating and using as a standard for present living. The thought and affirmation of "I am appreciation" will change lives. Publicize the thought your group chooses, display it, use it frequently in conversation and watch what happens.

Let's All Sing Like the Birdies Sing — Invite pet birds to attend the session and listen to their reaction. The merriment features colorful streamers, special bird songs plus bird whistles that anyone can play with a smile.

Flower Power — Everyone identifies with flowers and gardens. Take a poll and announce the residential favorite. This is a picturesque session with wonderful scents. It has everyone blooming.

OPTIONAL PROGRAMS

Universal Mothers Unite — The emphasis on Mother's Day is partly on one's biological mother, however, this program applauds the acts of mothering. These still occur as one enumerates those in their lives that do good motherly deeds for them. In addition, they are encouraged to keep on mothering others since motherhood is a fine profession.

Memorable Memorial Day — Spring may peak during another month in your locale so this series may be useful at another time. Whenever and wherever it is, welcome it.

BLOOM WHERE YOU'RE PLANTED

May Theme —   **WELCOME SWEET SPRINGTIME**

Today's Theme —   **Spring Has Sprung**

Advanced
Preparation:
- Prepare individual foam plates with spring flowers pasted on them.
- Make enough copies of the large print songsheet of "The Best Things In Life Are Free." This is included at the end of this week's session plan.
- Invite aides and volunteers to wear pastel colors and live spring flowers.
- Gather a collection of songs about spring.

Pre-Session: Volunteers should wear pastel colors and a fresh flower. Piano music is played as everyone enters the room. Suggested songs: "Welcome Sweet Springtime," "Tip Toe Through the Tulips," "When It's Springtime in the Rockies," "Singin' in the Rain." and "Country Gardens." (The music to "Country Gardens" is included on page 206.)

Opening: Announce the monthly theme of WELCOME SWEET SPRINGTIME and today's specific theme of SPRING HAS SPRUNG. Note the present weather conditions and then teach this song to the tune of "Hail, Hail, the Gang's All Here."
>   Hail, hail the gang's all here,
>   Never mind the weather, here we are together.
>   Hail, hail the gang's all here,
>   Let the music start, RIGHT NOW.
Sing three times.

To the tune of "Happy Birthday," sing to each other with: (The music is included under "Good Morning to You" on page 61.)
>   Happy springtime to you, happy springtime to you,
>   Happy springtime, dear neighbor, happy springtime to you.
Point to each other. Aides should shake hands, sing, greet.

Exercise: Distribute the foam paper plates that have pre-pasted daffodils, hyacinths, and other spring flowers. Instruct residents to hold up the plate as their flower is called. To the tune of "Where is Thumbkin?", sing the following song:

Leader	Where are the spring lovers, where are the spring lovers?
Response	HERE WE ARE, HERE WE ARE.
Leader	How are you today, friends?
Response	VERY WELL, WE THANK YOU.
Leader	God bless you.
Response	GOD BLESS YOU.

Additional verses — Where are the dandelion lovers, tulip lovers, rain lovers, worm lovers, optimists?

Exercise leader should lead simple exercises using the plates with:
"Tip Toe Through the Tulips — easy 2 beat.
"When It's Springtime in the Rockies" — waltz tempo.
"When You Wore a Tulip and I Wore a Big Red Rose" — faster 2 beat.
Finale — flower shower when everyone tosses plate at the leader.

Reminiscence: Ask the questions:
- What is your favorite part about springtime?
- Is it flowers, birds, weather, baseball, or energy.
- Do you miss your spring housecleaning?
- Exactly what did you do?
- Do people clean that much now?"

Write down the most interesting responses for the in-house newspaper.

Education:
- The first day of spring is usually thought of in March on the first day of the vernal equinox, when day and night hours are equal. In the Northern Hemisphere, it is 9.41 A.M. E.S.T. which also is the beginning of autumn in the Southern Hemisphere. Daylight length is virtually the same everywhere except at the poles.[1]
- One can attend the following festivals: National Cherry Blossom in Washington DC., Pear Blossom in Oregon, the Dogwood festival in Atlanta, or the Spring Wildflower Pilgrimage in Tennessee. Other flower festivals include the Azalea, Tulip, and Trillium. There are also spring celebrations for maple syrup, kites, roosters, Mayfests, sheep shearing, and the world Cow Chip Throwing Festival. In London, England, there are 22 acres of flowers at the Chelsea Flower Show. The entire show is sold at the end, including the sod.[2]

Group
Discussion: Are the best things in Springtime free?

Group Singing: Use large print songsheet of "The Best Things in Life Are Free."

Song
Identification: Name the following springtime melodies:

    April Showers
    Let's All Sing Like the Birdies Sing *
    I'll Be With You in Apple Blossom Time
    When You Wore a Tulip and I Wore a Big Red Rose
    The Trail of the Lonesome Pine
    Singin' in the Rain
    Blue Skies
    In The Garden §
    When It's Springtime in the Rockies
    Jeannine, I Dream of Lilac Time

*   Music is included on page 200.
§   A songsheet is included at the end of the PLANTING MORE THAN SEEDS [May] weekly session plan.

---

[1] *Chases Annual Events* (1993) p. 136.
[2] *Chases Annual Events* (1993) pp. 134-221.

Solo Time: Poetry read by resident as follows:[1]

                        Spring has sprung, the grass has riz,
                        I wonder where my allergy is?

                  Piano solo: "Welcome Sweet Springtime" or "Melody in F" by Rubenstein, "Spring Song" by Mendelssohn.

Rhythm Band: "The Trail of the Lonesome Pine" — gentle 3 beat.
                  "When It's Springtime in the Rockies" — all play on the first of three beats.
                  "Let's All Sing Like the Birdies Sing" — piano solo, instruments respond whenever there is a "tweet, tweet" part. (Music is included at the end of the LET'S ALL SING weekly session plan.)
                  "The Blue Danube Waltz" — piano solo with instruments playing on third and then first beat of second and third measure. Repeat. Listen carefully.

Closing: "Hallelujah" chorus from Handel's *Messiah* — welcome spring with joyous sound using all the rhythm and melodic instruments.

Assignment: Think about the many experiences spring has brought through the years. Enjoy the past memories and give thanks that a new springtime adventure is on it's way. Report any signs of spring indoors or outdoors that are seen, smelled or felt.

Music
Resources: *Everybody's Favorite Songs* (1933)
                  "Welcome Sweet Springtime" or "Melody in F" p. 12
              Masterpieces of Piano Music (1918)
                  "Spring Song" p. 104
              Great Music's Greatest Hits (1982)
                  "The Blue Danube Waltz" p. 50
              Family Song Book of Faith and Joy (1981)
                  "The Best Things in Life Are Free" p. 66
              Selections from the Messiah (1986)
                  "Hallelujah Chorus" p. 30
              Legit Fake Book (1990)
                  "When It's Springtime in the Rockies" p. 361
              Ultimate Fake Book (1981)
                  "The Trail of the Lonesome Pine" p. 591

---

[1] Poem by Joan Shaw.

MUSIC MENU

SPRING HAS SPRUNG

1. *April Showers*

2. *I Talk to the Trees*

3. *April in Paris*

4. *Spring Song (Mendelssohn)*

5. *When It's Springtime in the Rockies*

6. *Whistle While You Work*

7. *In the Garden*

8. *Singin' in the Rain*

9. *Moonlight and Roses*

10. *Take Me Out to the Ball Game*

11. *The Teddy Bear's Picnic*

12. *May the Good Lord Bless and Keep You*

*Pick your spring favorite,
I'll gladly play it.*

THE BEST THINGS IN LIFE ARE

FRIENDSHIP

FRESH AIR

SUNSHINE

FREE

THE MOON BELONGS TO EVERYONE

THE BEST THINGS IN LIFE ARE FREE.

THE STARS BELONG TO EVERYONE

THEY GLEAM THERE FOR YOU AND ME.

THE FLOWERS IN SPRING

THE ROBINS THAT SING

THE SUNBEAMS THAT SHINE

THERY'RE YOURS, THEY'RE MINE

AND LOVE CAN COME TO EVERYONE

THE BEST THINGS IN LIFE ARE FREE.

– B.G. DESYLVA, LEW BROWN

May Theme —   **WELCOME SWEET SPRINGTIME**

Today's Theme —   **Planting More Than Seeds**

Advanced
Preparation:

- Props should include:
  - straw hat,
  - hoe or pitch fork,
  - bonnet and colander,
  - stuffed dog, cat, mouse,
  - platter of cheese cut in cubes,
- Gather together a collection of farm songs and include music to "The Happy Farmer," and "Garden Song" which is found on page 194.
- You will need a soloist to sing "Garden Song" at Solo Time.

Pre-Session: Volunteers should wear gardening clothes, work gloves. Decorate with garden tools. Pianist plays "Welcome Sweet Springtime" and "How Ya Gonna Keep 'Em Down on the Farm"

Opening: Song to the tune of "On Top of Old Smokey."
     Thank God for the sunshine, thank God for the dew,
     Thank God for your friendship and blessings on you.
Point to each other, sing several times.

Announce theme of springtime planting. It is more than planting seeds, it is also planting good thoughts that take root.

Exercise: "The Happy Farmer" all clap hands to the beat.
Exercises are all motions used in planting:

Anvil chorus — digging motion (dynamic movement).
"Battle Hymn" — raking motion (smoothly).
"Whistle While You Work" — planting motion (wrist action).
No music — imitate rain water by clucking tongue, then pat leg, faster.
     Reverse by slow pat, clucking slowly, arms up to represent sunshine.

Guided Imagery: Start with a discussion of seeds the residents may have planted years ago. Since seed planting in the ground is difficult now, have them plant seed thoughts.

Residents should close their eyes. As soft music is playing have them breathe deeply and sigh a few times. In the quietness announce that is is time to plant the thought "Everyday I feel better and better." Say it several times as the leader and then invite them to join in.

Residents should open their eyes. Question them about their feelings on planting. Remind them that with positive thinking, their garden is growing and they can repeat this imagery anytime by themselves.

Education: • The US Department of Agriculture announced that farming is the nation's largest commercial industry. It employs 20% of the American work force.
                  • One farmer now provides food and fiber for 79 people compared with 31 people in 1963.
                  • One hour of farm labor produces sixteen times as much food as it did 60 years ago.
                  • There is more productivity with new plant fertilizers, pesticides, and irrigation techniques being introduced.
                  • The average cost of wages, machinery, and taxes have gone up by 125% in the last ten years. The farmer gets less than he did 20 years ago.
                  • The US supplies mainly soybeans, grapefruit, corn, sorghum, oranges, poultry, beef, cotton, and wheat to the world.[1]
                  • 50 years ago, the US had over 6 million farms with an average of 152 acres. In 1989, there were 2.4 million farms with an average of 456 acres.[2]
                  • Home gardeners plant mostly tomatoes, followed by peppers, green beans, cucumbers, onions, lettuce, and squash.[3]

Song
Identification: What can we plant from these song titles?

                  OATS, PEAS, BEANS and BARLEY Grow
                  Jimmy Crack CORN
                  Peter COTTONtail
                  Give Me the Simple Life (You say POTATOES)
                  I'm a Lonely Little PETUNIA in the ONION Patch
                  Here We Go 'Round the MULBERRY bush
                  TREES
                  Waltz of the FLOWERS

Solo Time: "Garden Song."

Special
Activity: To the tune of "The Farmer's in the Dell":
                  Choose a farmer and let him wear a straw hat and escort him up front. Present him with a hoe or pitch fork. Then let the farmer choose a wife. Present her with a bonnet and colander. Let the wife choose a dog. Dog holds a stuffed animal and then chooses a cat. The cat holds a stuffed animal and chooses a rat. Rat get a cute stuffed mouse and chooses the cheese. Entire group sings the song throughout this activity. Cheese gets presented with platters of pre-cut cubes of cheese that are passed for all to eat while singing "we all love the cheese."

---

[1]   Points 1-6 in the Education Section provided by US Department of Agriculture, Office of Information. *Nation's Largest Industry*, rev. 1984. pp. 3-6.
[2]   *World Almanac* (1992) "Agriculture, U.S. Farms (1992)" p. 160.
[3]   Rupp. R. (1987) *Blue Corn and Square Tomatoes*, pp. 1, 2.

Optional Song
Identification: As the story is read, residents call out the song title:
One day _____ [Name] went out to her garden singing ["Oh What a Beautiful Mornin'"]. She looked around and realized ["I've Got the Sun in the Morning and the Moon at Night"]. She noticed that the grass was wet with ["Du, Du, liegst Mir im Herzen"]. The sun got brighter and hotter and the garden seemed to talk to her and say ["How Dry I Am"]. [Name], being a good Christian woman said, ["I Believe with Every Drop of Rain That Falls My Garden Grows"]. Her faith was so strong that soon ["Raindrops Keep Falling on my Head"] followed by ["April Showers"]. [Name] was ["Singin' in the Rain"]. She encouraged everyone to ["Let's All Sing Like the Birdies Sing"]. The next thing she knew was that all the drenched plants reacted to her singing and they ["Stand Up, Stand Up for Jesus"]. [Pardon the grammar.] What a glorious series of events followed by nature's own pollinator, ["The Flight of the Bumblebee"]. That is the end of the story except for the birds and the bees and you know what happens then.

Rhythm Band: "Old MacDonald Had a Farm" — use animal names or plant names or the names of the rhythm band instruments. Enjoy the humor, such as:

> Old MacDonald had a farm, e-i, e-i, o.
> And on his farm he had some hollyhocks, e-i, e-i, o.
> With a hollyhock here, and a hollyhock there,
> Here a holly, there a holly, everywhere a hollyhock....etc.

"Jimmy Crack Corn" — lively 2 beat with a strong emphasis.
"How Ya Gonna Keep 'Em Down on the Farm" — merrily played 2 beat.

Closing: Group singing of "Bless This House" — A songsheet is included at the end of the GROUND-HOG DAY [February] weekly session plan.)

Assignment: Recall the thought planted and give it your attention. Know that it will sprout and flower. Caring and believing are necessary. Next week's theme is LET'S ALL SING LIKE THE BIRDIES SING. Remember how the beautiful blue jay sounds? Everyone is a singer.

Music
Resources: *Mitch Miller Community Song Book* (1962)
     "On Top of Old Smokey" p. 5
Tune Book Songs (1982)
     "Garden Song" p. 183a
Everybody's Favorite Songs (1933)
     "Welcome Sweet Springtime" (Melody in F) p. 12
Masterpieces of Piano Music (1918)
     "The Happy Farmer" (Schumann) p. 97
Greatest Legal Fake Book (1985)
     "How Ya Gonna Keep 'Em Down on the Farm" p. 187
     "Jimmy Crack Corn" p. 270
Children's Song Book (1988)
     "Peter Cottontail" p. 243

GARDEN SONG

Words & Music by David Mallet

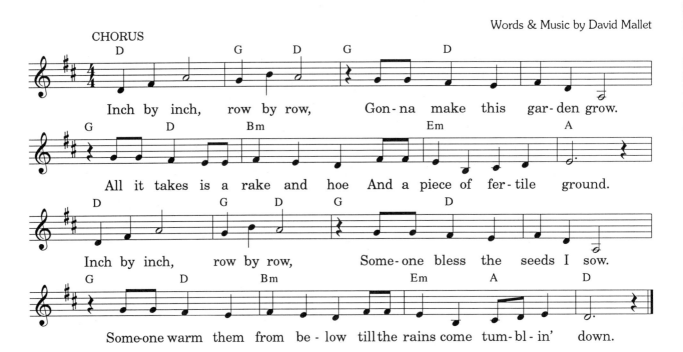

Inch by inch, row by row, Gon-na make this gar-den grow.

All it takes is a rake and hoe And a piece of fer-tile ground.

Inch by inch, row by row, Some-one bless the seeds I sow.

Some-one warm them from be - low till the rains come tum-bl - in' down.

1. Pulling weeds and picking stones,
   Man is made of dreams and bones.
   Feel the need to grow on my own,
   'Cause the time is close at hand.
   Grain for grain, sun and rain,
   Find my way in nature's chain
   To my body and my brain,
   To the music from the land

2. Plant your rows straight and long,
   Thicker than with prayer and song,
   Mother Earth will make you strong
   If you give her love and care.
   Old crow watchin' hungrily
   From his perch in yonder;
   In my garden I'm as free
   As that feathered beak up there. *Chorus.*

Planting Songs

1. *Oh What a Beautiful Mornin'*
2. *Sunshine in my Soul*
3. *How Ya Gonna Keep'em Down on the Farm?*
4. *In an Old Dutch Garden*
5. *Under the Anheuser Bush*
6. *<u>Oats</u>, <u>Peas</u>, <u>Beans</u> and <u>Barley</u> Grow*
7. *Give Me the Simple Life ("You Say <u>Potatoes</u>")*
8. *In the Garden*
9. *Country Gardens*
10. *The Happy Farmer (Schumann)*
11. *Peter <u>Cottontail</u>*
12. *Jimmy Crack <u>Corn</u>*
13. *Here We Go 'Round the Mulberry <u>Bush</u>*
14. *Garden Song*
15. *I Believe*

You pick 'em - I'll play 'em!

In the Garden

1. I come to the garden alone,
    While the dew is still on the roses;
    And the voice I hear,
    Falling on my ear,
    The Son of God discloses.

2. He speaks, and the sound of His voice
    Is so sweet the birds hush their singing,
    And the melody that He gave to me
    Within my heart is ringing.

3. I'd stay in the garden with Him
    Though the night around be falling,
    But He bids me go;
    Through the voice of woe,
    His voice to me is calling.

CHORUS:

    And He walks with me,
    And He talks with me,
    And He tells me I am His own,
    And the joy we share
    as we tarry there,
    None other has ever known.

    – C. Austin Miles (1912)

May Theme —   **WELCOME SWEET SPRINGTIME**

Today's Theme —   **Let's All Sing Like The Birdies Sing**

Advanced
Preparation:
- Invite anyone with a bird to bring it to the group session.
- Cut out 5 pieces of cardboard with large individual letters of R-O-B-I-N on them.
- Props will include:
  - 8-inch individual crepe paper streamers of red, blue, yellow, white colors, the colors of birds,
  - plastic bird whistles for each person all assembled on trays and pre-filled with water,
- Find a record of bird sounds.
- Make a collection of "bird" songs.
- Make enough copies of "Let's All Sing Like the Birdies Sing." Music is included on page 200.

Pre-Session: Residents enter room with a recording of bird sounds and also live birds singing.

Opening: Announce the theme of LET'S ALL SING LIKE THE BIRDIES SING. Discuss the beauty of the blue jay who pretends he has a lovely voice. Everyone should sing, like a blue jay or a canary. It is healthy.

Exercise: Pass out colorful streamers — pretend to be redbirds, bluebirds, canaries, doves with matching colored crepe paper.
"Red, Red Robin" — red streamers start flying.
"Bluebird" — add the blue streamers and wave to the music.
"Hot Canary" — yellow streamers added.
"Let There Be Peace of Earth" — white streamers representing doves.
Change hands, let group respond to tempo changes. End gently.

Reminiscence: Talk about birdwatchers, favorite birds, birds as pets, birds they are aware of now. Take a poll of the favorite bird. If live birds were brought into the room, note their reactions. Call attention to the research project ahead during the rest of the program and find out what music the birds prefer.

Group Singing: Invite 5 people to come up front and each hold up a letter. Sing the "Bingo" song using the new words. Hold up the appropriate letter as it is sung.

There was a gal who had a bird and Robin was it's name-o,
R-O-B-I-N, R-O-B-I-N, R-O-B-I-N, and Robin was it's name-o.

The second time go faster, or choose 5 other letter holders.

Solo Time: Poem, "Not In Vain" by Emily Dickinson[1] — discuss the significance of
                    helping others no matter how small the gesture may be.

                         If I can stop one heart from breaking,
                         I shall not live in vain:
                         If I can ease one life the aching,
                         Or cool one pain,
                         Or help one fainting ROBIN
                         Unto his nest again
                         I shall not live in vain.

Education: • There are over a million birdwatchers and they are increasing over the last
                      ten years according to the National Audubon Society.
                    • Spring migration is the best time for birding. This is a good year to watch
                      and listen.
                    • The house finch, a small reddish bird, is spreading nationally.
                    • There are more Canadian Geese now in the US.[2]

Song
Identification: Songs with specific bird/s in the title: Songs about birds:

                    Listen to the MOCKING BIRD   Lullaby of BIRDland
                    BLUE BIRDS Over the White Cliffs   Let's All Sing Like the BIRDIES Sing
                    WOODPECKER Song   The Love Nest
                    Bye Bye BLACKBIRD   When My Sugar Walks Down the
                    Red, Red ROBIN   Street, (all the little birdies go
                    SPARROW in the Treetop   tweet-tweet-tweet.)
                    PARTRIDGE in a Pear Tree   When It's Springtime in the Rockies
                    BLUEBIRD   (all the birds sing)
                    La Paloma (The DOVE)   Only a BIRD in a Gilded Cage
                    Under the Double EAGLE
                    His Eye is on the SPARROW
                    Christopher ROBIN
                    MOCKING BIRD Hill

Solo Time: To the tune of "Country Gardens" — Music is included on page 206.

                         How many songbirds fly to and fro
                         In an English country garden?
                         We'll tell you now of some that we know
                         In an English country garden.
                         Bob-o-link, cuc-koo and quail,
                         Tanager and cardinal,
                         Bluebird, lark and thrush and nightingale.
                         There is joy in the spring when the birds begin to sing,
                         In an English country garden.

----

[1] *One Hundred and One Famous Poems* (1958) p. 30.
[2] Information on birds from a personal interview with Phoebe Snetsinger, an outstanding birder in the St. Louis area — April 14, 1989.

Rhythm Band: Pass out plastic bird whistles pre-filled with water. Announce that the water is harmless. Play these songs as response songs tweeting with bird whistles. For example:

Leader	Let's all sing like the birdies sing.
Response	TWEET 5 times.
Leader	Let's all sing like the birdies sing.
Response	TWEET 5 times.
Leader	Let's all warble like nightingales ,
	Give your throat a treat,
	Take your time from the birds,
	Now you all know words and
Response	TWEET 5 times.

"Old MacDonald Had a Farm" — change to a person's name.

Leader	Susie Queesie had a home
Response	TWEET 5 times.
Leader	And in her home she had some birds,
Response	TWEET 5 times.
Leader	With a
Response	TWEET, TWEET
Leader	here and a
Response	TWEET, TWEET
Leader	there.
	Here a
Response	TWEET,
Leader	there a
Response	TWEET,
Leader	everywhere a
Response	TWEET, TWEET.
Leader	Susie Queesie had a home
Response	TWEET 5 times.

"Listen to the Mocking Bird" — TWEEEEEET
"The Blue Danube Waltz" — TWEET, TWEET, (pause) TWEET TWEET.
"Chiapanecas" — TWEET, TWEET.
     Chorus — all warble merrily in 3/4 time.
"Tit-Willow" from *The Mikado* — TWEET on alternate lines.

Closing: Group singing of "Let's All Sing Like the Birdies Sing."

Assignment: Increase awareness of the springtime bird life. Invite residents to listen for the first song in the morning, enjoy sounds during the day, go outdoors more often, listen for night sounds.

Music
Resources: *The Best Fake Book Ever* (1990)
                    "Let's All Sing Like the Birdies Sing" p. 367
                 One Thousand and One Jumbo (1985)
                    "Country Gardens" p. 386
                    "Listen to the Mocking Bird" p. 468
                    "La Paloma" p. 464
                    "Blue Danube Waltz" p. 373
                 Children's Song Book (1988)
                    "Bingo" p. 124
                 Great Latin American Song Book (1985)
                    "Chiapanecas" p. 4

LET'S ALL SING LIKE THE BIRDIES SING

Robert Hargreaves &   Tolchard Evans
Stanley J. Damerell

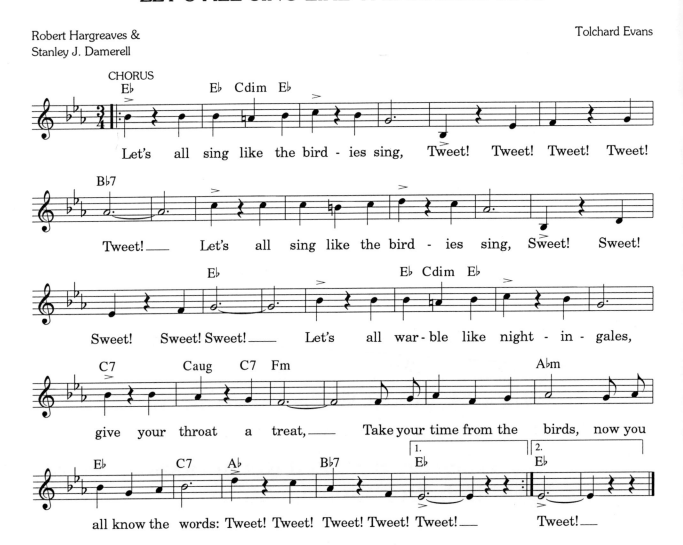

Choose your favorite BIRD SONG

music menu music menu music menu

1. Let's All Sing Like the <u>Birdies</u> Sing

2. Listen to the <u>Mocking Bird</u>

3. <u>Sparrow</u> in the Tree Top

4. His Eye is on the <u>Sparrow</u>

5. Bye Bye <u>Blackbird</u>

6. <u>Turkey</u> in the Straw

7. The Love <u>Nest</u>

8. <u>Blue Bird</u> of Happiness

9. When It's Springtime in the Rockies
(and the <u>Birds</u> Sing All the Day)

10. When My Sugar Walks Down the Street
All the <u>Birdies</u> Go Tweet-Tweet-Tweet

11. When the Red, Red <u>Robin</u> Goes
Bob, Bob, Bobbin' Along

———

The piano will sing it for you!

Turkey in the Straw

1. As I was a gwine on down de road
   with a tired team and a heavy load,
   I cracked my whip and the leader sprung,
   Says I goodbye to the wagon tongue.

2. Went out to milk and I didn't know how,
   Milked a goat instead of the cow
   A monkey sittin' on a pile of straw,
   Winkin' at his mother-in-law.

3. Met a big catfish comin' down the stream
   Says the big catfish "What does you mean?"
   Caught the big catfish right on the snout,
   Turned Mister Catfish inside out.

REFRAIN:

   Turkey in the straw (whistle)
   Turkey in the straw (whistle)
   Roll 'em twist 'em up a high tuck-a-haw,
   and hit up a tune called "Turkey in the Straw".

– American Folk Song (ca. 1834)

May Theme — **WELCOME SWEET SPRINGTIME**

Today's Theme — **Flower Power**

Advanced
Preparation:
- Prepare individual foam paper plates with spring flower pictures pasted on them. Lightly scent them.
- You will need music to "Welcome Sweet Springtime," "Sweet Adeline," "Hi Lily, Hi Lo."
- Bring fresh flowers to the session.
- Collect "flowery" songs together.
- Have a copy of the poem "Daffodils" by William Wordsworth[1] to be read during the Guided Imagery section.

Pre-Session: Volunteers are invited to wear a fresh flower to increase conversation as they escort residents. Pianist plays "Country Gardens," "Welcome Sweet Springtime," "When You Wore a Tulip and I Wore a Big Red Rose," "I'll Be with You in Apple Blossom Time," "Flower Song" by Gustav Lange.

Opening: Song — "Good Morning Springtime" to the tune of "Goodnight Ladies."

Good morning springtime, good morning springtime,
Good morning springtime, we're glad to see you now.
Merrily we sing along, sing along, sing along,
Merrily we sing along as we start the day.

Announce the theme of FLOWER POWER.

Guided Imagery: Invite residents to follow a brief relaxation exercise, close their eyes and experience the sight of a field of flowers. Read "Daffodils" by William Wordsworth.

Recognition: Anyone with a first or last name of a flower receives a flower to wear. Interview on the choice of the name.

Exercise: Using the foam paper plates:
"When You Wore a Tulip and I Wore a Big Red Rose" — window wiper motion — follow leader.
"Tea for Two" — (represents the tea rose) — follow leader:
8 taps on knees for introduction.
1. Right shoulder — 8 taps, lap 8 taps, repeat.
2. Head — 8 taps, knees 8 taps, repeat.
3. 2 large circles — 16 taps, repeat first line.
Finale — flower shower — everyone tosses their plate at leader at the count of five.

---

[1] *New Oxford Book of English Verse* (1972) p. 491.

Reminiscence: Flowers represent renewed life in spring, they are an expression of love as a gift, they send a positive message for all and add beauty to the world. Discuss their favorite flowers. Take a poll, announce it, post it. Ask about their gardens or famous gardens they had visited. Ask if they ever sent or received flowers. Relate.

Group Singing: "Sweet Adeline" sung as a response song.

Leader	Sweet Adeline
Response	SWEET ADELINE,
Leader	Sweet Adeline
Response	SWEET ADELINE,
Leader	At night dear heart,
Response	AT NIGHT DEAR HEART
Leader	For you I pine
Response	FOR YOU I PINE
Leader	In all my dreams
Response	IN ALL MY DREAMS
Leader	Your fair face beams
Response	YOUR FAIR FACE BEAMS
Leader	You're the **flower** of my heart, sweet Adeline.
Response	SWEET ADELINE.

Repeat song by singing in unison. Encourage natural harmony.

Education:
- The Chinese probably were the first to grow roses in gardens around 2700 B.C.
- The oldest living rose is about 1000 years old, growing on the wall of Hildescheim Cathedral in Germany.
- The largest rosebush grows in Tombstone, Arizona, with 6 inch diameter stems and the head covers 700 square yards.
- Portland, Oregon is known as the Rose City with it's annual festival.[1]
- People who enjoy roses are called rosarians.
- The goddess of Spring and Flowers is Flora.
- The best selling bedding plant in 1989 was impatiens by 45% of greenhouse respondents. It formerly was petunias.[2]

Song
Identification: Name the flower in the following song titles:

My Wild Irish ROSE *	DAISY, DAISY
Give Me One Dozen ROSES	Hi LILY, Hi-Lo
I'm a Lonely Little PETUNIA	EDELWEISS
in the Onion Patch	White CORAL BELLS
The BLUE BELL of Scotland	To a Wild ROSE

*
EVERYTHING'S COMING UP ROSES [January]

A songsheet is included at the end of the weekly session plan.

---

1 Facts on roses from Michigan Bulb Company, "Fantastic Facts on Roses." Holland, Michigan, 1989.
2 *Greenhouse Manager Magazine*, April 1989, p. 9. "Bedding Plants" by Kay Sallee.

Song Identification: (Cont.)	I'm Looking Over a Four Leaf CLOVER	LAVENDER'S Blue Sweet VIOLETS

When You Wore a TULIP and I Wore a Big Red ROSE
Finale — Waltz of the FLOWERS

Solo Time: "Country Gardens" — English folk tune. The music is included on page 206.

> How many kinds of sweet flowers grow
> In an English Country Garden?
> We'll tell you now of some that we know
> Those we miss you'll surely pardon.
> Daffodil, heart's ease and phlox,
> Meadow sweet and lady smocks,
> Gentian, lupine and tall hollyhocks,
> Roses, foxglove and snowdrops and blue forget-me-nots,
> In an English Country Garden.

Recognize familiar flower names in the song. Ask about travels to England. Recall other famous gardens.

Rhythm Band: "Hi Lily, Hi Lo" — first play waltz tempo with a strong first beat. Second time use a slower tempo — half the group play first beat, other half the after beats of 2 and 3.
"Edelweiss" — same procedure only softly. It is a delicate flower.
"Waltz of the Flowers" — play any beats up in the air if possible.
"The Blue Bell of Scotland" — bells only.
"I'm Looking Over a Four Leaf Clover" — peppy 2 beat for all.

Closing: All sing "God Bless America" which includes all the flowers.

Assignment: Think about the significance of flowers in life. Choose a favorite memory and share with a friend. Ask "Do flowers have power?"

Music Resources:
One Thousand and One Jumbo (1985)
    "Country Gardens" p. 386
    "Waltz of the Flowers" p. 284
    "The Blue Bell of Scotland" p. 278
Great Music's Greatest Hits (1982)
    "To a Wild Rose" p. 176
Legal Fake Book (1979)
    "Sweet Adeline" p. 277
    "I'm Looking Over a Four Leaf Clover" p. 138
Masterpieces of Piano Music (1918)
    "Flower Song" p. 354
Treasury of Best Loved Songs (1989)
    "Hi-Lily, Hi-Lo" p. 152
Ultimate Fake Book (1981)
    "Edelweiss" p. 294

COUNTRY GARDENS

English Folk Tune

How man-y kinds of sweet flow-ers grow in an Eng-lish coun-try gar - den?
How man-y song-birds fly to and fro

We'll tell you now of some that we know, those we miss you'll sure-ly par - don.

Daf - fo - dil, heart's ease and phlox, Mead - ow - sweet and la - dy - smocks,
Bob - o - link, cuck - oo and quail, Tan - a - ger and car - di - nal,

Gen - tain, lu - pine and tall hol - ly - hocks, Ro - ses, fox - glove and snow - drops,
Blue - bird, lark and thrush and night - in - gale, There is joy in the spring when the

Blue for - get - me - nots, in an Eng - lish coun - try gar - den.
birds be - gin to sing

FLOWER POWER

1. IN THE GARDEN

2. LAVENDER'S BLUE

3. WHITE CORAL BELLS

4. THE BLUE BELL OF SCOTLAND

5. WALTZ OF THE FLOWERS

6. I'LL BE WITH YOU IN APPLE BLOSSOM TIME

7. WHEN YOU WORE A TULIP AND
I WORE A BIG RED ROSE

8. ROSES OF PICARDY

9. COUNTRY GARDENS

10. DAISY BELL

TELL ME YOUR FAVORITE
I'LL "SET IT TO MUSIC"

Holiday Theme — **MOTHER'S DAY**

Today's Theme — **Universal Mothers Unite**
(Optional)

Advanced
Preparation:
- Write out the letters M-O-T-H-E-R on separate large sheets of colorful cardboard.
- Write quotations on separate pieces of cardboard with author on the back side facing audience, and pass them out for residents to practice.
- You will need the music to "Mother." A songsheet is included at the end of this week's session plan and the music is included on page 212.Make sure you have enough copies of the songsheet for the group.

Pre-Session: Invite everyone who has a mother to attend. Pianist plays "I Want a Girl—Just Like the Girl that Married Dear Old Dad," "I Love You Truly," and other appropriate songs. (A songsheet is included at the end of the I LOVE YOU AND ME [February] weekly session plan.)

Opening: Announce the theme of MOTHER'S DAY and that it includes everyone who had a mother and also everyone who helped to mother their child or someone else's. Include volunteer work, acts of mothering. All who qualify should raise their hands after the piano plays a fanfare. Group singing of "Goodnight Ladies" with the new words:

> Praise to the ladies, praise to the ladies,
> Praise to the ladies on Mother's Day each year.
> Merrily we sing along, sing along, sing along,
> Merrily we sing along to mothers everywhere.

Guided Imagery: Lead a brief relaxation exercise, instruct them to image someone they helped to mother, perhaps a neighbor's child or an animal on the farm, or a nurse's aide that needs advice. Suggest they give thanks for that opportunity. Remind everyone that mothering is universal and it is never too late to help another. Open eyes.

Exercise: To the tune of "Here We Go 'Round the Mulberry Bush" — exercise with the motions involved in motherhood such as:
1. Wash the clothes — up and down motion.
2. Iron the clothes — sideways motions.
3. Sweep the floor — strong pull downward.
4. Chased the mouse — fast foot motions.
5. Hugged the kids — hug yourself.
6. Threw a kiss — large arm extensions.
7. Today it's push a button on the microwave.

Reminiscence: Use these chants and then interview. The answers can be philosophical, materialistic or just memorable.

Reminiscence: (Cont.)	Mothers are special, yes, it's true. What did your mother give to you? The golden rule is helping others. Tell us how you helped your mother?
Group Singing:	"M-O-T-H-E-R" — words by Howard Johnson, music by T. Morse, 1913.

M is for the million things she gave me,
O means only that she's growing old.
T is for the tears were shed to save me,
H is for her heart of purest gold.
E is for her eyes with lovelight shining.
R means right, and right she'll always be.
Put them all together, they spell mother,
A word that means the world to me.

Rewrite the words as a group activity — such as M is for muffins. Collect the ideas. Refine them, rhyme them later and print locally.

Education:
- Mother's Day falls on the second Sunday in May. It was first observed on May 10, 1908 in Grafton, W. Virginia. It's founder was Anna Jarvis, a spinster. In 1908 she worried about neglect of the mother by children.
- She promoted carnations as the official flower due to their sweetness, purity and endurance. Today, red ones indicate that your mother is still living, white ones that she has passed on.
- Originally, it was a religious holiday (our's is not) which worshipped the feminine principle of life, and honored Mary, the mother of God. The tradition of Mothering Sunday, the fourth Sunday of Lent, began in 1644.[1]

Supply the foreign words for mother: English — mother; French — *mere*; German — *mutter*; Italian and Spanish — *madre*; Romanian — *mama*; Swedish — *moder*; Russian — *mat'*; Polish — *matka*; Greek — *mite'ra*. Stutterers in every language have trouble saying the word for mother.

Song Identification: All these songs are about mother, name them:

I Want a Girl—Just Like the Girl that Married Dear Old Dad
Oh You Beautiful Doll
MOTHER Machree
MA! He's Making Eyes At Me
My MAMMY
Pistol Packin' MAMA
Old MOTHER Hubbard

[1] All points in the Education section from Myers, R. (1972) *Celebrations* "Mother's Day" pp. 143-150.

Solo Time: Quotations read by pre-arranged residents using large cards with author on one side and quotation on the other for them to read.
  • "All that I am or hope to be I owe to my mother." — Lincoln.
  • "The future destiny of the child is always the work of the mother." — Napoleon.
  • "An ounce of mother is worth a pound of clergy." — Spanish proverb.
  • "God could not go everywhere, and therefore he made mothers." — Old Jewish saying.
  • "Adam did not call Eve his wife but called her mother, meaning mother of all living creatures." — Luther.[1]
  • "Mama's name was Mary and if your mother was an old-fashioned woman and named Mary you don't need to say much for her, everybody knows already." — Will Rogers.[2]
  • Famous mothers: Ma Bell, Whistler's mother, Jolson's Mammy, Mother Machree (1910, sung by John McCormick), Mother Hubbard.

Rhythm Band: Celebrate motherhood with joyous sound and cooperation.
  "Oh You Beautiful Doll" — gentle 2 beat. (A songsheet is included at the end of the OH YOU BEAUTIFUL DOLL [August] weekly session plan.)
  "My Mammy" — fairly lively tempo.
  "I Want a Girl—Just Like the Girl that Married Dear Old Dad" — play extra loud every time the word 'girl' appears in the song. (A songsheet is included at the end of the HERE COMES THE GROOM [June] weekly session plan.)

Closing: Use cue cards held by individuals leading the cheer "Give me an M" — all yell "M", continue spelling M-O-T-H-E-R and end with "what does that spell? Are we still mothering in many ways?" All shake instruments.

Assignment: Offer to be someone's other mother or adopted grandmother.

Resources: *Legit Fake Book* (1990)
                       "M-o-t-h-e-r" p. 234
                   Ultimate Fake Book (1981)
                       "I Wanna Girl....." p. 253
                       "My Mammy" p. 398
                       "Pistol Packin' Mama" p. 447
                   Greatest Legal Fake Book (1985)
                       "Oh You Beautiful Doll" p. 387
                       "Mother Machree" p. 362

---

[1] Quotations 1-5 from Edwards, T. (1936) *New Dictionary of Thoughts*, pp. 409-410.
[2] Smith, L. (1978) *The Mother Book*, p. 23.

M-O-T-H-E-R
(A Word That Means The World To Me)

Howard Johnson   Theodore Morse

MUSIC MENU
FOR

MOTHER'S DAY

1. *I Want a Girl-Just Like the Girl*
That Married Dear Old Dad

2. *Oh You Beautiful Doll*

3. *Mother Machree*

4. *My Mammy*

5. *Always*

6. *M-O-T-H-E-R*

7. *I Love You Truly*

8. *Pistol Packin' Mama*

9. *Beautiful Thoughts of Love*

10. *Ma! He's Making Eyes at Me*

11. *May the Good Lord Bless and Keep You*

CHOOSE YOUR FAVORITE
I'LL APPLY THE MOTHERLY TOUCH

MOTHER

by Howard Johnson

M is for the million things she gave me.

O means only that she's growing old.

T is for the tears were shed to save me.

H is for her heart of purest gold.

E is for her eyes with lovelight shining.

R means right, and right she'll always be.

Put them all together, they spell mother,
a word that means the world to me.

Holiday Theme — **MEMORABLE MEMORIAL DAY**
(Optional)

Advanced
Preparation:
- Props you will need for the holiday celebration include:
    - long rolls of crepe paper, red, white and blue,
    - many small flags, and one very large flag,
    - camera.
- Encourage all to wear red, white, or blue.
- Arrange for a soloist to read the poem "In Flanders Field" by John McCrea.

Pre-Session:
Greet each person with a small flag. Armed forces music playing as residents enter: — "The US Field Artillery March" (Caissons Go Rolling Along) "Anchors Aweigh," "The Marines Hymn."

Opening:
Announce the bitter-sweet observance of Memorial Day honoring those that died for our country and gave us the freedom and liberty we presently enjoy. Opening song: "America" sung softly and with feeling. (A songsheet of verses 2 and 3 is included at the end of the OUR HISTORY IN SONG [July] weekly session plan.) Second song to celebrate freedom: Chorus from "The Battle Hymn of the Republic" (Glory, Glory, Hallelujah).

Exercise:
Distribute streamers in long rows of color. Front row is one continuous row of red. Next row is white and then the next, blue. Instruct to listen carefully for directions. Also note colorful effect in the room due to everyone's cooperation.
"Stars and Stripes Forever" — sway side to side, colors at shoulders.
"You're a Grand Old Flag" — colors overhead. Stress lyrics "forever in peace may you wave." (A songsheet is included at the end of this week's session plan.)
"Columbia, the Gem of the Ocean" — alternate colors. (A songsheet is included at the end of the GO FORTH ON THE FOURTH OF JULY [July] weekly session plan.)
O Columbia, the gem of the ocean — red streamers up overhead;
The home of the brave and the free — red down at end of line;
The shrine of each patriot's devotion — white colors overhead;
A world offers homage to thee — white down at end of line;
Thy mandates make heroes assemble — blue overhead;
When liberty's form stands in view — blue down at end of line;
Thy banners make tyranny tremble — everyone tremble, shake;
When borne by the red, white and blue — no action.

Chorus: play and sing music slowly, each section raises their color as it is sung by the entire group:
Three cheers for the RED (up and down), WHITE etc. — 3 times;
Thy banners make tyranny tremble — shake;
When borne by the RED, WHITE and BLUE.

Reminiscence:
Discuss those who have died for their country. Praise the relatives for their ordeal and sacrifice. Ask about use of the flag, visiting cemeteries, decorating graves.

Reminiscence (Cont.)	Conclude with the positive fact that they truly died for their country and we all enjoy the sacrifice by living in the "land of the free and home of the brave."
Group Singing:	Unfurl a large flag and sing the "The Star Spangled Banner," followed by a heartfelt salute to the flag. Remind the group that the new pledge contains the words "under God."
Education:	• Memorial Day is also known as Decoration Day. • Officially it is observed on May 30, since on May 30 in 1868, General Logan commanded that the graves of the soldiers be decorated. Originally it honored those who died in the Civil War but now it honors all war dead. Now the legal public holiday falls on the last Monday in May.[1]
Solo Time:	Poetry reading "In Flanders Field" by Lt. Col. John McCrea.[2]
Song Identification:	Name these songs of the Armed Forces: Caissons Go Rolling Along The Marines Hymn Anchors Aweigh This is the Army, Mr. Jones I'm Popeye the Sailor Man Up in the Air Junior Birdsmen Goober Peas The US Air Force Song (The ArmyAir Corp Song)
Rhythm Band:	Celebrate our heritage by recalling Memorial day parades with these songs: "American Patrol" — imitate a parade approaching, play softly, increase volume as parade nears, follow dynamics of the music. "There's Somethin' About a Hometown Band" — play joyfully. "You're a Grand Old Flag" — several flag wavers up front lead band. "Stars and Stripes Forever" — as above with flag unfurled.
Closing:	All sing "God Bless America" with grateful hearts for the past and present.
Assignment:	Appreciate one's heritage. Consider our American history and all who made it possible for us to live in the land of the free. Name at least five people that have made life more meaningful.

Music Resources:	*Wee Sing America* (1988)
	        Most patriotic music
	Golden Book of Favorite Songs (1946)
	        "Columbia, the Gem of the Ocean" p. 6
	Ultimate Fake Book (1981)
	        "American Patrol" p.30
	        "There's Somethin' About a Hometown Band" p. 567

---

1   *Information Please Almanac* (1992) p. 586.
2   *One Hundred and One Famous Poems* (1958) p. 11.

MEMORIAL DAY

1. Anchors Aweigh

2. The Marines Hymn

3. The Star Spangled Banner

4. Stars & Stripes Forever

5. You're a Grand Old Flag

6. The U.S. Field Artillery March
   (Caissons Go Rolling Along)

7. The U.S. Air Force Song

8. Columbia, the Gem of the Ocean

9. There's Something About a Soldier

10. Let There Be Peace on Earth

11. America, the Beautiful

12. American Patrol

PICK YOUR FAVORITE

You're a Grand Old Flag

You're a grand old flag,

You're a high flying flag:

And forever in peace may you wave;

You're the emblem of the land I love,

The home of the free and the brave.

Ev'ry heart beats true under Red, White and Blue,

Where there's never a boast or brag;

But, should auld acquaintance be forgot,

Keep your eye on the grand old flag.

– George M. Cohan (1906)

WEDDINGS

June Celebrations

CELEBRATIONS
MUSICAL GAMES

June is the month for Celebrations. Name two familiar songs in each of the following events. Then see if you can think of a third answer or sing the songs. The answers are upside down.

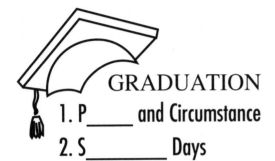

GRADUATION

1. P_____ and Circumstance
2. S_____ Days

3. Stars and S_____ Forever
4. Columbia, the Gem of the Ocean
   (The _____, _____, and _____)

FATHER'S DAY

5. My Heart Belongs to D_____
6. I Want a G_____ - Just Like the G_____ that Married Dear Old D_____

WEDDINGS

7. Here Comes the B_____
8. W_____ B_____ are Breaking Up that Old Gang of Mine

BASEBALL

9. Take Me Out to the B_____
10. National A_____

---

1. Pomp 2. School 3. Red, White, Blue 4. Stripes 5. Daddy 6. Girl, Girl, Dad 7. Bride 8. Wedding Bells 9. Ball Game 10. Anthem

CELEBRATIONS
JUNE

"Let's celebrate." The words ring a good sound no matter what the occasion. People want to attend, to participate, or just witness someone else having a good time. The month of June has several traditional reasons that will be honored and adapted at the same time.

Graduation Now and Then — Everyone has memories of someone's graduation but this program gives everyone a diploma. Enjoy leading the group as they realize all the aspects of life they have "graduated from." They truly are older and wiser and have experienced many changes for the better during their lifetimes. They have graduated from lamplights, toys, baby faces, hitching old dobbin and, of course, school. Concepts of segregation or the women's roles can also be addressed since there have been vast improvements in many areas of human behavior. The diploma included in this book should have a date inscribed and perhaps some official signatures. It is a cherished souvenir. For some, it is their first diploma ever.

Dads are Dandy — Father's Day can have both pleasant and unpleasant memories so this program stresses the acts of "fathering." You can still honor the men present as well as all fathers but continue on with the concepts of fathering and those in our present lives that are so kind and helpful.

Here Comes the Groom — June is still the most popular month for weddings so it is a good time to review the past and present. Be prepared to face the issues of the changes taking place. We all need to keep current. A style show or wedding pictures enliven this theme. Use an electronic organ stop on a portable piano for a wonderful sound.

Take Me Out to the Ball Game — Incorporate your area team or group favorite. A soft bat and ball will provide the indoor exercise and a lot of laughs. A local Little League may be willing to help or the staff softball team needs to come out and give a cheer.

OPTIONAL PROGRAM

Flag Day — It's a Grand Old Flag — Make sure everyone gets a flag to keep since it is especially meaningful. Try to obtain a superlarge one for this program since it is impressive to see one closely and then pledge wholeheartedly.

CELEBRATE LIFE

June Theme —   **CELEBRATIONS**

Today's Theme —   **Graduation Now and Then**

Advanced
Preparation:
- At the end of this week's session plan there is a diploma. Make copies of printed diplomas for everyone with "CONGRATULATIONS GRADUATE. YOU ARE FILLED WITH THE WISDOM OF THE AGES." Date. Roll up and tie with a ribbon. Place diplomas in a basket. A sample is included at the end of this week's session plan.
- Borrow cap and gown or choir robe.
- You will need the music to "Pomp and Circumstance" by Elgar, "Guadeamus Igitur," (1782), "Hallelujah" chorus of George Handel from the *Messiah.*
- Invite a high school graduate to speak.
- Have someone organized to sing their old college or high school graduation song for Solo Time

Pre-Session: Invite everyone to attend and receive a diploma. Pianist should play "Pomp and Circumstance" or "Guadeamus Igitur" as everyone assembles.

Opening: Announce the theme of GRADUATION NOW AND THEN. Tell the following story:
                    An elderly lady was asked if she was growing old. She replied, "No, I'm getting older and growing."
                    Repeat in unison. Affirm the truth together "I am older and wiser."

                    Sing the following song to the tune of "If You're Happy and You Know It" after praise is given for the knowledge that comes with advancing years.
                    Verses:
                    1. If you're smarter and you know it, clap your hands;
                    2. .... shake your head.
                    3. .... shout hoorah.

Exercise: Cross arms across chest and raise up straight. Repeat motion to the "Hallelujah" chorus of Handel. Everyone sing the word 'Hallelujah' repeatedly. Music written in 1742.

Reminiscence: Discuss former grade school and high school graduations. Recall any memories of anyone's graduation. Interview to find the oldest graduate. Talk about the early women in college. Introduce a current high school graduate to relate all the current news and advances.

Solo Time: Pre-arrange to have someone sing their college or high school graduation song.

Group
Discussion: Discuss the fact that, as we age, we graduate from more than formal education of the school room. Use the following songs as a game to stimulate thinking.

Song
Identification: Part One:
What has one graduated from in the following songs?

You Must Have Been a Beautiful Baby
Baby Face (would you want your baby face still?)
School Days *
Oats, Peas, Beans and Barley Grow (we choose what we eat)
Hello Dolly
Toyland
Playmates

* A songsheet is included at the end of the DEAR OLD SCHOOL DAYS [September] weekly session plan.

Part Two:
As we age we graduate from certain behavior patterns. Let the following songs be a clue. Discuss.

Put on Your Old Grey Bonnet (hitch old dobbin to the shay) *
Are You From Dixie? (segregation)
Smoke Gets In Your Eyes (choice of smoking, public smoking areas)
I Don't Want to Play in Your Yard (negativity)
Come, Josephine, in my Flying Machine (airplanes to jets to rockets.)

* A songsheet is included at the end of the REACH OUT AND TOUCH [April] weekly session plan.

Also, residents have graduated from cutting grass, emptying garbage, fixing the roof.

Rhythm Band: All join in with expressive tempos to celebrate the awareness of the value of aging with its graduation.
"Sweetheart of Sigma Chi" — 3/4 time.
"Whiffenpoof" — 3/4 time; play strongly on the first beat, feeling of one beat per measure.
"Guadeamus Igitur" — play strongly, proudly. 1782 - oldest student song.
College songs such as Illinois, Notre Dame, Michigan, or your area.

Recognition: Pianist plays "Pomp and Circumstance" as diplomas are awarded by two staff members or aides to everyone attending. A sincere "congratulations" should be given to everyone.

Closing: Repeat former exercise with diploma in one hand. Cross arms over chest, extend up straight overhead as everyone sings "Hallelujah."

Assignment: Invite residents to consider other aspects of life that didn't receive formal graduation but were nevertheless milestones. End your thinking with the fact that one is now older and wiser.

Music
Resources: *Great Music Greatest Hits* (1982)
                     "Pomp and Circumstance" p. 229
                Treasury of Best Loved Songs (1981)
                     "Whiffenpoof Song" p. 192
                     "Sweetheart of Sigma Chi" p. 170
                     "Hello Dolly" p. 60
                     "Smoke Gets in Your Eyes" p. 46
                     "Toyland" p. 215
                Song Session Community Song Book (1953)
                     "Guadeamus Igitur" p. 126
                Selections from the Messiah (1986)
                     "Hallelujah Chorus" p. 30
                Tune Book Songs (1982)
                     "If You're Happy and You Know It" p. 212
                Wee Sing and Play Musical Games (1986)
                     "Playmates" p. 59

music menu

Graduation

You've graduated from

1. School Days
2. Toyland
3. Put On Your Old Grey Bonnet (Hitch Old Dobbin)
4. Playmates
5. Hello Dolly
6. Baby Face
7. The Outhouse Blues
8. The Old Lamp Lighter
9. Collegiate
10. Your College Song
11. Pomp and Circumstance
12. Gaudeamus Igitur

Choose your favorite.

CONGRATULATIONS
GRADUATE

YOU ARE FILLED WITH
THE WISDOM OF THE AGES

June Theme — **CELEBRATIONS**

Today's Theme — **Dads Are Dandy**

Advanced
Preparation:

- Prepare a chair decorated as a throne for the king.
- Aides and volunteers will need to be reporters, armed with pencils and pads.
- Print on separate pieces of cardboard the letters of F-A-T-H-E-R.
- Prepare a collection of songs about dads.

Pre-Session: Aides should greet all attending by wearing straw hats and bow ties. Piano music heard as people assemble "Oh My Papa," Daddy's Little Girl," "I Want a Girl—Just Like The Girl that Married Dear Old Dad," and "My Heart Belongs to Daddy."

Opening: Sing to the tune of "Where Is Thumbkin?"

Leader	Where are the Ladies, Where are the Ladies?
Response	HERE WE ARE, HERE WE ARE.
Leader	How are you today, friends?
Response	VERY WELL WE THANK YOU.
Leader	God Bless You.
Response	GOD BLESS YOU.

Additional verses — Where are the Gentlemen, fathers, grandfathers?

Special
Recognition: Proclaim a King for a day. Residents vote or staff chooses, knowing past history and need for recognition. King sits up front and observes the celebration.

Exercise: Do the exercises to the tune of "Here We Go 'Round the Mulberry Bush", substituting activities that fathers did. Do the appropriate motions such as chopping wood, snow shoveling, driving the car, paying bills, hugging wife. Allow discussion time.

Guided Imagery: Lead a brief relaxation exercise, instruct them to image someone they helped to mother, perhaps a neighbor's child or an animal on the farm, or a nurse's aide that needs advice. Suggest they give thanks for that opportunity. Remind everyone that mothering is universal and it is never too late to help another. Open eyes.

Reminiscence: Teach the chant to the group:
Father, Daddy, Papa, Dad,
What did he do that made you glad?
Interview. Shake a hand while chanting for more personal approach.

Group Singing: "I Want a Girl—Just Like the Girl that Married Dear Old Dad."
Question: Ask if any man married a gal like his mother. (A songsheet is included at the end of the HERE COMES THE GROOM [June] weekly session plan.)

Group Chant: Have 6 people come up front and hold the letters of F-A-T-H-E-R up high when you lead the chant for "Give me an F" — they should yell "F", give me an A, etc. End with "What does that spell?" Who do we appreciate?"

Song Writing: Create a new song based on the song "M-o-t-h-e-r" (Music is included on page 212.) Use the letters of F-A-T-H-E-R. Have reporters write down their suggestions. Assemble song at a later date since time will not permit the chance to make it rhythmical or rhyme. Publish results. An example is included at the end of this week's session plan.

Education:
• Father's Day is always the third Sunday in June.
• It was first suggested as a holiday by Mrs. John Dodd of Spokane, Washington, in 1910. Though supported by President Calvin Coolidge, Father's Day was not proclaimed a national holiday until 1966. Mother's Day, in contrast, was officially proclaimed a holiday in 1908.[1]

Song
Identification: Songs about fathers.

For He's a Jolly Good Fellow	Oh My PAPA
My Heart Belongs to DADDY	DADDY
DADDY Sang Bass	DADDY'S Little Girl
Faith of our FATHERS	DADDY Won't You Please Come Home
The Hat Me FATHER Wore	Everybody Works But FATHER
Beat me, DADDY, Eight to the Bar	
DADDY Has a Sweetheart and Mother is Her Name	
Dance of the Hours (Hello Muddah, Hello Faddah)	

Solo Time: "When I was a boy of 14, my father was so ignorant I could hardly stand to have the man around. But when I got to be 21, I was astonished at how much the old man had learned in 7 years."[2]

Rhythm Band: "Daddy's Little Girl" — gentle 3/4 time.
"Let Me Call You Sweetheart" — livelier waltztime.
"Stouthearted Men" — strong 2 beat, emphatic.
"Hello Muddah, Hello Faddah" — piano only, instrumental response 2 beats.
"Seventy-six Trombones" — in honor of all who were like fathers — march tempo.

[1] *Chases Annual Events* (1992) p. 210.
[2] *American Treasury* (1955) "Advice to Youth" by Samuel Clemens, p. 984.

Rhythm Band: (Cont.)	"For He's a Jolly Good Fellow" — end of third line hold the beat of 'fellow' and play instruments loud and long. (A songsheet is included at the end of the PRESIDENTS' DAY—HAIL TO THE CHIEFS [February] weekly session plan.)
Closing:	Use instruments and chant: Give me an F — Give me an A — etc. What does that spell? Who do we thank? Closing song to the tune of "If You're Happy and You Know It" sing "If you're thankful [for your dad] and you know it, say 'thank you.'" Announce next week's celebration of WEDDINGS which are always so popular in June. All wedding pictures and treasures welcomed.
Assignment:	Think of those who are still fathering not only children but the ideals of fatherhood. Give thanks for the men who assist you now with banking, investing, transportation, and other needs. Tell them personally that you appreciate their "fathering."

Music
Resources:
	Legal Fake Book (1979)
	    "My Heart Belongs to Daddy" p. 400
	    "Oh My Papa" p. 422
	    "Daddy Won't You Come Home" p. 58
	One Thousand and One Jumbo (1985)
	    "Hello Muddah, Hello Faddah" (or "Dance of the Hours") p. 260
	The Best Fake Book Ever (1990)
	    "Daddy" p. 132
	    "Daddy's Little Girl" p. 136

MUSIC MENU

DADS ARE DANDY

1. OH MY PAPA
2. DADDY'S LITTLE GIRL
3. STOUTHEARTED MEN
4. IF I WERE A RICH MAN
5. MY HEART BELONGS TO DADDY
6. POP GOES THE WEASEL
7. I LOVE YOU TRULY
8. FAITH OF OUR FATHERS
9. OUR FATHER
(THE LORD'S PRAYER)
10. I WANT A GIRL JUST LIKE THE GIRL
THAT MARRIED DEAR OLD DAD

CHOOSE YOUR FAVORITE POP MUSIC
I'LL PLAY IT FOR YOU

F IS FOR THE FAITH HE SOUGHT TO SHOW ME

A 'S FOR ALL HIS WAYS THAT WERE SO GREAT

T IS FOR THE THANKS WE FEEL WE OWE HIM

H IS FOR THE HOME WE CELEBRATE

E IS FOR HIS EFFORTS USED TO GUIDE ME

R IS FOR ROYAL, KING HE'LL ALWAYS BE

PUT THEM ALL TOGETHER, THEY SPELL

FATHER

MY "DAD" WHO MEANS SO MUCH TO ME

Written by the residents during music therapy!

June Theme — **CELEBRATIONS**

Today's Theme — **Here Comes The Groom**

Advanced
Preparation:
- Props will include:
  - electronic piano with organ capability,
  - bridal gowns,
  - any wedding pictures,
  - camera,
  - appropriate decorations,
  - top hat (tails) for the groom.
- Organize a soloist to be the Groom for the day.
- You will need reporters with pencils and pads.

Pre-Session: Remind everyone to bring any wedding souvenirs. Greet residents with organ music playing "I Love You Truly," "Oh Promise Me," "Get Me to the Church on Time."

Opening: Announce the theme of celebrating all weddings and giving more recognition to the groom. Opening song of "It's Love That Makes The World Go 'Round." (Music is included on page 70.)
Verses:
1. It's love that makes the world go 'round.
2. It's brides that make the world go 'round.
3. It's grooms that make the world go 'round.
4. It's you that makes the world go 'round (point to each other)
5. It's us that make the world go 'round (with hands up in the air)

We are all an important part of a wedding.

Exercise: All based on motions associated with weddings.
1. Running around — arms to and fro as in running to the music of "Get Me to the Church on Time."
2. Replying "I do," — nod head to the music of "Oh What a Beautiful Mornin'."
3. Throwing rice — extend arm and throw repeatedly to Mendelssohn's "Wedding March."
4. Welcome to the family — crossed arms go in and out several times to the music of "I Love You Truly." (A songsheet is included at the end of the I LOVE YOU AND ME [February] weekly session plan.)

Reminiscence: Aides should be beside residents to encourage responses that can be shared over the microphone.
- Do you recall something special about your wedding?
- Expenses?
- Did anyone elope?
- Where did you go for your honeymoon?
- How many years married?
- What music did you have at your wedding?

Reminiscence: Wedding music to be played for easier recollection:
(Cont.)   Oh Promise Me
                          Ich liebe Dich
                          Because
                          I Love You Truly
                          Bridal Chorus from *Lohengrin,* "Here Comes The Bride"
                          Wedding March — Mendelssohn

                  Today's music:
                          Pachelbel Canon   Evergreen
                          Perhaps Love   The Rose
                          Theme from "Masterpiece Theater"

Solo Time: Quotation: In 1766 Oliver Goldsmith, vicar of Wakefield said "I chose my wife, as she did her wedding gown, for qualities that would wear well.[1]

Solo Time
Special Activity: Bridal fashion show of old gowns and a recent bride. Designate one man to represent all the splendid grooms. He wears the top hat and tails. Today's theme is HERE COMES THE GROOM so make this distinction an honor. Accompany procession with organ music, everyone singing "Here comes the groom" and then complete song with just la, la. Then sing "Here comes the bride." Soloist sings a wedding song during the fashion show.

Education:
- In marriage, Roman style circa A.D. 100, the bride wore a tunic-style dress, saffron veil, dyed to match her shoes, with orange blossoms in her hair and she carried a bouquet of wheat. After the ceremony the couple shared wedding cake, then the bride's father scattered the crumbs over their heads symbolizing fertility. The groom carried his bride over the threshold of their new home.
- Today's custom — before 1850, women wore their best dress. Other countries wear colorful ones. Brides are choosing white and also soft pastels for their gowns. It was the bride's day since historically her role changed the most. Now both wear rings, not necessarily diamonds. They throw rice, grass seed, bird seed or release balloons. Many couples live together before the marriage ceremony. Marriage is life's biggest hopeful adventure.
- Interview a new bride. Ask about today's vows, honeymoon spots, cakes, cars, finances, and what they throw at the finale.[2]

Group Game: Name these famous couples:[3]
                   Romeo and (Juliet)   Fibber McGee and (Molly)
                   Eddie Cantor and (Ida Lopino)   George Burns and (Gracie Allen)
                   Scarlett O'Hara and (Rhett Butler)   Dagwood and (Blondie)
                   Nelson Eddy and (Jeanette MacDonald) Clark Gable and (Carole Lombard)
                   Jack Benny and (Mary Livingstone)   George Bush and (Barbara Pierce)

---

1   Edwards, T. (1936) *New dictionary of Thoughts,* p. 699.
2   All points in Education section from *St. Louis Post Dispatch.* June 15, 1989, p. 12WF. "Weddings. More Than We Know. Tradition Carries the Day" by Sara Lowen.
3   Karras, B. (1985) *Down Memory Lane,* p. 186.

Song
Identification: For Me and My Gal (Judy Garland and Gene Kelly)
                  The Girl That I Marry
                  Love and Marriage (Maguire Sisters)
                  That Old Gang of Mine
                  In the Chapel in the Moonlight (Rudy Valley)
                  I'll Dance at Your Wedding
                  Hawaiian Wedding Song
                  I Want a Girl—Just Like the Girl that Married Dear Old Dad
                  Makin' Whoopee

Rhythm Band: "For Me and My Gal" - bells only.
                  "The Girl That I Marry" — gentle 3/4 beat.
                  "I Wanna Girl—Just Like the Girl that Married Dear Old Dad" — peppier 2/4
                      all play. (A songsheet is included at the end of this week's session plan.)
                  "Here Comes the Bride" — piano solo, instruments respond at the end of
                      line.
                  "Get Me to the Church on Time" — everyone plays joyously, with vigor.

Closing: Ask for advice for today's bride and groom. Reporters should write it down to
                  to be published as an extra publication. Close with the song "It's Love That
                  Makes the World Go 'Round."

Assignment: Enjoy recalling favorite weddings. Treasure those memories since they are
                  among your souvenirs. Continue to think about advice for newlyweds since all
                  present possess much more experience and wisdom than they do. Next
                  week's theme to celebrate is America's favorite sport, baseball.

Music
Resources: *Great Music's Greatest Hits* (1982)
                      "Bridal Chorus" p. 238
                      "Wedding March" p. 240
                  Wings of Song (1984)
                      "It's Love" p. 354
                  Ultimate Fake Book (1981)
                      "I Love You Truly" p. 238
                      "Get Me to the Church on Time" p. 180
                      "Oh What a Beautiful Mornin'" p. 421
                  Treasury of Best Loved Songs (1981)
                      "For Me and My Gal" p. 178
                  One Thousand and One Jumbo (1985)
                      "Makin' Whoopee" p. 101

JUNE WEDDING
MUSIC

1. WEDDING MARCH (BRIDAL CHORUS FROM LOHENGRIN)

2. I LOVE YOU TRULY

3. OH PROMISE ME

4. BECAUSE

5. EVERGREEN

6. PERHAPS LOVE

7. FOR ME AND MY GAL

8. MAKIN' WHOOPEE

9. THE GIRL THAT I MARRY

10. I'LL DANCE AT YOUR WEDDING

11. THE WEDDING OF THE PAINTED DOLL

12. GET ME TO THE CHURCH ON TIME

13. I WANT A GIRL-JUST LIKE THE GIRL
THAT MARRIED DEAR OLD DAD

14. MENDELSSOHN'S WEDDING MARCH

TELL ME YOUR FAVORITE AND I'LL PLAY IT FOR YOU

I Want a Girl - Just Like the Girl that Married Dear Old Dad

I want a Girl - just like the girl - that married dear old Dad

She was a pearl and the only girl that Daddy ever had -

A good old fashioned girl with heart so true,

One who loved nobody else but you,

I want a Girl - just like the girl that married dear old Dad.

– Will Dillon & Harry Von Tilzer (1911)

June Theme — **CELEBRATIONS**

Today's Theme — **Take Me Out to the Ball Game**

Advanced
Preparation:

- Props to include:
    - baseball jersies,
    - hats for all volunteers,
    - foam ball,
    - foam bat,
    - baseball cards,
    - souvenirs,
    - US flag.
- Organize a soloist to read the poetry selection at Solo Time.

Pre-Session: Volunteers escort residents to this celebration wearing uniforms and promoting today's indoor game. Background music consists of "In The Good Old Summer Time," "Take Me Out to the Ball Game," "Seventy-six Trombones" and any other marches.

Opening: Announce theme and open with the tradition of every game by singing the "The Star Spangled Banner" with resident holding the flag. At the end have group yell "play ball." Everyone just yell. Prolong yelling.

Exercise: All actions used in a baseball game set to music.
1. Warm up — rub hands together to the music of "Enjoy Yourself, It's Later Than You Think."
2. Pitch — right handed to the music of "In the Good Old Summer Time."
    left handed — same song.
    underhanded — same song.
    (A songsheet is included at the end of this week's session plan.)
3. Batting practice — clasp hands, swinging motions to the music of "Little Annie Rooney."
    Switch hitter — other hands to the same music — slow, determined.
4. Catching a fly ball — cup hands, sway to the music of "In The Good Old Summer Time."
5. Running the bases — run in place to music of "Supercalafragilistic- expialidocious"
6. Chewing gum — give jaws a good workout to the music of "Old Gray Mare.

Reminiscence: Discuss any or all of the following:
- Any souvenirs or treasures to be shared;
- favorite baseball players through the years;
- baseball cards, collecting;
- favorite sports announcers;
- memories of games attended;
- no interest at all in the sport - that's OK too!

Group Singing: Songs to inspire the team to the tune of "My Bonnie Lies Over the Ocean."

You have such a wonderful memory,
You have such a wonderful mind.
(repeat)
Chorus:
Praise God, praise God, you have such a wonderful memory.
Praise God, praise God, you have such a wonderful mind.

All sing "Take Me Out to the Ball Game."
(First, practice the countdown — "1, 2, 3 strikes you're out.")

Education:
- The origin of baseball probably lies in a game called rounders played by village boys in England.[1]
- The game was invented by Abner Doubleday in 1839, Cooperstown, New York, which is now the site of the Baseball Hall of Fame.[2]
- Fun and exercise were the goals. Winning was unimportant.[1]
- The first professional team was the Cincinnati Red Stockings.[2]
- Brooklyn Dodgers and New York Yankees were fierce rivals. The Dodgers left for California.[1]
- The first World Series game was in 1903.[1]
- The rules have changed slightly over the years.[2]
- In St. Louis, ticket prices today are $5.50 general admission, $9.50 reserved seats, $4.00 for bleacher seats, and $12.00 for box seats.[3]
- Over 2.5 million fans attended the games in St. Louis in 1991.[3]
- In 1988, the average salary for a ball player was $439,000.[1]
- The game is often played in school fields, sand lots, backyards, stadiums. It is formed into Little Leagues, local teams, professional teams and is more than a national sport, it's worldwide.

Song
Identification: Tell what kind of transportation is being taken to get to the ball park. The song title suggests the way.

In My Merry OLDSMOBILE *
WALKIN' My Baby Back Home
Up, Up and Away (My beautiful BALLOON)
Come, Josephine, in my FLYING MACHINE
The TROLLEY Song
Darktown Strutters' Ball (I'll be down to get you in a TAXI)
Daisy Bell (a BICYCLE built for two)
On the Atchison, Topeka, and the Santa Fe (TRAIN)
Only Make Believe (imagine)
Dream (When You're Feeling Blue) (dream)

*   A songsheet is included at the end of the YOU AUTO REMEMBER YOUR AUTOMOBILE [September] weekly session plan.

[1] *American Heritage*, April 1991,42(2):19. "The Business of America: The American Game" by John Steele Gordon.
[2] *Information Please Almanac* (1992) "Sports—Baseball" p. 950.
[3] *Media Guide* (1992) St. Louis National Baseball Club. Interview with secretary September 21, 1992.

Solo Time: Poetry excerpt of "Casey at the Bat" — Ernest Thayer.[1]

There was ease in Casey's manner as he stepped into his place.
There was pride in Casey's bearing and a smile on Casey's face.
And when, responding to the cheers, he lightly doffed his hat
No stranger in the crowd could doubt "'twas Casey at the bat."
....There is no joy in Mudville, mighty Casey has struck out.

Special Activity: Someone should be the batter using the foam bat. Ask for a volunteer to stand before the group. A second volunteer can pitch, crowd can cheer. No running required but keep the score, take turns with additional participants.

Good batter should hit a few foam rubber free balls to the assembled group. Anyone can catch them. Remind the residents that the balls are harmless.

Rhythm Band: "On the Atchison, Topeka, and the Santa Fe" — all play
"Daisy, Daisy" — play with a strong downbeat.
"In My Merry Oldsmobile" — gentle 3 beat.
"The Trolley Song" — Sticks first, bells added, shakers, tambourines, drums.
"Take Me Out to the Ball Game" — entire band.

Closing: Song to the tune of "Goodnight Ladies."

Goodbye sportsfans, goodbye sportsfans,
Goodbye sportsfans, we'll see you at the park.
Merrily we roll along, roll along, roll along,
Merrily we roll along, we've had a merry day.

Assignment: Think about the physical and mental exercise that a ballplayer has to do to stay in good condition. What do you need to do? Is it worth it? Decide on your course of action and you too will have a "winning score."

Next month's theme is AMERICA, THE BEAUTIFUL. All are welcome to contribute their thoughts and suggestions for the programs.

Music
Resources: *Family Song Book of Faith and Joy* (1981)
        "The Star Spangled Banner" p. 250
Popular Songs That Live Forever (1982)
        "Take Me Out to the Ball Game p. 222
Ultimate Fake Book (1981)
        "In the Good Old Summer Time" p. 291
        "Walkin' my Baby Back Home" p. 607
        "Come, Josephine, in my Flying Machine" p. 107
Legit Fake Book (1990)
        "On the Atchison, Topeka, and the Santa Fe" p. 260

---

[1] *Treasury of the Familiar* (1950) p. 278.

TAKE ME OUT TO THE

BALLgAME

music menu music menu music menu music menu

1. National Anthem

2. Take Me Out to the Ball Game

3. I Love a Parade

4. In the Good Old Summer Time

5. There's Somethin' About
   a Hometown Band

6. Seventy-Six Trombones

7. Meet Me in St. Louis, Louis

8. Enjoy Yourself, It's Later Than You Think

9. The Beer Barrel Polka

10. Supercalafragilisticexpialidocious

11. Walkin' My Baby Back Home

You call it - I'll hit it!

In the Good Old Summer Time

In the Good Old Summer Time,

In the Good Old Summer Time,

Strolling thro' the shady lanes

with your baby mine:

You hold her hand and she holds yours,

And that's a very good sign

That she's you tootsey wootsey

In the Good Old Summer Time.

– Ren Shields (1902)

June Theme —   **CELEBRATIONS**

Today's Theme —   **It's a Grand Old Flag**

Advanced
Preparation:
- Props to include:
    - a large flag,
    - small flags for everyone,
- Cut some red, blue and white streamers, enough for every individual participating.
- Prepare large print songsheets of flag songs "Columbia, the Gem of the Ocean" (or "Three Cheers for the Red, White and Blue"), "There are Many Flags," and "You're a Grand Old Flag." A songsheet at the end of this week's session plan provides the words to all three. A separate songsheet of "Columbia, the Gem of the Ocean" is included at the end of the GO FORTH ON THE FOURTH OF JULY [July] weekly session plan; and a separate songsheet for "You're a Grand Old Flag" is included at the end of the MEMORABLE MEMORIAL DAY [May] weekly session plan.)
- A soloist will be needed for the poetry reading.
- Gather together your music for patriotic songs.

Pre-Session: Greet each resident with a red, white, or blue streamer as you escort them to the group celebration. Assist with tying streamer around waist, wrist, neck, wheelchair or walker if they wish. Pre-taped march music should be playing.

Opening: Announce the theme of IT'S A GRAND OLD FLAG or THREE CHEERS FOR THE RED, WHITE, AND BLUE.

Exercise: Using streamers in hand encourage arm movements with music of "Three Cheers for the Red, White, and Blue." As the song is sung, the appropriate color is raised and lowered. Do slowly.
(Chorus)
Three cheers for the red, white, and blue
Three cheers for the red, white, and blue
The flag of America forever,
Three cheers for the red, white, and blue.

Reminiscence: Recall the flag in the early schoolhouse, in the town square, post office, and other places including memorials. Discuss proud moments with it. Review proper care of the flag. Allow plenty of time since there are many associations.

Group Activity: 2 or 3 residents hold up the largest flag possible. Group recites the Pledge of Allegiance. It is a privilege to pledge so suggest it be done slowly and with feeling. Recall how many times they have had this freedom of choice.

This pledge was written by Francis Bellamy in 1892 to celebrate the 400th anniversary of the discovery of America.

Education:
- The word "flag" means any kind of banner or standard. It is derived perhaps from the Anglo-Saxon word *floegan*, "to fly or float in the wind."
- The army calls it the national flag. The navy calls it the national ensign. When carried by the infantry (foot) it is called the colors. When carried by the cavalry (horse, car) it is called the standard.
- The Grand Union flag under Benjamin Franklin had 13 stripes, including the crosses of St. George, the Patron Saint of England, and St. Andrew, the Patron Saint of Scotland. It was hoisted by George Washington in 1776, at Cambridge Mass.
- Congress passed this resolution: "Resolved: That the Flag of the United States be thirteen stripes: alternate red and white; that the union be thirteen stars, white on a blue field, representing a constellation." George Washington asked Betsy Ross to make this flag in Philadelphia. It was first flown on June 14, 1777.
- The next flag was of 15 stars and stripes. Francis Scott Key wrote about it during the War of 1812. What he wrote is still our National Anthem. Many feel it should be changed. Take a poll.
- The flag today symbolizes the oneness of the nation. The 13 stripes represent the original colonies, with 50 stars for the states in the union. Ask what the colors stand for: Red = valor; white = purity; blue = justice. The stars represent a new constellation which has arisen or a new nation. The hope was that the stars would be like the constellation Lyra, named for the lyre (a musical instrument), a symbol of peace and harmony.[1]

Group Singing: Use the songsheet included of large print patriotic songs or lead the following by rote since they are familiar to many:

> Three Cheers for the Red, White, and Blue
> You're a Grand Old Flag
> There Are Many Flags
> The Star Spangled Banner

Song Identification: Name these patriotic songs and sing some of them:

> America *
> Stars and Stripes Forever
> America, the Beautiful §
> Battle Hymn of the Republic
> March of the Men of Harlech
> Columbia, the Gem of the Ocean
> Yankee Doodle

* A songsheet for verses 2 and 3 is included at the end of the OUR HISTORY IN SONG [July] weekly session plan.

§ A songsheet is included at the end of the THANKSLIVING [November] weekly session plan (verses 1 and 2) and at the end of the OUR HISTORY IN SONG [July] weekly session plan for verses 2 and 3).

[1] All points in the Education section from *Girl Scout Handbook* (1933) p. 61-67

Solo Time: Poetry reading of "The Flag Goes By"[1] by Henry Bolcomb Bennett and "America for Me"[2] by Henry Van Dyke - 8 stanzas.

Rhythm Band: "Stars and Stripes forever" — stirring march.
               "You're a Grand Old Flag" — sing and play.
               "Yankee Doodle" — sticks only (1st verse) , bells only (2nd verse) , shakers, (3rd verse) drums (4th verse), and all together for the last verse.
               "American Patrol" — start softly as parade nears, mimic music.

Closing: Use rhythm instruments and voice for a rousing finale of "America." Announce the ending should last a long, vibrant time as everyone sings and plays 'Let freedom riiiiiiiiiing.'

Assignment: Enjoy recalling associations with the flag. Share them with others during the day. Question your visitors. Display your flag proudly.

Music
Resources: *Golden Book of Favorite Songs* (1946)
                   "There Are Many Flags" p. 98
                   "March of the Men of Harlech" p. 102
                   "Columbia, the Gem of the Ocean" p. 6
               Wee Sing America (1988)
                   "You're a Grand Old Flag" p. 10
                   "Three Cheers for the Red, White, and Blue" p. 11
                   "Stars and Stripes Forever" p. 12
               Ultimate Fake Book (1981)
                   "American Patrol" p. 30

---

[1] *One Hundred and One Famous Poems* (1958) p. 131.
[2] Ibid. p. 50.

Our Flag

1. God Bless America

2. Count Your Blessings

3. Star Spangled Banner

4. This Land is Your Land

5. There Are Many Flags

6. America, the Beautiful

7. You're a Grand Old Flag

8. Stars and Stripes Forever

9. National Emblem March

10. March of the Men of Harlech

11. Columbia, the Gem of the Ocean
(The Red, White and Blue)

I need YOU to choose the music.

I'll give it a
RRRRROUSING RRRRRENDITION !!!

PATRIOTIC SONGS

There are Many Flags

There are many flags in many lands
There are flags of every hue
but there is no flag however grand
like our own red, white and blue.

Then hurrah for the flag
Our country's flag
It's stripes and white stars too
There is no flag in any land
like our own red, white and blue.

Columbia, the Gem of the Ocean

O Columbia the gem of the ocean
The home of the brave and the free
The shrine of each patriot's devotion
a world offers homage to thee.

Thy mandrates make heros assemble
When liberty's form stands in view
Thy banners make tyranny tremble
when borne by the red, white and blue.

Three cheers for the red, white and blue
Three cheers for the red, white and blue
Thy banners make tyranny tremble
When borne by the red, white and blue.

- David T. Shaw, T.A. Beckett

You're a Grand Old Flag

You're a grand old flag
You're a high flying flag
And forever in peace may you wave.

You're the emblem of
The land I love
The home of the free and the brave.

Every heart beats true
Under red, white and blue
Where there's never a boast or brag.

But, should auld acquaintance be forgot,
keep your eye on the grand old flag.

- George M. Cohan

MUSICAL GAME FOR JULY
GOD BLESSED AMERICA

The game is to figure out the song titles from different parts of the United States. The main clue is missing but surely, you know the song. Then figure out which part of th US is the best. The answers are upside down and no fair peeking.

NORTH
1. _____Doodle
2. I'm a _____ _____ Dandy
3. Moonlight in _____

VT

SOUTH
4. Deep in the Heart of _____
5. Sweet _____ Brown
6. _____ Mud

GA

EAST
7. Carry Me Back to Ole _____
8. _____ in the Morning
9. The Sidewalks of _____

NY

CA

WEST
10. _____, Here I Come
11. On the Atchison, Topeka and the _____
12. Little Grey Home in the _____

MIDWEST
13. _____Waltz
(Harry Truman's favorite)

NEW STATE
14. My Little Grass Shack in _____

Add up your score. If you got ten correct you get four stars. If you got all of them, then it's your turn to write the next puzzle!

REMEMBER TO BLOOM WHERE YOU ARE PLANTED

ANSWERS: 1. Yankee 2. Yankee Doodle 3. Vermont 4. Texas 5. Georgia 6. Mississippi 7. Virginny (Virginia) 8. Carolina 9. New York 10. California 11. Santa Fe 12. West 13. Missouri 14. Hawaii Best one is HERE!

AMERICA, THE BEAUTIFUL
JULY

The theme of patriotism is one that reaches every heart. The elderly enjoy the status of being Americans and proudly celebrate the fact for the entire month. Programs, decorations and speakers are easily arranged with the following suggestions.

Our History in Song — This program gives everyone the opportunity to sing their favorite patriotic anthems. Large print songsheets for the unfamiliar verses are a good visual aid. Let the roof be raised and the rafters ring in appreciation of America.

They Fought for Freedom — Our heritage includes the brave men and women who fought for the freedom we presently enjoy. Loved ones should still be honored even though many years have passed since their involvement. The wars also inspired many songs that we still sing with pride.

North, South, East, and West — The chant continues with "tell me which one is the best." This program encourages conversation and participation regarding various sections of our country. Be prepared for strong opinions and end up with the central theme that America is Beautiful.

My Hometown — Reflect on individual hometowns that are still filled with memories. Use the nametags depicting the town's name. It stimulates conversation for days and there are always people who discover they are from the same state or city. Celebrate the fact that Americans are encouraged to bloom where they are planted and that the present place of residence gives us all the opportunity.

OPTIONAL PROGRAM

Go Forth on the Fourth of July— An in-house parade that is anticipated all year long as well as providing a vivid memory afterwards. Often it is the first time a resident has had an opportunity to be in a parade. Being a participant can be a valuable goal for the physical therapy department, yet everyone can parade whether they are in a wheelchair, use a walker, or only have limited use of their legs. The key to success is organization and volunteer help. It is worth the effort.

AMERICA IS BEAUTIFUL — YOU MAKE IT THAT WAY

July Theme —   **AMERICA, THE BEAUTIFUL**

Today's Theme —   **Our History in Song**

Advanced
Preparation:
- Make copies of the large print songsheet of the 2nd and 3rd verses of "America, the Beautiful" and "America" which is included at the end of this week's session plan.
- Find some old sheet music for decoration and reminiscence.

Pre-Session: Pianist plays "Yankee Doodle," "I'm a Yankee Doodle Dandy," "Oh What a Beautiful Mornin'," "America, the Beautiful."

Opening: Welcome everybody and announce the theme of AMERICA, THE BEAUTIFUL, especially our history. After honoring Independence Day, take the time to appreciate one's heritage through music. First, sing "Little Sir Echo" as a response song:

Leader	Little Sir Echo, how do you do? Hello.
Response	HELLO
Leader	Hello
Response	HELLO.
Leader	Little Sir Echo will answer you. Hello
Response	HELLO
Leader	Hello
Response	HELLO.
Leader	Hello
Response	HELLO
Leader	Hello
Response	HELLO.
Leader	Won't you come over and play:
Response	AND PLAY.
Leader	You're a nice little fellow I know by your voice But you're always so far away.
Response	AWAY.

Exercise: The USA was founded on not only the Declaration of Independence but hard work. The following songs have related exercises and are easily sung without songsheets.
"I've Been Working on the Railroad" — everyone hammer with energy.
"Billy Boy" (Can She Bake a Cherry Pie?) — strong rolling-pin motion.
"I'm Gonna Leave Old Texas Now" — echo/response, shoulders up and down.
"Pick a Bale of Cotton" — motion of throwing over the shoulders.
"Bill Bailey Won't You Please Come Home" — imitate typing a Western Union message — finger exercise.

Education and
Group Singing: YANKEE DOODLE
- This was sung by the British soldiers to make fun of the poorly clad and awkward colonial soldiers during the French and Indian war of 1754-1763. 20 years later the Colonists marched to victory at Lexington with this music. Five years later Cornwallis marched to it at Yorktown to surrender his sword and his army to General Washington. It became popular during the Revolutionary War of 1775. The words are not meaningful but the tune is catchy and popular. A doodle is a simple fellow.[1]
- Sing first verse twice.

AMERICA
- The words were written in 1832 by Rev. Samuel Francis Smith of Boston who liked the music "God Save the King." It was written in a half hour on a scrap of paper as a hymn based on an English folk song of the 16th century. It was then sung as an anthem, a prayer for the British king in 1745 and used by many nations. "America" was first sung at a children's 4th of July celebration in Boston but did not become popular until the Civil War.[2]
- Print and sing all 3 verses.

AMERICA, THE BEAUTIFUL
- In 1893 Katherine Lee Bates wrote the poem after being inspired by the fine view from Pikes Peak, Colorado. She chose a melody that was originally a hymn written by Samuel Ward in 1882. Over 60 people had offered to write a new one. When being honored for the work Miss Bates replied, "It is not work to write a song, it is a great joy."[3]
- Print and sing 3 verses.

Reminiscence: Discuss our country's songs. Ask if anyone has a favorite song and why it is meaningful. Talk about learning patriotic songs in school and the method used, number of verses and accompaniment. Ask about elocution. Check if hymns were sung in school. Discuss separation of church and state. Encourage sharing these memories.

Song
Identification: Name the following songs you probably first learned in school:

The Star Spangled Banner
Rock-a-Bye Baby
All Through the Night (Welsh lullaby)
Bingo (a contraction of bandog, a mastiff watchdog, England)
Go Tell Aunt Rhody — (sung as Aunt Patsy in the South)
Mary Had a Little Lamb (1830)
Twinkle, Twinkle, Little Star
The Muffin Man — (popular in England, like today's ice cream man)
Farmer in the Dell
Skip to my Lou

---

[1] *Golden Book of Favorite Songs* (1946) — Preface to "Yankee Doodle" p. 8.
[2] Ibid. Preface to "America" p. 3.
[3] Ibid. Preface to " America, the Beautiful" p. 7.

Rhythm Band: This demonstrates the teacher's early musical influence and that everyone is musical.

> "Yankee Doodle" — drum solo or sticks.
> "I'm A Yankee Doodle Dandy" — everyone 2/4 time.
> "When the Saints Go Marching In" — sticks first, add bells, then shakers, then tambourines, and lastly drums. Finale should have cymbal crashes after the first line "Oh when the saints" crash, crash.
> "Battle Hymn of the Republic" — everyone plays merrily and joins in the singing of the chorus, "Glory, glory, Hallelujah."

Closing: Acknowledge the roots of our patriotism including our ancestors, politicians, warriors, historians, and our first music teachers. Take a poll to determine the song that is the group's favorite patriotic song and announce it as the closing song. Sing the first verse with eyes closed and then repeat with open eyes and heartfelt joy.

Assignment: Continue to think about the songs that we learned. when we were young They are all stored in our massive brain computer and since everyone has lived a long time, the computer is very full and it may take a bit longer to retrieve the information. This is normal. Ask each other during the day or later in the week if their brain computer worked and if they recalled an early song.

Music
Resources: *Greatest Legal Fake Book of All Times* (1985)
> "Little Sir Echo" p. 307

CHILDREN'S SONGS:
Fireside Book of Children's Songs (1966)
PATRIOTIC SONGS:
Family Song Book of Faith and Joy (1981)
Wee Sing America (1988)
Golden Book of Favorite Songs (1946)
SONG HISTORY:
Golden Book of Favorite Songs (1946)
(See prefaces to songs for history)
> "America" p. 3
> "America, the Beautiful" p. 7
> "Yankee Doodle" p.8

MUSIC MENU

Our History in Song

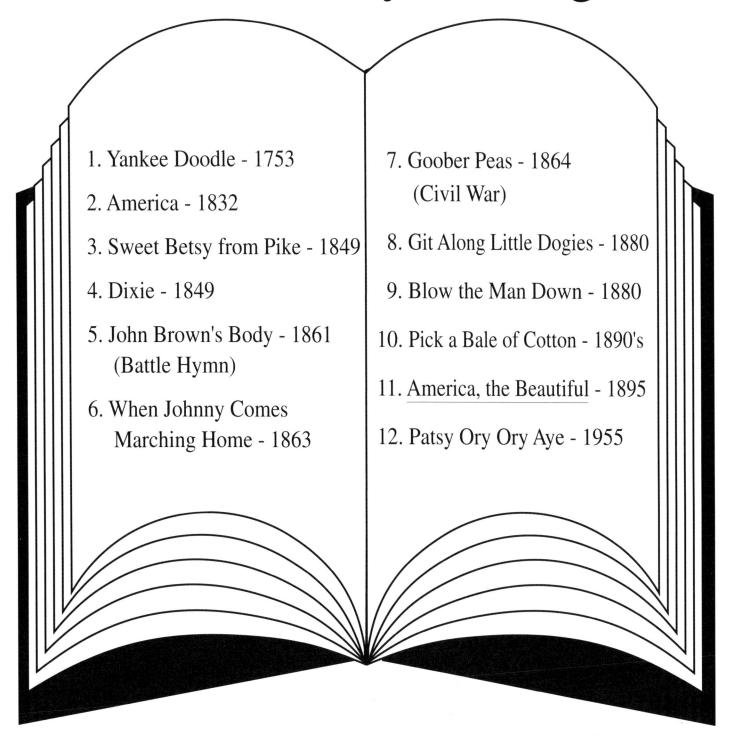

1. Yankee Doodle - 1753

2. America - 1832

3. Sweet Betsy from Pike - 1849

4. Dixie - 1849

5. John Brown's Body - 1861
   (Battle Hymn)

6. When Johnny Comes
   Marching Home - 1863

7. Goober Peas - 1864
   (Civil War)

8. Git Along Little Dogies - 1880

9. Blow the Man Down - 1880

10. Pick a Bale of Cotton - 1890's

11. America, the Beautiful - 1895

12. Patsy Ory Ory Aye - 1955

CHOOSE YOUR FAVORITE -
WE'LL MAKE HISTORY TOGETHER!

SONGSHEET

HERE ARE EXTRA VERSES
AMERICA

2. MY NATIVE COUNTRY, THEE
   LAND OF THE NOBLE FREE, THY NAME I LOVE.
   I LOVE THY ROCKS AND HILLS
   THY WOODS AND TEMPLED HILLS;
   MY HEART WITH RAPTURE THRILLS
   LIKE THAT ABOVE.

3. OUR FATHER'S GOD, TO THEE
   AUTHOR OF LIBERTY
   TO THEE WE SING.
   LONG MAY OUR LAND BE BRIGHT
   WITH FREEDOM'S HOLY LIGHT;
   PROTECT US BY THY MIGHT,
   GREAT GOD OUR KING.

AMERICA, THE BEAUTIFUL

2. O BEAUTIFUL FOR PILGRIM FEET
   WHOSE STERN, IMPASSIONED STRESS
   A THOROUGHFARE FOR FREEDOM BEAT
   ACROSS THE WILDERNESS.
   AMERICA, AMERICA
   GOD MEND THY EVERY FLAW
   CONFIRM THY SOUL IN SELF-CONTROL
   THY LIBERTY IN LAW.

3. O BEAUTIFUL FOR PATRIOT DREAM
   THAT SEES BEYOND THE YEARS
   THINE ALABASTER CITIES GLEAM
   UNDIMMED BY HUMAN TEARS.
   AMERICA, AMERICA
   GOD SHED HIS GRACE ON THEE
   AND CROWN THY GOOD
   WITH BROTHERHOOD
   FROM SEA TO SHINING SEA.

July Theme —	**AMERICA, THE BEAUTIFUL**
Today's Theme —	**They Fought for Freedom** **Songs of World War One and Two**

Advanced
Preparation:

- Make enough copies of the large print songsheet of WWI songs which is included at the end of this week's session plan.
- Print bold smiling faces on some yellow paper plates.
- Prepare pictures on cardboard depicting each part of the song "Smiles." These placards will be needed in Exercise section and the Rhythm Band section. (A songsheet is included at the end of the EVERYONE LOVES A SMILE [February] weekly session plan.)
- Props will include:
  - duffle bag,
  - paper and pen,
  - large mirror.
- Aides will need to act as reporters — see Opening section.
- Ask families for old sheet music.

Pre-Session: Pianist plays "Over There," "It's a Long Way to Tipperary," "When Johnny Comes Marching Home Again," "Anchors Aweigh."

Opening: Announce the fact the America is beautiful because of its heritage including those who have died for our country. War is not a pleasant subject but it does contain many happy associations, including the music. The theme THEY FOUGHT FOR FREEDOM will focus on the memorable music of both world wars that is an American legacy.

Opening song "Pack Up Your Trouble" — ask everyone to write down their trouble and you circulate a kit bag for the slips of paper. Aides needed to encourage answers, write and deposit. (A songsheet is included at the end of this week's session plan.)

Exercise: Sing the song "Smiles" as a solo.
1. Use the yellow smile plates as masks. Every time the word 'smile' is sung, the masks go in front of the face, then down. Anyone depressed should sit up front and enjoy the entire scene. Note effect on behavior.
2. All sing song together. Smiling plates go overhead and down in rhythm. Leader uses placards that describe each part of the song— example happy, blue, tender meaning. End with a large mirror.

Education: **WWI**
- 1917 Germany, suffering from British blockade, declared almost unrestricted submarine warfare on January 31.
- US cut diplomatic ties with Germany on February 3 and formally declared war April 6, 1917.
- 1 million American troops were sent to Europe.
- The war ended on November 11, 1918.

WWII
- On December 7, 1941, Japan attacked Pearl Harbor.
- US declared war on Japan the next day; and then Germany and Italy on December 11.
- On May 7, 1945, Germany surrendered.

Reminiscence: Memories may be shared including volunteer efforts, civil defense, USO activities and reunions.

Group Singing: Rationale by Frank Peat:

"The soldiers and sailors of every war create and sing certain songs in which they find spiritual unity. Sometimes their songs are somber, sentimental, gay or rollicking. We at home sing these same songs with those men overseas because we want to be united to them and feel that we too are a part of the great spiritual forces which sustain them. They produce a national morale unequalled anywhere in the world."[1]

Pack up Your Trouble (a reminder that they are packed)
K-K-K-Katy *
When Johnny Comes Marching Home
Over There *
Don't Sit Under the Apple Tree
It's a Long Way to Tipperary *
There's a Long, Long Trail *

* All these songs are included on a songsheet at the end of this week's session plan.

Song
Identification: I'm In Love with a Beautiful Nurse
Hinky Dinky Parlay Voo (Mad'moiselle from Armentières)
I Want to Go Home
I'm in the Army Now
Oh How I Hate to Get Up in the Morning
Round Her Neck She Wore a Yellow Ribbon
The Rose of No Man's Land
My Buddy
Keep the Home Fires Burning

Rhythm Band: "Round Her Neck She Wore a Yellow Ribbon" — strong downbeat.
"When Johnny Comes Marching Home" — peppy 2 beat, use drum roll.
"Anchors Aweigh" — stirring march.
"The US Field Artillery March" (Caissons Go Rolling Along) — sticks only, add other instruments.
"Smiles" — smile, sing and play for this finale. Use the placards held by a few residents for visual impact.

---

[1]   This quotation from the Foreword to *Legion Airs — Songs of "Over There" and "Over Here"* (1932)

Solo Time: Quotation: "The way to win an atomic war is to make certain it never starts." General Omar Bradley.[1]

Closing: All join in singing "Till We Meet Again." Join hands and sway to the music. Hum or sing along. (A songsheet is included at the end of this week's session plan.)

    Ask if anyone wants their troubles back from the old kit bag.

Assignment: Think of some more songs that were learned as a result of the war. Suggest residents ask their grandchildren if they know them. If they don't, residents might teach them one as a link between the generations.

Resources: *Legion Airs Songs* (1932)
        "Pack Up Your Trouble" p. 24
        "K-K-K-Katy" p. 22
        "Over There" p. 6
        "It's a Long Way to Tipperary" p. 20
        "There's a Long, Long Trail" p. 8
        "The Rose of No Man's Land" p. 10
        "Smiles" p. 36
        "Keep the Home Fires Burning" p. 12
    Family Song Book of Faith and Joy (1981)
        "When Johnny Comes Marching Home" p. 248

---

[1] Safire and Safir (1982) *Good Advice*, p. 354.

The Best of World War I & World War II

1. Over There

2. It's a Long Way to Tipperary

3. Pack Up Your Trouble in Your Old Kit Bag
   and Smile, Smile, Smile

4. The Rose of No Man's Land

5. Keep the Home Fires Burning

6. When Johnny Comes Marching Home

7. Smiles

8. K- K-K-Katy

9. My Buddy

10. Don't Sit Under the Apple Tree

11. Anchors Aweigh

12. Till We Meet Again

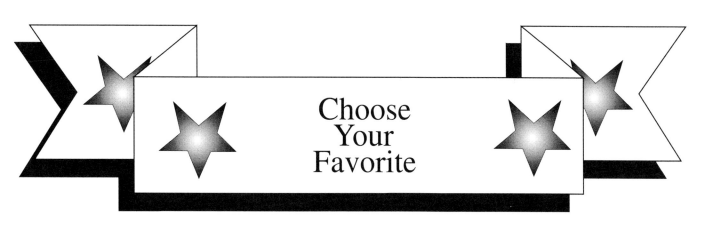

Choose
Your
Favorite

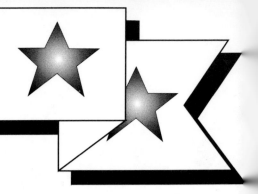

WORLD WAR I SONGS

PACK UP YOUR TROUBLE

PACK UP YOUR TROUBLE
IN YOUR OLD KIT BAG
AND SMILE, SMILE, SMILE
WHILE YOU'VE A LUCIFER
TO LIGHT YOUR FAG
SMILE BOYS THAT'S THE STYLE
WHAT'S THE USE OF WORRYING
IT NEVER WAS WORTH WHILE
SO, PACK UP YOUR TROUBLES
IN YOUR OLD KIT BAG
AND SMILE, SMILE, SMILE.

- George Asaf (1915)

IT'S A LONG WAY TO TIPPERARY

IT'S A LONG WAY TO TIPPERARY
IT'S A LONG WAY TO GO
IT'S A LONG WAY TO TIPPERARY
TO THE SWEETEST GIRL I KNOW
GOODBYE PICCADILLY
FAREWELL LEICESTER SQUARE
IT'S A LONG, LONG WAY TO TIPPERARY
BUT MY HEART'S RIGHT THERE.

- Jack Judge, Harry Williams (1912)

K-K-K-KATY

K-K-K-KATY, BEAUTIFUL KATY
YOU'RE THE ONLY G-G-G-GIRL
THAT I ADORE
WHEN THE M-M-M-MOON SHINES
OVER THE COWSHED
I'LL BE WAITING AT THE
K-K-K-KITCHEN DOOR.

- Geoffrey O'Hara (1918)

TILL WE MEET AGAIN

SMILE THE WHILE YOU KISS ME SAY ADIEU
WHEN THE CLOUDS ROLL BY I'LL COME TO YOU
THEN THE SKIES WILL SEEM MORE BLUE
DOWN IN LOVERS LANE MY DEARIE
WEDDING BELLS WILL RING SO MERRILY
EVERY TEAR WILL BE A MEMORY
SO WAIT AND PRAY EACH NIGHT FOR ME
TILL WE MEET AGAIN.

- Raymond B. Egan (1918)

THERE'S A LONG, LONG TRAIL

THERE'S A LONG, LONG TRAIL
AWINDING INTO THE LAND OF MY DREAMS
WHERE THE NIGHTINGALES ARE
SINGING AND A WHITE MOON BEAMS
THERE'S A LONG, LONG NIGHT
OF WAITING UNTIL MY DREAMS ALL COME TRUE
TILL THE DAY WHEN I'LL BE
GOING DOWN THE LONG, LONG
TRAIL WITH YOU.

- Stoddard King (1913)

OVER THERE

OVER THERE, OVER THERE,
SEND THE WORD, SEND THE WORD OVER THERE
THAT THE YANKS ARE COMING
THE YANKS ARE COMING
THE DRUMS RUM TUMMING EVERYWHERE
SO PREPARE, SAY A PRAYER
SEND THE WORD, SEND THE WORD TO BEWARE
WE'LL BE OVER, WE'RE COMING OVER
AND WE WON'T BE BACK TILL
IT'S OVER OVER THERE.

- George M. Cohan (1917)

July Theme — **AMERICA, THE BEAUTIFUL**

Today's Theme — **North, South, East, West**

Advanced
Preparation:
- Find a large map of the US with flags to pinpoint relevant areas.
- You will need a collection of songs about the states.
- Prepare yellow foam plates with smiley faces drawn on them.
- Make enough copies of the large print songsheet of "What did Delaware?" This is included at the end of this week's session plan.

Pre-Session: Pianist plays "By the Beautiful Sea," "Climb Every Mountain," "On the Atchison, Topeka, and the Santa Fe," "See the USA in Your Chevrolet," "In My Merry Oldsmobile." (Music to "See the USA in Your Chevrolet" is included on page 348; A songsheet of "By the Beautiful Sea" is included at the endof the A TRIP TO SUNNY ITALY [January] weekly session plan; and a songsheet of "In My Merry Oldsmobile" is included at the end of the YOU AUTO REMEMBER YOUR AUTOMOBILE [September] weekly session plan.)

Opening: Sing song to the tune of "It's a Long Way to Tipperary."

> It's a good time to get acquainted, it's a good time to know
> Who is sitting close beside you and to smile and say hello.
> Goodbye that lonesome feeling, goodbye woes and cares.
> When we all shake hands and smile together
> There's music in the air.

Announce the theme of AMERICA, THE BEAUTIFUL as the country is explored North, South, East, West in today's program.

Exercise: Using yellow smile plates:
"The Sidewalks of New York" — large fanning motions, east side, west side.
"Dixie" — tap leg with plate in rhythm, listen for its sound.
"Missouri Waltz" or "Beautiful Ohio" — large circular motions.
"California Here I Come" — intro — count of 8 beats as a group, proceed with 8 taps on head, 8 on shoulder, 8 on leg, etc.

Group Activity: Leader teaches chant. Whoever answers gets to chant it to another person or else this is done as a group.

North, South, East, West, tell me which one is the best?

Guided Imagery: Direct a short relaxation technique suggesting that everyone close their eyes. Ask them to think about the United States and recall it's beauty. Pianist plays "America, the Beautiful" softly in the background.

Reminiscence: Ask residents to name the states where they have lived, place a banner on a large map to note it and then ask if they think that part of America is beautiful.

Group Singing
(or Solo)

Use large print songsheets of "What Did Delaware?" The music is included on page 267.
1. What did Del-a-ware, boys, what did Del-a-ware? — (six times)
   I ask you now as a personal friend what did Del-a-ware?
   She wore her New Jersey, boys (six times)
   I tell you now as a personal friend she wore her New Jersey.
2. What did Idaho, boys.........she hoed her Maryland, boys.
3. What did Ioway, boys.........she weighed a Washington, boys.
4. What did Tennessee, boys.........she saw what Arkansas, boys.
5. What did Massachew, boys.........she chewed her conecti-cud, boys.

Song
Identification:

First, name some states that have a song written about them. Then name the states in the song titles:

KENTUCKY Babe
Sweet GEORGIA Brown
ALABAMY Bound
TENNESSEE Waltz
MISSOURI Waltz
Back Home Again in INDIANA
PENNSYLVANIA Polka
MISSISSIPPI Mud
Deep in the Heart of TEXAS
CAROLINA Moon
OKLAHOMA
Moonlight in VERMONT
MAINE Stein Song
Blue HAWAII

Rhythm Band:

"Missouri Waltz" — easy 3/4 tempo.
Excerpts from state songs above for various instrumental groupings.
"Washington Post March" — all join in.

Closing:

All join in singing "America, the Beautiful." (See songsheets included at the end of the OUR HISTORY IN SONG [July] and the THANKSLIVING [November] weekly session plans.) Announce next week's program.

Assignment:

Suggest residents ask friends and relatives their opinion of what makes America beautiful and where it is the prettiest.

Music
Resources:

Wee Sing Silly Songs (1984)
   "What Did Delaware" p. 16
Ultimate Fake Book (1981)
   "It's a Long Way to Tipperary" p. 306
   State songs about Kentucky, Indiana, Pennsylvania, Mississippi, Vermont, Oklahoma, California, and Carolina
One Thousand and One Jumbo (1985)
   "Washington Post March" p. 577

WHAT DID DELAWARE?

Traditional

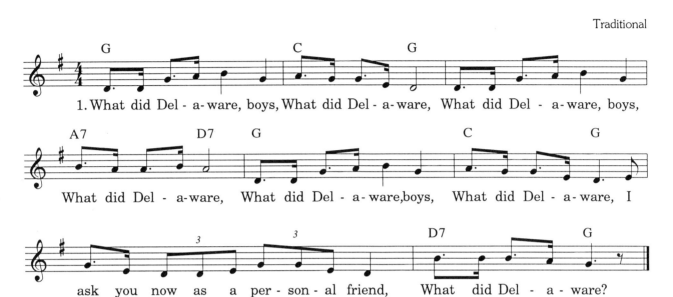

1. What did Del - a-ware, boys, What did Del - a-ware, What did Del - a-ware, boys,
What did Del - a-ware, What did Del - a-ware,boys, What did Del - a-ware, I
ask you now as a per - son - al friend, What did Del - a - ware?

> She wore her New Jersey, boys. (six times)
> I tell you now as a personal friend,
> She wore her New Jersey.
>
> 2. What did Idaho, boys . . .
> She hoed her Maryland, boys . . .
> 3. What did Ioway, boys . . .
> She weighed a Washington, boys . . .
> 4. How did Wiscon-sin, boys . . .
> She stole a New-bras-key, boys . . .
> 5. What did Tennessee, boys . . .
> She saw what Arkansaw, boys . . .
> 6. How did Flora-die, boys . . .
> She died in Missouri, boys . . .
> 7. Where has Oregon, boys . . .
> She's gone to Okahom, boys . . .
> 8. What did Mass-a-chew, boys. . .
> She chewed her Connecti-cud, boys.

Music Menu

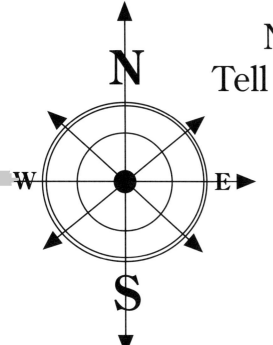

North, South, East, West,
Tell me which you like the best!

1. Kentucky Babe
2. Alabamy Bound
3. Tennessee Waltz
4. Pennsylvania Polka
5. Mississippi Mud
6. Carolina Moon
7. Oklahoma
8. Missouri Waltz
9. Sweet Georgia Brown
10. The Sidewalks of New York
11. Back Home Again in Indiana
12. California, Here I Come
13. Deep in the Heart of Texas

Wonderful country! Wonderful music!

WHAT DID DELA-WARE?

1. What did Dela-ware, boys?
   (sung six times)
   I ask you now as a personal friend,
   what did Dela-ware?

   She wore her New Jersey, boys
   (sung six times)
   I tell you now as a personal friend
   She wore her New Jersey

2. What did Ida-ho, boys..........
   She hoed her Mary-land, boys..........

3. What did Io-way, boys..........
   She weighed a Washing-ton, boys....

4. What did Tenne-ssee, boys..........
   She saw an Arkan-sas, boys..........

5. What did Massa-chew, boys..........
   She chewed her Connecti-cud, boys...

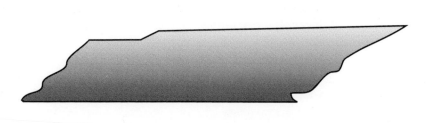

July Theme —   **AMERICA, THE BEAUTIFUL**

Today's Theme —   **My Hometown**

Advanced
Preparation:

- Make some 5-inch silhouettes of a house with some construction paper. A template is included at the end of this week's session plan.
- You will need copies of the large print songsheet of "Dear Hearts and Gentle People" included at the end of this week's session plan.
- Prepare some paper plates with roses pasted on them.
- Extra aides will be needed to print names of towns on the house silhouettes and then to tape them on each person. Scotch tape and magic markers will be required. Aides should also attend wearing their own hometown's name emblazoned on a house-shaped badge.

Pre-Session: Pianist plays "Dear Hearts and Gentle People," "There's Somethin' About a Hometown Band," "God Bless America." Aides greet people with name of their hometowns pinned on their lapel to start conversations.

Opening: Hometowns make America beautiful, the theme for today. Open with the songs "He's Got the Whole World in His Hands."
Verse:
1. He's got the whole world in His hands.
2. He's got my hometown in His hands.
3. He's got every city in His hands.
4. He's got [the town you are in now] in His hands.

Acknowledge the friendship that was in the hometown and is also in the present place of residence.

Exercise: Using rose paper plates, ask residents immediately if there were rose arbors, gardens, or flower shows in their hometown.
"Yellow Rose of Texas" — count 8 aloud and then tap 8 counts to each area, knees, elbows, shoulders, head and back down.
"Church in the Wildwood" — same motions, all sing chorus.
"School Days" — circular motions. (A songsheet is included at the end of the DEAR OLD SCHOOL DAYS [September] weekly session plan.)
"Finale — fling plate at group leader at count of three.

Group Singing: Use the large print songsheets of "Dear Hearts and Gentle People." Discuss words.

Solo Reading: Vocal solo or to be read as poetry — "There's Somethin' About a Hometown Band" by John Nagy, Milt Lane, Don Canton.

There's somethin' about a Home Town Band that makes you want to shout.
There's somethin' about a Home Town Band, that brings the neighbors out.
Your sister may be the majorette who leads them down the street.
Ta-ra-ta-ta boom, ta-ra-ta-ta goes your heart with their marching feet!
Wherever you live throughout the land,
There's somethin' about a Home Town Band.

It may be the Elks, it may be the moose, it may be the Shriners' Band,
The Fire Department, Police Department, or may be the College Band,
It may be the Lions, or the Legionaires, or may be the High School Band,
And if I've forgotten to mention one, Attention, that one's grand!
Whevever you live throughout the land,
There's somethin' about a Hometown Band.

Reminiscence: Find out the names of everyone's hometown, write it boldly on the pre-cut houses and tape on each person. Introduce those who have the same towns or states. Discuss some of the following points to stimulate recall:
1. Name the favorite store.
2. Was there a soda fountain?
3. Do you remember door to door salesmen?
4. Did you have telephone service?
5. Did the town have bells?
6. Where was the mail delivered?
7. Describe the fire department.
8. Name a friendship that is treasured.

Education: • In 1990, United Van Lines reports that the average person has 12 moves in a lifetime.[1]
• 46 million or 17% of the US population moves yearly within the US.
• In 1987-1988, 33% of those people who moved were aged 20-29.
• Only 4.7% of people over age 75 moved in 1991.
• Fewer people moved in 1991.[2]

Song
Identification: Name the town or city in the following songs:

GARY, Indiana
I Left my Heart in SAN FRANCISCO
NEW YORK, New York
KANSAS CITY
Erie Canal (BUFFALO)
CHATANOOGA Choo Choo
CHICAGO
Big "D" (DALLAS)
Do You Know What It Means to Miss NEW ORLEANS
SIOUX CITY Sue
Meet me in ST. LOUIS, LOUIS

Rhythm Band: "Dear Hearts and Gentle People" — everyone plays in honor of their town.
"The Little Brown Church" — bells only.
"Grandfather's Clock" — sticks only.
"Erie Canal" — shakers, castanets only.
"There's Somethin' About a Hometown Band" — call out each section.
"Seventy-six Trombones" — everyone play.

---

[1] Provided by the Public Affairs Department, United Van Lines, St. Louis, MO. Phone interview, Oct. 9, 1992.
[2] Points 2-5 in the Education section from *Statistical Abstracts of the United States* (*Us Dept. of Commerce* 1991 111th Edition #25. "Population - Mobility Status 1987-1988." p. 19.

Closing: Chorus of "Small World." Sing several times all holding hands recognizing the value of friendship no matter where you live. Friendship makes America beautiful.

Assignment: Give thanks for your hometown. Enjoy the memories but realize it has changed.

Next month's theme is IN THE GOOD OLD SUMMER TIME and PRECIOUS PORCHES will be honored. Think about favorite porches.

Music
Resources: *Family Song Book of Faith and Joy* (1981)
           "Dear Hearts and Gentle People" p. 8
        Ultimate Fake Book (1981)
           "There's Somethin' About a Hometown Band" p. 567
        Golden Book of Favorite Songs (1946)
           "The Little Brown Church" p. 11
        All American Song Book (1984)
           "Grandfather's Clock" p. 122
        Disney Collection of Songs (1990)
           "Small World" p. 55

My Hometown

1. Dear Hearts and Gentle People
2. There's Somethin' About a
   Hometown Band
3. Back Home Again in Indiana
4. Sioux City Sue
5. The Sidewalks of New York
6. Do You Know What it Means to Miss
   New Orleans
7. We're Loyal to You Illinois
8. Big "D"
9. I Left My Heart in San Francisco
10. Meet me in St. Louis, Louis
11. Back in Your Own Back Yard
12. Small World

Tell Me Your Favorite

SONGSHEET

DEAR HEARTS AND GENTLE PEOPLE

I love those dear hearts and gentle people
who live in my home town
because those dear hearts and gentle people
will never, ever let you down.

They read the good book
from "Fri" 'til Monday
that's how the weekend goes.
They've got a dream plan
they'll build there someday
with picket fence & ramblin' rose.

I feel so merry each time that I recall
that my happy heart keeps laughing like a clown.
I love the dear hearts and gentle people
who live and love in my hometown.

- Bob Hilliard (1950)

Hometown

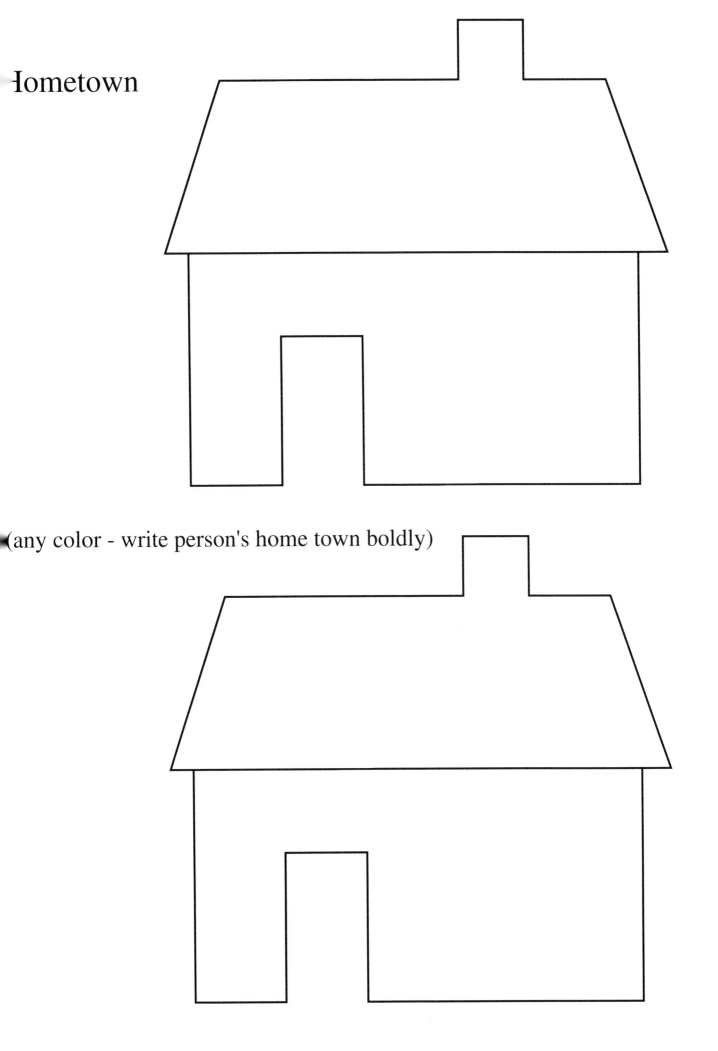

(any color - write person's home town boldly)

July Theme —   **AMERICA, THE BEAUTIFUL**

Today's Theme —   **Indoor Parade - Go Forth on the Fourth of July**
                   An Annual Celebration

Purpose: The purpose is to provide an opportunity to celebrate our national heritage, a
                   time of reflection and joy and to increase awareness of our many freedoms.
                   Use mobility as a goal involving the staff, families, and community. Establish
                   friendships and tour the facility during the parade.

Advanced
Preparation: • Plan with staff an appropriate date and time.
                   • Publicize the date early to increase anticipation. Use a countdown poster —
                     "Only 5 days until......," "Only 4 days until........."
                   • Encourage staff, residents, and families to wear patriotic colors.
                   • Have 2 or 3 copies of pre-taped music.
                   • Decorate chairs, canes, walkers with flags, patriotic streamers and balloons.
                     This is easily done by a scouting group the day before.
                   • Contact volunteers to assist with wheelchairs, and to provide extra support.
                     This is another chance for the community to serve.
                   • Have a flag or patriotic handout for every marcher and room stop over.
                   • Make lapel signs with "reporter" on them and then assign aides or
                     volunteers as reporters to interview the marchers at the conclusion of the
                     parade.

Decorations: • Activity department or community service group can help residents make
                     colorful red, white and blue flowers, and flag arrangements that can be used
                     for room doors or for other decorations.
                   • Fill red, white, and blue helium balloons and attach them to wheelchairs,
                     canes or wrists.
                   • Decorate bulletin boards with anything patriotic.

Music: Pre-taped music to include:

                       God Bless America
                       Columbia, the Gem of the Ocean (Three Cheers for the Red, White, and
                           Blue) *
                       This Land is Your Land
                       Battle Hymn of the Republic
                       America, the Beautiful §
                       America †

                   *   A songsheet is included at the end of this week's session plan.
                   § A songsheet (verses 2 and 3) is included at the end of the OUR HISTORY IN SONG [July]
                   weekly session plan and (verses 1 an d 2) at the end of the THANKSLIVING [November] weekly
                   session plan.
                   † A songsheet (verses 2 an 3) is included at the end of the OUR HISTORY IN SONG [July]
                   weekly session plan.

Song
Identification   There are Many Flags *
(Cont.)   Yankee Doodle
                        I'm a Yankee Doodle Dandy
                        Count Your Blessings §
                        Stars and Stripes Forever

        *   A songsheet is included at the end of the IT'S A GRAND OLD FLAG [June] weekly session
             plan.
        §   A songsheet is included at the end of the THANKSGIVING [November] weekly session plan.

Planning
of Parade: • Invite residents to help with the planning. Encourage them to decorate, help
                          someone else.
                        • Send a letter of invitation to families. No observers allowed — all must
                          participate!
                        • Plan with staff who is eligible to march or be escorted.
                        • Put a symbol on the doors of those residents who are not to be disturbed by
                          a visit from the marchers or who are not to be included in parade.

Day of the Parade:
                        • Announce over the intercom where and when to meet.
                        • Escort anyone to general meeting place that has been pre-arranged. Taped
                          music or piano music should be playing.
                        • Any additional decorations.

GO FORTH ON THE FOURTH OF JULY OPENING PROGRAM

                        Welcome everyone to the annual event. Open with the following song of
                        introduction to the tune of "Where is Thumbkin?"

                        Leader   Where are the volunteers, where are the volunteers?
                        Response   HERE WE ARE, HERE WE ARE.
                        Leader   How are you today, friends?
                        Response   VERY WELL WE THANK YOU.
                        Leader   God bless you.
                        Response   GOD BLESS YOU

                        Continue song by identifying residents, staff, families, scouts. Last verse should
                        be "Where are the Marchers?"

Education: • The Declaration of Independence was written by Thomas Jefferson and
                          signed on July 4th 1775 in Independence Hall, Philadelphia.
                        • 56 delegates to the Second Continental Congress signed it. John Hancock
                          signed his name so large that he said King George III could read it without
                          his glasses.[1]
                        • Ask for feedback.

---

[1]   Points 1 and 2 in the Education section from Ashworth, E. (1982) *Let's Talk,* p. 35.

Parade
Warm-up:

- Pass out flags, streamers for motion. Warm up with a march.
- Choose several parade leaders depending on group size and number of wheelchairs. Give the parade leaders a tall flag to hold high.
- Give each group a name. For example, one group could be called "Stars," another "Stripes."
- Assign areas for each group of marchers. The size of the group determines the area to be covered. Do not attempt to involve everyone to cover the entire facility. The area assigned should be fairly small. This can be both an exhilarating and a tiring activity for many.

GO FORTH PARADE

- Music begins on various tape players, one in the meeting place, another in the hall farther away, or else all on the intercom.
- The march units are called by their group names and then begin.
- Everyone is encouraged to sing along with the tape and let their voices celebrate Independence Day.
- Marchers leave a flag in every room they visit. Do not stay, continue with march but offer to come back.
- Return to general meeting area for light refreshments.
- Collect any props they do not wish to keep.
- Have volunteers with "reporter" sign on their lapel interview some of the happy marchers.
- Print event in local newspaper.

Closing:

Stay and visit. Escort back to room. Collect unwanted decorations. Thank everyone for the official celebration.

Music
Resources:

Wee Sing America (1988)
The entire book is appropriate

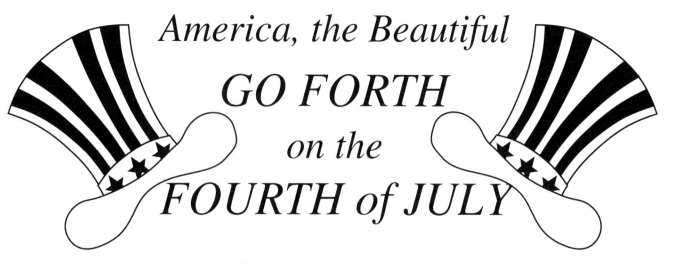

America, the Beautiful
GO FORTH
on the
FOURTH of JULY

1. YANKEE DOODLE

2. I'M A YANKEE DOODLE DANDY

3. AMERICA, THE BEAUTIFUL

4. AMERICA
(MY COUNTRY, 'TIS OF THEE)

5. GOD BLESS AMERICA

6. STARS AND STRIPES FOREVER

7. BATTLE HYMN OF THE REPUBLIC

8. COLUMBIA, THE GEM OF THE OCEAN

9. THERE ARE MANY FLAGS

10. THIS LAND IS YOUR LAND

11. COUNT YOUR BLESSINGS

12. THE STAR SPANGLED BANNER

Run your favorite up the flagpole, I'll salute it in rhythm.

COLUMBIA, THE GEM OF THE OCEAN

O Columbia, the Gem of the Ocean,
The home of the brave and the free,
The shrine of each patriot's devotion,
A world offers homage to thee!

Thy mandates make heroes assemble,
When Liberty's form stands in view,
Thy banners make tyranny tremble
When borne by the red, white and blue.

Chorus:

When borne by the red, white and blue,
When borne by the red, white and blue,
Thy banners make tyranny tremble
When borne by the red, white and blue.

- Thomas A. Becket (1843)

August

In the Good Old Summer Time

Musical Game for the Good Old Summer Time

There are lots of memories associated with the back porch as well as the front porch. There are also many songs that tell about some of the activities we enjoyed on porches. Fill in the blanks and then check the activities you enjoyed most. The answers are upside down.

1. Sippin' _____ Thru a Straw

2. C_____ Up a Little Closer

3. I'm Forever Blowing _____

4. S_____ on a Star

5. I W_____ a Happy Tune

6. S_____ in the Rain

7. Count Your _____

8. Last Night On the Back Porch - I _____ Her Most Of All

9. Aunt Dinah's _____ party

10. Show Me The Way To Go _____

1. Cider 2. Cuddle 3. Bubbles 4. Swinging 5. Whistle 6. Singin' 7. Blessings 8. Loved 9. Quilting 10. Home Good for you!

IN THE GOOD OLD SUMMERTIME
AUGUST

Warning — These programs are all overloaded with enjoyable activities, associations, and meaningful music. Use discretion when planning what to use for your facility.

Summer time is generally regarded as a happy time, at least a warm one. The following innovative programs will have everyone involved and recalling those hazy, lazy days especially if the leader presents them with a relaxed attitude.

Porches Were Precious — Everyone had a porch years ago and all kinds of activities took place there. Restore them with the many suggestions provided but leave lots of time for individual responses.

Ye Olde Piano Recital — Fears and tears as well as smiles were all a part of the olde piano recitals. Update everyone by inviting a few students to perform both the old standards and the new songs and then take a bow. A good leader can make everyone at ease and the recital will be the best ever.

Oh You Beautiful Doll — So much has changed through the years but not some of our favorite dolls. Invite a group of preschoolers with their dolls for an intergenerational activity that will be dear to everyone's heart.

Animal Friends — 100 well-behaved stuffed animals will be an enlightening experience in the good old summertime. Enjoy the dear old teddy bears but also let the children educate everyone on the latest animals on the toy market. Warning — it is hard to say goodbye to a new friend especially when it is soft and huggable.

Ice Cream — Real Cool — August ends with the chance to cool off with not only ice cream but cooling thoughts. Be sure to take a poll of the favorite flavor and try to arrange for several homemade ice cream makers for that perfect taste.

SUMMER TIME AND THE LIVING IS EASY — THANKS TO YOU

August Theme —   **IN THE GOOD OLD SUMMER TIME**

Today's Theme —   **Porches Were Precious**

Advanced
Preparation:
- Props will include:
  - Individual folded paper fans, personal fans, and electric fan,
  - bubble soap and wands.
  - music collection related to theme,
  - tape of "I'm Forever Blowing Bubbles" played 20 times,
  - watermelon scratch and sniff seals or other summer scent.
- You will need copies of "Bless This House" songsheet. (A songsheet is included at the end of the THANKSGIVING [November] weekly session plan.)

Pre-Session: Pass out fans to everyone. Use as a stimulus to attend group session. Theme music "In the Good Old Summer Time" is played as people enter the room.

Opening: Announce the theme for the month, IN THE GOOD OLD SUMMER TIME which includes precious memories of the front and back porch. Porches welcomed people years ago. Use "Make New Friends but Keep the Old" as the opening song.

Exercise: Use the paper fans or real hand fans for the following:
"In the Good Old Summer Time" — large fanning motion to the beat. (A songsheet is included at the of this week's session plan.)
"Playmates" — much faster beat in 2/4 rhythm.
"Yes Sir, That's My Baby" — very fast fanning action.

In honor of the traditional porch rocking chair try gentle rocking motion to this music:
"Rock-a-Bye Baby" — sway with arms cradling baby.
"Rock-a-Bye Your Baby with a Dixie Melody" — clasp arms and sway merrily side to side.
"Rock Around the Clock Tonight" — strong shoulder motions, jive-like.

Education:
- Americans call it a porch and in Greece and Rome it is a *portico*, in Italy a *Piazza* and in Spain a *patio*.
- It has been associated with shelter, coolness, fresh air and memories.
- Rod MacLeish wrote in the *Washington Post*:[1]

> "We don't use porches on houses any longer because we've forgotten how to do those things for which the porch was a natural setting......spontaneous visiting, public courting, shared silences and random conversation to no end except its own pleasure.... We began to abandon the porch when radio came into our lives. We went indoors to listen to it. Then television came and gripped us. Then air conditioning made indoors more tolerable."

[1]   *Washington Post* Dec. 1, 1974, p. 8. "In Praise of Porches" by R. MacLeish.

Solo Time: Poetry excerpts: "In Praise of Porches" by Hadley Read.[1]

> First off our neighbors would have scoffed if we ever had the nerve to call our plain back porch a gracious patio. And served us right. No fancy thing at best, that porch... but a special kind of place when one looks back... (old back porch).
>
> A place where at the edge
> > you scraped your muddy overshoes
> > when coming in from the chores.
> A place to sit and wince with pain
> > when Mom poured kerosene on cuts we got
> > from going barefoot in the rain.
> A place to make a kite in spring
> > to carve a pumpkin in the fall
> > to watch the stars on summer nights
> > and marvel at the wonder of it all
> We never could have done those things
> If we had called that place a patio.

Reminiscence: The traditional front porch signified "I'm home, come sit a spell." Talk about the following points — this will stimulate the memory:
- Was that true for most porches?
- Recall where porches were located.
- Was it inviting?
- Was there a railing? A stoop?
- What was under the porch?
- Were there flowers or vines?
- Tell about the activities that took place there.

Group Singing: "Last Night on the Back Porch—I Loved Her Most of All"

> I love her in the morning, I love her at night
> I love her, yes I love her when the stars are shining bright.
> I love her in the springtime, I love her in the fall
> But last night on the back porch I loved her best of all.

Song Identification: Music title gives a clue to the porch activity.

Sippin' Cider Thru a Straw	Swinging on a Star
Whispering	Lazybones
Cuddle up a Little Closer, Lovey Mine	I Whistle a Happy Tune
	Singin' in the Rain
Ma! He's Making Eyes at Me	Food Glorious Food
Lullaby and Good Night	Count Your Blessings
Show Me the Way to Go Home	I'm Forever Blowing Bubbles

---

[1]   H. Read (1977) *Morning Chores and Other Times Remembered*, p. 8.

Sensory
Stimulation: Pass out watermelon scratch and sniff seals.

Special Activity: Pass out bubble pipes and wands. Announce that a little soap and water is harmless. Blow bubbles while taped background music is playing. Encourage singing along with the tape. Finale — blow bubbles underneath ceiling fan or in front of portable fan for massive effect. Encourage catching, singing, smiling.

Rhythm Band: "Hail to the Chief" — march in honor of Warren Harding who ran his presidential election from his front porch. (The music is included on page 108.)
"Last Night on the Back Porch—I Loved Her Most of All" — peppy 2 beat with deliberate ending.
"Cuddle Up a Little Closer, Lovey Mine" — softer, gentler 2 beat.
"Whispering" — soft as possible.
"Count Your Blessings" — all play with feeling. (A songsheet is included at the end of the THANKSGIVING [November] weekly session plan.)

Closing: Using songsheets, sing "Bless This House." Many of the activities we did on the porches are now indoors so we continue the tradition in that sense. Next week's theme is YE OLDE PIANO RECITAL with 4 young students coming to play.

Assignment: Enjoy the memories associated with porches. If you could add a porch to this facility, where would you put it and what activity would you encourage considering everyone's abilities?

Music
Resources: *Family Song Book of Faith and Joy* (1981)
                      "I'm Forever Blowing Bubbles" p. 32
                   Ultimate Fake Book (1981)
                      "Hail to the Chief" p. 198
                      "Last Night on the Back Porch—I Loved Her Most of All" p. 341
                      "In the Good Old Summer Time" p. 271
                      "Yes Sir, That's my Baby" p. 638
                   Legal Fake Book (1979)
                      "Cuddle Up a Little Closer, Lovey Mine" p. 57
                   All American Song Book (1984)
                      "Whispering" p. 15
                   Tune Book Songs (1982)
                      "Count Your Blessings" p. 113
                   Wee Sing and Play Musical Games (1986)
                      "Playmates" p. 59
                   Songs of the 1950s (1988)
                      "Rock Around the Clock" p. 198
                   Greatest Songs of 1890-1920 (1990)
                      "Rock-a-Bye Your Baby with a Dixie Melody" p. 42

Front Porch Activities

1. Swinging on a Star
2. Sippin' Cider Thru a Straw
3. Ma! He's Making Eyes at Me
4. Cuddle Up a Little Closer, Lovey Mine
5. Whispering
6. Brahms' Lullaby
7. Aunt Dinah's Quilting Party
8. Singin' in the Rain
9. I Whistle a Happy Tune
10. Count Your Blessings
11. Last Night on the Back Porch - I Loved Her Most of All
12. In the Good Old Summer Time

Choose your favorite.
I'll play it for the whole neighborhood!

IN THE GOOD OLD SUMMER TIME

In the Good Old Summer Time,

In the Good Old Summer Time,

Strolling thru' the shady lanes with your baby mine;

You hold her hand and she holds yours,

And that's a very good sign

That she's your tootsey wootsey

In the Good Old Summer Time.

– Ren Shields (1902)

August Theme —   **IN THE GOOD OLD SUMMER TIME**

Today's Theme —   **Ye Olde Fashioned Piano Recital**

Advanced
Preparation:
- Arrange for four young pianists and their teacher to perform and bow.
- Prepare 2 sets of piano nametags that say "I Taught" and "I Played." A template for both is included at the end of this week's session plan.
- Offer large cookies as a snack for performers.
- Prepare large flash cards for "Do-Re-Mi" song.
- Get hold of, if possible, a portable Casio keyboard for Demonstration section.

Pre-Session: Pianist plays familiar recital tunes such as "The Happy Farmer," "The Glow Worm," Beethoven's "Minuet in G," "Spinning Song."

Opening: Welcome everyone to the piano recital. Open with the song "Make New Friends but Keep the Old." Sing first in unison, then as a round in 2 parts with 2 leaders. Introduce and interview piano teacher.

Exercise: All are associated with playing piano. Remember the teacher said these exercises were good for you. They still are.
1. Hand out front — start with thumb and "play" each finger while counting 1, 2, 3, 4, 5 — 5, 4, 3, 2, 1. Hands separately then together.
2. Former pianists do the entire scale 1, 2, 3, 1, 2, 3, 4, 5.
3. Shake out nervousness — Tarantella music — everyone shakes.
4. Pretend solo time "The Glow Worm" — exercise all fingers irregularly.
5. Second piece — Tschaikowsky Piano Concerto — chords hand over hand. All take a bow. Practice bending from the waist.

Group Singing: Names of the scales Do, Re, Mi, Fa, Sol, La, Ti, Do, followed by "Do-Re-Mi." Group calling out "Doe," while leader says "A deer...."

Group	DOE
Leader	A deer, a female deer
Group	RAY
Leader	A drop of golden sun.
Group	ME
Leader	A name I call myself
Group	FAR
Leader	A long long way to run
Group	SEW
Leader	A needle pulling thread
Group	LA
Leader	A note to follow sew
Group	TEA
Leader	A drink with jam and bread
All	THAT WILL BRING US BACK TO DOE.

Special Activity: Teacher proudly presents her class, Children introduce themselves and their music, perform admirably and then bow.

Reminiscence: Memories of former piano recitals.
   • Recall the name of any teachers.
   • How long were the lessons?
   • Were rewards given?
   • Was punishment involved?
   • How long was the practicing? Did you cheat?
   • Recall the name of the piano.
   • Recall piano pieces, recitals.
   • Discuss the popularity of piano rolls.
   • Ask if any of the residents regret not taking lessons.

Special Activity: Honor all former piano teachers with a large construction paper piano to be taped on them saying "I Taught." Applaud. Honor everyone who ever played the piano with the paper piano "I Played."

Education:
   • Piano sales are up with 1,116,495 pianos sold in 1992, according to the American Music Conference.[1]
   • The price ranges from $2,000 - $100,000.
   • We export 45%.
   • 3 largest US makers are Steinway, Baldwin, and Kimball.
   • There is a new emphasis on learning for fun or just for recreation.
   • Composing and improvisation lessons are given today.
   • Classes for seniors are popular.
   • New electronic pianos are always in tune, portable and inexpensive plus they have versatile sounds.[2]
   • A lesson in 1992 costs $10-12 for a half hour.
   • The old adage "practice makes perfect" is no longer taught. Now it is "perfect practice makes perfect."

Demonstration: With a portable Casio keyboard, demonstrate the various sounds of which the keyboard is capable. For example, organ, clarinet, rhythm instruments, etc. Discuss computer music.

Song
Identification: Name these recital songs:

Chopsticks   Für Elise (Beethoven)
The Happy Farmer   Minuet in G (Bach)
Long Long Ago   Musetta's Waltz - (*La Bohème* -
The Glow Worm   Puccini)
Minuet in G (Beethoven)   Country Gardens
Spinning Song

---

[1]   American Music Conference 1992. *Review of US Music Industry,* p. 8.
[2]   Points 2-8 in Education section from *Los Angeles Times* August 1, 1988, Business—Part IV, pp. 1-2. "Pianos in Tune with the Times" by N. Yoshihara.

Rhythm Band: If the piano students know any of the songs, they should join in.
"Chopsticks" — sticks only, add bells, shakers, etc. till all join in.
"Country Gardens" — easy 2/4 beat. (The music is included on page 206.)
"Spinning Song" — play on the downbeat, increase tempo.
"The Happy Farmer" — with loud cymbal crashes at end of phrases. (The music is included on page 194.)
"Music Music Music" — all play merrily.

Closing: Old and new friends join in singing "Bless This House." (A songhseet is included at the end of the THANKSGIVING [November] weekly session plan.) Invite pianists to come again.

Assignment: Ask friends and families for any old piano books of yours or favorite songs that you would like to hear again.

Music
Resources:

Great Music's Greatest Hits (1982)
    Minuet in G (Bach) p. 8
    Tschaikowsky's Piano Concerto p. 5
    Musetta's Waltz p. 120
    "Für Elise" p. 189
    "Country Gardens" p. 212
Ultimate Fake Book (1981)
    "Music, Music, Music" p. 392
    "Do-Re-Mi" p. 126
    "Tarantella" p. 552
    "The Glow Worm" p. 192
One Thousand and One Jumbo (1985)
    "The Happy Farmer" p. 266

THE HAPPY FARMER

R. Schumann, Op. 68, No. 10

Ye Olde Fashioned Piano Recital

1. Long Long Ago
2. Country Gardens
3. The Happy Farmer (Schumann)
4. Anitra's Dance (Grieg)
5. Barcarolle (Offenbach)
6. Evening Prayer (Humperdink)
7. The Glow Worm
8. Tales from the Vienna Woods
9. Tarantella (John Thompson)
10. Minuet in G (Beethoven)
11. Missouri Waltz
12. Spinning Song

Choose your favorite "old chestnut".

August "Piano Recital"

August Theme — **IN THE GOOD OLD SUMMER TIME**

Today's Theme — **Oh You Beautiful Doll**

Advanced
Preparation:
- Invite a preschool class to attend and bring their dolls, Raggedy Ann and Andy.
- Invite families and residents to contribute.
- Provide light refreshments,
- Prepare a collection of "doll" songs.

Pre-Session: Children and their teachers greet residents with dolls waving their hands. Background music softly playing. Include "Oh You Beautiful Doll," "Toyland," "Paper Doll."

Opening: Welcome everyone. Children should sit up front with their dolls. Open with the song "Make New Friends." This applies to everyone attending including the dolls. Sing several times and eventually as a 2-part round using two leaders.

> Make new friends, but keep the old
> One is silver and the other gold.

Children introduce their dolls over the microphone. Residents tell about theirs. Distribute dolls so everyone has one for exercise as well as reminiscence.

Exercise: "Rock-a-Bye Baby" — our first association with dolls, rock.
"Toyland" by Victor Herbert — bounce dolls on lap.
"Dance with a Dolly" — be creative, let the dolls dance.

Reminiscence: Ask residents if they had a favorite doll:
- What was its name?
- What were its clothes like?
- Where was the doll kept?
- What happened to her?
- Do you still love her?

Group Singing: "Playmates" — teach by rote slowly.

> Say, say oh playmate come out and play with me
> And bring your dollies three, climb up my apple tree,
> Cry down my rainbarrel, slide down my cellar door,
> And we'll be jolly friends forever more.

Education:
- Dolls are still important at any age. Doll collecting and doll houses are very popular. The origin comes from "playing mother."
- Ancient dolls came from Egypt around 2000 B.C. Greek and Roman clay dolls have been discovered.
- The first real dolls were wooden from England in 1720.
- Famous dolls include Dydee who would drink and wet, Shirley Temple, Kewpie, Quints, and Raggedy Ann and Andy in 1918.[1]

---

[1] Points 1-4 in Educatino section from Ashworth, E. (1982) *Let's Talk*, pp. 27, 28.

Education: (Cont.)	• Barbie dolls have been popular since 1959 so she is now 34 years old. In 1990, 95% of American girls aged 3-11 owned Barbie dolls. People have spent $700 million on her. She is international.[1] • Dolls are made of corn cobs, raw hide, whittled from wood, china, rag, paper and wax.[2]
Song Identification:	The following songs are all abut dolls. Call out the title or sing along.

> Paper DOLL
> Dance with a DOLLY
> Hello DOLLY
> Baby Face
> Toyland
> Cradle Song (R. Schumann)
> Waltzing DOLL
> The Wedding of the Painted DOLL
> Oh You Beautiful DOLL *
> Satin DOLL
> Playmates

* A songhseet is included at the end of this week's session plan.

Special Activity:	Children take back their dolls and march around the room with them in between chairs to the music of Victor Herbert's "Toyland" or the "March of the Toys."
Rhythm Band:	All dolls are put away and rhythm instruments are passed out for a grand time of making music together. "Twinkle, Twinkle Little Star" — simple children's song, easy 2 beat. "Dance with a Dolly" — faster 2 beat. "March of the Toys" — piano introduction 8 measures. Call out names of instrument for various sections. "Seventy-six Trombones" — stirring march for the finale.
Closing:	All sing "Reach out and Touch." Space children between adults whenever possible. Sing several times. (The music is included on page 172.) Announce next week's theme is ANIMAL FRIENDS and over 100 stuffed animals want to meet everyone. Learn about the oldest and newest toys.
Assignment:	Let residents think about today's session and decide which is their favorite doll, new or old and then figure out why.

[1] *Forbes*, Jan. 7, 1991, p. 66 "Barbie Does Budapest" by Gretchen Morgenson.
[2] Recommended reading on dolls Boehn, Max von. (1972) *Dolls*.

Music
Resources:
        Great Music's Greatest Hits (1982)
           "March of the Toys" p. 155
        Treasury of Best Loved Songs (1981
           "Toyland" p. 215
           "Paper Doll" p. 264
        Legal Fake Book (1979)
           "Oh You Beautiful Doll" p. 212
        Ultimate Fake Book (1981)
           "Dance with a Dolly" p. 118
        Wee Sing and Play Musical Games (1986)
           "Playmates" p. 59
        Sheet Music, Charles Brown, Ashford, and Simpson, Jobete Music Co.
Hollywood, CA. (1970)
           "Reach Out and Touch"

Dolls

1. *Oh You Beautiful Doll*

2. *Dance with a Dolly*

3. *Hello Dolly*

4. *Paper Doll*

5. *Pretty Baby*

6. *Baby Face*

7. *Satin Doll*

8. *Toyland*

9. *The Doll Dance*

10. *I Love You Truly*

11. *March of the Toys*

12. *The Wedding of the Painted Doll*

Request Your Favorite Song

OH YOU BEAUTIFUL DOLL

Oh! You Beautiful Doll
You great big beautiful doll,
Let me put my arms about you,
I could never live without you,

Oh! You Beautiful Doll
You great big beautiful doll,
If you ever leave me,
how my heart will ache,
I want to hug you but I fear you'd break,
Oh! Oh! Oh! Oh!
Oh! You Beautiful Doll!

– A. Seymour Brown (1911)

August Theme — **IN THE GOOD OLD SUMMER TIME**

Today's Theme — **Animal Friends**

Advanced
Preparation:
- Invite family or troop to bring stuffed animal collection, all sizes, new and old.
- Provide collection of animal songs.
- Prepare a tape of animal sounds.

Pre-Session: Children walk to each person and greet with a stuffed animal and ask them to carry it to the group session. Background music playing as people enter room includes "Talk to the Animals," "Do-Re-Mi," "The Teddy Bear's Picnic," and "Camptown Races."

Opening: Song sung first to the children and then to the animal to the tune of "On Top of Old Smokey."

> Thank God for the sunshine, thank God for the dew,
> Thank God for your friendship, and blessings on you.

Exercise: Children introduce themselves and talk about some of the animals. Distribute so everyone exercises with an animal of their choosing. Exchange animals for more variety later on.

Reminiscence: Discover who had a favorite teddy bear or other animal.
- Where is it now?
- Is it still beloved?
- What were the names of favorite animals?
Let the children enter discussion and name their favorites too.

Education:
- Children should introduce new animals on the market from the past five years.
- 1989 — Garfield the Cat "Stuck on You" was the #1 best-selling animal. Talking Mickey Mouse is very popular at $29 in 1992.[1]
- The teddy bear is best for security more so than a blanket.[2]

Group Singing: "Bill Grogan's Goat" as an Echo/Response song.

Leader	There was a man
Response	THERE WAS A MAN
Leader	Now please take note
Response	NOW PLEASE TAKE NOTE
Leader	There was a man
Response	THERE WAS A MAN
Leader	Who had a goat

---

[1] Points 1 and 2 in Education section from Animal Kingdom and Children's Palace, St. Louis, MO. — Phone interview, September 8, 1990.
[2] *Rocky Mountain News* (Denver) July 5, 1989, p. 39. "Teddy Bear Still Top Dog for Children's Security, Expert Says.," col. from AP New York.

Group Singing: (Cont.)	Response	WHO HAD A GOAT
	Leader	He loved that goat
	Response	INDEED HE DID
	Leader	He loved that goat
	Response	JUST LIKE A KID.
	Leader	One day that goat
	Response	FELT FRISK AND FINE
	Leader	Ate three red shirts
	Response	RIGHT OFF THE LINE
	Leader	The man he grabbed
	Response	HIM BY THE BACK
	Leader	And tied him to
	Response	THE RAILROAD TRACK.
	Leader	Now when that train
	Response	HOVE INTO SIGHT
	Leader	That goat grew pale
	Response	AND GREEN WITH FRIGHT
	Leader	He heaved a sigh
	Response	AS IF IN PAIN
	Leader	Coughed up those shirts
	Response	AND FLAGGED THE TRAIN.

Group song — "He's got the Whole World in His Hands" use animal names such as "lovely, lovely lambs" and "prancing, dancing horses."

Group Chant: I like animals, yes sir-ee
If you could be an animal what would you be?[1]

Ask group to repeat chant with you. Shake hand of person you wish to interview. Aides circulate and receive more responses.

Song Identification: Name the animal in the following song titles or the animal described later on in the music after you hear the melody.

Pop Goes the WEASEL	Mary had a Little LAMB
Me and My Teddy BEAR	Baa Baa Black SHEEP
Hey Diddle Diddle, The CAT and the Fiddle	Go Tell Aunt Rhody
	Three Little KITTENS
Rudolph the Red-Nosed REINDEER	MARES Eat Oats
Three Blind MICE	Hickory, Dickory, Dock
TIGER Rag	Puff the Magic DRAGON
HORSEY, Keep Your Tail Up	It's Not Easy Being Green
BEAR Went Over the Mountain	Mickey MOUSE Theme
Jingle Bells	Yankee Doodle
Alley CAT	Swinging on a Star

---

1   Wenrick, N. (1972) *So Much More Than a Sing a Long*, p. 3.

Song Identification: (Cont.)	SHEEP May Safely Graze (J.S. Bach) The Blue Tail FLY Old Grey MARE Old MacDonald Had a Farm Lonely GOATherd Oh Where Oh Where Has My Little DOG Gone? * * A songsheet is included at the end of this week's session plan.
Sound Identification:	Play tape of animal sounds to be identified.[1]
Group Game:	Finish the following bits of wisdom with an animal:

Wise as an (owl)   Slow as a (snail)
Clever as a (fox)   Stubborn as a (mule)
Strong as a (horse, ox)   Hungry as a (bear)
Quick as a (fox)   Busy as a (bee)
Happy as a (clam)

Closing:	Hug the animals while the music is played to "Cuddle up a Little Closer, Lovey Mine." Can be sung as a solo. Then all animals are collected with the plan that they will visit again next year.

Rhythm Band:	All animals should be up front to watch the entire group play with the rhythm instruments. This is an intergenerational activity. More instruments may be necessary.
	"Old MacDonald Had a Farm" — substitute instruments for animal names:
	    For example:
	    'In his band he had some bells' — just the bells play. Continue with various instruments. Use name of your facility.
	"Bingo" — all sing "There was a farmer had a dog and Bingo was his name O" — spell the letters in the song with instruments, no words.
	"The Teddy Bear's Picnic" — everyone play and include crashing cymbal at end of line one, line two, and final line.

Closing:	Sing to the tune of "Goodnight Ladies:"
	
	    Goodbye children........ we're happy that you came.
	    Merrily we sing along...... we're happy that you came.
	
	Sing in like manner to the animals.

Assignment:	Encourage more thought concerning the animal they would like to be, if that were possible. Consider the traits. Share these thoughts with each other during the next few days.

---

[1] "Sounds of Animals" Folkways Records, FX6124.

Music
Resources: *Wee Sing Silly Songs* (1984)
                       "Bill Grogan's Goat" p. 42
                   Legal Fake Book (1979)
                       "Cuddle Up a Little Closer, Lovey Mine" p. 57
                       "The Teddy Bear's Picnic" p. 284
                   Children's Song Book (1988)
                       "Bingo" p. 124
                       "Pop Goes the Weasel" p. 187
                       "Hey Diddle Diddle" p. 226
                       "Puff the Magic Dragon" p. 161
                       "Hickory, Dickory, Dock" p. 232
                       "Yankee Doodle" p. 250
                       "It's Not Easy Being Green" p. 10

Music Menu

1. In the Good Old Summer Time
2. Me and My Teddy Bear
3. The Teddy Bear's Picnic
4. (How Much is That) Doggie in the Window?
5. Three Little Fishes
6. Bill Grogan's Goat
7. Hickory, Dickory, Dock
8. The Old Grey Mare
9. Camptown Races
10. Horsey, Keep Your Tail Up
11. Old MacDonald Had a Farm
12. Do - Re - Mi (Doe, a Deer)
13. Home on the Range
14. Always (I'll Be Loving "Ewe", Always)

Request your favorite - I'll make it sing!

OH WHERE, OH WHERE HAS MY LITTLE DOG GONE

German Folk Tune

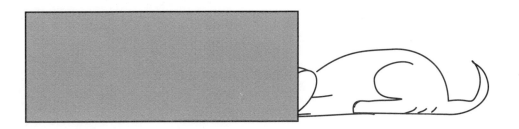

Oh where, oh where has my little dog gone?

Oh where, oh where can he be?

With ears cut short

and his tail cut long,

Oh where, oh where can he be?

– Septimus Winner (1847)

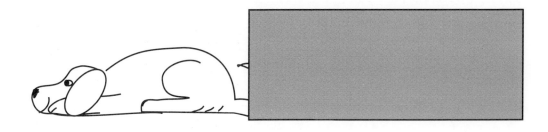

August Theme — **IN THE GOOD OLD SUMMER TIME**

Today's Theme — **Ice Cream — It's Cool**

Advanced
Preparation:
- Cut out and prepare big 4-inch ice cream paper cone nametags in popular flavors (colors). A template for this is included at the end of this week's session plan. Aides can act as reporters and help tape these to residents.
- Gather together homemade ice cream ingredients, machines and volunteers. You will also need small bowls, spoons, and napkins.
- A collection of songs that infer coldness is appropriate for this week.

Pre-Session: Greet everyone by wearing a straw hat and large ice cream cone name tag. Background music: "In the Good Old Summer Time," "Let It Snow, Let It Snow, Let It Snow," and "Frosty the Snow Man."

Opening: "In the Good Old Summer Time." Read the refrain as poetry. (A songsheet is included at the end of the PORCHES WERE PRECIOUS [August] weekly session plan.)

> There's a time each year that we always hold dear,
> Good old summer time.
> With the birds and the trees and the sweet scented breezes,
> Good old summer time.
> When your day's work is over then you are in clover,
> And life is one beautiful rhyme.
> No trouble annoying, each one is enjoying the good old summer time.

Chorus: teach by rote, all join in singing.

> In the good old summer time, in the good old summer time
> Strolling through the shady lanes with your baby mine;
> You hold her hand, she holds yours
> And that's a very good sign
> That she's your tootsey wootsey in the good old summer time.

Questionnaire: Take a poll of who is warm. Note the number.

Exercise: Cross arms over chest, expand out and in to the chant:
    I scream, you scream, we all scream for ice cream.
Repeat until everyone is involved.

Reminiscence: Name the ingredients in homemade ice cream (eggs, sugar, vanilla, whipped cream, salt). Discuss who used to make it. Find out if anyone had an ice box with an ice man. Recall early ice cream cones, shapes, flavors. Talk about ice cream parlors, soda jerks.
Short quiz: What was: cow-juice — (milk)
                        fizz — (carbonated water)
                        o.j. — (orange juice)
                        white cow — (vanilla milk shake)
                        brown cow — (chocolate ice cream in shake)

Reminiscence
(Cont.)

Recall good humor men. Invite residents to name the famous ice cream places in their city.

Take a poll of favorite flavors. Attach (using scotch tape) vanilla paper cones to all those favoring that flavor. Continue in like manner with other favorites to increase conversation for the entire day.

Group Activity:

Volunteers and residents make homemade ice cream together or have it made before the session and add finishing touches. Avoid ice cream sundaes. Savor the simple flavor of plain vanilla. Point out the joy of simplicity. Serve at this time. While eating ask about the ways people kept cool years ago.

Education:

- Alexander the Great in 4 B.C. created the first ice cream treat called *macedoine.*
- In 54 A.D. Nero Ceasar sent runners into the mountains for snow which he flavored with fruits.
- Italy served it in the 16th century, then France.
- In 1790, George Washington spent $200 on it. Dolly Madison served it on President Madison's 2nd inauguration in 1812.
- In 1987, retail sales topped $9 billion in the U.S., the equivalent of 44 pints per person.
- The consumption in Australia is second only to ours.[1]
- The top flavors are vanilla (32%), chocolate, neapolitan, vanilla fudge, and cookies and cream.
- Children like peanut butter swirl and bubble gum.
- The cone started in St. Louis at the 1904 World's Fair. Some say that they ran out of dishes and put the ice cream in a belgian waffle. Today's cone price is $1.18 at Baskin Robbins in St. Louis; 95 cents for a kid's size.[2]

Solo Time:

Poetry reading from Rachel Field's "The Ice Cream Man."[3]

When summer's in the city and bricks a blaze of heat
The ice cream man with the little cart goes trundling down the street.

Beneath his round umbrella oh, what a joyful sight,
To see him fill the cones with mounds of cooling brown and white.

Vanilla, chocolate, strawberry or chilly things to drink
From bottles full of frosty fizz green, orange, white or pink.

His cart might be a flower bed or roses and sweet peas
The way the children cluster round as thick as honeybees.

Song: "Ice Cream Song" (Howard Johnson's *Children's Song Book)*

---

[1] Points 1-6 in Education section from *St. Louis Post Dispatch*, Aug. 23, 1987, p. D1. "Comfort and Joy" by Patricia Corrigan.
[2] Points 7-9 from an interview with Tom Cuccia, District Manager for Baskin Robbins, August 14, 1992, St. Louis MO.
[3] *Favorite Poems Old and New* (1957) p. 249.

Song
Identification: Name these cold songs:

                              Winter Wonderland
                              Let It Snow, Let It Snow, Let It Snow
                              Frosty the Snow Man
                              Baby, It's Cold Outside
                              In the Cool, Cool, Cool of the Evening
                              Jingle Bells

Rhythm Band: "Jingle Bells" — bells only
"Let It Snow, Let It Snow, Let It Snow" — everyone with a peppy 2 beat.
"The Blue Danube Waltz" (wintertime) — piano solo with instruments responding on 2nd and 3rd beats. All play together at ending 3/4 time.
"Over the River and Through The Woods" — strong downbeats, all play extra long and extra loud on the word "snow." (A songsheet is included at the end of the THANKKSGIVING [November] weekly session plan.)
"Battle Hymn of the Republic" — celebrate coldness with a glory hallelujah.

Closing: Now take a poll and see if anyone warmed up. End with the closing song of "Bless This House." (A songsheet is included at the end of the THANKSGIVING [November] weekly session plan.)

Assignment: Suggest the residents think cold thoughts and see if it is cooling. One's mind is powerful. Remind residents to use it.

Music
Resources: *Family Song Book of Faith and Joy* (1981)
          "In the Good Old Summer Time" p. 182
          "Battle Hymn of the Republic" p. 280
Great Music's Greatest Hits (1982)
          "The Blue Danube Waltz" p. 50
Merry Christmas Song Book (1981)
          "Let It Snow, Let It Snow, Let It Snow" p. 128
          "Over the River and Through The Woods" p. 136
          "Frosty the Snow Man" p. 99
Festival of Popular Songs (1977)
          "Winter Wonderland" p. 70
Children's Song Book (1988)
          "Ice Cream Song" p. 143

ice cream - real cool

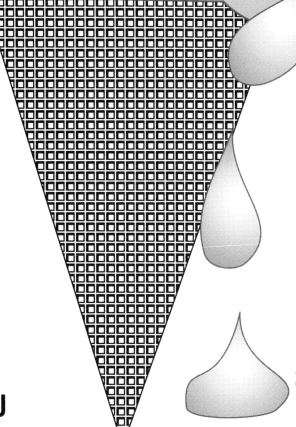

1. Cool Water
2. Frosty the Snow Man
3. In the Good Old Summer Time
4. Baby, It's Cold Outside
5. In the Cool, Cool, Cool of the Evening
6. Louise (Every Little Breeze)
7. Let There Be Peace on Earth
8. Mountain Greenery
9. Winter Wonderland
10. Let It Snow, Let It Snow, Let It Snow

MUSIC MENU

SELECT YOUR FLAVORITE

August "Ice Cream"

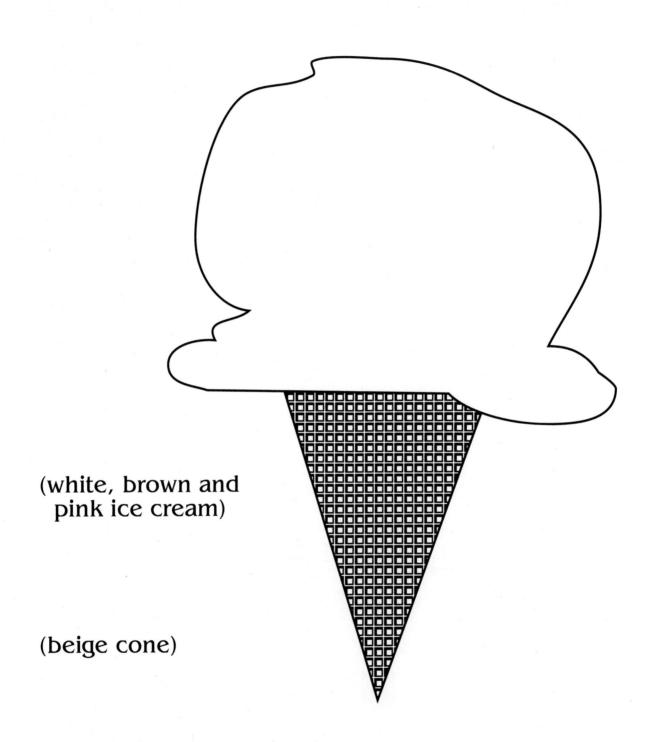

(white, brown and
pink ice cream)

(beige cone)

September

Olde Fashioned Favorites

September Musical Game
Old Fashioned Favorites

Match the song with the picture.
Then sing them.
(The answers are upside down.)

A

G

1. Around the World (in Eighty Days)
2. In My Merry Oldsmobile
3. God Bless America
4. (Oh, My Darling) Clementine
5. Tea for Two
6. Indian Love Call
7. The Old Oaken Bucket
8. All Alone (Irving Berlin)
9. My Bonnie Lies Over the Ocean
10. Mozart piano piece

H

D

B

E

I

C

F

J

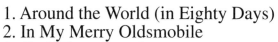

Answers: One-A, Two-G, Three-H, Four-J, Five-D, Six-I, Seven-H, Eight-C, Nine-B, Ten-E

OLDE FASHIONED FAVORITES
SEPTEMBER

Half of the fun is recalling the good old days and the other half is looking at the current times. "There is a lot of water that has gone under the bridge" in most cases. The following programs will stimulate the mind as well as the body. The order can easily be rearranged for your convenience. The contents are overloaded so enjoy your preparation time. The results will be New Fashioned.

Labor Day — A Labor of Love — Honor everyone on this national holiday since laboring is a fact of life. Explore many professions including the privilege of volunteering. This is an excellent time to honor various employees who are faithful laborers of love.

Dear Old School Days — Education has seen many changes yet our heartfelt thanks go back to our early teachers. Dwell on the impact they had and honor all those who once taught school, Sunday school, or music.

Styles up to the Ankle — If everyone wears their oldest dress there will be many smiles. As you remember the old styles it will soon be apparent that many of them are back again. There is lots to sing about.

Give Me That Old Time Religion — This is an ecumenical program that is enhanced with an electronic piano with organ effect and a violinist or other string players. Group singing will raise your roof and that includes learning new songs of other faiths.

You Auto Remember Your Automobile — Elderly people have vivid and hilarious memories about this topic. Their generation saw the birth and adolescent period of cars and the conversations need to be preserved from those early days.

OPTIONAL PROGRAM

Ragtime Review — "The real American folksong is the rag" according to Irving Berlin.[1] There are many old fashioned songs and recollections of the ragtime era. Surely there is a pianist in your area that would be happy to demonstrate the music and activate the mind. Reporters need to record this memorable period of American music.

OLD BUT NOT FORGOTTEN

---

[1] Song title "The Real American Folk Song (is a rag)" from the musical *Ladies First*. Lyrics by Ira Gershwin, music by George Gershwin. The song itself is in *The Original, Legal, Musicians Fake Book* (1980) p. 144.

September Theme —**OLD FASHIONED FAVORITES**

Today's Theme —   **A Labor of Love**

Advanced
Preparation:
- Obtain work hats of various professions.
- Find props/tools such as shovel, stethoscope, legal pad, paint brush, apron, telephone, book, hoe, wrench, sewing supplies, whistle, baby bottle, hammer and nails, chalk and eraser, Bible.
- Find a box to hold the tools.
- Make nametags designed as a prize ribbon. A template for this is included at the end of this week's session.
- Volunteers/aides will need magic markers.

Pre-Session: Greet residents wearing one of the workers hats and nametags telling of your profession. Pianist plays songs such as "Whistle While You Work," "Work for the Night is Coming," "Nice Work if You Can Get It," and "Heigh-Ho" (Heigh-Ho, It's Off to Work We Go).

Opening: Opening song is "If You're Happy and You Know It." The music is included on page 322.
Verse:
1. If you're happy and you know it, clap your hands.
2. If you've worked and you know it, nod your head
3. If you labored and you know it, give a groan.
4. If you're thankful and you know it, say "thank you."

Exercise: The song "Here We Go 'Round the Mulberry Bush" — sing and participate:
Verse:
1. This is the way we washed our clothes (strong arm motions)
2. This is the way we dried our clothes (reach high to hang)
3. This is the way we ironed our clothes (strong sideways motions)
4. Now they have improved our clothes (sing and clap at the same time)

Education:
- Labor Day recognizes all laborers on the first Monday in September since 1882 in all states. In April 1991, over 6% of our population was unemployed, however, that does mean that 94% were working.[1]
- The National Labor Organization has over 10.5 million members.[2]
- As the partial list is read, hands should raise when their profession is mentioned and a nametag made for them by an aide: Auto, bakery, boilermakers, bricklayers, carpenters, textile workers, electrical and electronic workers, fire fighters, food, Government employees, hotel, iron, letter carriers, machinists, mine workers, nurses, office employees, oil and chemical, engineers, painters, paper, plumbers, police, retail stores, sheet metal, state, county, municipal workers, teachers, teamsters and transportation workers. Any others should be recognized with a nametag listing their profession.

---

[1] *Information Please Almanac* (1992) "Business and the Economy" p. 59.
[2] Ibid. "National Labour Organizations" p. 51.

Group Singing: "Whistle While You Work" from *Snow White and the Seven Dwarfs.*

> Whistle while you work (whistle)
> Put on that grin and start right in to whistle loud and long.
> Just hum a merry tune (hum)
> Just do your best, then take a rest and sing yourself a song.

Special Activity: Honor all laborers with the philosophy of Kahlil Gibran that "Work is love made visible."[1] Discuss.

Reminiscence: Recall either your profession or some jobs that you did when you were younger that were pleasurable. Include gardening, parenting, volunteering work. Discuss if any of these jobs still exist.

To stimulate recall, pull various professional tools from a box such as a stethoscope, paint brush, *Wall Street Journal*, druggist's pills, chalk and eraser, baby bottle, garden tools, camera, and any others.[2]

Solo Time: Invite guests to say a few words about their present profession such as director of activities, administrator, director of nursing, maintenance personnel, dietician, and physical therapist.

Song
Identification: Name the labor involved in these songs.

> I've Been Working on the Railroad (engineer, railroad worker)
> Farmer in the Dell (farming)
> School Days (teaching) *
> Where Oh Where Has my Little Dog Gone (dog catching)
> The Sidewalks of New York (cement mixing)
> Aunt Dinah's Quilting Party (quilting)
> I Don't want to Set the World On Fire (fire fighting)
> I'm Gonna Sit Right Down and Write Myself a Letter (letter carriers)
> Git Along Little Dogies (cowboys, ranching)
> Pick a Bale of Cotton (cotton pickers)
> Anvil Chorus (smith)

> *   A songsheet is included at the end of the DEAR OLD SHOOL DAYS [September] weekly session plan.

Rhythm Band: "Work for the Night is Coming" — majestic 4/4 time.
"Heigh-Ho" — Call out the names of the instruments to be featured. First shakers, then sticks, bells, drums. For the last verse, all play together.
"Anvil Chorus" — divide group into half. Use two leaders. One group plays on the downbeat, the other on the afterbeat.
"Seventy-six Trombones" — strong march honoring Labor Day.

---

[1]   Gibran, K. (1968). *The Prophet.*, "On Work" p. 28.
[2]   The basic idea for this section came from Karras, B. (1985) *Down Memory Lane*, p. 144.

Closing: Group singing of "God Bless America" honoring Labor Day.

Assignment: Wear your badge all day honoring your profession. Talk about your work with pride realizing that you have lived a long, full life and have seen many changes but labor truly makes America great. Consider any employees that are presently laboring and thank them.

Music
Resources: *Children's Song Book* (1988)
                        "Whistle While You Work" p. 62
                        "Heigh-Ho" p. 66
                        "Here We Go 'Round the Mulberry Bush" p. 216
                    Golden Book of Favorite Songs (1946)
                        "Work for the Night is Coming" p. 58
                    Great Music's Greatest Hits (1982)
                        "Anvil Chorus" p. 218
                    Remembering the Fifties (1992)
                        "Seventy-six Trombones" p. 96
                        "I'm Gonna Sit Right Down and Write Myself a Letter" p. 498
                        "Pick a Bale of Cotton" p. 516

IF YOU'RE HAPPY AND YOU KNOW IT

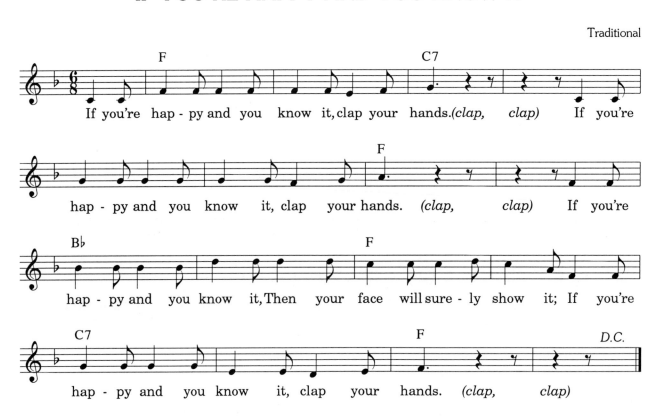

A LABOR OF LOVE

1. ANVIL CHORUS

2. WITH THESE HANDS

3. DON'T FENCE ME IN

4. HOW GREAT THOU ART

5. AMERICA, THE BEAUTIFUL

6. WHISTLE WHILE YOU WORK

7. GOD OF CONCRETE, GOD OF STEEL

8. THE STRENUOUS LIFE (SCOTT JOPLIN)

9. WORK FOR THE NIGHT IS COMING

10. I'VE BEEN WORKING ON THE RAILROAD

11. HEIGH-HO (HEIGH HO, IT'S OFF
    TO WORK WE GO)

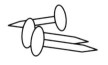

PLEASE PUT ME TO WORK,
I LOVE TO PLAY THE PIANO!

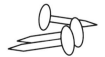

September "Labor Day"

Write in their profession

any color

add blue ribbon

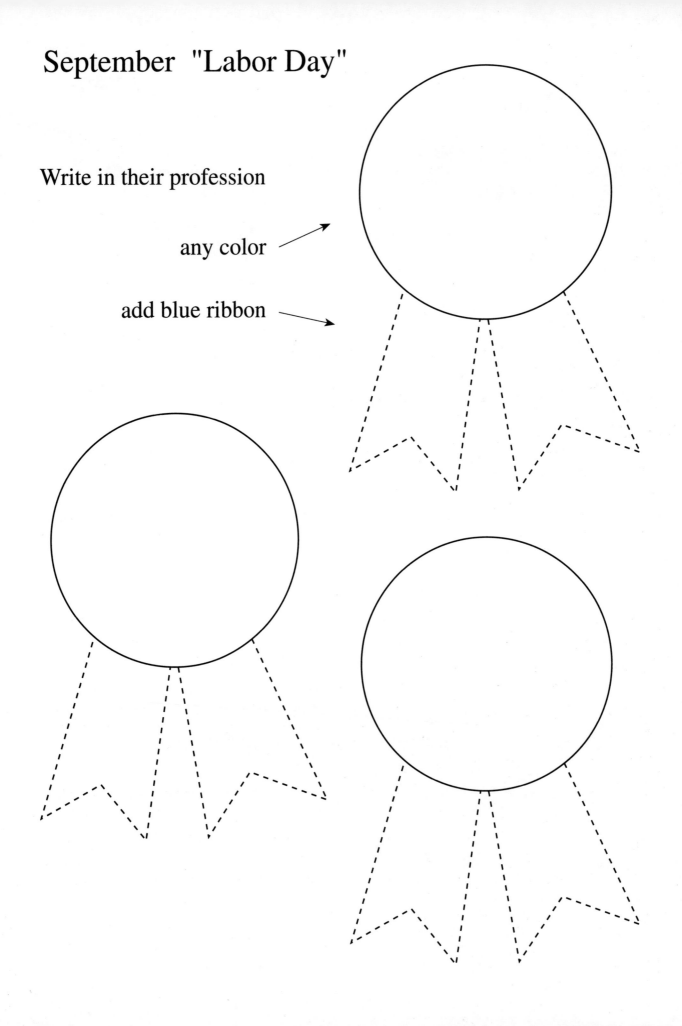

September Theme — **OLD FASHIONED FAVORITES**

Today's Theme —   **Dear Old School Days**

Advanced
Preparation:
- Provide a flag.
- Make letters of the alphabet on separate pieces of cardboard.
- Props for this session will include: bell, chalkboard, chalk, marbles, jump rope, hickory switch, dunce cap, lunch box, apple, quill, ink well.
- Make large paper red apple nametags. There is a template for this at the end of this week's session plan.
- Suggest that helpers wear old fashioned blouses.
- Make generic report cards with large "A+" on the outside and "student of life" inside. A template for this is included at the end of this week's session plan.
- Locate music to "A - You're Adorable."

Pre-Session: Pianist plays music "School Days," "Long Long Ago," and the "The Old Oaken Bucket."

Opening: Ring the school bell and announce the theme. Group singing of "School Days" softly the first time and proudly the second time. (A songsheet is included at the end of this week's session plan.)

Exercise: Pass out separate letters of the alphabet randomly or in order. Leader sings the "ABCD Alphabet Song" and each person holds up their respective letter as high as they can. Increase tempo second time.

Leader sings or recites this song with group responding with letters;

A - you're adorable, B- you're so beautiful, C - you're a cutie full of charms, D - you're a darling and E - you're exciting and F - you're a feather in my arms. G - you look good to me, H - you're so heavenly, I - you're the one I idolize, J - we're like Jack and Jill, K - you're so kissable, L - is the love light in your eyes. M-N-O-P I could go on all day. Q-R-S-T alphabetically speaking you're OK. U - made my life complete, V - means you're very sweet double-U-X-Y-Z. It's fun to wander through the alphabet with you to tell you what you mean to me. (1948)

Special
Recognition: Honor all teachers with a big red apple nametag announcing "I am a teacher" since one never stops teaching. Add a star to the apple of the person who taught the longest.

Reminiscence: Props decorate the room or else pull them from a box, such as chalk, chalkboard, eraser, marbles, book, lunch box. Ask residents questions such as these below to stimulate discussion.
- Did anyone attend a one-room school house?
- How did you get to school?

Reminiscence: • Was your schoolhouse red? (paint was cheaper)
(Cont.)   • Did you have a favorite teacher?
                       • How was the class disciplined?
                       • Did you ever give an apple to the teacher?

Special Activity: Create a school session. First pledge to the flag. Announce that today is a
                    review day in arithmetic, English, geography, history.

                    Arithmetic:
                       • How many zeros in a million? (6)
                       • How far is it to the sun? (93 million miles)
                       • How many in a baker's dozen? (13)
                       • How much is 6+6+3-2? (13)
                    English:
                       • What is a homonym? (Two words that sound the same, e.g. to/too)
                       • What is an adjective? (A word that modifies a noun, e.g. FAT cat)
                    Geography:
                       • Name the state capital of Illinois? (Springfield)
                       • Name the largest river in the US. (Mississippi)
                    History:
                       • What territory did T. Jefferson purchase to double the size of the US?
                         (Louisiana territory)
                       • What does the 'S' stand for in Truman's middle name? (Nothing)
                    Spelling:
                       • Spell Ohio - O-H-ten, Mississippi (M-I crooked letter).
                    Added quiz on foreign languages:
                       • What is *à la mode*? (Ice cream on top)
                       • What does *et cetera* mean? (And so on)
                       • What does *arrivederci* mean? (Goodbye, see you again)
                       • How about *e pluribus unum*? (Out of many, one. Motto of the US).

Education: • Students today study English, math, science, social studies, fine arts,
                      practical arts, gym and elective units.[1]
                    • In 1990, about 4% of the high school students dropped out of school in
                      America.[2]
                    • Now we find that people with more education live longer, have better jobs,
                      have less stress, are more engaged in life, and are receptive to new ideas.[3]
                    • People between the ages of 55 and 75 have the highest level of education
                      of any group in history. They are knowledge workers having moved from a
                      society of production of goods to one occupied with information and the
                      provision of services.[4]
                    • So keep on learning since education has so many benefits.

---

[1]   From a personal interview in 1990 with Keri Frost, a junior in the Kirkwood (MO) School District.
[2]   US Bureau of the Census Current *Population Report Series P.* No 409 p. 20.
[3]   *Futurist*, June 1984, p. 35. "Retirement to Re-Engagement" by M. Kouri.
[4]   *Next* May/June 1981, p. 8. "Living Longer" by R. Conniff.

Song
Identification: Name the teaching concept in each song:

> Alphabet Song (learning the alphabet)
> B-I-N-G-O (spelling)
> Do-Re-Mi (music notes)
> America (history)
> One Little, Two Little Indians (arithmetic)
> I'm Gonna Sit Right Down and Write Myself a Letter (writing)
> Dry Bones (biology)
> Jesus Loves You (Bible)
> School Days (reading, writing and arithmetic)
> London Bridge / A Tisket a Tasket (games)

Group Singing: "Golden Rule" song to the tune of the "Battle Hymn of the Republic"

> Leader: I do unto others as I'd have them do to me (2 times)
>   I do unto others as I'd have them to do me but I always do it first.

Group then sings with conviction.

Awards: Pianist plays Elgar's "Pomp and Circumstance March" while everyone receives a report card with an A+ for being a student of life.

Rhythm Band: "Pomp and Circumstance" — solid slow 2.
"B-I-N-G-O" — leader sings, group responds on letter part — 5 sounds.
"You're a Grand Old Flag" — stirring march. (A songsheet is included at the end of the MEMORABLE MEMORIAL DAY [May] weekly session plan.)
"School Days" — joyous 3 beat.

Closing: Singing of "Bless This House" with the realization that the facility is a place of learning every day to those who are curious. (A songsheet is included at the end of the THANKSGIVING [November] weekly session lpan.)

Assignment: Encourage residents to recall a teacher who was especially meaningful and mentally give him or her thanks. Then they might recall a lesson or truth that this special teacher imparted that is still important. Suggest they share this with others. Next week the theme is STYLES UP TO THE ANKLE so encourage all to wear their oldest clothing or jewelry.

Music
Resources:

> *Ultimate Fake Book* (1981)
>   "School Days" p. 481
> *Unforgettable Musical Moments* (1987)
>   "A-You're Adorable" p. 122
> *Wee Sing Silly Songs* (1984)
>   "Dry Bones" p. 14
> *Wee Sing Children's Songs and Fingerplays* (1986)
>   "B-I-N-G-O" p. 25
> *Great Music's Greatest Hits* (1982)
>   "Pomp and Circumstance" p. 229

SCHOOL DAYS SONGS

1. <u>School</u> Days
2. Songs My Mother <u>Taught</u> Me
3. I'd Like to <u>Teach</u> the World to Sing
4. <u>Alphabet</u> Song
5. <u>Do</u> - <u>Re</u> - <u>Mi</u>
6. <u>Inch</u>worm
7. Sweet Sixteen
8. Whiffenpoof Song
9. The Sweetheart of Sigma Chi
10. Collegiate
11. Pomp and Circumstance

And now it's time for music!

SCHOOL DAYS

When We Were A Couple Of Kids

Nothing to do, Nellie Darling
Nothing to do you say,
Let's take a trip on memory's ship,
Back to the bygone days
Sail to the old village schoolhouse,
Anchor outside the school door,
Look in and see,
there's you and there's me,
A couple of kids once more.

CHORUS:

Schoolday, schooldays,
dear old golden ruledays
Readin' and 'ritin' and 'rithmetic,
Taught to the tune of a hickry stick,
You were my queen in calico,
I was your bashful barefoot beau,
And you wrote on my slate,
I love you Joe,
When we were a couple of kids.

– Will D. Cobb (1907)

September "School Days"

brown stem   ⟶

green leaves   ⟶

red apple   ⟶

I AM A
TEACHER

I AM A
TEACHER

I AM A
TEACHER

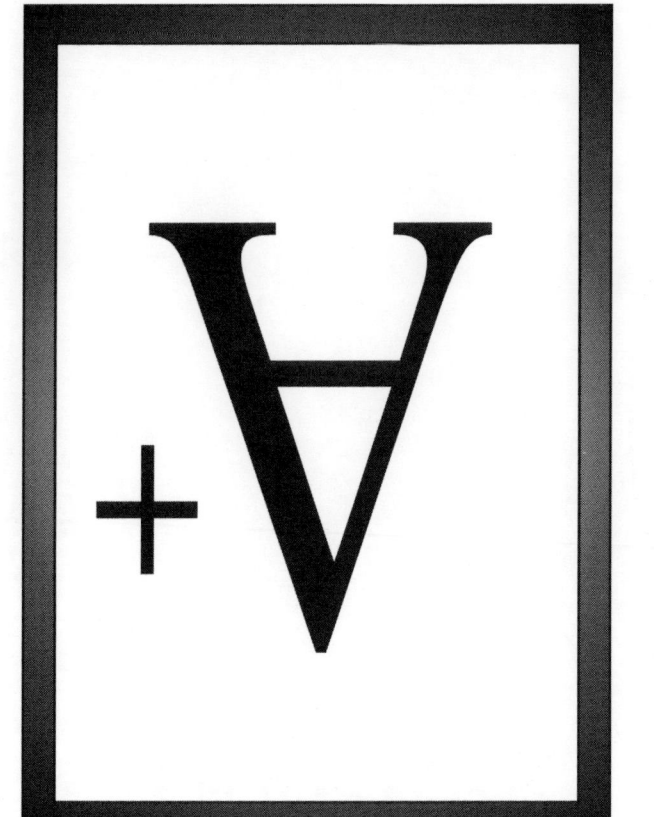

A
STUDENT
of
LIFE

September Theme — **OLD FASHIONED FAVORITES**

Today's Theme —   **Styles up to the Ankle**

Advanced
Preparation:
- Announce in the newspaper that everyone should wear their oldest clothes or antique jewelry.
- Prepare a collection of sheet music or pictures of old styles.
- Make smiling yellow paper plates.
- Make copies of the large print songsheet of "Five Foot Two, Eyes of Blue" which is included at the end of this week's session plan.

Pre-Session: Pianist plays "Oh You Beautiful Doll," "Five Foot Two, Eyes of Blue" "Pretty Baby," "Second Hand Rose," "You Must Have Been a Beautiful Baby." All helpers wear dated clothing.

Opening: Opening song of "Hail, Hail, the Gang's All Here."

> Hail, hail the gang's all here, never mind the weather,
> Here we are together, hail, hail the gang's all here,
> Let the music start RIGHT NOW.

Sing several times.

Exercise: Use the yellow smiling plates. Styles bring smiles.
Music:
"Pretty Baby" — wave plate side to side, change hands, both hands.
"Five Foot Two, Eyes of Blue" — count eight beats all together, music starts.
     Leader models actions — change every 8 measures.
     Fanning motion with both hands, push-pull both hands.
     Tap leg, tap head, be creative.
Finale — at the count of 3, pitch the plate at the leader.

Solo Time: To the tune of "Smiles" (origin unknown)

> There are styles up to the ankle,
> There are styles that show the knee.
> There are styles that make the people wonder
> What the women want the men to see.
> There are styles that have a naughty meaning,
> That the eyes of men alone may see.
> But the styles that Eve wore in the garden
> Are the styles that appeal to me.

Group Singing: "Five Foot Two, Eyes of Blue" — use large print songsheets.

Reminiscence: Pass out song covers or pictures of styles to increase memory and associations. Ask the residents the following questions:

Reminiscence: (Cont.)	• Did you or your mother *ever* sew? • Did you make something you didn't like or else simply loved? • Talk about fabrics used including flour sacks. • Did parents *ever* make you change clothes? • Discuss these styles: bustle, leg-o-mutton sleeves, galoshes, union suit, leggings, Gibson girl look, turned-down hose, argyle socks, middy blouse, bobbed hair, knickers, removable men's collars, cloche hat, slicker, raccoon coat, parasol, gloves. There is no need to cover all topics so allow time for a well paced discussion.

Special Activity: Everyone has a chance to model or explain the old clothes they are wearing. Make it a mini fashion show.

Education:

• Styles for senior citizens are classic, not matronly.
• 2-piece dresses and jackets are versatile.
• 1990s fashion for seniors will be tailored pants, tunic tops, tailored skirts with elastic waistbands and overblouses in soft comfortable fabrics.
• Leather shoes will be less popular. Canvas cloth shoes, like today's athletic shoes will be available in flats and heels for greater comfort. They are ideal for tourists and women who stand on their feet a lot.[1]

Song Identification: These songs contain styles or articles of clothing.

> BUTTONS and BOWS
> Alice Blue GOWN
> Easter Parade (in your Easter BONNET)
> BUTTON up your OVERCOAT
> School Days (queen in CALICO)*
> Dance with a Dolly with a Hole in Her STOCKING
> Second Hand Rose (wears SECOND HAND CLOTHES)
> All of God's Children Got SHOES (Mary Jane's?)
> BELL BOTTOM TROUSERS
> STRING OF PEARLS
> Itsy Bitsy Teenie Weenie Yellow Polka Dot BIKINI.

* A songsheet is included at the end of the DEAR OLD SCHOOL DAYS [September] weekly session plan.

Rhythm Band: "Alice Blue Gown" — everyone play softly, waltz tempo.

"The Blue Danube Waltz" — pianist plays opening bars, rhythm band responds with afterbeats. Example: Piano plays "Danube so blue" — answered by "ding dong, ding dong." At the conclusion instruct when they should all play in unison 3/4 time. This takes concentration and cooperation.

---

[1] All points in the Education section from *West County Journal* (St. Louis), July 12, 1989, p. C3. "Senior Styles Classic, Not Matronly" by Carter Osborne.

Rhythm Band: (Cont.)	"Oh Them Golden Slippers" — peppy 2/4 tempo, tap feet at the same time, exaggerate.
	"Smiles" — all play joyously, smiling over all the styles they've known. (A songhseet is included at the end of the EVERYONE LOVES A SMILE [February] weekly session plan.)

Closing:

Decide on a style that everyone is glad is extinct. To the tune of "Goodnight Ladies" sing your own version such as:

Goodbye flappers, goodbye flappers, goodbye flappers,
We're glad that you have gone.
Merrily we sing along, sing along, sing along,
Merrily we sing along, we sing our silly song.

Assignment:

Enjoy recalling some of those humorous styles as well as some of the favorite ones. Talk about them with each other and be sure and tell the grandchildren what they missed. Next week's theme is GIVE ME THAT OLD TIME RELIGION. Your assignment is to recall a song from your church that you still love.

Music
Resources:

Treasury of Best Loved Songs (1981)
    "Five Foot Two, Eyes of Blue" p. 122
    "Alice Blue Gown" p. 204
Family Song book of Faith and Joy (1981)
    "Pretty Baby" p. 28
    "You Must Have Been a Beautiful Baby" p. 138
    "Smiles" p. 34
One Thousand and One Jumbo (1985)
    "Oh Them Golden Slippers" p. 252
    "Bell Bottom Trousers" p. 374
    "Itsy Bitsy Teenie Weenie Yellow Polka Dot Bikini" p. 73

MUSIC MENU

STYLES
STYLES
STYLES
STYLES

1. *OH YOU BEAUTIFUL DOLL*

2. *BELL BOTTOM TROUSERS*

3. *ALICE BLUE GOWN*

4. *BUTTONS & BOWS*

5. *SECOND HAND ROSE*

6. *PUT ON YOUR OLD GREY BONNET*

7. *FIVE FOOT TWO, EYES OF BLUE*

8. *PRETTY BABY*

9. *DANCE WITH A DOLLY*

10. *SCHOOL DAYS (CALICO)*

11. *ITSY BITSY TEENIE WEENIE*
YELLOW POLKA DOT BIKINI

12. *BUTTON UP YOUR OVERCOAT*

TELL ME YOUR FAVORITE SONG

FIVE FOOT TWO, EYES OF BLUE

FIVE FOOT TWO, EYES OF BLUE
BUT OH WHAT THOSE FIVE FOOT COULD DO!
HAS ANYBODY SEEN MY GAL?

TURNED UP NOSE, TURNED DOWN HOSE
FLAPPER? YES SIR, ONE OF THOSE.
HAS ANYBODY SEEN MY GAL?

NOW IF YOU RUN INTO A FIVE FOOT TWO
COVERED WITH FUR,
DIAMOND RINGS AND ALL THOSE THINGS,
BETCHA LIFE IT ISN'T HER!

BUT COULD SHE LOVE, COULD SHE WOO,
COULD SHE, COULD SHE, COULD SHE COO!
HAS ANYBODY SEEN MY GAL?

– Sam M. Lewis (1925)

September Theme — **OLD FASHIONED FAVORITES**

Today's Theme — **Give Me That Old Time Religion**

Advanced
Preparation:
- Make nametags in the shape of a church and have "I taught Sunday School" and "I Taught Religion" written on them. A template for this is included at the end of this week's session plan.
- Aides/volunteers will need tape to attach the nametags to the residents.
- Organize a string soloist to perform at Solo Time.
- Gather a collection of Sunday School songs, Jewish songs, and songs of any other specific religions that are represented.
- Try and obtain a pump organ or use the organ voice on a Casio piano.

Pre-Session: Pianist plays "The Little Brown Church," "Give Me That Old Time Religion," and "Onward Christian Soldiers."

Opening: Open with the song "He's Got the Whole World in His Hands." Clap hands while singing:
Verse:
1. He's got the whole world in His hands..
2. He's got all the ladies......etc.
3. He's got all the gentlemen..... etc.

Exercise: Continue with the opening song adding exercise:
4. He's got all the nurses...... (sway side to side)
5. He's got all the visitors...... (wave wildly)
6. He's got all the staff...... (both hands up high and sway)
7. He's got everybody....... (arms out and in)

Group Singing: "Give Me That Old Time Religion" — teach by rote.
Give me that old time religion (sung 3 times)
It's good enough for me.
It was good for our mothers, it was good for our fathers
It was good for our mothers, and it's good enough for me.
(Repeat first two lines)

"Swing Low, Sweet Chariot" — 2 parts, so divide the group in half.
'A' group sings the traditional melody led by a leader.
'B' group sings simple bass line over and over with it's leader.

SWING LOW, SWEET CHARIOT

African-American Spiritual

Ostinato sings this continually.

Swing low char-i-ot, swing low char-i-ot.   Swing low sweet char-i-ot.

"Zum Gali, Gali" — 2 parts, add new words.
'A' group sings "Zum gali, gali, gali, zum gali, gali.
'B' group sings " Let us face each day with cheer
                            Without fret or frown or fear."

"The Little Brown Church" — group singing.
Ask if anyone went to a brown church? In a vale?

Solo Time: Violin, viola, or cello solo of "Kol Nidre," "You'll Never Walk Alone," "Let
                          There Be Peace on Earth," or the Jewish national anthem ("Rock of Ages").
                          Play both Christian and Jewish melodies and stress their beauty through the
                          ages.

Reminiscence: With closed eyes, concentrate on your old church and review any memories.
                          Recall any sermons or baptisms. Talk about revivals, Sunday Schools, and
                          singing. Remember church socials. Ask the residents if anyone had a woman
                          in the pulpit.

Education: • What do Americans have more confidence in? 59% said religious
                            institutions. The next strongest was the military at 58% according to a
                            Gallup Poll. The Supreme Court ranked third with a 56% level of trust.[1]
                          • In 1990, 7 out of 10 people belonged to a church, and Americans favored
                            public schools offering a variety of religious studies in school. 94% believed
                            in a higher power known as God or Spirit, and 71% believed in life after
                            death and the number is steadily growing[2]
                          • The Bible is the most widely read book in America.[3]

Special
Recognition: Honor all Sunday School teachers or religious leaders of any faith with the
                          nametag that states "I was a Sunday School teacher" or "I Taught Religion" if
                          that is more appropriate. Suggest they wear it proudly all day long.

Song
Identification: These are familiar religious songs so encourage residents to sing along.

                              Jesus Wants me for a Sunbeam
                              When the Roll is Called up Yonder *
                              Onward Christian Soldiers
                              Rock of Ages (2 versions, Christian and Jewish)
                              Jesus Loves Me
                              This Little Light of Mine
                              Amazing Grace
                              Give Me That Old Time Religion
                          Take any requests.

                          *   A songsheet is included at the end o fthe THE SMELLS OF CHRISTMAS [December] weekly
                               session plan.

1   *Gallup Poll Monthly*, December 1988, #279, p. 31. "Confidence in Institutions."
2   *Gallup Poll Monthly*, June 1990, #297, p. 33. "More Americans Now Believe in a Power Outside Themselves."
3   *Gallup Poll Monthly*, November 1990, # 302, p. 39. "The Bible is Still Widely Read and Studied."

Rhythm Band: "The Little Brown Church" — sing and play.
               "When the Saints Go Marching In" — using rhythm instruments:
                   When the BELLS go chiming in
                   When the SHAKERS go shaking in. etc.
               "Give Me That Old Time Religion" — joyfully celebrate with instruments.
               "Hava Nagila" — watch the tempo changes.
               "Battle Hymn of the Republic" — sing and celebrate.

Closing: Thank everyone for contributing by recalling their religious heritage. Close with the song "Shalom."

               Shalom my friends, shalom my friends, shalom, shalom.
               Till we meet again, tell we meet again, shalom, shalom.

               Shake each hand as you sing, encouraging all to join in or at least say "Shalom" to each other.

Assignment: Enjoy the memories of your own religion and also realize that today's program honored all religions. Abraham Lincoln said "Whatever you are, be a good one."[1] Keep your mind and heart open to the spiritual values of all faiths. Seek and ye will find.

Music
Resources: *Ultimate Fake Book* (1981)
                   "Give Me That Old Time Religion" p. 181
                   "Zum Gali, Gali" p. 669
               Wee Sing Bible Songs (1986)
                   "He's Got the Whole World In His Hands" p. 41
               Family Song Book of Faith of Joy (1981)
                   "When the Roll Is Called Up Yonder" p. 144
                   "When the Saints Go Marching In" p. 240
                   "The Little Brown Church" p. 162
               Wee Sing Around the Campfire (1984)
                   "Swing Low, Sweet Chariot" p. 30
               One Thousand and One Jumbo (1985)
                   "Hava Nagila" p. 431
               Tune Book Songs (1982)
                   "Shalom" p. 150a
               Jewish Folk and Holiday Songs (1978)
                   "Rock of Ages" p. 14
               Song Session Community Song Book (1958)
                   "Rock of Ages" p. 106

---

[1]   Safire, W. and L. Safir (1982) *Good Advice*, p. 291.

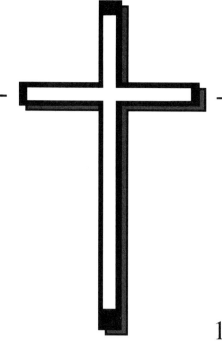

Music Menu

Give Me That *Olde Time Religion*

1. AMAZING GRACE

2. HAVA NAGILA

3. DEEP RIVER

4. SHALOM CHAVERIM

5. JESUS LOVES ME

6. HATIKVAH - NATIONAL ANTHEM

7. SWING LOW, SWEET CHARIOT

8. HIS EYE IS ON THE SPARROW

9. JUST A CLOSER WALK WITH THEE

10. JOSHUA FIT DE BATTLE OF JERICHO

11. THE LITTLE BROWN CHURCH

12. LET THERE BE PEACE ON EARTH
    (AND LET IT BEGIN WITH ME)

 Request the one you love.

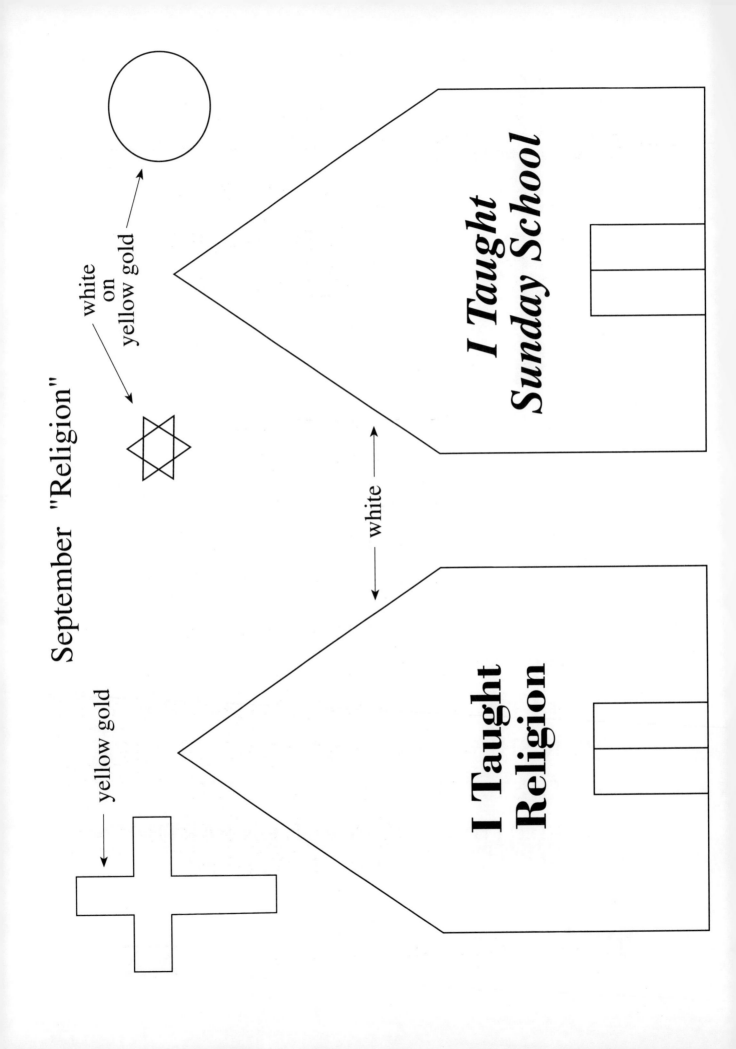

September "Religion"

yellow gold

white on yellow gold

white

I Taught Sunday School

I Taught Religion

September Theme — **OLD FASHIONED FAVORITES**

Today's Theme — **You Auto Remember Your Automobile**

Advanced
Preparation:
- Make enough copies of the large print songhseet of "In My Merry Oldsmobile" is included at the end of this week's session plan.
- Organize a vocal soloist for car song.
- Prepare a collection of songs about transportation.
- Decorate the room with pictures of automobiles.
- Invite someone with an old car to park it outside.
- Prepare one blue ribbon of paper or fabric.

Pre-Session: Pianist plays car songs such as "See the USA in Your Chevrolet," and "In My Merry Oldsmobile." (The music to "See the USA in Your Chevrolet" is included on page 348.)

Opening: Sing an adapted round as follows:
1. Sing "Row, Row, Row Your Boat" in unison.
2. Teach new words to this melody:
    Start, start, start your car
    Start it with a crank.
    Merrily, merrily, merrily, merrily,
    There's gas inside the tank.
3. Add some motions of cranking it up and driving.
4. Sing it as a two-part round using two leaders up front.

Exercise: These exercises are done to "In My Merry Oldsmobile" music.
1. Cranking up the motor.
2. Driving the steering wheel — exaggerate wheel motions.
3. Bumpy road conditions — exercise shoulders.
4. Flat tire — pump hand down to imitate a jack.
5. Waiting for a bus — sit motionless and smile.

Education:
- AAA Club of Missouri forecasts that in the future all states will have re-testing around age 75 to 80 for license renewal. Presently there is no age limit. This test will require a road exam, written test, and eye test. Some states already have these tests at different ages.[1]
- US Big 3 car manufacturers are General Motors, Ford, and Chrysler who have the largest car markets in the world. GM is the largest and Ford is the strongest.[2]
- Imports Honda and Toyota are reliable cars purchased by Americans. To meet this competition, the US is building better cars now that are safer, with higher performance and durability according to Consumer Reports in 1992.[3]

---

[1] Personal interview with Mike Right, Director of Public Affairs, AAA Club of Missouri on October 5, 1992.
[2] *Maclean,* August 1, 1988, p. 26. "Car Wars 1988" by T Fennell.
[3] *Consumer Reports*, April 1992, 57(4):210. "The 1992 Cars."

Solo Time: Sung or recited — song of 1928 by Clarence Gaskill:

I'm wild about horns on automobiles that go ta-ta-ta-ta-ta-ta-tah.
I used to own a Model A, I got it from a guy named Ray
And every time it started up it sounded like this Hey, Hey.
I'm a nut, I'm a pest but the one that I love best
I'm wild about horns on automobiles that go Whaaaaaaaa, oooga ooga.

or

Stephen got even, he really go even when he sold his automobile
He took his boat and then he set out to see
To find a little girlie who would sit on his knee
Oh, oh the boat started chugging and he started hugging
And those wild waves they did rolllllllllll.
Steven sure got even when he sold his fliver,
There never was a girlie who could walk the river.
Stephen got even, he really got even when he sold his automobile.

Group Singing: "In My Merry Oldsmobile" and "See the USA in Your Chevrolet." Use large print songsheet of "In My Merry Oldsmobile" provided.

Special Activity: Enjoy making the sound of an "Oog ha" automobile. Turn this into a contest. Winner receives a big blue ribbon.

Guided Imagery: Encourage everyone to close their eyes, and lead a brief relaxation exercise. Slowly play "In My Merry Oldsmobile" as background music as they recall any old car from their memory bank. With eyes opened, proceed to the next part of the program.

Reminiscence: Find out if anyone remembered an old car that they hadn't thought about in years. Name of car, color, or model can be mentioned. Ask a few questions to stimulate the memory:
- How smooth was the ride?
- Did it have a rumble seat?
- How much did the car cost?
- What was the price of gas then?
- What ever happened to it?

Song
Identification: Cars are only one mode of transportation. The following song titles suggest other ways of getting places:

Daisy Bell (a BICYCLE built for two)
The SKATERS (Waltz)
On the Atchison, Topeka, and the Santa Fe (RAILROAD)
The SURREY With the Fringe on Top
I'm Out to Get You on a SLOWBOAT to China
Come, Josephine, in my FLYING MACHINE

Song
Identification: Darktown Strutters' Ball (I'll be down to get you in a TAXI)
(Cont.) The Wheels on the BUS Go Round and Round
WALKIN' my Baby Back Home

Rhythm Band: "Daisy Bell" — strong beat to unify group
"Coming Round the Mountain" — echo/response activity. (The music to this
    is included on page 457, adapted to fit "I Feel The Christmas Spirit".)
    She'll be playing silver bells when she comes — bells only
    She'll be playing wooden sticks..... continue with others.
    She'll be hearing everybody..... all play.
"The Skaters (Waltz)" — easy 3 beat.
"On the Atchison, Topeka, and the Santa Fe" — crisp short sounds.
"Darktown Strutters Ball" — jive.

Closing: Give thanks for the world of wheels including wheelchairs. Transportation
includes walkers, legs and encouragement from physical therapists plus will
power. Close by singing "Bless This House" keeping this all in mind. (A
songsheet is included at the end of the THANKSGIVING [November] weekly
session plan.)

Music
Resources: *Family Song Book of Faith and Joy* (1981)
    "In My Merry Oldsmobile" p. 194
Great Music's Greatest Hits (1982)
    "The Skaters (Waltz)" p. 45
Popular Songs That Live Forever (1982)
    "Darktown Strutters' Ball" p. 230
Ultimate Fake Book (1981)
    "The Surrey with a Fringe On Top" p. 536
T.V. Theme Song Sing-Along Song Book (1984)
    "See the USA in Your Chevrolet" p. 28
Legit Fake Book (1990)
    "On the Atchison, Topeka, and the Santa Fe" p. 260
All American Song Book (1984)
    "Daisy Bell" p. 141
"Stephen Got Even" and "I'm Wild about Horns" — no longer in print but ask
anyone over 60!

SEE THE U.S.A. IN YOUR CHEVROLET

Leon Carr and Leo Corday

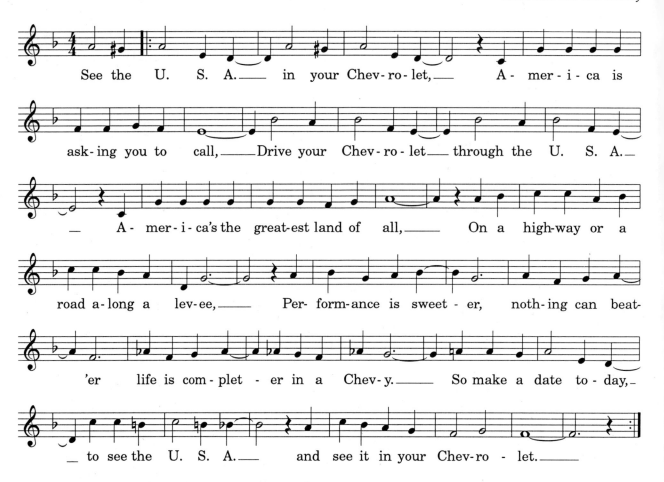

See the U. S. A.___ in your Chev-ro-let,___ A-mer-i-ca is ask-ing you to call,___Drive your Chev-ro-let__ through the U. S. A.___ A-mer-i-ca's the great-est land of all,___ On a high-way or a road a-long a lev-ee,___ Per-form-ance is sweet-er, noth-ing can beat-'er life is com-plet-er in a Chev-y.___ So make a date to-day,__ to see the U. S. A.___ and see it in your Chev-ro-let.___

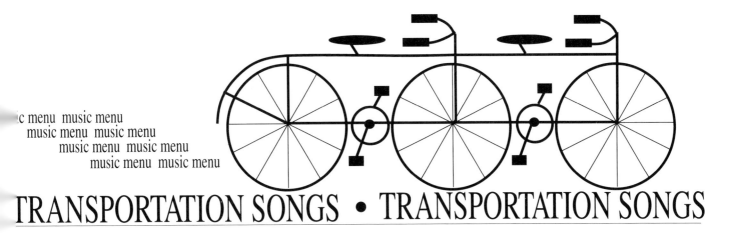

c menu music menu
music menu music menu
music menu music menu
music menu music menu

TRANSPORTATION SONGS • TRANSPORTATION SONGS

1. DAISY BELL (BICYCLE BUILT FOR TWO)

2. THE SKATERS (WALTZ)

3. ON THE ATCHISON, TOPEKA, AND THE SANTA FE

4. THE SURREY WITH THE FRINGE ON TOP

5. RED SAILS IN THE SUNSET

6. COME, JOSEPHINE, IN MY FLYING MACHINE

7. IN MY MERRY OLDSMOBILE

8. THE TROLLEY SONG

9. WAIT FOR THE WAGON

10. I'VE BEEN WORKING ON THE RAILROAD

11. WHILE STROLLING THROUGH THE PARK ONE DAY

12. SEE THE U.S.A. IN YOUR CHEVROLET

Tell me your favorite way to go, I'll play it!

In My Merry Oldsmobile

Come away with me, Lucille,

In my merry Oldsmobile.

Down the road of life we'll fly,

Automobiling, you and I.

To the church we'll swiftly steal

Then our wedding bells will peal.

You can go as far as you like with me

In my merry oldsmobile.

- Vincent P. Bryan (1905)

September Theme — **OLD FASHIONED FAVORITES**

Today's Theme — **Ragtime Review**
(Optional)

Advanced
Preparation:
- Commit a ragtime pianist.
- Encourage aides to wear vintage clothing.
- Find some old Ragtime sheet music covers.
- Prepare a large songsheet of "Hello! Ma Baby" which is included at the end of this week's session plan.
- Provide paper and pencils for interviewing.

Pre-Session: Pianist plays or recording of ragtime music is played as residents enter.

Opening: Group singing of "Hello! Ma Baby." Encourage them to greet each other with a hearty "Hello."

Exercise: Leader demonstrates simple wrist exercise to the music of Scott Joplin's "The Entertainer," Flap left wrist 8 times, flap right wrist 8 times, clap hands 8 times, fling arms out and clap 8 times.

Education:
- Ragtime existed in spirit before 1900. It was leisure time music for the slaves. They had no instruments but their heels and hands.
- The piano was the instrument most often heard and the popularity was in saloons. Compositions featured a basic, straight rhythm in one hand and a syncopation in the other so that the music always had energy in it.[1]
- The American Federation of Musicians passed a resolution to suppress and discourage such music in 1901.[2]
- At the World's Fair of 1904 in St. Louis, John Phillip Sousa declared "Ragtime is an established feature of American music, it will never die."[3]
- The fad grew and children enjoyed taking lessons learning how to rag any tune. Ragtime was popular in Europe. The most famous ragtime composer was Scott Joplin and today such music can be heard in fancy concert halls, park programs and high school orchestras. It was displaced by jazz and vocal blues.[4]
- Edward Berlin, the author of *Ragtime* says: "Whatever the fate of Ragtime music, whether it remains in the public focus or again recedes to historical obscurity, it leaves a legacy of rhythmic vitality."[5]

Solo Time: Ragtime pianist demonstrates different styles of rags by Scott Joplin for both education and enjoyment.

Waltz — "Bethena" — a concert waltz (1905)
March and two step — "Cleopha" (1902)

---

[1] Berlin, E. (1980) *Ragtime*, pp. 21, 22.
[2] Blesh and Janis (1971). *The **All** Played Ragtime*, p. 135.
[3] Berlin, E. (1980) *Ragtime*, p. 49.
[4] Schafer, W. and J. Riedel (1974) *The Art of Ragtime*, p. 44.
[5] Berlin, E. (1980) *Ragtime*, p. 196.

Solo Time: Mexican slow rag — "Solace" used in the movie *The Sting* (1909)
(Cont.)   Dance with Words — "Pine Apple Rag" (1908)
                    Stomp — "Rag-Time Dance" — a stoptime two step. All participate with a
                        clap. Use a leader.
                    Demonstration — how to rag any tune.

Reminiscence/
Interviews/Group
Discussion: Aides should also interview individually and write down names and reactions
                    for the local monthly news or separate publication. Ask questions like the
                    following ones to stimulate group discussion:
                    • What memories does anyone recall with ragtime music?
                    • Where did your first hear it?
                    • How does it make you feel?
                    • Does anyone not like ragtime?
                    • Were you allowed to dance to this music?
                    • Is it an important part of American Music?
                    • Do you have a favorite rag?

Visual Aid: Circulate old sheet music or covers of ragtime music. These artistic covers
                    stimulate much conversation. Slide projector could be considered. Pianist can
                    play a rag softly in the background.

Song
Identification: Name the following songs with ragtime in them:

                        Alexander's Ragtime Band
                        Twelfth Street Rag
                        Hello! Ma Baby
                        Ragtime Cowboy Joe
                        Darktown Strutters' Ball
                        Waiting for the Robert E. Lee
                        Golliwog's Cakewalk (Debussy)
                        That International Rag
                        Maple Leaf Rag

Rhythm Band: "Alexander's Ragtime Band" — everyone play.
                    "The Entertainer" — two leaders needed:
                        First two measures half the room plays;
                        Next two measures, the other half responds.
                        Repeat 3 times and all play together on last 4 bars.
                        This pattern can be used throughout the entire rag.
                    "Waiting for the Robert E. Lee" — not too fast, all play.
                    "Hello! Ma Baby" — with instruments, vocalist and banjo.

Closing: All sing "God Bless America" in honor of the land of ragtime.

Assignment: Enjoy your memories of the ragtime era and realize that is is a part of one's heritage. The assignment is to ask the grandchildren if they are familiar with ragtime. Introduce them to it since you are well versed in its rhythms.

Music
Resources:

Collected Piano Works of Scott Joplin (1972)
     "Maple Leaf Rag" p. 25
     "Bethena" p. 113
     "Cleopha" p. 47
     "Pine Apple Rag" p. 175
     "Stoptime Rag" p. 221
     "Solace" p. 185
Family Song Book of Faith and Joy (1981)
     "Hello! Ma Baby" p. 190
Legit Fake Book (1990)
     "Ragtime Cowboy Joe" p. 286
     "Darktown Strutters' Ball" p. 72
Popular Songs That Live Forever (1982)
     "Twelfth Street Rag" p. 244

MUSIC MENU

1. THE ENTERTAINER

2. TWELFTH STREET RAG

3. DILL PICKLES

4. WAITING FOR THE ROBERT E. LEE

5. ALEXANDER'S RAGTIME BAND

6. RAGTIME COWBOY JOE

7. ST. LOUIS TICKLE

8. THAT INTERNATIONAL RAG

9. GOLLIWOG'S CAKEWALK

10. MAPLE LEAF RAG

11. "REQUEST ANY RAG"

WHICH ONE DO YOU LIKE?

SONGSHEET

HELLO! MA BABY

HELLO, MY BABY, HELLO MY HONEY

HELLO, MY RAGTIME GAL

SEND ME A KISS BY WIRE

BABY, MY HEART'S ON FIRE

IF YOU REFUSE ME,

HONEY YOU'LL LOSE ME

THEN, YOU'LL BE LEFT ALONE

OH, BABY, TELEPHONE

AND TELL ME I'M YOUR OWN

HELLO, HELLO, HELLO THERE

– Ida Emerson & Joseph Howard (1889)

October

HEALTH IS CONTAGIOUS !

an apple a day

HEALTH
IS
CONTAGIOUS
Musical Game

This is the perfect month to praise your wonderful body even if parts of it don't work perfectly. It is time to praise your original parts as well as the replacements due to modern medicine. The following songs all have body parts in the title and are worth praising. You can draw a line to the corresponding part. Good luck. The answers are upside down.

1. I'm Gonna Wash that Man Right Outa My _____

2. When Irish _____ are Smiling

3. He's Got the Whole World in His _____

4. Tip _____ Through the Tu___

5. Five _____ Two, _____ of Blue

6. Peg o' My _____

7. Baby _____

8. Raindrops Keep Falling on My _____

9. Nobody _____ the Trouble I've Seen (a pun)

10. Full Moon and Empty _____

11. I Love _____ Truly

ANSWERS: 1. Hair 2. Eyes 3. Hands 4. Toe, lips 5. Foot, Eyes 6. Heart 7. Face 8. Head 9. Nose 10. Arms 11. You, You are worth praising!

HEALTH IS CONTAGIOUS
OCTOBER

Start this month with a large sign proclaiming the fact that health is contagious. Health, good cheer, optimism, and energy all spread quickly throughout the facility when family, friends, staff and residents all take this attitude. Everyone will be affected by this theme with good results.

Note that Halloween is programmed as a happy experience. Several of the songs are introduced the week preceding the holiday so that familiarity adds to the success of the Halloween program

Healthy Food — Dear to every stomach is this subject. One can enjoy the facts of aging regarding foods and eat heartily and sensibly. This is the big day for the dietician.

Healthy Hands — Older hands represent both years of work and caring. Emphasize gratitude for the years of service as well as the activities that they can presently do, even if limited.

Healthy Hearts — Everyone with a heart is invited to this program. This is a time of celebration of life and love.

Healthy Bones — Where else would we hang our clothes? This program precedes Halloween with its skeleton, however, the skeleton has a cute face and everyone sings "Them Bones, Them Bones, Them Strong Bones" as a way of increasing awareness of the effect of positive words regarding health.

Healthy Fun — The benefits of laughter have been proven to improve one's health. Laughter is contagious. This program will have everyone feeling better. Anyone depressed is especially welcomed for a health treatment.

OPTIONAL PROGRAM

A Healthy Halloween — Health, laughter, fun, and active bones, hands and hearts combine for a grand finale for this month in the Halloween program. It is more beneficial than "trick or treating."

YOU'VE CAUGHT THE HEALTH BUG

NOW SPREAD THE GERM OF THE IDEA

October Theme —   **HEALTH IS CONTAGIOUS**

Today's Theme —   **Healthy Food**

Advanced
Preparation:
- Get the dietician involved, helping to provide a few healthy foods.
- Provide napkins.
- Collect related songs about various foods.
- Make some large fruit nametags for volunteers. A template is included at the end of this week's session plan.

Pre-Session: Pianist plays "Yes! We Have No Bananas," "Ida, Sweet as Apple Cider," "Give Me the Simple Life" (You say tomatoes, I say tomatoes), and "Oats, Peas, Beans and Barley Grow." Aides wear nametags of various fruits.

Opening: Announce the theme that HEALTH IS CONTAGIOUS and that everyone attending will feel better while healthy thoughts are shared and spread during the next hour. Opening song sung to the tune of "We Wish You a Merry Christmas," Point to each other while singing.

> I wish you a healthy autumn, I wish you a healthy autumn,
> I wish you a healthy autumn and a happy today.

Second song in praise of food that has contributed greatly towards one's health — sing in unison. (Note how it descends down the scale.) The music is included on page 364.

> For health and strength and daily food we give thee thanks, oh Lord.
> ("Oh Lord" or else change to "right now.")

Using two leaders, sing as a round.

Exercise: Food give us the energy to do the Hokey-Pokey:
1. You put your right hand in, you take your right hand out,
   You put your right hand in and you shake it all about.
   You do the Hokey-Pokey (hands above head and sway)
   While you sing and shout
   "That's what it's all about."
2. You put your left hand in.......
3. You put both hands in....
4. You put your feet in.....

Other verse suggestion: shoulders, neck, and head. Pace this according to the group level that day. Do not overdo.

Solo Time: This is the dietician's big opportunity to address their residents with the facts of food life. Address the changes in taste that come about with medication, aging, and appetite.

Education:
Residents can individually read the facts to the group:
- Water is the most important nutrient in the diet. Average adult contains 45 quarts of water in the body. Drink 6-8 glasses a day, especially between meals, for transportation of nutrients.
- Carbohydrates are the most important source of energy. They fuel our muscles, brain tissue, and nervous system so eat whole grain foods, barley, rice, fruits and vegetables including the skins.
- Fats provide insulation for the body but too much causes fatty deposits on the walls of the arteries and increase chances of a heart attack. Fats should compile 30% of your daily calories.
- Protein builds muscles and repairs cells. Renew daily with meat, dairy products, fish, eggs, and dried beans.
- Minerals and fiber are still important to aid blood clotting, keep bones strong, regulate the heart, prevent cancer and arteriosclerosis.
- Fewer calories are needed as we age.
- Slow down, chew carefully, taste and enjoy what you eat.
- Decrease in food intake and energy is common over age 70.[1]
- Drugs can decrease food intake by depressing appetite, taste, smell. Some drugs can stimulate appetite.[2]

Special Activity:
Refreshment such as a fruit platter can be served with the realization that as one slowly eats the food and deeply appreciates its value, it not only tastes better but is beneficial to the body.

Reminiscence:
While everyone is savoring a simple food, discuss the foods mother or dad felt were important to your health. Recall foods that were given as folk remedies such as castor oil, garlic, and others. This chant can be used for rhythmic activity and memory recall. Chant as a group or chant individually as you shake a hand and await their reply.

> Good food makes you feel so fine
> Tell me one that's on your mind.

Group Singing:
"Sippin' Cider Thru a Straw" as an echo response song (1919)

Verse 1:

Leader	The prettiest girl
Response	THE PRETTIEST GIRL
Leader	I ever saw
Response	I EVER SAW
Leader	Was sippin' ci-
Response	WAS SIPPIN' CI-
Leader	Der thru a straw
Response	DER THRU A STRAW

Continue with the following verses, the responses simply echoing exactly what the leader says.

---

[1] Points 1-8 in the Education section from Porcino, J. (1984) *Growing Older, Getting Better,* p. 206-223.

[2] Whitfield, P. (1984) *Hearing, Taste and Smell,* pp. 64-85.

Group Singing: Verse 2:
(Cont.)   Leader   I told that girl
                          I didn't see how
                          she sipped that cider
                          Thru a straw

                 Verse 3:
                 Leader   And cheek to cheek
                          And jaw to jaw
                          We sipped that cider
                          Thru a straw.

                 Verse 4:
                 Leader   And now I've got
                          Me a mother-in-law
                          From sippin' cider
                          Thru a straw.

Song
Identification: Recall the food mentioned in the song title:

Billy Boy (Can She Bake a CHERRY PIE?)   Yes! We Have no BANANAS*
In the Shade of the old APPLE Tree   HOT CROSS BUNS
Don't Sit Under the APPLE Tree   Ida, Sweet as APPLE CIDER
Put Your Arms Around Me, HONEY   TURKEY in the Straw
12 Days of Christmas (partridge) (pear)   GOOBER PEAS
LETTUCE Fall in Love (pun - Let us)   EGGSactly Like You
MEAT me in St. Louis, Louis
       (pun - Meet)
Coming Round the Mountain (chicken dumplings, now chocolate pizza)
Take Me Out to the Ball Game (Buy me some PEANUTS and CRACKERJACK)

* Songsheet included at the end of the HOW'S YOUR TASTE, BUD [April] weekly session plan.

Rhythm Band: "Turkey in the Straw" — slow and deliberate. The second time speed up. (A
                 songsheet is included at the end of the LET'S ALL SING LIKE THE BIRDIES
                 SING [May] weekly session plan.)
                 "Shortnin' Bread" — Softly except on the words 'Shortnin' Bread' every time.
                 "Billy Boy" (Can She Bake a Cherry Pie?) — play merrily at a fast tempo.
                 "Take Me Out to the Ball Game" — strongly on "1, 2, 3 strikes you're out."
                 End with all instruments celebrating with sound.

Closing: Teach a new song "I Feel Wonderful" with the fact that perhaps all parts of
                 the body don't feel ideal but many parts still are worth praising. Sing several
                 times. The music is included on page 364.
                 1. I feel wonderful, I feel wonderful, for this is a glorious day
                     I feel wonderful, I feel wonderful, and I'm going to STAY THAT WAY
                 2. YOU feel wonderful — point to each other.
                 3. WE feel wonderful — arms up in the air.

Assignment: Enjoy recalling the many delicious foods and chose two that are particular favorites. Then decide if they are healthy ones. Next week the theme is HEALTHY HANDS. Imagine the fun ahead.

Music
Resources: *Mitch Miller Community Song Book* (1962)
                   "Shortnin' Bread" p. 20
               One Thousand and One Jumbo (1985)
                   "Sippin' Cider Thru a Straw" p. 543
               Wings of Song (1984)
                   "I Feel Wonderful" p. 343
               Popular Songs That Live Forever (1982)
                   "Take Me Out to the Ball Game" p. 222
               Children's Song Book (1988)
                   "Billy Boy" (Can She Bake a Cherry Pie?) p. 220
                   "The Hokey-Pokey" p. 204
               Sing Together 3rd Edition (1973)[1]
                   "For Health and Strength" p. 175

---

[1] This round is reproduced in *Sing Together* from *Graded Rounds and Catches*. J. Curwen & Sons Ltd. used by permission of G. Schirmer, Inc.

I FEEL WONDERFUL

Charles King
adapted by Charles Gabriel

I feel won-der-ful, I feel won-der-ful for this is a glo-ri-ous day

I feel won-der-ful, I feel won-der-ful and I am going to stay that way.

FOR HEALTH AND STRENGTH

(Two-part Round)

Grace

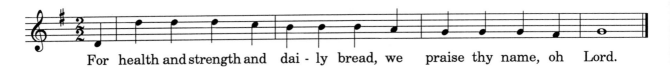

For health and strength and dai-ly bread, we praise thy name, oh Lord.

HEALTHY FOOD

1. OATS, PEAS, BEANS & BARLEY GROW

2. BILLY BOY (CAN SHE BAKE A CHERRY PIE?)

3. YES! WE HAVE NO BANANAS

4. SIPPIN' CIDER THRU A STRAW

5. HOT CROSS BUNS

6. EGGSACTLY LIKE YOU

7. MEAT ME IN ST. LOUIS, LOUIS

8. PUT YOUR ARMS AROUND ME, HONEY

9. DON'T SIT UNDER THE APPLE TREE

10. TURKEY IN THE STRAW

11. TAKE ME OUT TO THE BALL GAME
    (PEANUTS AND CRACKERJACK)

12. THE LORD'S PRAYER (DAILY BREAD)

REQUEST YOUR FAVORITE FOOD SONG

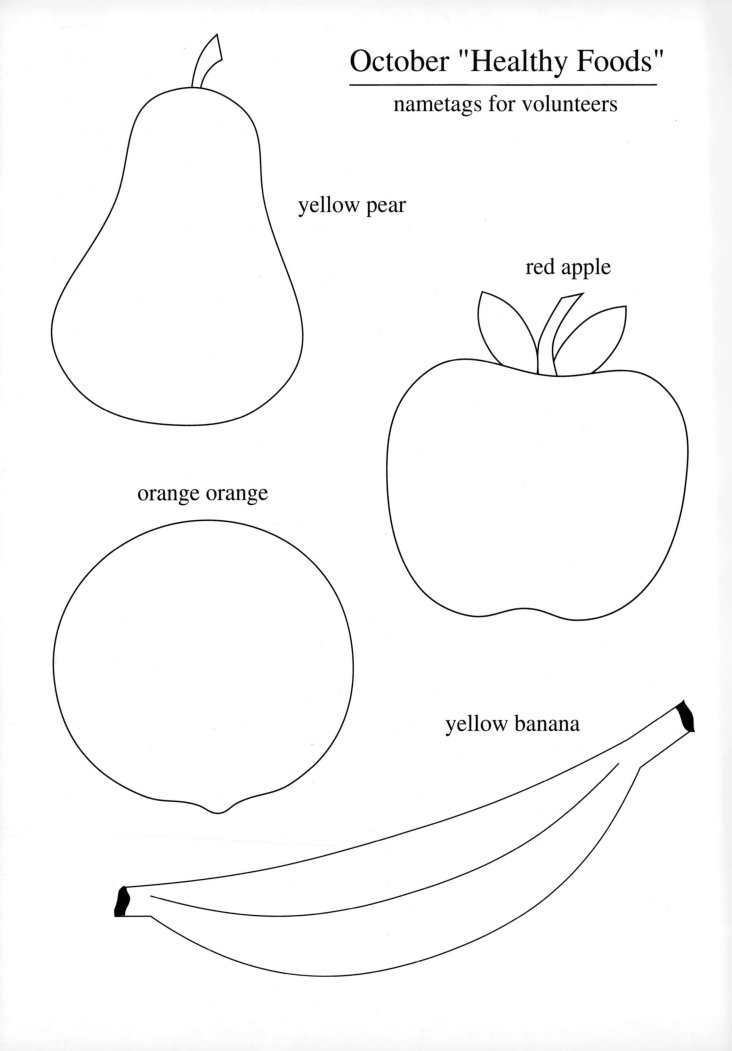

October "Healthy Foods"

nametags for volunteers

yellow pear

red apple

orange orange

yellow banana

October Theme — **HEALTH IS CONTAGIOUS**

Today's Theme — **Healthy Hands**

Advanced
Preparation:

- Make some paper hands out of construction paper. A template for this is included at the end of this week's session plan.
- Provide scotch tape, a marking pen, and volunteers.
- You will need a solo vocalist for Solo Time.

Pre-Session: Volunteers wear nametag of a paper hand that says "volunteer," pianist plays "He's Got the Whole World in His Hands," and "Reach Out and Touch" (Somebody's Hand).

Opening: To the tune of "Till We Meet Again" — follow directions as leader sings: (A songsheet is included at the end of the THEY FOUGHT FOR FREEDOM [July] weekly session plan.)

> Smile a while and give your face a rest. (smile)
> Stretch a while and ease your weary chest. (stretch)
> Reach your HANDS up towards the sky. (raise hands overhead)
> While you watch them with your eye. (look at hands up there)
> Smile a while and shake a leg there, sir. (shake a leg)
> Now lead forward, backward as you were
> Then reach out to someone near, shake his HAND and smile.

Exercise: Announce the theme that health is still contagious. Health can be improved with a healthy handshake as well as appreciation for all that our hands have done. Group singing of "I've Got Music in My Hands." The music to this is included on page 75.

> I've got music in my hands and it's keeping me alive,
> Keeping me alive, keeping me alive.
> I've got music in my hands and it's keeping me alive,
> Music is keeping me alive.

Clap on the beat continually. Exercise strongly with other verses — shoulders, elbow, wrists. End with hands overhead.

Group Singing: Pass around good health with one word, "Gesundheit" which means good health in German. Volunteers pass their energy along shaking hands as everyone sings this song. (Music is included on page 50.)

> Gesundheit, gesundheit, gesundheit, gesund. — Repeat

Reminiscence: Group should seriously look at their hands stretched out before them and appreciate all they have accomplished. Discuss what they have done such as cooking, bakeoffs, sewing, entertaining, gardening, quilting, wood working, sports, photography, remodeling, dealing with pets, collecting, and soothing.

Reminiscence: (Cont.)	Volunteers write down on a paper hand one example of each persons accomplishments with their hands, (no names) and attach with scotch tape.
Solo Time:	Poetry reading. The title and author is unknown.

> Today when I am old, I look at my hands,
> Wrinkled, arthritic, empty, trembling.
> But God says "What is that in your hand?"
> I hold it out and look again and lo it is filled with his gifts
> That I cup my two hands together and still they overflow
> With his love for me to share with others.

Song Identification:	Be aware that hands can still do many things such as are found in the song titles:

> Goodbye, My Coney Island Baby (wave goodbye)
> Rock-a-Bye Baby (hold and rock)
> Anvil chorus (hammer)
> The Sidewalks of New York (east side, west side, give directions)
> I'm Gonna Sit Right Down and Write Myself a Letter (write)
> Chopsticks (Play piano with one finger. Do finger exercises, practice scale,
>   play some chords in the air. Former pianists are obvious.)
> Kiss Me Again (blow a kiss to a friend)
> Tea for Two (drink tea)
> Put on a Happy Face (dab powder)
> Lovely Hula Hands (dance with hands)
> Standin' in Need of Pray'r (pray)

Education:	• "Old age does not deny us our humanity, our capacity to respond to others. As we age we seek satisfaction in daily deeds rather than a grand design."[1]
	• "Our hands and hearts are still useful. Older volunteers bring great dignity to the cause of aging America." Some of the volunteer work being done by the elderly is reading to the blind, driving for Meals on Wheels, election workers, teacher aides, day care assistance, nursing home and hospital volunteers, and literacy projects. Perhaps best of all, hands can offer the gift of friendship.[2]
Solo Time:	Vocalist to sing "Take My Hand, Precious Lord," or "With These Hands."
Rhythm Band:	"I've Got Music in My Hands" — play on the beat, loud response at the end of the word "alive."
	"Chopsticks" — solo time for all the stick players.
	"Anvil Chorus" — play afterbeats strongly.
	"He's Got the Whole World in His Hands" — sing and play together.
	John Phillip Sousa march — let your hands choose it.

---

[1] *Fifty Plus* May 1988, p. 88. Back Talk: "Our Time for Giving" by Dr. Robert Coles.
[2] *Fifty Plus* March 1988, p. 4-5. The Editor's Column: "Three Cheers for Older Heroes." by Bard Lindeman.

Closing: Sing:
                    Reach out and touch somebody's hand
                    Make this a better place, and you can.

               Sing repeatedly with volunteers joining all hands till the entire room is swaying and celebrating. (The music is included on page 172.)

Assignment: Offer your hand of friendship to five people not in this room Help them to appreciate their hands which are so often taken for granted. Tell others that HEALTH IS CONTAGIOUS

               Next week's program is on having a HEALTHY HEART. Everyone with a heart is invited to come.

Music
Resources: *Family Song Book of Faith and Joy* (1981)
                    "Till We Meet Again" p. 52
                    "Take My Hand Precious Lord" p. 28
                    "With These Hands" p. 97
                    "He's Got The Whole World in His Hands" p. 226
                    "Put on a Happy Face" p. 58
       Tune Book Songs (1982)
                    "Standin' In Need of Pray'r" p. 37
       Great Music's Greatest Hits (1982)
                    "Anvil Chorus" p. 218
       Ultimate Fake Book (1981)
                    "Lovely Hula Hands" p. 356
       One Thousand and One Jumbo (1985
                    "Kiss me Again" p. 461
                    "I'm Gonna Sit Right Down and Write Myself a Letter" p. 92
       Sheet Music, Charles Brown, Ashford, and Simpson, Jobete Music Co. Hollywood, CA. (1970)
                    "Reach Out and Touch"

MUSIC MENU

OUR THEME IS
HANDS
WHAT THEY CAN DO

1. GOODBYE, MY CONEY ISLAND BABY (WAVE)

2. TEA FOR TWO (DRINK TEA)

3. ANVIL CHORUS (HAMMER)

4. I'M GONNA SIT RIGHT DOWN
   & WRITE MYSELF A LETTER

5. PUT ON A HAPPY FACE (DAB POWDER)

6. BILLY BOY (CAN SHE BAKE A CHERRY PIE?)

7. TURKEY IN THE STRAW (CLAP)

8. BLESS THIS HOUSE (PRAY)

9. I'VE GOT MUSIC IN MY HANDS

10. LOVELY HULA HANDS

11. TAKE MY HAND, PRECIOUS LORD

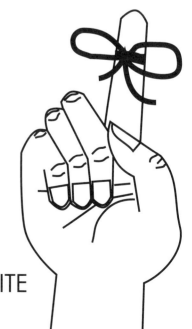

DON'T FORGET TO POINT OUT YOUR FAVORITE
SO MY HANDS CAN PLAY IT FOR YOU.

October "Healthy Hands"

any color
print volunteer work

October "Healthy Heart"

I DID IT

red

October Theme — **HEALTH IS CONTAGIOUS**

Today's Theme — **Healthy Hearts**

Advanced
Preparation:
- Make some red hearts out of construction paper with the words "I DID IT" on them. A heart template is included at the end of the HEALTHY HANDS [October] weely session plan. One could also duplicate the template "I DID IT" heart and underline the words in red.
- Use one or two baskets to hold the paper hearts. For ease in distribution, pre-cut the tape and tape one third of it to the rim of each basket. No pins are necessary. Just tape the heart on all who participated.
- Invite a physical therapist as a guest speaker.
- Provide a collection of heart songs and some old sheet music with romantic covers.

Pre-Session: Pianist plays "Let Me Call You Sweetheart," "Dear Hearts and Gentle People," "My Heart Belongs to Daddy," and "Young at Heart."

Opening: Announce the theme that HEALTH IS CONTAGIOUS and good health requires appreciating our heart. Open with the song "Open Up Your Heart" with actions. If the music is unobtainable, use as a chant. (A songsheet is included at the end of the HELLO YELLOW [March] weekly session plan.)

Let the sunshine in, face it with a grin.
Smilers never lose and frowners never win.
So let the sunshine in, face it with a grin.
Open up your HEART and let the sunshine in.

Exercise: Physical therapist or aerobics instructor leads light exercises. Pre-arrange the music with them. Use heart songs listed below. Everyone who participates receives a red paper heart taped to them that proclaims I DID IT. Everyone else will ask about it all day.

Education: By physical therapist.
- February has been proclaimed as American Heart Month since 1964.
- With proper care we can celebrate our hearts every day.
- At birth, it weighed 2/3 of an ounce. It now weighs 9-11 ounces. It is as big as your fist and beats 70 times a minute or 100,000 times a day.
- 5 quarts of blood pass through the four chambers every 60 seconds. By the age of 70, 51 million gallons of blood have circulated and your heart has beaten 2.5 billion times.[1]
- Decrease cholesterol and salt and eat large amounts of vegetables, grain, and fruit.[2]
- Your heart needs good food, exercise, and gratitude.

---

[1] Points 3 and 4 fn the Education section from *World Book Encyclopedia* (1991) Vol. H. p. 137.
[2] Porcino, J. (1984) *Growing Older, Getting Better*, p. 241.

Group Singing: "Let Me Call You Sweetheart" — no songsheets needed. Follow with a short discussion on the importance of loving someone and how it is good for both the physical and emotional heart.

Reminiscence: Invite residents to name some sweethearts, special friends, employees, or favorite pets that are still loved. They are treasured memories and dear to the heart. Discuss why these people were so special. What made them endearing? Note the effect of recalling the names and the person on the physical body.

Guided Imagery: Lead a short relaxation exercise, encourage everyone to close their eyes and picture someone they love. Then softly sing "Let Me Call You Sweetheart" again keeping an image of the loved one in mind. Open eyes and realize the importance of heartfelt relationships.

Visual Aid: Circulate copies of old sheet music with heartfelt covers, titles and pictures. Even the smell brings memories.

Solo Time: Choose any heart song and have a resident sing it. "Hearts and Flowers" on the violin is a good alternative.

Song
Identification: These songs all have HEART in the title.

Peg o' My HEART *	A Dream is a Wish Your HEART Makes
StoutHEARTed Men	HEARTaches
HEART of My HEART	None But the Lonely HEART
Young at HEART	Two HEARTS in Three Quarter Time
Will You Remember (SweetHEART)	With a Song in My HEART
SweetHEART of Sigma Chi	Deep in My HEART, Dear
My HEART Belongs to Daddy	I Left My HEART in San Francisco
Good Night SweetHEART	HEARTS and Flowers
Dear HEARTS and Gentle People	Open Up Your HEART
HEART and Soul	Yours is my HEART Alone

                  *   A songsheet is included at the end of this week's
                  session plan.

Rhythm Band: "Stouthearted Men" — strong accents.
                  "Deep in the Heart of (name of your town)" — sing your town's name.
                  "Heart of My Heart" — gentle 2 beat.
                  "Dear Hearts and Gentle People" — livelier tempo. (A songsheet is included at the end of the MY HOMETOWN [July] weekly session plan.)
                  "Open Up Your Heart" — open up your hearts and sing along.

Closing: Sing this adapted song to the tune of "I've Got Music in My Hands" — the music is on page 75.

                      I've got music in my HEART and it's keeping me alive
                      Keeping me alive, keeping me alive.
                      I've music in my HEART and it's keeping me alive

Music is keeping me alive.

Assignment: Suggest residents thank their heart for all it has done for them. Encourage them to tell their friends that health is contagious and that their heart is getting better all the time. Remind them to feed it good thoughts, praise, the right food, exercise, and good music!

Music
Resources: *Family Song Book and Faith and Joy* (1981)
"Dear Hearts and Gentle People" p. 8
"Yours is My Heart Alone" p. 178
"Stouthearted Men" p. 168
Ultimate Fake Book (1981)
"My Heart Belongs to Daddy" p. 400
"Let me Call You Sweetheart" p. 330
Treasury of Best Love Songs (1981)
"Young at Heart" p. 235
One Thousand and One Jumbo (1985)
"Hearts and Flowers" p. 431
Sheet music: Stuart Hamblen, Shawnee Press. Delaware Water Cap. PA 18327 (1955)
"Open Up Your Heart"

Hearty Music

1. Heart of My Heart
2. Hearts and Flowers
3. Stouthearted Men
4. Young at Heart
5. Deep in My Heart, Dear
6. Yours is My Heart Alone
7. Peg o' My Heart
8. None but the Lonely Heart
9. Dear Hearts and Gentle People
10. Open up your Heart
11. Two Hearts in Three Quarter Time
12. With a Song in My Heart
13. Will You Remember (Sweetheart)
14. Good Night, Sweetheart
15. Let Me Call You Sweetheart

Select Your Favorite

Peg o' My Heart

Peg o' My Heart,
I love you, don't let us part,
I love you, I always knew,
it would be you,
Since I hear your lilting laughter,
it's your Irish heart I'm after.

Peg o' My Heart,
Your glances make my heart say
"How's chances,"
Come, be my own,
Come make your home in my heart.

– Alfred Bryan (1913)

October Theme — **HEALTH IS CONTAGIOUS**

Today's Theme — **Healthy Bones**

Advanced
Preparation:

- Prepare a paper or plastic skeleton hanging on a stand wearing a cute mask.
- Prepare paper body parts of a heart, smile, hand, foot, eyes, hair, liver, nose, arm, neck, teeth, lips, chin.
- You will also need the music to "Dry Bones."
- Make apple cider for everyone.
- Make a few paper bone nametags for the volunteers to advertise the theme and their name. A template for this is included at the end of this week's session plan.
- Organize music and a soloist for "The Thank You Song."

Pre-Session: Volunteers wear a large paper bone with their name on it. Pianist plays "Dry Bones" and "I've Got Music in My Hands."

Opening: This opening song is adapted from "Vive la Compagnie" as a response song, with the group responding.

Leader	Let every good fellow now join in the song
Response	VIVE LA COMPAGNIE
Leader	**Health** to each other and pass it along
Response	VIVE LA COMPAGNIE
All	Vive L'a, Vive l'a, Vive l'amour (3 times)
	Vive la compagnie

Leader	A friend on the left and a friend on the right
Response	VIVE LA COMPAGNIE
Leader	In one and good fellowship let us unite
Response	VIVE LA COMPAGNIE
All	Vive L'a, Vive l'a, Vive l'amour (3 times)
	Vive la compagnie

Announce the theme of HEALTH IS CONTAGIOUS and good health means strong bones.

Exercise and
Group Singing: To the tune of "Dry Bones" use the model skeleton with the cute face on it, all sing:

Them bones, them bones, them STRONG BONES (sing 3 times)
Let's sing a song of praise
    The foot bone's connected to the leg bone
    The leg bone's connected to the knee bone
    The knee bone's connected to the thigh bone
    The thigh bone's connected to the back bone

Exercise and
Group Singing: The back bone's connected to the neck bone
(Cont.)   The neck bone's connected to the head bone
                          End each section with "Let's sing a song of praise."
                      Chorus:
                          Them bones, them bones, them strong bones
                          Them bones, them bones, them strong bones
                          Them bones, them bones, them strong bones
                          Let's sing a song of praise.

                      1. Point to parts on the model,
                      2. Exercise those parts — all shake on bone part as sung.

Education: • Between the ages of 30 and 35, our bones have reached their maximum
                         growth. Then there is a steady decline until age 70 with no further loss.
                         Loss of calcium in the bone causes women to lose 3/4 inch in height
                         around age 60 and another half inch around age 70.
                      • By the age of 75, 50% of all white women have osteoporotic vertebral
                         fractures. Osteoporosis means porous bones. One out of 4 women over 50
                         suffer from osteoporosis. The affliction may be due to family history, high
                         caffeine, or heavy smoking, but the exact cause is still unknown.
                      • Exercise slows down bone loss and even builds new tissue. Walking and
                         swimming are recommended plus vitamin D, ice cream, and lots of water.[1]

Solo Time: "The Thank You Song" from the musical production of *Maggie Flynn*.

Song
Identification: Cover the skeleton model with corresponding paper part by attaching with
                      scotch tape as the song is identified.

                          Peg o' My Heart *
                          Smiles
                          He's Got the Whole World in His Hands
                          Five Foot Two, Eyes of Blue †
                          I'm Gonna Wash That Man Right Outa my Hair
                          When the Organ Played at Twilight (liver)
                          Nobody Knows the Trouble I've Seen (pun — nose)
                          Full Moon and Empty Arms
                          It Aint Gonna Rain No Mo' (wash my neck)
                          All I Want for Christmas is my Two Front Teeth
                          Tip Toe Through the Tulips (toe and two lips)
                          Chin Chin Cheree (actually Chim Chim)
                          Dry Bones

                      *   A songsheet is included at the end of the HEALTHY HEARTS [October] weekly session
                      plan.
                      † A Songsheet included at the end of the STYLES UP TO THE ANKLE [September] weekly
                         session plan.

_____

[1] All points in Education section from Porcino, J. (1984) *Growing Older, Getting Better*, pp. 227-234.

Rhythm Band: "Smiles" — Everyone play, dedicate it to the model up front. (A songsheet is included at the end of the EVERYONE LOVES A SMILE [February] weekly sesion plan.)
"Shortnin' Bread" — play very softly except on the words "shortnin' bread."
"He's Got The Whole World in His Hands" — use instrument names instead of 'whole world'.
"Ida, Sweet as Apple Cider" — lilting 2 beat.
"Battle Hymn of the Republic" — All sing and play "Glory, Glory Hallelujah."

Special Treat: Apple cider for all. Drink to good health.

Closing: Group singing of "I've Got Music in My Hands" adapted for this program — everyone sing and clap. (The music is included on page 75)[

I've got music in my bones, and it's keeping me alive,
Keeping me alive, keeping me alive.
I've got music in my bones, and it's keeping me alive,
Music is keeping me alive.

Continue with other body parts for verses or else end with the healthy thought of "I've got calcium in my bones."

Assignment: Suggest that residents think what their bones have done all these years: Praise them. Help them plan on how they are going to keep them healthy. Encourage them to make 3 resolutions and not to wait until New Year's Day, but to "Do it today."

Music
Resources: *Wee Sing Silly Songs* (1984)
                    "Dry Bones" p. 14
                 Wee Sing Around the Campfire (1984)
                    "Vive La Compagnie" p. 9
                 Legit Fake Book (1990)
                    "Ida, Sweet as Apple Cider" p. 159
                    "Shortnin' Bread" p. 301
                 Family Song Book of Faith and Joy (1981)
                    "Smiles" p. 34
                 Sheet music by H. Luigi and G. Weiss. Norman Leyden Choral Series, Valando Music, New York (1970)
                    "The Thank You Song"

Music Menu

Songs to Celebrate the Wonderful Parts of our BODIES

1. Full Moon and Empty Arms
2. Baby Face
3. Peg o' My Heart
4. Side By Side
5. Dry Bones
6. Tip Toe Through the Tulips
7. Five Foot Two, Eyes of Blue
8. Jeanie with the Light Brown Hair
9. Nobody Nose de Trouble I've Seen
10. Put Your Arms Around Me, Honey
11. When the Organ Played at Twilight
12. He's Got the Whole World in His Hands

Tell me your favorite,
I'll play it for you.

October "Healthy Bones"

print name of volunteer

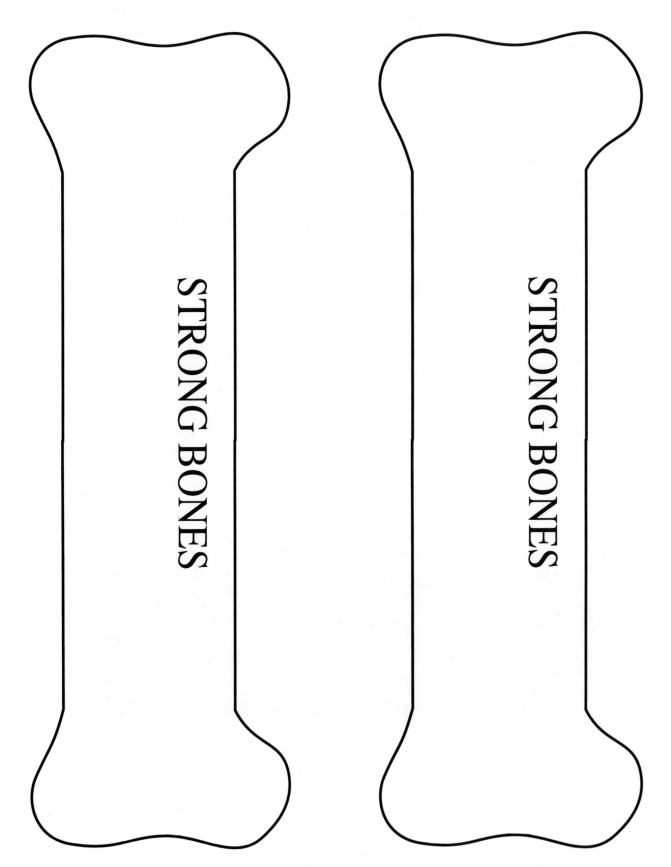

October Theme — **HEALTH IS CONTAGIOUS**

Today's Theme — **Healthy Fun**

Advanced
Preparation:
- Prepare a paper or plastic skeleton hanging on a stand wearing a cute mask. (If the previous week's program was used, then the same skeleton would work well.)
- Obtain a large paper or real pumpkin.
- Cut out orange and black streamers cut in 16 -inch lengths.
- Provide songs depicting costumes.
- Invite volunteers to wear their own funny hats.
- Props will include:
  - large pumpkin as a prize,
  - a camera,
  - a mirror.

Pre-Session: Volunteers wear funny hats of their own creation. Pianist plays "Deck the Halls" while everyone assembles.

Opening: Halloween sounds — moans, groans, ahhhhs, and sighs. Practice going up and down the scale with oooohs. It's fun.

Education:
- When you laugh, scientists believe that the brain is stimulated and pours out endorphins, powerful pain relievers. Adrenalin floods the bloodstream, stimulating the heart and lungs. Norman Cousins, Editor of the *Saturday Review* and author of many health related books calls it "internal jogging."[1]
- When you stop laughing arteries and muscles relax thus reducing blood pressure, aiding digestion, and relieving depression.[2]
- The *Readers Digest* still carries a section called "Laughter is the Best Medicine."

Solo Time: Invite anyone to share a joke. Have a few ready such as the fact that when former president Reagan went to the hospital and was on his way to surgery, his last words were "Please tell me you're Republicans."

Reminiscence: Think about a time that struck you as funny. Share it and recall the affect it had on you then and now.

Exercise: Distribute the orange and black individual streamers and exercise to this song adapted to "Deck the Halls" as a response song.

Leader	Deck the walls with orange and black
Response	FA LA LA LA LA LA LA LA LA.
Leader	Halloweeen time now is back
Response	FA LA LA LA LA LA LA LA LA.

---

[1]   *St. Louis Post Dispatch*, August 29, 1987. D section, p. 1. "Why Laughter is the Best Medicine" by Victor Cohn.
[2]   Ibid. p. 7.

Exercise: Leader   Don we now our funny hats
(Cont.)   Response   FA LA LA... etc.
                   Leader   They should scare the 'fraidy cats
                   Response   FA LA LA... etc.
                   (Repeat as needed)

Group Singing: Sing as a solo while group does the actions to the tune of "O Du lieber,
                Augustin" or "Did You Ever See a Lassie":

                Solo: Oh once I had a pumpkin, a pumpkin, a pumpkin,
                        Oh once I had a pumpkin with no face at all (faces blank)
                        With no eyes and no nose and no mouth and no teeth (all point)
                        Oh once I had a pumpkin with no face at all (faces blank)

                        So I made a jack-o-lantern, jack-o-lantern, jack-o-lantern
                        So I made a jack-o-lantern with a big funny face (do it)
                        With big eyes, big nose, big mouth, and big teeth (all point)
                        So I made a jack-o-lantern with a big funny face. (Don't be shy!)

Special Activity: Halloween can be fun. Now is the time to enter the personal jack-o-lantern
                   contest. A pumpkin is given to the person making the funniest face on
                   themselves. Look in the mirror. Encourage all to be a living jack-o-lanterns and
                   glow. Capture with a camera and display later.

Song
Identification: Name these songs that all depict a Halloween costume. Kids associate
                 costumes with fun even if they are spooky.

                        Alice Blue Gown
                        Alley Cat
                        Ghost Riders in the Sky
                        Baby Elephant Walk
                        Gypsy Love Song
                        Indian Love Call
                        If I Were a Rich Man
                        This is the Army, Mr. Jones
                        You're in the Army Now
                        Pony Boy
                        Daring Young Man on the Flying Trapeze
                        I Don't Want to Get Well — I'm In Love with a Beautiful Nurse
                        School Days (several answers) *

                *   A songsheet is included at the end of the DEAR OLD SCHOOL DAYS [September] weekly
                    session plan.

Rhythm Band: "Inka Dinka Doo" — nonsense song — play deliberately.
               Creative sound — all make a sound with instruments that duplicates Fibber
                   McGee's closet door being opened with contents rattling to the floor.

Rhythm Band: (Cont.)	"Dry Bones" — Leader sings song and points to parts on the skeleton bravely standing up front. Group plays their instrument at or near same part of their own body.

      The foot bone connected to the leg bone — start playing instrument fairly low.

      The leg bone connected to the knee bone — continue singing moving instrument up higher.

      Complete song with verses about the thigh bone, back bone, neck bone and head bone with instruments going higher. End song with

           Them bones, them bones, them strong bones,
           Let's sing a song of praise.

"Seventy-six Trombones" — all join in merrily playing anywhere.

Closing:

To the tune of "We Wish You Merry Christmas."
Verse:
1. I wish you a funny Halloween, I wish you a funny Halloween (point to each other)
I wish you a funny Halloween and a funny today.
2. I wish me a funny Halloween (point to self)
3. I wish us a happy Halloween (sing with arms overhead)

Assignment:

Encourage residents to enjoy the Halloween season. It shouldn't be taken seriously. Remind them that fun and laughter are healthy. Suggest they keep a twinkle in the eye that keeps others guessing. That kind of health is contagious.

Music Resources:

Wee Sing Silly Songs (1984)
    "Dry Bones" p. 14
Popular Songs That Live Forever (1982)
    "Seventy-six Trombones" p. 18
Sigmund Spaeth's Song Session (1958)
    "O Du lieber Augustin" p. 124
Ultimate Fake Book (1981)
    "Deck the Halls" p. 130
    "Alley Cat" p. 22
Legit Fake Book (1990)
    "Alice Blue Gown" p. 13
Family Song Book of Faith and Joy (1981)
    "Gypsy Love Song" p. 161
Country Western Song Book (1983)
    "Ghost Riders in the Sky" p. 193
Children's Song Book (1988)
    "John Jacob Jingleheimer Schmidt" p. 134

music menu

HEALTHY
FUN
SONGS

1. INKA DINKA DOO
2. *three little fishes*
3. **BIBBIDY-BOBBIDY-BOO**
4. Mary had a William Goat (Mary Had a Little Lamb)
5. *horsey, keep your tail up*
6. SOLOMON LEVI
7. John Jacob Jingleheimer Schmidt
8. **FOUND A PEANUT**
9. *supercalifragilisticexpialidocious*
10. Fibber McGee's Closet
    (sound)

11. TA-RA-RA **BOOM** DE-AY

*Tell me which one **you** would like to have **fun** with!*

Ta-Ra-Ra-Boom-De-ay

A sweet Tuxedo girl you see,
Queen of swell society,
Fond of fun as fond can be,
When it's on the strict Q. T.
I'm not too young, I'm not too old,
Not too timid not too bold,
Just the kind you like to hold,
Just the kind for sport I'm told.

I'm a blushing bud of innocence,
Papa says at big expense,
Old maids say I have no sense,
Boys declare I'm just immense,
Before my song I do conclude,
I want it strictly understood,
Tho' fond of fun, I'm never rude,
Tho' not too bad I'm not too good.

CHORUS:

Ta-ra-ra-Boom-de-ay,
Ta-ra-ra-Boom-de-ay,
Ta-ra-ra-Boom-de-ay
Ta-ra-ra-Boom-de-ay,
Ta-ra-ra

– Henry J. Sayers (1891)

October Theme — **HEALTH IS CONTAGIOUS**

Today's Theme — **A Healthy Halloween**

Advanced
Preparation:

- You will need to organize volunteers in costume.
- An adult and 2 children dressed as smiling ghosts under simple sheets would be appropriate for this program.
- Design 12 individual poster boards with "The 12 days of Halloween" illustrated on them: a moon shining, flying witch, crazy costume, owl, cat, pumpkin, broomstick, ghosts, spooky noise, bat, tired mother, and a trick or treater.

Pre-Session: Pianist plays "Whistle a Happy Tune," "Oh What a Beautiful Mornin'," and "Great Day."

Opening: Open with the theme announcement that HALLOWEEN IS FUN. Ask everyone to get in the mood with a moan, groan, ahhhhs, and finally practice going up and down the scale with ooooooooooooos. Explain the benefits of this form of expression.

Exercise: Leader sings the following song to the tune of "Deck The Halls" while the audience answers with the traditional "Fa la la.. etc". In the second verse, reply with long "boos." Encourage as many actions as are appropriate. Sing slowly for greater benefits with the physical exercise. Small ghosts should be ready to enter on their cue.

Leader	Deck the halls with scary cats (make a scary face)
Response	FA LA LA LA LA LA LA LA LA
Leader	Ghosts and pumpkins and big black bats (indicate largeness with rounded arms)
Response	FA LA LA LA LA LA LA LA LA
Leader	Add some broomsticks and witches' hats (sweep or don hat)
Response	FA LA LA LA LA LA LA LA LA
Leader	All we need is tape and tacks (hammer motions)
Response	FA LA LA LA LA LA LA LA LA

Leader	Halloween ghosts are flying around (fly with arms)
Response	BOOOOOOOOOOOOOO!
Leader	High in the air and near the ground (arms high and low)
Response	BOOOOOOOOOOOOOO!
Leader	Here come the spooky ghosts and ghouls (watch doorway)
[Costumed children enter and float around room]	
Response	BOOOOOOOOOOOOOO
Leader	Tell me now if you were fooled
Response	BOOOOOOOOOOOOOO

Sing a second time as friendly ghosts float among residents.

Education:
- Halloween or All Hallows Eve combines the Druid autumn festival and Christian costumes.
- It was the beginning of Hallowtide and embraces the season of the Feast of All Saints on November 1 and the Feast of all Souls, November 2.
- It was in the 6th century that the thoughts of ghosts, spirits, and witches began.
- Superstitions have disappeared. Now it is also known as Trick or Treat or Beggars Night.[1]

Reminiscence: Share memories of past celebrations including some of the vandalism. Talk about homemade costumes, treats, and parties. Allow plenty of time for expression and then update on the changes, such as collecting for UNICEF, X-raying candy, store-bought costumes, children's parades, parents accompanying, price of masks.

Solo Time: "Alice Blue Gown" — representing many of the costumes worn throughout the years as princesses, ladies at a ball, Cinderella, beauty queens and royalty.

Group Singing: To the tune of "The 12 Days of Christmas". Give each person a cardboard with their day numbered and pictured on it. For greater strength in sound have three people on a part. Pre-arrange the fifth day with your strongest singer. The entire group is the first day.

| Leader | On the first day of Halloween, my true love gave to me |
| Response (all) | A MOON SHINING IN A BARE TREE. (Leader holds up picture) |

Leader	On the second day of Halloween, my true love gave to me
Group Two	TWO FLYING WITCHES (holding up the picture)
All	AND A MOON SHINING IN A BARE TREE.

Leader	On the third day of Halloween, my true love gave to me
Group Three	THREE HOOTY OWLS
Group Two	TWO FLYING WITCHES
All	AND A MOON SHINING IN A BARE TREE.

Continue in like manner with as many groups as are successful. Aim for at least five with the following order: four fraidy cats, five big fat pumpkins, six flying broomsticks, seven smiling ghosts, eight spooky noises, nine crazy costumes, ten scary bats, eleven tired mothers, twelve trick or treaters and a moon shining in a bare tree.

Rhythm Band: "The Farmer In the Dell" — adapted to "the witch hears the bells," continue naming other instruments.
"Dry Bones" — sticks only — sing along on chorus using "strong" bones.
"Hall of the Mountain King" — start slowly, add loud cymbals at the end of the 8th measure. Play on the piano or use a good recording.
"Great Day" — celebrate Halloween with this joyful song (1929)

---

[1] All points in Education section form *Chases Annual Events* (1992) p. 369.

Closing: To the tune of "We Wish You A Merry Christmas":
1. I wish you a healthy Halloween (point to each other)
   I wish you a healthy Halloween
   I wish you a healthy Halloween and a happy today.
2. I wish me a healthy Halloween (point to self)
3. I wish us a healthy Halloween (all hands up overhead)

Assignment: Enjoy this Halloween more than any other as you witness friends, children, employees, enjoying the festive aspects of it.

Music
Resources: *Legit Fake Book* (1990)
        "Great Day" p. 473
    Treasury of Best Loved Songs (1981)
        "Alice Blue Gown" p. 204
    Wee Sing Silly Songs (1984)
        "Dry Bones" p. 14
    Wee Sing for Christmas (1986)
        "Twelve Days of Christmas" p. 12
        "Deck the Halls" p. 7
    Sheet Music, Edvard Grieg, Opus 64, No. 4. Schirmer/Hal Leonard, Milwaukee WS (1926)
        "In the Hall of the Mountain King"

Healthy Halloween BOO-sic Menu

Halloween Costumes

1. Alley Cat
2. Alice Blue Gown
3. Baby Elephant Walk
4. Colonel Bogey March
5. Gypsy Love Song
6. Indian Love Call
7. If I Were a Rich Man
8. My Special Angel
9. Oh You Beautiful Doll
10. Parade of the Wooden Soldiers
11. The Hawaiian Wedding Song
12. The Old Lamp-Lighter

Choose your favorite and have it played by the "Get Well Witch".

November
a Month of Praise

A Musical Game for November

"Count your blessings, name them one by one." That is good advice from a familiar song. The song titles suggest more things we can be thankful for especially during this month of Praise. The answers are upside down.

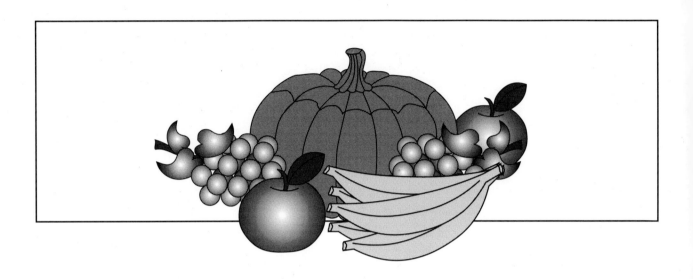

1. Blue _____

2. America (My _____ 'Tis of Thee)

3. You are My _____

4. Make New _____ (but Keep the Old)

5. You're a Grand Old _____

6. You Must have been a Beautiful _____

7. There are _____ that Make Us Happy

8. I _____ You Truly

9. Let There be _____ on Earth

10. T_____ in the Straw

1. Skies 2. Country 3. Sunshine 4. Friends 5. Flag 6. Baby 7. Smiles 8. Love 9. Peace 10. Turkey. Now name two more of your blessings.

A MONTH OF PRAISE
NOVEMBER

The power of positive words has been well established by documentation.[1] Can you imagine your whole facility using them for an entire month? The theme and programs encourage constructive, encouraging words by the residents, staff, employees, families, friends, and the community. It becomes a month of thanks-living as well as thanksgiving.

Praise for Autumn — If fall leaves are unavailable in your part of the country, have them mailed to your facility by an understanding friend. The results are well worth the effort. Actual oak leaves or paper ones when worn as a visual aid will proclaim to all that "I am oak-kay." That is worth praising.

Praise for the Harvest — Harvesting food is a typical program. This one contains memories of canning and freezing all those goodies. In addition, one can harvest thoughts and memories. Once they are collected, there is a lot to praise. Group dynamics work well here.

Praise for Thanksliving — In preparation for the national holiday of Thanksgiving, this program will prepare everyone. Being thankful is an everyday event even though there may be health challenges. There is so much to praise and it is easy in this land of freedom.

Thanksgiving — Turkey time and turkey tunes all encompassed with the joy of friendship make this a true celebration. Families are heartily welcomed to join in this time of praise. The music menu is designed to be folded in half and placed on dining room tables for conversation and music requests.

OPTIONAL PROGRAM

Praise for Music — All kinds of music motivates and stimulates people in all parts of the earth. Enjoy taking a poll of your residents, and recalling all that music symbolizes. Recognize the freedom to choose as well as the effects of music. Music works.

PRAISE IS PRICELESS

---

[1] Author recommends Bright, R. (1991) *Music in Geriatric Care: A Second Look*.

November Theme — **A MONTH OF PRAISE**

Today's Theme —   **Praise for Autumn**

Advanced
Preparation:
- Make a poster with various leaves pasted on it.
- Glue some real leaves onto paper plates.
- Make leaf-shaped nametags for everyone from real or paper leaves with "I'm Oak-Kay" written on them. A template is included at the end the PRAISE FOR MUSIC [November] weekly session plan.
- Aides /volunteers will need scotch tape for attaching nametags.
- Prepare a collection of songs with various trees in the title.
- Make copies of the songsheet "Shine On Harvest Moon" which is included at the end of this week's session plan.

Pre-Session: Volunteers greet everyone wearing their oak leaf that says "I'm oak-kay." Background music plays as they enter the room which has been decorated with a large bouquet of autumn leaves.

Opening: Opening song is to the tune of "We Wish You a Merry Christmas." Sing:
                      We wish you a happy autumn,
                      We wish you a happy autumn,
                      We wish you a happy autumn, and a happy today.

                  Point to each other, establish eye contact.

Exercise: With the leaf plates:
                  "Shine on Harvest Moon" — slowly raise plates like the moon rising.
                      Continue to hold the plate up there, descend and then repeat.
                  "Tie a Yellow Ribbon Round the Ole Oak Tree" — plates left-right.
                  "Missouri Waltz" — waltz your leaves around to the 3 count rhythm.
                  "Seventy-six Trombones" — march — Imitate the action of a slide trombone.
                      1. Push/pull out in front.
                      2. Push/pull high in the air.
                      3. Push/pull towards the floor.
                  Leaf storm — pitch leaves at therapist.

Poetry: Encourage the residents to supply the missing words in this poem "Trees" by Sergeant Joyce [Kilmer][1]

                      I think that I shall never [see]
                      A poem as lovely as a [tree].
                      A tree whose hungry [mouth] is pressed
                      Against the earth's sweet flowing [breast].
                      A tree that looks at [God] all day
                      And lifts her leafy [arms to pray].

---

[1] *Treasury of the Familiar* (1950) p. 583.

Poetry: (Cont).	A tree that may in [summer] wear A nest of [robins] in her hair. Upon whose bosom [snow] has lain, Who intimately lives with [rain]. Poems are made by fools like [me] But only [God can make a tree].
Display:	Set up a leaf board of various local leaves or have a friend mail some other leaves from the east coast or northern United States.
Reminiscence:	Encourage residents to recall their favorite tree: • Where was it located? • Was it climbable? • Who planted it? • Did its leaves require raking? • Did one jump in the leaves? • Did it have fruit or flowers or a birds nest? • Does it still exist? Suggest that one's life is similar to a tree. We put down roots, we spread our branches and add to the family tree. In other words, living a long time and reflecting on all the good things life has offered makes one feel "oak-kay" in spite of physical concerns. With scotch tape, attach to residents' shirts and dresses leaf badges that read "I'm Oak-Kay." When asked about these badges, they can simply reply "Parts of me are perfect."
Special Activity:	Take a poll of the group's favorite tree. Use popular local trees but also include Christmas trees. Ask if anyone prefers an artificial tree. Announce results in the in-house newspaper.
Group Singing:	"Shine On Harvest Moon."
Education:	• Trees are the oldest and most massive living thing on earth. • The small, gnarled bristlecone pines in California are the oldest trees, about 4600 years old. Redwoods are only 2200 years old, the tallest is 368 foot and weighs 6000 tons. • A tree is defined as a perennial woody plant 20 foot tall with an erect trunk and well defined canopy. • Some shrubs are vines that can be trained to fit that definition.[1] • Patients in hospital rooms with a natural view had shorter postoperative stays, fewer pain killers, and a better evaluation from the nurses. • People's physical and mental well being can be directly tied to the quality of the environment, with trees being a significant factor.[2]

---

[1] Points 1-4 in Education section from *Encyclopedia of Science and Technology* (1987) Vol. 18, p. 512 "Trees."
[2] Points 5-6 from *American Forests* July/Aug 1988, p. 6. "Making Cities Livable for Trees" by N. Sampson.

Song
Identification: Name the trees or parts of a tree that are in the following song titles. Some
                    are puns.

                        MAPLE Leaf Rag
                        The Old OAKen Bucket
                        Tie a Yellow Ribbon Round the Ole OAK Tree.
                        CHESTNUTs Roasting on an Open Fire ("The Christmas Song")
                        Don't Sit Under the APPLE Tree
                        ELMer's Tune
                        Love Me or LEAF Me (pun)
                        I'm Going to LEAF Old Texas Now (pun)
                        Tit-WILLOW
                        Tip Toe Through the TULIPS
                        Billy Boy (Can She Bake a CHERRY Pie?)
                        Back Home Again in Indiana (Indiana sycamore tree)
                        ASH Grove
                        Under the BAMBOO Tree

Rhythm Band: "Don't Sit Under the Apple Tree" — cymbal crashes after the word "me".
                    "Ash Grove" — bells only
                    "Tip Toe Through the Tulips" — sticks only.
                    "Billy Boy" (Can She Bake a Cherry Pie?) — castanets only.
                    "Shine On Harvest Moon" — everyone sings and plays simultaneously.
                    March of your choice to celebrate autumn.

Closing: Group sings "Bless This House" as it prepares for the fall season. A songsheet
                    is included at the end of the THANKSGIVING [November] weekly session plan.

Assignment: Wear your oak leaf all day long and proclaim to the world that your are oak-
                    kay. Watch their reaction.

Music
Resources: *Popular Songs That Live Forever* (1982)
                        "Seventy-six Trombones" p. 18
                        "Shine On Harvest Moon" p. 228
                    Legit Fake Book (1990)
                        "Don't Sit Under the Apple Tree" p. 84
                        "Elmer's Tune" p. 88
                        "Under the Bamboo Tree" p. 352
                        "Love me or Leave Me" p. 224
                    Festival of Popular Songs (1977)
                        "Missouri Waltz" p. 108
                    Golden Book of Favorite Songs (1946)
                        The Old Oaken Bucket" p. 106
                    One Thousand and One Jumbo (1985)
                        "Tit-Willow" p. 595

Music Menu

Tree Songs

Praise for Autumn Praise for Autumn Praise for Autumn Praise for Autumn Praise for Autumn

1. Maple Leaf Rag
2. The Old Oaken Bucket
3. The Trail of the Lonesome Pine
4. Peacherine Rag
5. Elmer's Tune
6. Trees
7. Tie a Yellow Ribbon Round the Ole Oak Tree
8. Around the Corner and Under the Tree
9. Don't Sit Under the Apple Tree
10. Indiana (Sycamore Tree)
11. Tit-Willow (The Mikado)
12. I'm Going to Leaf Old Texas Now
13. I'm Tying the Leaves So They Won't Come Down

Go out on a limb for your favorite!

Shine On Harvest Moon

Shine on, shine on harvest moon
up in the sky.

I ain't had no lovin' since January,
February, June or July.

Snow time ain't no time to
sit around and croon.

So shine on, shine on harvest moon
for me and my gal.

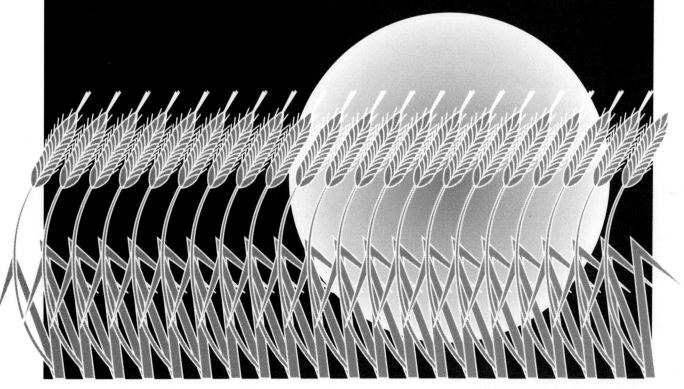

Jack Norworth (1908)

November Theme — **A MONTH OF PRAISE**

Today's Theme — **Praise for the Harvest**

Advanced
Preparation: You will need:
- the paper plates with real leaves glued on them that were used for last week's programs,
- a collection of fall songs,
- a poetry reader for solo time.

Pre-Session: Volunteers wear fall colors, their names on real leaves for a nametag. Pianist plays "Bringing In the Sheaves," "Autumn Leaves," and "Falling Leaves."

Opening: The opening song sung to the tune of "We Wish You a Merry Christmas."
Verse:
1. I wish you a happy autumn (point to each other)
   I wish you a happy autumn
   I wish you a happy autumn starting right now.
2. I wish me a happy autumn....(point to yourself)
3. I wish us a happy autumn....(hands thrust upward)

Exercise: Using the leaf paper plates, everyone with maple leaves should wave their plate up high. Follow with other species native to your area.
"Bringing in the Sheaves" — or raking up the leaves. Plates at the side, use swinging arms as in raking.
"I'll Be With You in Apple Blossom Time" — 3/4 tempo — circles.
"Put Your Arms Around Me, Honey" — do contact with the body in units of 8 — head, chest, lap. Listen for the sound of the contact. Use more energy if sound is too soft.
Finale of falling leaves — at the count of three get good arm extension and toss the plate at the leader up front.

Guided Imagery:Lead a short relaxation exercise with eyes closed. Group softly sings "America, the Beautiful". Suggest people imagine the scenes the music provides such as spacious skies, amber waves of grain. At the end of the music everyone can open eyes and relate the scenery or the feelings. (A songhseet of verses 1 and 2 is included at the end of the THANKSLIVING [November] weekly session plan; and verses 2 and 3 are included at the end of the OUR HISTORY IN SONG [July] weekly session plan.)

Solo Time: Read the poem "Apple Song" by Frances Frost.[1]

> The apples are seasoned
> And ripe and sound.
> Gently they fall
> On the yellow ground.

---

[1] *Favorite Poems Old and New* (1957) p. 239.

Solo Time: The apples are stored
(Cont.)   In the dusky bin
                    Where hardly a glimmer
                    Of light creeps in.

                    In the firelight, winter
                    Nights, they'll be
                    The clear sweet taste
                    Of a summer tree!

Reminiscence: Discuss the foods that were harvested years ago and the labor involved. Be
                    sure and stimulate recall on home canning of foods. Contrast it later with
                    modern food distribution. Talk about harvesting other aspects of life such as
                    collecting good thoughts, counting one's blessings, and appreciating the fact
                    that one has lived a long life and has much to harvest in retrospect.

Education: • Getting foods to the factory for processing as soon as it is harvested is
                      important in order to retain the nutritional value, according to the
                      Encyclopedia Americana.[1]
                    • Canning is still the largest single segment of the food processing industry.
                    • Nicolas Appert, a French candymaker was the first to can in 1780.
                    • In 1856 Louis Pasteur proved that heat served as the agent to destroy
                      microorganisms that caused spoilage.
                    • In 1851 we had the first ice machine for refrigeration. Clarene Birdseye
                      invented quick freezing in 1925.
                    • Much food was dried in World War I in order to provide unspoiled food to
                      the soldiers. In World War II, the process to make instant coffee and dried
                      milk was developed.[2]
                    • Food today can be dried, frozen, canned, smoked, salted, fermented,
                      pickled, coated, chemically preserved, fat imbedded, or eaten.

Song
Identification: Name what is being harvested in these songs:
                    Food:
                        TURKEY in the Straw *
                        MEAT me in St. Louis, Louis (pun)
                        Yes! We Have no BANANAS †
                        Ida, Sweet as APPLE Cider
                        Goober PEAS
                        Don't Sit Under the APPLE Tree
                        Over the River and Through the Woods (Hurrah for the PUMPKIN pie) §

                    *   A songsheet included at the end of the LET'S ALL SING LIKE THE BIRDIES SING [May]
                        weekly session plan.
                    †   A songsheet is included at the end of the HOW'S YOUR TASTE, BUD [April] weekly session
                        plan.
                    §   A songsheet is included at the end of the THANKSGIVING [November] weekly session plan.

---

1   *Encyclopedia Americana* (1990) Vol. 11, pp. 526-527. "Historic Food Preservation" by George Bergstrom.
2   Points 2-6 in Education section from *World Book Encyclopedia* (1991) Vol. 7(F), pp. 341-344. "How Food is Processed" by Margaret
    McWilliams.

Song
Identification: **Other:**
(Cont.)
                Partridge in a PEAR Tree
                Count Your BLESSINGS *
                Make New FRIENDS but Keep the Old
                MEMORIES

        *   A songsheet included at the end of the THANKSGIVING [November] weekly session plan.

Rhythm Band: Harvest some American songs using rhythm instruments!
                "Bringing in the Sheaves" — celebrate the harvest.
                "Dixie" — jolly 2 beat — celebrate cotton and the south.
                "Peacherine Rag" — peaches. Celebrate the American composer, Scott
                     Joplin, with a strong 2 beat.
                "Memories" — enjoy 3/4 time.
                "Do-Re-Mi" (Doe a Deer) — harvest deer, play strongly on the first beat of
                     each section.
                "Stars and Stripes Forever" — joyous march.

Closing: Harvest friendships by singing "Make New Friends but Keep the Old (One is
                silver and the other is gold)." Announce next week's theme.

Assignment: Invite residents to reflect on the things harvested, especially the emotional
                ones, like grandchildren, good feelings, warm memories. Suggest all rejoice in
                longevity and the opportunity to gather so many experiences. It is important
                to praise the gift of life.

Music
Resources:
                Ultimate Fake Book (1981)
                     "Do-Re-Mi" p. 126
                     "Dixie" p. 133
                Family Song Book of Faith and Joy (1981)
                     "Bringing in the Sheaves" p. 130
                Collected Piano Works of Scott Joplin (1972)
                     "Peacherine Rag" p. 30
                Great Music's Greatest Hits (1982)
                     "Stars and Stripes Forever" p. 220
                Mitch Miller Community Song Book (1962)
                     "Memories" p. 85

Harvesting Songs

1. **Turkey** in the Straw
2. Put your Arms Around Me, **Honey**
3. Ida, Sweet as Apple **Cider**
4. Goober **Peas**
5. Over the River and Through the Woods
   (Hurrah for the **Pumpkin** Pie)
6. Yes! We Have No **Bananas**
7. **Meat** Me in St. Louis, Louis
8. Jimmy Crack **Corn**
9. In the Shade of the Old **Apple** Tree
10. Shine on **Harvest** Moon
11. America, the Beautiful -
    (With Amber Waves of **Grain**)
12. **ROLL** Out the Barrel -
    (The Beer Barrel Polka)

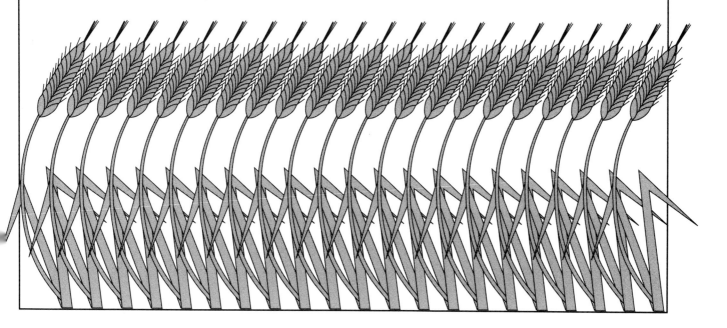

Let's gather in the good old songs. Request your favorite.

November Theme —   **A MONTH OF PRAISE**

Today's Theme —   **Thanksliving**

Advanced
Preparation:
- Set up the room allowing space for the wheelchair dance. Adapt for any 4 people who are unlikely to dance but could do so with assistance such as those with canes or walkers.
- Organize:
  - a reader for the poetry,
  - a soloist for "The Thank You Song,"
  - a collection of songs of praise.
- Make enough copies of the large print songsheet of "America, the Beautiful," a copy of which is included at the end of this week's session plan. (Verses 2 and 3 are set out on a large print songsheet at the end of the OUR HISTORY IN SONG [July] weekly session plan.)
- Make a poster with the letters of THANKSLIVING printed downward. You will need a black pen to write in answers in the Reminiscence section.

Pre-Session: Pianist plays "We Gather Together," "Come, Ye Thankful People, Come," "Bringing in the Sheaves," and "Count Your Blessings."

Opening: Announce the theme of Praise for THANKSLIVING and that every day is an opportunity to give thanks.

Teach the round "For Health and Strength and Daily Bread." Begin in unison, note how the melody simply descends the scale. Use two leaders and sing as a round. If successful make it a 3-part round. Praise the group for singing 3 parts, something they cannot do alone. The music is included on page 364

Exercise: An assisted wheelchair dance with everyone clapping in rhythm to "Turkey in the Straw." (A songsheet is included at the end of the LET'S ALL SING LIKE THE BIRDIES SING [May] weekly session plan.) are included Pianist plays song and controls tempo. 4 residents and 4 volunteers need to be in a large circle. Push chairs all toward center for 8 beats, backwards 8 beats, round the circle 16 beats. Repeat entire procedure with same group or a new one. Give praise for the enjoyment of the dance that the entire group shared.

Solo Time: Poetry reading — excerpts from "Landing of the Pilgrim Fathers" by Felicia Hemens.[1]

The breaking waves dashed high on a stern and rock bound coast
And the woods against a stormy sky their giant branches tossed.

And the heavy night hung dark. The hills and waters oer
When a band of Pilgrims moored their bark on a wild New England shore.

Aye, call it holy ground, the soil where first they trod
They have left unstained what there they found - freedom to worship God.

---

[1] *Favorite Poems Old and New* (1957) p. 92.

Education: • Our country was founded on the power of praise which can be traced back
                              to the pilgrims. In spite of hardships they were thankful and the fine
                              tradition of thanksgiving was founded.
                            • The pilgrims came from Holland aboard the *Mayflower* and landed in
                              Plymouth Rock, Mass. in 1620. 101 sailed but a year later, only 55
                              survived due to pneumonia, typhoid, and scurvy.
                            • They had a good harvest and thanked God in a 3 day celebration.[1]
                            • An Indian chief and 90 braves showed up with wild turkeys, geese, ducks,
                              and 5 deer. The women cooked for three entire days and ended up with
                              enough food for a week.[2]
                            • 70 acres of corn survived which was new to the pilgrims. They also ate
                              oysters, clams, eels, beans, wild plums, dried cherries, and gooseberries.
                              Pilgrims were too leary to eat cranberries and pumpkins yet since these
                              were new foods.[2]

Guided Imagery: Lead a short relaxation exercise encouraging everyone to close their eyes.
                Slowly read the words to "America, the Beautiful" and have them image the
                scenes. Let the mood of the poetry present a calmness and peace to the
                group. Enjoy the silence at the end. Open eyes and softly sing.

Group Singing: "America, the Beautiful" — use large print songsheet.

Reminiscence: Make a Thanksliving list of all the things you are thankful for. They must begin
                with one of the letters of the word t-h-a-n-k-s-l-i-v-i-n-g. Write the responses
                including the person's name. Leave poster up for the rest of the month and
                print the results in the local paper.

Song
Identification: Tell what there is in the following songs played on the piano that suggest an
                aspect of life for which to be thankful.

                        You Are My SUNSHINE
                        Count Your BLESSINGS *
                        MUSIC MUSIC MUSIC
                        Make New FRIENDS but Keep the Old
                        Put Your ARMS Around Me, Honey (hugs)
                        I LOVE You Truly
                        You're a Grand Old FLAG §
                        My COUNTRY 'Tis of Thee
                        Give Me That Old Time RELIGION
                        M is for the Many Things She Gave Me (mother)]
                        Sleep, BABY, Sleep
                        GREAT DAY
                        Oh What a BEAUTIFUL MORNIN'

                *   A songsheet included at the end of the THANKSGIVING [November] weekly session plan.
                § A songsheet is included at the end of the MEMORABLE MEMORIAL DAY [May] weekly
                   session plan.

---

[1] Points 1-3 in Education section from Myers, R. (1972) *Celebrations*, "Perilous Journey to America" p p. 273-277.
[2] Points 4-5 from *World Book Encyclopedia* (1991) Vol. 19(T) pp. 229-230. "Thanksgiving Day" by Joan Gunderson.

Rhythm Band: "Enjoy Yourself—It's Later Than You Think" — all play appreciatively.
                 "Dance of the Hours" (Hello Muddah) — echo response song, group plays on
                        beats 2 and 3 using a leader for visual cues.
                 "Chiapanecas" — as above, residents play on beats 2 and 3. At the chorus all
                        play in 3/4 time.
                 Any march by John Phillip Sousa — joyous coordinated ending.

Closing: To the tune of "Goodnight Ladies":
                 Verse:
                 1. I am thankful, I am thankful, I am thankful, thankful for RIGHT NOW.
                     Merrily we sing along, sing along, sing along.
                     Merrily we sing along, thankful for RIGHT NOW.
                 2. You are thankful...... (point to each other)
                 3. We are thankful.... (clap hands)

                 Thank everyone for the opportunity to express themselves in our land of
                 freedom and plenty. Invite them to the special Thanksgiving session.

Assignment: Continue with the attitude of THANKSLIVING no matter what the challenges.
                 Every day is a gift. The assignment is to praise 3 things more later today with
                 a twinkle in the eye.

Music
Resources: *One Thousand and One Jumbo* (1985)
                        "Dance of the Hours" p. 260
                 Ultimate Fake Book (1981)
                        "Chiapanecas" p. 92
                 Golden Book of Favorite Songs (1946)
                        "America, the Beautiful" p. 7
                 Mitch Miller Community Song Book (1962)
                        "Come, Ye Thankful People, Come" p. 37
                 Legit Fake Book (1990)
                        "Turkey in the Straw" p. 331

BLESSINGS

music menu

Praise for Thanksliving

1. *Come Ye Thankful People*
2. *Doxology (Old Hundredth)*
3. *We Gather Together*
4. *Count Your Blessings*
5. *Always (Irving Berlin)*
6. *Now Thank We All Our God*
7. *America (My Country 'Tis of Thee)*
8. *Oh What a Beautiful Mornin'*
9. *America, the Beautiful*
10. *Bless This House*

Let this thankful musician
play your favorite.

AMERICA, THE BEAUTIFUL

Oh, beautiful, for spacious skies,
For amber waves of grain,
For purple mountain majesties
Above the fruited plain.

Chorus:
America! America!
God shed his grace on thee,
And Crown thy good with brotherhood
From sea to shining sea.

Verse 2:
Oh Beautiful, for patriot dream
That sees beyond the years,
Thine alabaster cities gleam,
Undimmed by human tears.

(Repeat Chorus)

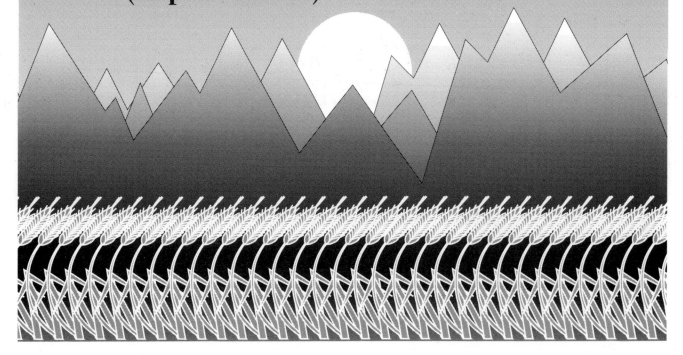

November Theme — **A MONTH OF PRAISE**

Today's Theme — **Thanksgiving**

Advanced
Preparation:
- Fold copies of the Music Menu in half for each table.
- Prepare paper plates with real leaves pasted on them. You may want to use the ones used in the IN PRAISE OF AUTUMN weekly session plan.
- Make copies of large print songsheets. "Count Your Blessings," "Over the River and Through the Woods," and "Bless This House" are all included at the end of this week's session plan.
- Make a collection of Thanksgiving songs.

Pre-Session: Pianist plays "We Gather Together," "Come, Ye Thankful People Come," and "Over the River and Through the Woods," as people gather.

Opening: Opening song "The More We Get Together" to the tune of "Did You Ever See a Lassie" — point to each other.

> The more we get together, together, together,
> The more we get together, the happier we'll be.
> For your friends are my friends, and my friends are your friends.
> The more we get together the happier we'll be.

Exercise: Pass out paper plates with real autumn leaves on them. The leader promotes exercise with these tunes on the piano.
"We Gather Together" — make large circles with plates, reverse 3/4.
'"Come, Ye Thankful People, Come" — rhythmical fanning motion in 2/4 time.
"Over the River and Through the Woods" — follow the leaders with 8 counts for each action — 8 taps on the chest, 8 on arms, 8 on legs.
Grand Finale — arm extension and tossing of plates directly at the leader at the count of 3.

Group Singing: Open with two rounds. Teach them in unison, then 2 parts with 2 leaders.

1. For health and strength and daily bread we give Thee thanks O Lord. (The music is included on page 364 (

2. Turkey Dinner — to the tune of "Frère Jacques" Start standing up.

> Turkey dinner, turkey dinner,
> Gather round, gather round.
> All of us were thinner, till we came to dinner.
> All sit down, All sit down.

Use large print songsheets.
"Over the River and Through the Woods"
"Count Your Blessings"

Solo Time: "Turkey Hunt" by Ann Hill, RN,[1] to the tune of "Up on the Housetop."

In from the garden the housewives run
Looking for that turkey gun.
Out to the barnyard, quick, quick, quick.
Thanksgiving dinner she will pick.

Bang, bang, bang, aim down the sight
Bang, bang, bang, oh good night.
Got a little careless and that's too bad
He was the best dog she ever had.

Education: • First, as a review of last week's session, ask the following:
- Name the boat the pilgrims sailed on? (Mayflower)
- How many came over? (101)
- Where did they land? (Plymouth Rock, Mass)
- How many survived the first year? (55)
- Who were the guests at the first thanksgiving? (91 Indians)
- What did they eat? (deer, lobster, corn, venison, turkey, fruits)
Education Continued:
• The first celebration was in 1621 and George Washington proclaimed it a national holiday in 1789.[2]

Reminiscence: Pianist plays "Thanks for the Memories." Leader encourages anyone to contribute from their memory bank.
• Does any particular Thanksgiving celebration remain vivid? Why?
• Did anyone ever kill a turkey?
• Describe the stuffing used to make the bird delicious.
• Did anyone go over the river and through the woods to grandmother's house by horseback or sleigh?
• Does anyone prefer something other than pumpkin pie?
• Do you think women still bake pumpkin pie from "scratch"?

Song
Identification: Name these favorite Thanksgiving songs.

Turkey in the Straw *
Come, Ye Thankful People, Come
We Gather Together
Now Thank We All Our God
Bringing in the Sheaves
The Landing of the Pilgrims
Count Your Blessings
Let There be Peace on Earth
America, the Beautiful §

*   A songsheet is included at the end of LET'S ALL SING LIKE THE BIRDIES SING [May] weekly   session plan.
§ A songsheet is included at the end of the THANKSLIVING [November] weekly session plan.

---

1   Ann Hill, R.N. Lyricist: Private Communication, October 1991.
2   *Chases Annual Events* (1992) p. 395. "Thanksgiving."

Rhythm Band: "Farmer in the Dell" — use the tune to sing "The Farmer had a band." Call out the various instruments, encourage careful listening. Sing instructions, for example: "The band had some bells."
"Bringing in the Sheaves" — easy 2 beat — all play.
"Turkey in the Straw" — faster tempo, speed up each verse.
"This Land is Your Land" — spirited march celebrating America.

Closing: All sing "God Bless America."

Assignment: Promote the idea that Thanksgiving is more than a one day holiday. Talk about it at the dinner table and then vow to be thankful for something every day.

Music
Resources: *Family Song Book of Faith and Joy* (1981)
  "This Land is Your Land" p. 282
Legit Fake Book (1990)z
  "Over the River and Through the Woods" p. 261
  "Turkey in the Straw" p. 331
Wee Sing for Christmas (1986)
  "Up on the Housetop" p. 46
Mitch Miller Community Song Book (1962)
  "Come, Ye Thankful People, Come" p. 37
Tune Book Songs (1982)
  "Let There Be Peace on Earth" p. 109
  "Count Your Blessings" p. 113

THANKSGIVING
Music Menu

1. Come Ye Thankful People

2. Over the River and Through the Woods

3. Let There Be Peace on Earth

4. The Landing of the Pilgrims

5. Bringing in the Sheaves

6. America, the Beautiful

7. Count Your Blessings

8. How Great Thou Art

9. Turkey in the Straw

10. We Gather Together

Over the River and Through the Woods

Over the river and through the woods,
To grandmother's house we go;
The horse knows the way to carry the sleigh
Through the white and drifted snow.
Over the river and through the woods-
Oh, how the wind doth blow!
It stings the toes and bites the nose,
As over the ground we go.

Over the river and through the woods
And straight through the barnyard gate.
We seem to go extremely slow-
It is so hard to wait!
Over the river and through the woods-
Now grandmother's cap I spy!
Hurrah for the fun! Is the pudding done?
Hurrah for the pumpkin-pie!

Count Your

BLESSINGS

When upon life's living
   You are tempest tossed,
When you are discouraged
   Thinking all is lost,
Count your many blessings
   Name them one by one,
And it will surprise you
   What the Lord has done.

Chorus:
Count your blessings,
   Name them one by one;
Count your blessings,
   See what God has done.
Count your blessings,
   Name them one by one;
Count your many blessings,
   See what God has done.

Bless This House

Bless this house, oh Lord, we pray.
Make it safe by night and day.

Bless these walls, so firm and stout,
Keeping want and trouble out.

Bless the roof and chimney tall.
Let thy peace lie over all.

Bless this door that it may prove
ever open to joy and love.

Bless these windows shining bright
Letting in God's heavenly light.

Bless this home that's filled with caring,
Loving, laughing, praying, sharing.

Bless the folk who all live here.
Keep them kind and free from fear.

Bless us all that we may be
Fit, oh Lord, to dwell with thee.

Bless us all that one day we
May dwell, oh Lord, with thee.

November Theme — **A MONTH OF PRAISE**

Today's Theme — **Praise for Music**
(Optional)

Advanced
Preparation:
• Prepare music note nametags for everyone with "I love _____" printed on them. (The musical preference will be filled in later, during the Special Activity.) A template for this is included at the end of this week's session plan.
• Provide pens and scotch tape.
• Select a soloist for the poetry reading.

Pre-Session:
Pianist plays "Music Music Music," "Music Alone Shall Live," "There's Music in the air."

Opening:
Opening song to the tune of "I've Got Music in my Hands." The music is included on page 75.
1. I've got music in my heart and it's keeping me alive,
   Keeping me alive, keeping me alive.
   I've got music in my heart and it's keeping me alive,
   Music is keeping me alive.
(Hand over heart and sing:)
2. I've got music in my soul and it's keeping me alive (close eyes and sway)
3. I've got music in my shoulders......(lift shoulders up and down)
4. I've got music in my hands.... (clap and sing)

Exercise:
Song with actions "Ich bin der Musikant" — music included on page 50
Ask German resident for help with pronunciation.[1]
Verse 1:

Leader	Ich bin ein musikant (I am a musician)
	Ich komm von _____ (Name of your town)
	Ich kann spielen (I can play)
Response	DU KANNST SPIELEN? (You can play?)
Leader	Auf der violine
Response	AUF DER VIOLINE
All	VIO, VIO, VIOLIN, VIOLIN, VIOLIN
	VIO, VIO, VIOLIN, VIO, VIOLIN. HEH!

(Add a loud HEH to the end of every verse)
Actions: sing and play violin using both arms correctly

Verse 2

Leader	Ich bin ein musikant (I am a musician)
	Ich komm von _____ (Name of your town)
	Ich kann spielen (I can play)
Response	DU KANNST SPIELEN? (You can play?)

---

[1] There are variations in the words since the German language has feminine and masculine nouns; so one uses *der violine, dem piano, ein conductor, dem bagpipe.* Source is Frederick Herzer, German specialist in Webster Groves, MO in a private communication, October 17, 1992.

Exercise:	Leader	Auf der bass viol
(Cont.)	Response	AUF DER BASS VIOL
	All	ZUMBA, ZUMBA, ZUMBA, ZUM, ZUMBA, ZUM, ZUMBA, ZUM.
		ZUMBA, ZUMBA, ZUMBA, ZUM ZUMBA, ZUMBA, ZU. HEH!

Action: pretend to use bass bow by moving arm back and forth at waist level.

Verse 3
Same format. Use "auf dem piano" for the instrument line and "plink plink, plink, plink...HEH!" for the last two lines.
Action: play pianistically either chords, scales, or one finger.

Verse 4
Same format. Use "Wie ein conductor" for the instrument line. For the two lines at the end, all should imagine the melody and conduct silently in the air with 4 beats to a measure. End with a HEH!
Action: follow the conductor and direct the music with one arm.

Verse 5
Same format. Use "auf dem bagpipe" (or dudelsack) for the instrument line and "wah, wah, wah, wah...HEH!" for the last two lines.
Action: hold nose for nasal sound while squeezing right arm into and out from the body.

Solo Time: Poetry reading of "The Arrow and the Song" by Henry W. Longfellow.[1]

I shot an arrow into the air, it fell to earth I know not where;
for, so swiftly it flew, the sight could not follow it in its flight.

I breathed a song into the air, it fell to earth, I know not where;
for who has sight so keen and strong, that it can follow the flight of song?

Long, long afterward, in an oak I found the arrow, still unbroke;
And the song, from beginning to end, I found again in the heart of a
friend.

Reminiscence: Recall any music in the past or present that you would label enjoyable. This includes playing music or listening. Ask the following questions to stimulate the memory.
- How important is music in one's life?
- Were you the musician in the family?
- What kind of music do you prefer? Rock, classical, folk, religious, country, marches, ragtime, easy listening?
- Has anyone's preference in music changed through the years?

Special Activity: On each paper nametag write the individual response to the type of music they love the most. Example: folk music. Attach with scotch tape to be worn all day.

---

1 *Treasury of the Familiar* (1950) p. 172.

Solo Time: Vocalist to sing "With a Smile and a Song," and "Without a Song."

Education: • Music can be defined as sound arranged into pleasing or interesting patterns.
                    • Music is one of the oldest arts. By 10,000 B.C. people discovered how to make flutes out of hollow bones.
                    • Singing began with the development of language.
                    • People use music to express feelings and ideas. Music also entertains, inspires, or relaxes.[1]
                    • In 1992, there were over 54,000 school music teachers giving instructions in band, orchestras, and choral groups in the USA.[2]
                    • "In the last 20 years there has been the acknowledgement of the value of music therapy for people who are not ill, as a helpful means of self-awareness and expression, perhaps even as a branch of preventative medicine."[3]

Song
Identification: Pianist plays the following songs that all have a musical instrument in the title. Anyone should call out the title and then someone should imitate the instrument. Encourage the entire group to "air play" the instrument for exercise and also to experience that position that musicians use most of their lives.

Seventy-six TROMBONES   Little DRUMmer boy
FIDDLER on the Roof   CLARINET Polka
Boogie Woogie BUGLE Boy   Two GUITARS
The HARP that Once Through   The Big Bass VIOL
    Tara's Hills The TRUMPET Shall Sound
When Yuba Plays the Rhumba   The Old PIANO Roll Blues
    on his TUBA
When the ORGAN played at Twilight
There's Somethin' About a Hometown BAND

Rhythm Band: Pass out rhythm instruments. Those that decline are encouraged to "air play" their favorite one.
                    "Fiddler on the Roof" — methodical, deliberate, strong beat.
                    "Old MacDonald Had a Band" — call out name of instruments.
                    "The Blue Danube Waltz" — piano solo, group plays afterbeats — use a leader.
                    "Clarinet Polka" — fast 2 beat.
                    "Seventy-six Trombones" — spirited march.
                    "There's Somethin' About a Hometown Band" — all join in.

Closing: Teach the song or round "Music Alone Shall Live." The music is included on page 428.

---

[1]   Points 1-4 in Education section from *World Book Encyclopedia* (1991), Vol. 13 (M) pp. 946-958. "Music" by R. M. Longyear.
[2]   Telephone Interview with Gail Crum, Information Services Manager of Music Educators October 13 1992, concerning *Educational Mailing List and Marketing Guide for the Muisc Educators National Conferenence*, published by Market Data Retrieval Co. Shelton, Conn.
[3]   Bright, R. (1991) *Music in Geriatric Care: A Second Look.* "History of Music Therapy" p. 15.

Closing: All things shall perish from under the sky, music alone shall live,
(Cont.)   Music alone shall live, music alone shall live, never to die.

Assignment: Reflect on the impact of music on one's life. Encourage residents to ask
                    themselves if they would like more music to be part of their daily living.
                    Suggest they make arrangements to join in group singing, take lessons, play
                    duets, have a Casio piano, use earphones and a Walkman, or mark good radio
                    stations.

Music
Resources: *Ultimate Fake Book* (1981)
                        "There's Somethin' About a Hometown Band" p. 567
                    Wee Sing Around the Campfire (1984)
                        "Music Alone Shall Live" p. 47
                    1001 Jumbo Words and Music (1985)
                        "The Blue Danube Waltz" p. 373
                    Children's Song Book (1988)
                        "With a Smile and a Song" p. 59
                    *Legit Fake Book (*1990)
                        "Without a Song" p. 375
                    Songs for Swinging Housemothers (1961)
                        "Ich bin der Musikant" p. 406

MUSIC ALONE SHALL LIVE

German Folk Song

All things shall per-ish un-der the sky Mus-ic a-lone shall live,
mus-ic a-lone shall live, Mus-ic a-lone shall live, nev-er to die.

Praise for
MUSIC

1. Do - Re - Mi

2. The Lost Chord

3. Say It with Music

4. Johnny One Note

5. Music Music Music

6. The Sound of Music

7. Rock and Roll Music

8. Two Hearts in Three Quarter Time

9. Melody in F (Rubinstein)

10. There's Music in the Air

11. A Pretty Girl is Like a Melody

12. The Music Goes 'Round and 'Round

13. Gee! But I Like Music With My Meals

**Please tell me your favorite
so that I can play and praise it.**

November – "Praise for Music"

"Praise for Autumn"

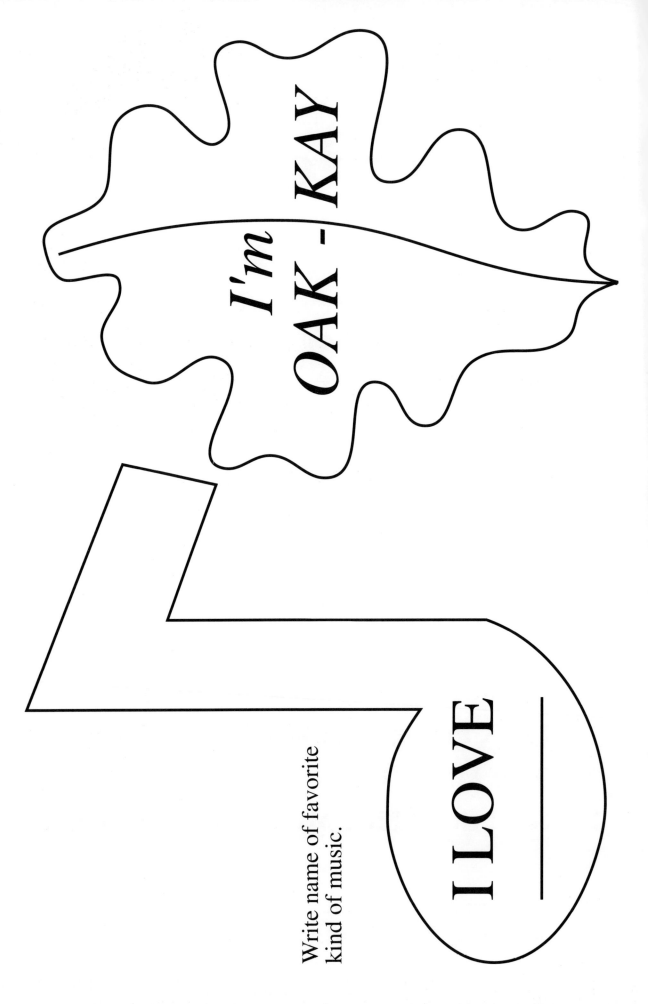

I'm OAK - KAY

Write name of favorite kind of music.

I LOVE _____

December

Holiday Happiness

A Musical Game for December

The following song titles will stir the five senses. After you name the song, see if you can smell it or picture it or even hear it. The answers are upside down.

SIGHTS OF CHRISTMAS
  1. _____ _____ is Coming to Town
  2. Rudolph the Red-Nosed _____
  3. Away in a _____

SOUNDS OF CHRISTMAS
  4. I Heard the _____ on Christmas Day
  5. _____, _____ Little Girl and Boyland
  6. Here We Come a _____

SMELLS OF CHRISTMAS
  7. O Christmas _____
  8. T_____ in the Straw
  9. The Trail of the Lonesome _____

SPIRIT OF CHRISTMAS
  10. Let There Be _____ on Earth
  11. O Come All Ye _____
  12. Silent _____

1. Santa Claus 2. Reindeer 3. Manger 4. Bells 5. Toyland
6. Caroling 7. Tree 8. Turkey 9. Pine 10. Peace 11. Faithful
12. Night. May your holidays be filled with music in your heart
and lips.

December Game
Extra Holiday Fun!

Dust off your holiday memories and answer the following music related questions:

1. What is the reindeer's name with the red nose?
2. What little town lies sweet and still?
3. Who did you see mommy kissing?
4. How many reindeer does Santa have?
5. How many can you name?
6. Who wrote the poem "The Night Before Christmas"?
7. What should we deck the halls with?
8. What color Christmas are you dreaming of?
9. Would you want a partridge in a pear tree for a gift?
10. Can you still go ho ho ho???

(The answers are upside down.)

HO HO HO

1. Rudolph 2. Bethlehem 3. Santa Claus 4. eight 5. Dasher, Dancer, Prancer, Vixon, Comet, Cupid, Donder, Blitzen 6. Clement Moore 7. Holly 8. white 9. the pear, yes 10. Good for you!

HOLIDAY HAPPINESS
DECEMBER

Holiday time for all religions and festivals are overloaded with activities and so are the following programs. Choose carefully what is best for your residents and facility. Since most programming for the month of December is easily provided by the community as entertainment, these programs are designed for involvement by the residents themselves. There is a lot of sensory stimulation suggested that is adaptable for all stages and ages of life. The emphasis here is on many aspects of the holidays so that everyone can celebrate the entire month. A staff planning meeting should be held early to make this a smooth month. There are opportunities for involvement for everyone in the following programs.

Shop early or make red Santa hats trimmed with fake fur and a bell for your volunteers. They wear them for every December session as a promotion and to identify themselves as truly "Santa's Helpers." Then they get to keep them as a memorable gift.

If your budget allows it, consider having Santa arrive by helicopter. This is a family, staff, community, and resident activity that is one of the highlights of the year. All ages watch the windows and listen for the whirr of the blades and the helicopter lands right before your eyes. Mr. and Mrs. Claus greet everyone. It is exciting and the cost is around $200 for this unforgettable event. If a helicopter is impossible, consider renting a horse and buggy with everyone singing "Here Comes Santa Claus." Armed with cameras, film, and flash bulbs, there will be winning photos.

The Sights of Christmas — Everyone can recall sights associated with the holidays and your volunteers will enjoy collecting familiar ones for this program. Your rhythm band will be a glorious sight in itself.

The Smells of Christmas — There are so many good smells associated with this season that even the weak noses will recall numerous ones. In addition, it makes everyone aware all month long of seasonal smells.

The Sounds of Christmas — Music, music, music. Gather lots of bells and fill your facility with the holiday sounds. There is joy in singing the carols and usually some harmonies to make the rafters ring.

The Spirit of Christmas — This is a quiet relaxing program that releases tension and any anxiety regarding the holidays. Let the community provide the glitter with their programs. You can offer the gift of the peace of Christmas.

Chanukah[1] — The Festival of Lights — This holiday commemorates the continuous dedication of a people to the practice that binds them together as a community. The program of observance, music, and a game of dreydl combines joy with solemnity.

---

[1] This spelling of "Chanukah" will be used throughout the text, although there are many different ways of spelling it. However, all song titles/book titles, etc. will be cited with the spelling used by the composer/author.

OPTIONAL PROGRAMS

Celebrate Christmas — Five Possibilities — These programs are designed for a Christmas Day program. They do not follow the usual format. You choose the one that best fits your residents. Remember that many people will be elsewhere or pre-occupied with numerous visitors. Those attending get a special program that is designed to be intimate and meaningful.

Goodbye Old Year, Hello New — Celebrate the fact that everyone made it through another year and enjoy the memories. Say goodbye to this old year and welcome the new one with Hello songs. Arrange for a real New Year's baby to appear and win everyone's heart.

THIS IS THE YEAR YOUR DREAMS COME TRUE
MAKE IT HAPPEN!

December Theme — **HOLIDAY HAPPINESS**

Today's theme — **The Sights of Christmas**

Advanced
Preparation:
- Props for the holiday happiness this week include:
  - roping tinsel in red, green, silver and gold,
  - a collection of holiday songs,
  - lots of jingle bells,
  - red holiday Santa caps for volunteers and staff.
- Prepare a Santa sack filled with various appropriate items such as bells, packages, baked goods, and decorations.
- Make copies, if need be, of "Must Be Santa," the music of which is included on page 440.

Pre-Session: Volunteers escort residents to session wearing red caps, and jingling a bell. Pianist plays "Deck the Halls," "Silver Bells," and "White Christmas."

Opening: Opening song adapted to the tune of "We Wish You a Merry Christmas." Sing the following verses with appropriate actions:
Verse:
1. Let's all do a little waving
   Let's all do a little waving
   Let's all do a little waving and spread Christmas cheer.
2. Let's all do a little clapping....
3. Let's all do a little hugging....(aides hug as many residents as possible)
4. Let's all do some more hugging (residents hug themselves)
5. Let's all do a little kissing....(blow kisses everywhere)

Exercise: Pass out colorful tinsel roping in long lines with all hands holding on. Teach the song "Deck the Halls" as follows. This can be sung as a response song.

Leader	Deck the halls with Christmas roping
Response	FA LA LA LA LA LA LA LA LA
Leader	There's no time for moans or moping
Response	FA LA LA LA LA LA LA LA LA
Leader	Don we now our gay apparel
Response	FA LA LA LA LA LA LA LA LA
Leader	Troll the ancient yuletide carol
Response	FA LA LA LA LA LA LA LA LA.

Add the actions of raising the tinsel overhead as a long line when the leader indicates the row that is involved. Raise and lower with each line of music so more lines participate. Repeat faster.

Group Singing: The sights of Christmas: Use the response song "Must Be Santa".

Leader	Who's got a beard that's long and white?
Response	SANTA'S GOT A BEARD THAT'S LONG AND WHITE.

Group Singing: (Cont.)	Leader	Who comes around on a special night?
	Response	SANTA COMES AROUND ON A SPECIAL NIGHT.
	All	Must be Santa, must be Santa, must be Santa, Santa Claus

Reminiscence: Suggest the residents recall any sights associated with the holiday season. Keep on the subject, postpone smells and sounds for other sessions. Include packages, creches, bells, baked goods, stores, decorations, choirs, wreaths, smiles. To stimulate recall, pull some of these items from the Santa sack, or place them around the room.

Song Identification: Pianist plays these songs that all have one of the sights of Christmas in the song title. Call out the answer.

Here Comes SANTA CLAUS
WHITE Christmas (snow)
Away in a MANGER
Silver BELLS
O Christmas TREE *
We THREE KINGS
Up on the HOUSETOP
SMILES
Here We Come a-Caroling
   (carol singers)
I'm Gonna Sit Right Down and
    Write Myself a LETTER
Silent NIGHT §

When you Wish Upon a STAR
Rudolph the Red-Nosed REINDEER
Youl LIGHT up My Life
I saw Mommy Kissing Santa Claus
   Underneath the MISTLETOE
Deck the Halls with Boughs of HOLLY
CHESTNUTS Roasting on an
   OPEN FIRE ("The Christmas Song")
Make New FRIENDS
I Ain't Got a Barrel of MONEY
Love Sends a Little GIFT of Roses
TOYland TOYland

*   A songsheet is included at the end of this week's session plan.
§ A songsheet is included at the end of the tTHE SPIRIT OF CHRISTMAS [December] weekly session plan.

Rhythm Band: "Row, Row, Row Your Boat" — to this tune sing the following song:
     Ring, ring, ring your bells, ring them loud and clear,
       To tell the children everywhere that Christmas time is near.
    Adapt to various instruments. For example:
     Hit hit hit your sticks, hit them loud and clear.....
"Silver Bells" — solo for bells that play after each phrase of music. For example: Silver bells (ringing), silver bells (ringing), it's Christmas time in the city (ringing).
"Rudolph the Red-Nosed Reindeer" — all play merrily.
"Smiles" — smile and play at the same time. Who smiles the longest? (A songsheet is included at the end of the EVERYONE LOVES A SMILE [February] weekly session plan.)
"Parade of the Wooden Soldiers" — Start softly, build, end softly.

Closing: All sing to the tune of "We Wish You a Merry Christmas"
    We wish you a happy holiday,
    We wish you a happy holiday,

Assignment:

We wish you a happy holiday that's starting RIGHT NOW
Encourage everyone to enjoy the sights they recall even if their present sight is limited. The assignment is to prepare for next week's session and start thinking about THE SMELLS OF CHRISTMAS. Think so much you can almost smell the items.

Music
Resources:

Wee Sing for Christmas (1986)
    "Must Be Santa" p. 54
    "Ring, Ring, Ring the Bells" p. 49
    "We Wish You a Merry Christmas" p. 8
    "Deck the Halls" p. 7
Treasury of Best Loved Songs (1981)
    "Toyland" p. 215
    "Side by Side" p. 119
Family Songbook of Faith and Joy (1981)
    "Love Sends a Little Gift of Roses" 180
Original Legal Musicians Fake Book (1980)
    "Silver Bells" p. 557
Sheet Music, Leonard Jessel, Edward Marcus Corporation, Radio City, NY. (1933)
    "Parade of the Wooden Soldiers"
Sheet Music, Irving Berlin, Irving Berlin Publishing Co/Hal Leonard, Milwaukee, WS. (1942)
    "White Christmas"

MUST BE SANTA

Hal Moore & Bill Fredericks

Hal Moore & Bill Fredericks

1. Who's got a beard that's long and white? San-ta's got a beard that's long and white.

Who comes a-round on a spe-cial night? San-ta comes a-round on a spe-cial night.

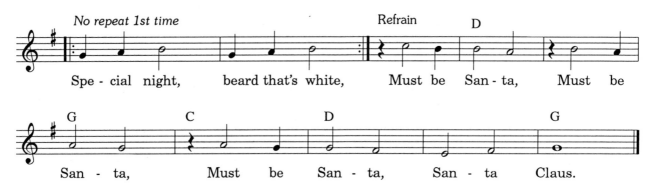

No repeat 1st time   Refrain

Spe - cial night,   beard that's white,   Must be San - ta,   Must be

San - ta,   Must be San - ta,   San - ta Claus.

2. Who's got boots and a suit of red?
Santa's got boots and a suit of red.
Who wears a long cap on his head?
Santa wears a long cap on his head.
Cap on head, suit that's red,
Special night, beard that's white,
(Chorus)

3. Who's got a great big cheery nose?
Santa's got a great big cheery nose.
Who laughs this way, "Ho, ho, ho?"
Santa laughs this way, "Ho, ho, ho."
Ho, ho, ho, cheery nose,
Cap on head, suit that's red,
Special night, beard that's white,
(Chorus)

4. Who very soon will come our way?
Santa very soon will come our way.
Eight little reindeer pull his sleigh.
Santa's little reindeer pull his sleigh.
Reindeer sleigh, come our way,
Ho, ho, ho, cheery nose,
Cap on head, suit that's red,
Special night, beard that's white,
(Chorus)

SIGHTS *of* CHRISTMAS

1. <u>Smiles</u>
2. Silent <u>Night</u>
3. Away in a <u>Manger</u>
4. I'm Gonna Sit Right Down and Write Myself a <u>Letter</u>
5. Here Comes <u>Santa Claus</u>
6. Love Sends a Little <u>Gift</u> of Roses
7. The Christmas Song (<u>Chestnuts</u> Roasting on an Open Fire)
8. Rudolph the Red-Nosed <u>Reindeer</u>
9. Here We Come a <u>Caroling</u>
10. Make New <u>Friends</u>
11. O Christmas <u>Tree</u>
12. <u>White</u> Christmas
13. Silver <u>Bells</u>

Tell me your favorite sight and song for this happy season.

O Tannenbaum

O Tannenbaum, O Tannenbaum, wie treu sind deine Blätter.

O Tannenbaum, O Tannenbaum, wie treu sind deine Blätter.

Du grunst nicht nur zur Sommerzeit,

Nein auch im Winter wenn es schneit.

O Tannenbaum, O Tannenbaum, wie treu sind deine Blätter.

– German Traditional

O Christmas Tree

O Christmas Tree, O Christmas Tree, thy leaves are so unchanging.

O Christmas Tree, O Christmas Tree, thy leaves are so unchanging

Not only green when summer's here,

But also when 'tis cold and drear.

O Christmas Tree, O Christmas Tree, thy leaves are so unchanging.

– English verse by James Ryder Randall (1861)

December Theme — **HOLIDAY HAPPINESS**

Today's Theme — **The Smells of Christmas**

Advanced
Preparation:
- Provide:
  - a fresh green evergreen bough for each person,
  - a fresh Christmas tree,
  - potpourri pot with Christmas aroma simmering as people gather.
- Punch holes in paper bags and in each one put one of the following: pumpkin pie spice, pine cones sprayed with scent, evergreens, sliced apples, cinnamon, ginger to represent gingerbread, peppermint, and popcorn.

Pre-Session: Volunteers wear a sprig of evergreens; pianist plays "O Christmas Tree," and "Deck the Halls."

Opening: Sing and point to each other singing, to the tune of "We Wish You a Merry Christmas"

> We wish you a happy holiday
> We wish you a happy holiday
> We wish you a happy holiday and especially RIGHT NOW.

Sing slowly, emphasizing the word YOU while pointing. Repeat several times. Announce today's theme of THE SMELLS OF CHRISTMAS.

Exercise: Pass out an evergreen bough to all. Encourage deep breathing savoring the aroma of fresh cut pine. To the tune of "Jimmy Crack Corn" sing the following with the appropriate actions.
1. Wave that branch up in the air
   Wave that branch up in the air
   Wave that branch up in the air, Christmas time has come.
2. Wave that branch and nod your head...
3. Wave that branch and give a twist......
4. Wave that branch around and around
5. Smell that branch now good and deep....

Group Singing: "O Christmas Tree." Any German Residents sing "O Tannenbaum." A sonsheet of "O Tannenbaum" is included at the end of the THE SIGHTS OF CHRISTMAS [December] weekly session plan.

> O Christmas tree, O Christmas tree, how evergreen your branches.
> they're green when summer days are bright,
> They're green when winter snows are white.
> O Christmas tree, O Christmas tree, how evergreen your branches.

Reminiscence: With closed eyes, encourage residents to concentrate on former Christmas trees.
- Were they hand cut?
- Think about the decorations. Did anyone use real candles on the tree?
- Was there ever a fire?
- How much did a tree cost years ago?
- Did anyone decorate a tree outdoors?
- Did you string popcorn?
- Did you ever have a cat climb the tree or knock it over?

With open eyes, share the scene and smells that were recollected.

Special Sensory
Activity: THE SMELLS OF CHRISTMAS. First talk about some of the favorite smells associated with the holidays. Following this discussion, see how many smells are hidden in the paper bags. Circulate the prepared bags and ask the residents to guess the contents: pumpkin pie spice, pine cones sprayed with scent, evergreens, sliced apples, cinnamon, ginger to represent gingerbread, peppermint, and popcorn.

Rhythmic
Chant: This is taken from the song "Fruitcake."

Group 1 chants in whole notes
"Sift the flour and fold in eggs."
Group 2 chants in quarter notes
"Now you add some lemon peel, I would say a cup or two, then some raisins, dates, and figs, just how much is up to you."
Group 3 says in eighth notes
"Cloves and spice will make it nice but don't forget the cinnamon."

After the parts are learned, you can use three leaders and do it simultaneously and make a "fruitcake."

Song
Identification: Name the smells suggested in these songs:

The Trail of the Lonesome PINE
CHESTNUTS Roasting on an Open FIRE ("The Christmas Song")
On the Good Ship LOLLIPOP
When the ROLL is Called up Yonder *
Shortnin' BREAD
TURKEY in the Straw §
Over the River and Through the Woods (Hurrah for the PUMPKIN PIE) †
TEA for Two

*   A songsheet is included at the end of this week's session plan.
§   A songsheet is included at the end of the LET'S SLL SING LIKE THE BIRDIES SING [May] weekly session plan.
†   A songsheet is included at the end of the THANKSGIVING [November] weekly session plan.

Song
Identification
(cont)
    Chanuka Song (Candles) — honor Jewish holidays also
    Don't Sit Under the APPLE Tree
    Take Me Out to the Ball Game (buy me some PEANUTS and CRACKERJACK)
    O CHRISTMAS TREE

Rhythm Band:
    "March of the Kings" (Bizet *Farandole*) — play slowly, majestically.
    "March of the Toys" — play in 8 measure sections calling out the various instruments, ending with everyone playing.
    "O Christmas Tree" — strong, joyous 3/4 celebration.

Closing:
    Repeat the opening song:
    Verse:
1. We wish you a happy holiday (pointing to each other)
   We wish you a happy holiday
   We wish you a happy holiday and especially RIGHT NOW.
2. I wish me a happy holiday.... (pointing to self)
3. I wish us a happy holiday...(raise up arms and emphasize the words RIGHT NOW by accenting with the arms)

Assignment:
    Invite recall of some of the same smells discussed today and encourage residents to picture a scene associated with the smell. Give thanks for your nose and the years of service it has given. Next week's session is called THE SOUNDS OF CHRISTMAS.

Music
Resources:
    Wee Sing for Christmas (1986)
        "March of the Kings" p. 28
        "We Wish You a Merry Christmas" p. 8 ("Bring Us Some Figgy Pudding")[1]
        "O Christmas Tree" p. 9
    Great Music's Greatest Hits (1982)
        "March of the Toys" p. 155
    Jewish Folk and Holiday Songs (1978)
        "Chanuka Song" p. 16
    Family Songbook of Faith and Joy (1981)
        "Tea for Two" p. 98
        "When the Roll is Called up Yonder" p. 144
    Legit Fake Book (1990)
        "Over the River and Through the Woods" p. 261
        "Shortnin' Bread" p. 301
    Sheet Music, P. Hageman and P. Leka, Belwin Mills. (1978)
        "Fruitcake"

---

[1] On the Music Menu, "Bring us Some Figgy Pudding" is listed as a song title, but is actually the first line of the second verse of this Christmas favorite.

The SMELLS of Christmas

1. O Christmas Tree

2. The Big Rock Candy Mountain

3. The Christmas Song
    (Chestnuts Roasting on an Open Fire)

4. The Trail of the Lonesome Pine

5. When the Roll is Called Up Yonder

6. Shortnin' Bread

7. Turkey in the Straw

8. Tea for Two

9. We Wish You a Merry Christmas
    (Bring Us Some Figgy Pudding)

10. Over the River and Through the Woods
    (Hurrah for the Pumpkin Pie)

Tell me your favorite aromatic melody!

When the Roll is Called Up Yonder

When the trumpet of the Lord shall sound
and time shall be no more,
And the morning breaks eternal, bright, and fair;
When the saved of Earth shall gather
over on the other shore,
And the roll is called up yonder, I'll be there.

On that bright and cloudless morning,
when the dead in Christ shall rise,
And the glory of His resurrection share;
When His chosen ones shall gather
to their home beyond the skies,
And the roll is called up yonder, I'll be there.

CHORUS:

When the roll is called up yonder,
When the roll is called up yonder,
When the roll is called up yonder,
When the roll is called up yonder, I'll be there.

– James M. Black (1893)

December Theme — **HOLIDAY HAPPINESS**

Today's Theme — **The Sounds of Christmas**

Advanced
Preparation:
- Gather together:
  - lots of bells,
  - a collection of holiday music,
  - large cards depicting the 12 days of Christmas with a numbered day on both sides of each card.
- Arrange mistletoe hanging from the ceiling.

Pre-Session: Volunteers greet everyone with sounds of jingling bells, pianist plays "Silver Bells," "I Heard the Bells on Christmas Day," and "Jingle Bells."

Opening: Either sing "We Wish You a Merry Christmas" with actions or alter the words to "We Wish you Happy Holidays and a Happy New Year." Announce the theme of THE SOUNDS OF CHRISTMAS — and singing is but one of them.

Exercise: Sing above song with these actions:
Verse:
(1.   Already sung above in the Opening section.)
2. Let's all do a little clapping
   Let's all do a little clapping
   Let's all do a little clapping and spread Christmas cheer.
3. Let's all do a little stretching...... (Note mistletoe above)
4. Let's all to a little waving.....
5. Let's all do a little kissing... (blow kisses to each other)

Group Singing: "Jingle Bells" — with an ostinato. Use the key of C major for the melody. Sing G to C alternately as an ostinato with the words "Hear those bells" on 2 half notes and a whole note led by a conductor. Rehearse this section first. When well established, have melody join in. Add some bells and put it all together for a joyous cooperative activity.

Solo Time: Everyone gets to be a poet as they complete the lines to the poem "The Night Before Christmas" by Clement Moore.[1] See separate page.

More Group
Singing: Sing "Must Be Santa" as a response song. Rehearse refrain first. The music is included on page 440. Use only a few verses.

Reminiscence: Invite recall of any sounds associated with Christmas time. Try to include choirs, bells, pinecones opening, cash register, music boxes, children, kitchen sounds, Salvation Army bell, sawing the Christmas tree, candles, carolers, wrapping packages, organ, ho-ho-ho, and,.......angels?

---

[1]   *One Hundred One Famous Poems* (1958) p. 150. The correct title of this poem is "A Visit From St. Nicholas." It is better known by it's more familiar title "The Night Before Christmas."

Song
Identification: Call out the sounds suggested in these song titles:

        Jingle BELLS
        I Heard the BELLS on Christmas Day
        Silver BELLS
        The Little DRUMmer Boy
        Here we Come a-CAROLING
        ANGELS We Have Heard on High*
        MUSIC MUSIC MUSIC
        When the ORGAN Played at Twilight
        Let it SNOW, Let It SNOW, Let It SNOW
        Must Be SANTA

       *   A songsheet is included at the end of this week's session plan.

Group Activity: Sing "The Twelve Days of Christmas" with 2 or 3 people on each part. as a
response song. Distribute the days. There is no need to use all 12 unless your
group is well coordinated and very large. Make sure the '5 gold rings' are a
solid singing group and a bit theatrical. This song was written in 1760.

Leader	On the first day of Christmas, my true love gave to me
Group 1 (All)	A PARTRIDGE IN A PEAR TREE.
Leader	On the second day of Christmas my true love gave to me
Group 2	TWO TURTLE DOVES
All	AND A PARTRIDGE IN A PEAR TREE.

Continue at least through six days with 3 french hens, 4 calling birds, 5 gold
rings, 6 geese a-laying, 7 swans a-swimming, 8 maids a-milking, 9 ladies
dancing, 10 lords a-leaping, 11 pipers piping, 12 drummers dancing AND A
PARTRIDGE IN A PEAR TREE.

Rhythm Band: Residents must listen carefully for directions from the leader. The tune is
"Row, Row, Row Your Boat."
1. Leader sings:
      Ring, ring, ring the bells, ring them loud and clear
      Tell the people everywhere that Christmas time is here.
   All sing the same verse with bells only ringing to the rhythm.
2. Leader sings:
      Play, play, play the sticks, play them loud and clear
      Tell the people everywhere that Christmas time is here.

Residents should continue carefully listening for different sounds in the band.

"Silver Bells" — bells only at the end of each phrase.
   Silver bells (ring) silver bells (ring)
   It's Christmas time in the city (ring)
   Ring a ling (ring) hear them ring (ring)
   Soon it will be Christmas day. (ring long)
"Joy to the World" — all play emphatically.

Closing: All sing "We Wish you a Merry Christmas" (or "We Wish You a Happy Holiday")
               Verse:
               1. I wish you a merry Christmas (point to self)
                   I wish you a merry Christmas,
                   I wish you a merry Christmas and a healthy New Year.
               2. I wish me a merry Christmas..... (point to self)
               3. I wish us a merry Christmas......(arms up high)

Assignment: The assignment is to continue to enjoy the sounds of Christmas time. Encourage all to discover 3 new sounds and report to each other of their new awareness.

Music
Resources: *Wee Sing for Christmas* (1986)
                   "Must Be Santa" p. 54
                   "Twelve Days of Christmas" p. 12
                   "We Wish You a Merry Christmas" p. 9
                   "Ring, Ring, Ring The Bells" p. 49
                   "Joy to the World" p. 15
               Original Legal Musicians Fake Book (1988)
                   "Silver Bells" p. 557

THE NIGHT BEFORE CHRISTMAS
by Clement C. Moore

'Twas the night before _____, when all through the _____
Not a creature was stirring, not even a _____;
The stockings were hung by the _____ with care,
In hopes that _____ soon would be there;
The children were nestled all snug in their _____,
While visions of _____ danced in their heads;
And Mamma in her _____, and I in my _____,
Had just settled our _____ for a long winter's nap,—
When out on the _____ there arose such a clatter,
I sprang from my _____ to see what was the matter.
Away to the window I flew like a _____,
Tore open the _____ and threw up the _____.
The moon on the breast of the new-fallen _____
Gave a luster of mid-day to objects below;
When what to my wandering eyes should appear,
But a miniature _____ and eight tiny _____,
With a little old driver, so lively and quick
I knew in a moment it must be _____.
More rapid than _____ his courses they came,
And he whistled and shouted, and called them by _____:
"Now, Dasher! now, D_____! now, Prancer and V_____!
On, Comet! on, C_____! on, Donder and B_____!
To the top of the porch, to the top of the _____,
Now dash away, dash away, dash away, all."
As dry leaves that before the wild _____ fly,
When they meet with an obstacle, mount to the _____,
So up to the house-top the coursers they flew,
With the sleigh full of _____, and St. Nicholas too.
And then in a twinkling I heard on the _____
The prancing and pawing of each little _____.
As I drew in my _____, and was turning around,
Down the _____ St. Nicholas came with a _____.
He was dressed all in _____ from his head to his _____,
And his clothes were all tarnished with ashes and _____;
A bundle of _____ he had flung on his _____,
And he looked like a pedlar just opening his _____.
His eyes, how they _____! his dimples, how _____!
His cheeks were like _____, his nose like a _____;
His droll little _____ was drawn up like a bow,
And the beard on his _____ was as white as the _____.
The stump of a _____ he held tight in his teeth,
And the smoke it encircled his head like a _____.
He had a broad _____ and a little round _____
That shook, when he laughed, like a bowl full of _____.
He was chubby and _____, and a right jolly old _____;
And I laughed, when I saw him, in spite of _____.
A wink of his eye and a twist of his _____
Soon gave me to know I had nothing to dread.
He spoke not a _____, but went straight to his work,
And filled all the _____; then turned with a jerk,
And laying his finger aside of his _____,
And giving a nod, up the _____ he rose.
He sprang to his _____, to his team gave a _____,
And away they all flew like the down of a _____;
But I heard him exclaim, ere he drove out of sight,
"Happy Christmas to all, and to all a _____"

The SOUNDS of Christmas

1. Jingle Bells

2. Silver Bells

3. Silent Night

4. Hallelujah Chorus

5. The Birthday of a King

6. Jolly Old St. Nicholas

7. O Come, Little Children

8. Here Comes Santa Claus

9. The Little Drummer Boy

10. Here We Come A-Caroling

11. Angels We Have Heard on High

12. I Heard the Bells on Christmas Day

13. Let It Snow, Let It Snow, Let It Snow

Let me hear about your favorite Christmas sounds.

Angels
We Have
Heard
on High

TRADITIONAL

Angels we have heard on high
Sweetly singing o'er the plains,
And the mountains in reply
Echoing their joyous strains.

Shepherds, why this jubilee?
Why your joyous strains prolong?
What the gladsome tindings be
Which inspire your heav'nly song?

Come to Bethlehem and see
Him whose birth the angels sing.
come adore on bended knee
Christ the Lord, the newborn King.

CHORUS:

Glo-ria in excelses Deo,
Glo-ria in excelses Deo.

– Traditional (c. 1855)

December Theme — **HOLIDAY HAPPINESS**

Today's Theme —   **The Spirit of Christmas**

Advanced
Preparation:
- Prepare long roping of tinsel in silver and gold.
- Arrange for a soloist to sing "Still, Still, Still," and a violinist or a vocalist to perform "O Holy Night." The music to "Still, Still, Still" is included on page 458.
- Make a selection of carols for the pianist, or a tape of carols.

Pre-Session: Soft Christmas music on the piano or tapes of "Away in a Manger," "O Little Town of Bethlehem," "The First Noel," and "Jesu Bambino."

Opening: Announce that it is a good time to get rid of all the tension associated with the holidays and that this session will guarantee a feeling of peace. Learn a new song to the tune of "Coming Round the Mountain." Music is included on page 457.

1. Medium Tempo:
I can feel the Christmas tension inside me
I can feel the Christmas tension inside me
I can feel the Christmas tension
I can feel the Christmas tension
I can feel the Christmas tension inside me.

2. Invite everyone to tense their muscles, then relax. Next take some deep breaths and slowly let it out, releasing tension. Sing slowly and softly "I can feel the CHRISTMAS SPIRIT inside me." (It is the spirit of love and peace.)

Exercise: Pass out the roping in long rows joining corners until the entire room is joined with the colorful tinsel. Families and volunteers will be needed to add strength. All join in the singing of "The First Noel" On the first beat of every measure, the group sways slowly from side to side with the tinsel. All arms and tinsel are raised over head on the final line "Born is the King of Israel."

Education:
- Christmas is a Christian festival celebrating the birth of Jesus of Nazareth. It is the most widely celebrated holiday of the Christian year and falls on December 25th. It is also known as the Feast of the Nativity.
- In the 4th Century the Western church chose the date perhaps to counteract the non-Christian festivals held around that time such as Yuletimes, festivals of David and the winter solstice.[1]
- The name Santa Claus is taken from the Dutch name for the 4th Century St. Nicholas given by the Colonial Manhattan Islanders.[2]

Reminiscence: Help the residents recall a time of being in a nativity play or seeing their children or grandchildren participate in one. Remember the songs, staging, and costumes, and especially the FEELINGS it brought.

---

[1]   Points one and two in the Education section from *Chases Annual Events* (1992) p. 423.
[2]   *Information Please Almanac* (1992) p. 587.

Solo Time: Soloist sings and old Austrian carol "Still, Still, Still One Can Hear the Falling Snow." Invite anyone to close their eyes and imagine the scene while it is being sung or else read as poetry. (Music is included on page 458.)

> Still, still, still one can hear the falling snow.
> For all is hushed, the world is sleeping.
> Holy Star its vigil keeping
> Still, still, still one can hear the falling snow.
>
> Sleep, sleep, sleep, 'tis the eve of our Saviour's birth.
> The night is peaceful all around you,
> Close your eyes ,let sleep surround you
> Sleep, sleep, sleep 'tis the eve of our Saviour's birth.
>
> Dream, dream, dream of the joyous day to come.
> While guardian angels without number
> Watch as you sweetly slumber.
> Dream, dream, dream of the joyous day to come.

Guided Imagery: Invite anyone to set aside the glitter of the holidays, the concern about gifts, the frustration of remembering everything and everybody, and all the commercial aspects of Christmas. Ask them "What is left?" The answer is peace. The following imagery will help everyone experience more peace in their lives.

Leader gently urges relaxation of sets of muscles. Trained leader is recommended for this activity. Good breathing releasing all tension is also suggested. As the group experiences a state of relaxation "Silent Night" is softly played on the piano. (A songsheet is included at the end of this week's session plan.) This is followed by a violin solo of "O Holy Night." Leader suggests that everyone keep their eyes closed a little longer and enjoy the feeling of peace within themselves and also in the room. Then open the eyes and slowly proceed to a group song.

Group Singing: "Peace Like a River." Sing it softly and slowly. Music is included on page 458.
1. I've got peace like a river, I've got peace like a river
    I've got peace like a river in my soul. (Repeat all words.)
2. I've got joy like a river..... etc. (Sing this slowly.)

Closing: Group sings closing song to the tune of "We Wish You a Merry Christmas."
    I wish you a peaceful Christmas.
    I wish you a peaceful Christmas.
    I wish you a peaceful Christmas and a peaceful New Year.
Encourage residents to turn to the person next to them and say "peace to you."

Assignment: Anytime there is a feeling of holiday tension including indigestion or over-eating, suggest residents recall today's session and get themselves back to the SPIRIT OF CHRISTMAS which is love and peace.

Music
Resources: *Ultimate Fake Book* (1981)
                "O Holy Night" p. 417
                "The First Noel" p. 168
            Tune Book Songs (1982)
                "Peace Like a River" p. 157
            Wee Sing for Christmas (1986)
                "Silent Night" p. 20
            Sheet Music, Austrian carol arranged by Norman Luboff, Lyrics by Marilyn
            Keith and Alan Bergman. Walton Music Corp. (1960)
                "Still, Still, Still"

I FEEL THE CHRISTMAS SPIRIT
(Tune: She's Coming 'Round the Mountain)

Words by Joan Shaw   American Folk Melody

I can feel the Christ-mas ten - sion in - side me. I can
I can feel the Christ-mas Spir - it in - side me. I can

feel the Christ-mas ten-sion in-side me. I can feel the Christ-mas ten-sion, I can
feel the Christ-mas spi-rit in-side me. I can feel the Christ-mas spi-rit, I can

feel the Christ-mas ten-sion, I can feel the Christ-mas ten-sion in-side me.
feel the Christ-mas spi-rit, I can feel the Christ-mas spi-rit in-side me.

PEACE LIKE A RIVER

Traditional

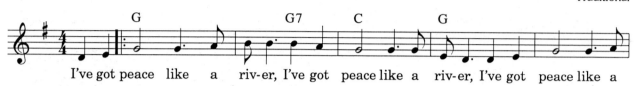

I've got peace like a riv-er, I've got peace like a riv-er, I've got peace like a

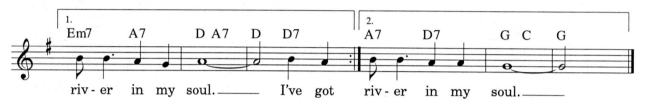

riv - er in my soul._____ I've got   riv - er in my soul._____

2. I've got love like an ocean
I've got love like an ocean
I've got love like an ocean in my soul.

3. I've got joy like a fountain
I've got joy like a fountain
I've got joy like a fountain in my soul.

STILL, STILL, STILL

Words by Marilyn Keith
& Dean Bergman

Austrian Carol

Still,__ still,__ still one can hear the__ fall - ing__ snow. For

all is__ hushed, the world is__ sleep-ing, Ho-ly__ Star its vi-gil keep-ing

Still,__ still,__ still one can hear the__ fall - ing__ snow.

Spirit of Christmas

1. O Holy Night
2. Away in a Manger
3. What Child is This?
4. Stille Nacht
5. O Little Town of Bethlehem
6. Hallelujah Chorus from
   Handel's "Messiah"
7. Angels We Have Heard on High
8. O Come, Little Children
9. The Birthday of a King
10. Still, Still, Still
11. Let There Be Peace on Earth
12. Your Favorite

Let your request be made known!

Stille Nacht
(Silent Night)

English

Silent night! Holy night! All is calm, all is bright.
Round yon virgin mother and child!
Holy infant, so tender and mild,
Sleep in heavenly peace,
Sleep in heavenly peace.

German

Stille nacht, heilige nacht!
Alles schläft, einsam wacht
nur das traute hochhelige Paar.
Holder Knabe im lockigen Haar,
schläft in himmlischer Ruh,
schläft in himmlischer Ruh.

– Joseph Mohr (1818)

December Theme — **HOLIDAY HAPPINESS**

Today's Theme — **Chanukah — The Festival of Lights**

Advanced
Preparation:
- Decorate the room with Chanukah symbols from a local store.
- Obtain a menorah, 9 candles, matches, 4" dreydl, and gelt for everyone (foil covered chocolates that resemble coins.)
- Ask Jewish children to join in the celebration.
- For the Education section, put all the points on large cards so as to distribute speaking parts.
- Provide potato latkes or jelly doughnuts as refreshments.

Pre-Session: Have a tape of lively Jewish music playing. For example "Tzena, Tzena," "Hava Nagila," "Matchmaker" and "Mazel Tov."

Opening: Greet each person with a handshake and "Hag sameach" which means "Happy Holidays."

Education: Children or Jewish residents should read the following background:
- Chanukah is a Jewish festival celebrating the victory of the Jewish people over the Syrians. It began in 175 B.C. when Antiochus Epiphanes ascended the throne.[1]
- Judea was under Syrian rule and the new monarch was so hungry for power and fame that he declared himself the living incarnation of the Greek god Zeus.
- Most Jews would not exchange their belief in one God. Antiochus was so obsessed with the idea of converting the population that he defiled the Temple and slaughtered hundreds of faithful Jews.
- In 165.B.C. after 3 years of fighting, the Jewish people, led by Judas Maccabeus marched to Jerusalem and overcame the enemy. They rededicated the Temple but found that the Syrians had taken most of the pure olive oil that was used to light the Menorah. There was only one day's supply left, and yet the menorah burned bright for 8 full days. This miracle has been celebrated ever since that day. Today we celebrate with both joy and solemnity.[2]

Observance: Jewish resident or guests light the 8 candles from the 9th or servant candle which should be placed higher that the rest in the menorah. Usually one candle is lit each day commemorating the miracle of light, however, if your program is on the fourth day, only three candles should be lit since the fourth should not be lit until sundown. A prayer for peace and justice would be appropriate.

Group Singing: "Rock of Ages."

Rock of ages, let our song praise Thy saving power

---

[1] Myers, R. (1972) *Celebrations* "Hanukkah" (sic) pp. 302-307.
[2] Points 2-4 in the Education section from Chiel, K. (1972) *The Complete Book of Hanukkah* "Hanukkah in History" pp. 2-6.

Group Singing; (Cont.)	Thou amidst the raging foes wast our sheltering tower. Furious they assailed us but Thine arm availed us And Thy word broke their sword when our own strength failed us.
Group Exercise:	All sing "I Have a Little Dreydl." Pianist continues to play the song. Give the dreydl to the first person and have them pass it along until the music stops. The one "caught" with the dreydl must raise arms up showing it to everyone. His prize is 6 pieces of gelt. Continue until there are four winners. Winners come forward to a game of dreydl. This traditional game is played only during Chanukah. The dreydl is a top with different Hebrew letters on each of its four sides. When spun, one of the letters will face up and instruct the player. If it is a "shin," the player must add his gelt to the pot; a "nun" means the player gets nothing; a "gimmel" means the player gets all; and a "hay" means that the player gets half. Keep at least six coins in the pot in case everything is won before all four players participate.[1]
Reminiscence:	The children can share their favorite Chanukah stories. They receive gifts each of the eight nights. Ask them about their favorite memories. Encourage adult discussion.
Group Singing:	One or two songs that have been chosen by the children could be sung here. All join in the festival favorites.
Closing:	Close the session with the group singing of "Hatikvah." Turn to the person beside you and say "Peace to you " or "L'Chaim." (A songsheet for "Hatikvah" is included at the end of this week's session plan.)
Refreshments:	Chocolate coins for everyone. Potato latkes or pancakes are the traditional Chanukah food which can be made earlier by volunteers or purchased at a deli and warmed up. Currently popular for a second choice are jelly doughnuts. Background music recommended for this include "Shalom," or "El-Shaddai."
Music Resources:	*Jewish Folk and Holiday Songs* (1978) "Hatikvah" p. 3 "Mazel Tov" p.11 "Rock of Ages" p.14 "Chanuka Song" p. 16 "Hava Nagila" p.6 *Songs We Sing* (1950) "I Have a Little Dreydl" p. 109 *Broadway Gold* (1982) "Shalom" p. 168 *Amy Grant's Greatest Hits* (1984) "El-Shaddai" p. 23 *Festival of Popular Songs* (1991) "Matchmaker" p. 188

---

[1] Personal interview with Jean Schneider, RMT at Jewish Center for the Aged, St. Louis, MO., August 18, 1992.

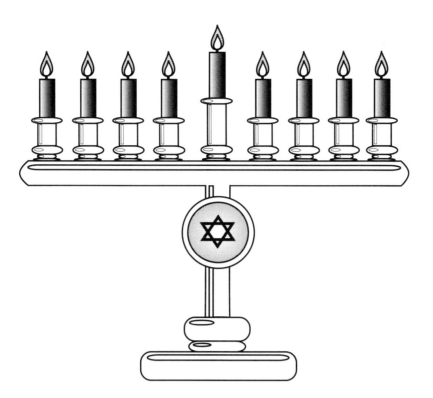

Chanukah Music Menu

1. Shalom
2. Hatikvah
3. El-Shaddai
4. Hava Nagila
5. Shalom Chaveyreem
6. I Have a Little Dreydl
7. Havenu Shalom Aleychem
8. Chanukah Oy Chanukah
9. Zum Gali Gali
10. Chanukah Song
11. Mazel Tov
12. Matchmaker

Hatikvah

Kalohd baleyvav p'neemah

Nefesh y'hoodee hohmeeyah,

Ool'fahahtey mizrach kahdeemah

Ahyin l' Tzeeyon tsohfeeyah;

ohd loh avdah tikvahteynu

Hatikvah shnoht ahlpahyim,

Lihyoht ahm chafshee b'ahrtsaynoo

b'ehretz Tzeeyon veerooshahlahyim.

Lihyoht ahm chafshee b'ahrtsaynoo

b'ehretz Tzeeyon veerooshahlahyim.

– (words) Naphtali Herz Imber (1895)

December Theme — **HOLIDAY HAPPINESS**

Today's Theme — **Celebrate Christmas — Five Possibilites**
(Optional)

Santa Comes by Helicopter

It truly is an intergenerational activity with the children, adults, and grandparents all anticipating Santa. Everyone joins in the singing of "Here Comes Santa Claus" and out of the skies comes a modern day version of that great man and his lady, Mrs. Santa. The cost is about $200 and worth a million. Santa knows everyone by name since it is a beloved volunteer or employee and he has a small gift for everyone.

Musical Christmas

Pianist invites residents with a personal invitation, either written or verbal, for a time of music reflecting the joy of Christmas Day. Music should include "O Come All Ye Faithful," "O Holy Night," "Hark the Herald Angels Sing," "It Came Upon the Midnight Clear," "O Little Town of Bethlehem," "Silent Night," "We Three Kings of Orient Are," "Angels We Have Heard on High," "Angels From the Realms of Glory," "Joy to the World," and ending with selections from the *Messiah*, especially the "Hallelujah Chorus." Singing can be encouraged, however songsheets should be **dis**couraged so everyone sings from the heart. Excellent arrangements are now available for piano with unusual chords and transitions. Run to your nearest music store and update your collection.

A Quiet Christmas

Peace on earth is experienced with adequate leadership. Invite anyone to attend and announce the goal of inner and outer peace. Suggest a short relaxation exercise. Invite a harpist or violinist to play some of the beloved Christmas songs. Absorb the beauty of the music and the moment. Close with "Let there be peace on earth and let it begin with me." Suggest that they take the peace they experienced and pass it along to others by quietly saying "Peace to you."

A Noisy Christmas

Not everyone gets invited out on December 25th so those that are indoors get to have a jolly time with Santa. Make sure he knows everyone by name. Mrs. Claus should come too and add to the merriment. Have them lead the songs of "Up on the Housetop," "Jolly Old St. Nicholas," "Here Comes Santa Claus," "Jingle Bells," "Rudolph the Red-Nosed Reindeer, and "We Wish You a Merry Christmas." If the group is creative, have them re-write "The Twelve days of Christmas" to apply to their feelings such as "'ten tons of laughter, nine nifty nurses,'"and so on.

Music Menu

Provide an attractive Christmas menu for each table. An example is included on the next page. Take requests from the families, children, residents and the staff and announce their names over the loudspeaker. Music and friendship fills the air.

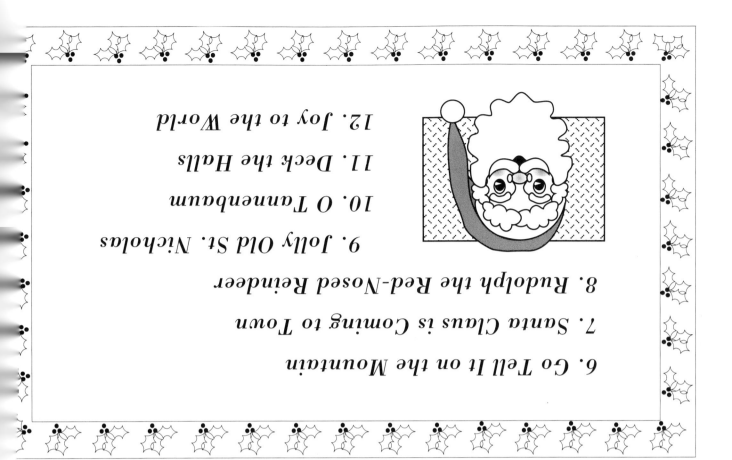

6. Go Tell It on the Mountain
7. Santa Claus is Coming to Town
8. Rudolph the Red-Nosed Reindeer
9. Jolly Old St. Nicholas
10. O Tannenbaum
11. Deck the Halls
12. Joy to the World

Music Menu for Christmas

1. O Holy Night
2. The Birthday of a King
3. The Little Drummer Boy
4. Hallelujah Chorus
5. The Christmas Song (Chestnuts Roasting on an Open Fire)

December Theme — **HOLIDAY HAPPINESS**

Today's Theme —   **Goodbye Old Year, Hello New**
(Optional)

Advanced
Preparation:
- Arrange for a few children to bring in their new Christmas toys and for a new baby to visit.
- Organize:plenty of reporters with pencils and pads,
- A celebration drink would be appropriate here.
- Props will include:
  - a collection of Goodbye and Hello songs,
  - 2 signs, one with the date of the old year, and one with the new.
  - a collection of silk scarves.

Pre-Session: Pianist plays Goodbye songs, such as "Aloha Oe" (Farewell to Thee) "Bye Bye Blackbird," "Bye Bye Blues," as everyone gathers.

Opening: Announce the theme of saying Goodbye to the old year and a warm welcome to the New. Open with the wisdom of the song "Make New Friends and Keep the Old" (one is silver, and the other is gold). Use two leaders and sing as a round 3 times each.

Exercise: Pass out silk scarves or colorful, glittery material for group exercise as everyone waves goodbye to the old year.
"Toot Toot Toosie (Goo' Bye)" — swing arms at side to the music.
"Bye Bye Blackbird" — Windshield wiper motions with scarves.
"Aloha Oe" (Farewell to Thee) — large, floating motions keeping the beat.
"So Long It's Been Good to Know You" — scarves up high waving goodbye.

Reminiscence: Reflect on what was good in the old year. Have the reporters write down the responses. Then discuss what anyone would like to see personally in the new year and record these answers.

Education: Invite any children present to show or demonstrate their new Christmas toys. Make this an intergenerational discussion and discover what toys are favorites with both generations such as building blocks, crayons, wooden toys, yo-yos, dolls, and teddy bears.

Group Singing: To the tune of "Goodnight Ladies," sing a farewell to the old year:

     Goodbye old year, goodbye old year,
     Goodbye old year, it's time for you to go.
     Merrily it rolled along, rolled along, rolled along,
     Merrily it rolled along, day by day by day.

Group Singing: (Cont.)	Hello new year, hello new year Hello new year, I welcome you today. Merrily you'll roll along, roll along, roll along. Merrily you'll roll along, I hope to stay that way.

Ask for any favorite songs of the old year sung during these sessions, or for any others that come to mind and sing as a group.

Song Identification: The following all have a goodbye or a farewell in the title. Identify it as quickly as possible. Display the sign of the old year.

GOODBYE Broadway, Hello France
BYE BYE Blackbird
BYE BYE BLUES
Toot Toot, Tootsie (GOO' BYE)
AUF WIEDERSEHN
SO LONG It's Been Good to Know You
SO LONG, FAREWELL

This next group is filled with Hello songs. Display the sign of the new year.

HELLO! Ma Baby
HELLO Muddah, HELLO Faddah ("The Dance of the Hours")
HELLO Young Lovers
HELLO, Central, Give Me Heaven
HELLO Dolly
Little Sir Echo (All responses are HELLO)

Rhythm Band: Welcome the new year with lots of rhythm instruments, encourage everyone to celebrate the fact that they have lived through the old one successfully and they will be given the gift of a brand new one.
"Hello! Ma Baby" — everyone joins in joyfully. (A songsheet is included at the end of the RAGTIME REVIEW [September] weeklysession plan.)
"Little Sir Echo" — pianist plays song, residents respond on the echo parts. Use a leader to direct group responses.
"Seventy-six Trombones" — spirited march.
"Stars and Stripes Forever" — welcomes in the new year.

Closing: "Auld Lang Syne": sing and play very deliberately with many long joyful sounds at the end. A songsheet is included at the end of this week's session plan.

Should auld acquaintance be forgot, and never brought to mind?
Should auld acquaintance be forgot, and days of auld lang syne?
For auld lang syne, my dear, for auld lang syne,
We'll take a cup of kindness yet, for auld lang syne.

Special Guest: A sweet new baby appears and greets everyone with the promise of a new year. A celebration drink is served.

Assignment: Invite participants to make only one new year resolution, write it down and begin living it today. Why wait?

Music
Resources: *Golden Book of Favorite Songs* (1946)
      "Auld Lang Syne" p. 37
Great Music's Greatest Hits (1982)
      "Stars and Stripes" p. 220
Legit Fake Book (1990)
      "Goodbye Broadway, Hello France" p. 121
      "Hello! Ma Baby" p. 144
      "Hello Young Lovers" p. 136
Ultimate Fake Book (1981)
      "So Long It's Been Good to Know You" p. 518
      "Bye Bye Blues" p. 65
      "So Long, Farewell" p. 516
Legal Fake Book (1979)
      "Auf Wiedersehn" p. 14
      "Bye Bye " p. 24
100 Hit Songs From Broadway's Greatest Musicals (1974)
      "Hello Dolly" p. 173
Popular Songs That Live Forever (1982)
      "Seventy-Six Trombones" p. 18

Music Menu

"GOODBYE"

(date)

Goodbye Old Year

1. Auf Wiedersehn

2. Bye Bye Blues

3. Bye Bye Blackbird

4. Toot, Toot, Tootsie (Goo' Bye)

5. So Long (It's Been Good to Know You)

6. Aloha Oe (Farewell to Thee)

"HELLO"

(date)

7. Hello! Ma Baby

8. Hello Young Lovers

9. Hello Dolly

10. Little Sir Echo (Hello)

11. Auld Lang Syne

Request your favorite
and I'll play it.

Auld Lang Syne

Should auld acquaintance be forgot
And never brought to mind?
Should auld acquaintance be forgot,
And days of auld lang syne?
For auld lang syne, my dear,
For auld lang syne;
We'll tak' a cup o' kindness yet,
For auld lang syne.

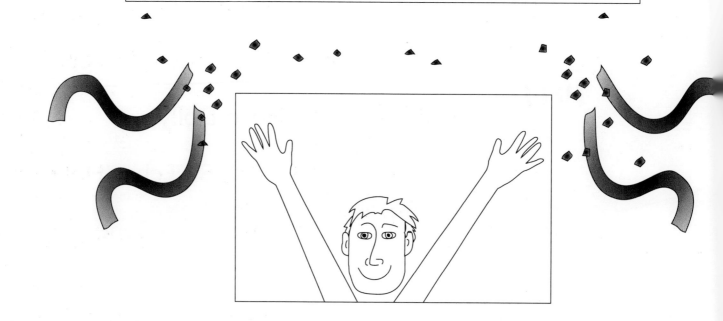

PART THREE

INDEX

General Index

Key to abbreviations
v.a. - visual aid (handout)

Page numbers in italics denote handout /perforated pages
Monthly titles are in bold print, and weekly session titles are in italics

Advanced Preparation, 15
America, the Beautiful
    General theme for July, 251-283
Animal Friends, 305-309
Apple v.a., *331*
"Apple Song," poem, 405-406
April, 149-182
    Theme: **It's a Sense-Sational Month**, 151
"Arrow and the Song," poem, 426
Assignment, 23.
    See individual programs
August, 285-316
    Theme: **In the Good Old Summer Time**, 287
Autoharp, 11
Automobiles, 345-350
Autumn, 400-404

Baseball, 239-243
Bell Band, 25
Birds, 197-201
Blue, 114-118
Blues, 114-118
Bone v.a., *384*
Bones, 397-384
Brides, 233-237
Bye Bye Blues, 114-118

Cars, 345-350
"Casey at the Bat," poem, 241
Celebrate Christmas — Five Possibilities, 465
Celebrations
    General theme for June, 219-250
Chants, 88, 209-210, 227, 265, 306, 361, 444
Chanukah — Festival of the Lights, 461-463
Church v.a., *344*
Christmas, 435-459, 465
Closing, 22-23
Colorful World, It's a, 111-148
Cost and Equipment, 9
Cruising Through January
    General theme for January, 31-61

Dads Are Dandy, 227-232
Dance, wheelchair, 53, 128, 411
Dear Old School Days, 325-332
December, 431-473
    Theme: **Holiday Happiness**, 435-436
Decoration Day, 215-217
Dietician, 360
Diploma v.a., *226*
Dolls, 299-303
Dreydl, game, 462

Easter Parade, 180-182
Education, 21
    See individual programs
Equipment, 9-12
Everyone Loves a Smile, 93-97
Everything's Coming Up Roses, 59-63
Exercise, 17
    See individual programs
Expanding your staff, 8
Extensions of the program, 23
Eyes, 163-169

Fall, 400-410
Fake Books, 11
Fashions, 333-338
Father's Day, 272-232
Favorites, 317-356
February, 65-109
    Theme: **It's a Love-ly Month,** 67
Flag Day, 245-250
Flower Power, 203-207
Food, 311-316, 360-366, 405-410
Format of the Program, 15
Fourth of July, 279-284
Freedom, 259-264
Friendship Poem, 69
Fruit nametags v.a., *366*
Fruitcake chant, 444
Fun, 385-389

Garden, 191-195, 203-209, 417-419
Germany, 47-51
Give Me That Old Time Religion, 339-344
Go Forth on the Fourth of July, 279--284
Goodbye Old Year, Hello New, 469-473
Graduation Now and Then, 222-226
Green, 127-132
Greeting, 17
    See individual programs
Groom, 233-237
Ground-Hog Day, 99-103
Group Discussion, 21
    See individual programs
Group Singing, 19-20
    See individual programs
"Growing Old is a Gentle Art," poem, 142
Guided Imagery, 17
Guided Imagery activities, 32,74, 163, 176, 191, 203, 209, 227, 265, 346, 374, 405, 412,456

Halloween, 385, 389, 391-395
Hail to the Chiefs, 105-109
Hands, 367-372; poem, 368; v.a., 372

Harvest, 405-410
Hawaii Bids You Welcome, 32-35
Health is Contagious
    General theme for October 357-395
Healthy Bones, 379-384
Healthy Fun, 385-389
Healthy Food, 360-366
Healthy Halloween, 391-395
Healthy Hands, 367-372
Healthy Hearts, 373-377
Helicopter, 465
Here Comes the Groom, 233-237
Hear Ye, Hear Ye, 152-155
Hearing, 152-155
Heart, 373-377; v.a., *372*
Hello Yellow, 133-139
Hello New Year, 469-473
History of America in Song, 254-258
Holidays
    New Year's, 469-473, 59-63
    Ground-Hog, 99-103
    Valentine's, 73-79
    President's Day, 105-109
    St. Patrick's, 127-129
    Easter, 209-214
    Flag Day, 245-249
    Mother's Day, 209-214
    Memorial Day, 215-217
    Father's Day, 227-231
    Fourth of July, 279-284
    Labor Day, 320-324
    Halloween, 385-396
    Veteran's Day, 259-264
    Thanksgiving Day, 411-424
    Christmas, 435-459, 465
    Chanukah, 461-463
Holiday Happiness
    General theme for December, 431-473
Hometown, 271-277
How's Your Taste, Bud?, 152-162

"I am in the pink" (tulip) v.a., *125*
"I am sunny" (starburst) v.a., *139*
"I did it" (heart) v.a., *404*
"I love music" (note) v.a., *404*
"I love _____" (heart) v.a., *79*
I Love You and Me, 68-71
"I taught _____" (apple) v.a., *331*
"I taught religion" (church) v.a., *344*
"I taught sunday school" (church) v.a., *344*
Ice cream cone v.a., *316*
Ice Cream—It's Cool, 311-316
"Ice Cream Man," poem, 312
Imagery, 17, *See also* Guided Imagery activities
"I'm oak-kay" (leaf) v.a., *404*
In Praise of Porches, 289
In the Good Old Summer Time
    General theme for August, 285-316
In the Pink, 119-125
Irish, 127-132
Italy, 37-46
Introduction, 3
It's a Colorful World
    General theme for March, 111-148

It's a Grand Old Flag, 245-250
It's a Love-ly Month
    General theme for February, 65-109
It's a Sense-Sational Month
    General theme for April, 149-179
It's Not Easy Being Green, 127-132

January, 29-63
    Theme: **Cruising Through January**, 31
Joy of Organization, 8
June, 219-250
    Theme: **Celebrations**, 221
July, 251-283
    Theme: **America, the Beautiful**, 253

Labor Day, 320-324; v.a,. 324
Labor Day v.a., *324*
Labor of Love, 320-324
Lace, 141-145
Ladies, 81-86
"Landing of the Pilgrim Fathers," poem, 411
Laughter, 385-389
Lavender and Old Lace, 141-145
Let's All Sing Like the Birdies Sing, 197-201
Lincoln, Abraham, 105-109
Love, 65-109
Love Those Ladies, 81-86
Love Those Stouthearted Men, 97-91

March, 111-148
    Theme: **It's a Colorful World**, 113
March Into Spring, 146-148
Marches
    March Into Spring, 145
    Easter Parade, 180-182
    Go Forth on the Fourth of July, 279-284
May, 183-218
    Theme: **Welcome Sweet Springtime**, 185
Memorable Memorial Day, 215-217
Memorial Day, 215-217
Men, 87-91
Month of Praise
    General theme for November, 387-429
Music, Praise for, 425-429
Music v.a., *414*
Music Games, 24, 30, 61, 112, 150, 184, 220, 252,
    281, 318, 358, 398, 432, 433
Music Menus, 23-24
    See every individual weekly program
Music Therapy Works, 7
    Examples, 8, 9, 10, 11, 16-19, 21-25
Music, Christmas, 465
My Hometown, 271-277

Names, 82-85, 88, 91
New Year's Day, 59-61, 469-473
"Night Before Christmas," poem, 452
Noisy Christmas, 465
November, 397-429
    Theme: **Month of Praise**, 399
North, South, East, West, 265-270
"Not In Vain," poem, 197-198
Note, music v.a., *404*

Occupations, 320-324
October, 357-395
    Theme: **Health is Contagious**, 359
Oh You Beautiful Doll, 299-303
Old Lace, 141-145
Old Year, 469-473
Olde Fashioned Favorites
    General theme for September, 317-356
Omnichord, 11
Organization, 8
Opening of Session, 16
Our History in Song, 254-258

Parades,
    Spring, 146-148
    Easter, 180-182
    Fourth of July, 279-284
Patriotic Songsheet, 250, 264
Pets, 305-309
Physical therapist, 373
Planting More Than Seeds, 191-195
Piano Recital, 293-298; v.a., *298*
Pink, 119-125
Porches Were Precious, 288-292
Purpose, 3
Praise for Autumn, 400-404
Praise for Music, 425-429
Praise for Thanksgiving, 417-424
Praise for Thanksliving, 411-416
Praise for the Harvest, 405-410
Preparation, 15
Pre-session, 15
Professions, 320-324, 88, 367-372
Promotional monthly sheet, 29, 60, 111, 149, 184, 219,
    251, 280, 312, 357, 397, 431
President's Day— Hail to the Chiefs, 105-109
Publicizing Your Theme, 9
Purple, 141-145

Quiet Christmas, 465

Ragtime Review, 351-356
Rationale and Goals, 3-7
Reach Out and Touch, 169-174
Recitals, 293-298
Relaxation, *see under* Guided Imagery, and Guided
    Imagery activities
Religion, 339-344; v.a., *344*
Reminiscence, 19
    See individual programs
Report card v.a., 332
Resources, 23, and Part Four, 485
Rhythm Band, 22
    See individual programs
Roses, 59-63, 175-179

School Days, 325,332; v.a., *331, 332*
Seeds, 191-195
Seeing is Believing, 163-167
Sensational month, 149-179
Senses, 149-179, 443-447
September, 317-356
    Theme: **Olde Fashioned Favorites**, 319
Sight, 163-167, 437-441

Sights of Christmas, 437-441
Singing, 19
Size of Group Session, 12-13
Smell, 175-179, 443-447
Smile, Everyone Loves a, 93-97
Solo Time, 21
    See individual programs
Song Identification, 21
    See individual programs
Sound, 152-155, 449-453
Sounds of Christmas, 449-453
South America Take it Away, 53-39
Spirit of Christmas, 455-467
Spring, 183-217, 197-201
Spring has Sprung, 186-190
Spring March, 146-148
Star v.a., *86, 92*
Stop and Smell the Roses, 175-179
Stouthearted Men, 87-91
Styles up to the Ankle, 333-338
Summer Time, in the Good Old, 285-316
Sunday school v.a., *344*

Take Me Out to the Ball Game, 239-243
Taste, 157-162
Teachers: school, 325,-331; piano, 293-298; religious,
    339-344
Thanksgiving, 417-424
Thanksliving, 411-416
There's Joy in Germany, 47-52
They Fought for Freedom, 259-264
Tone Bells, 11
Travel, 29-57, 265-270
Trees: program, 400-401; poem, 400-410; v.a., *404*
Trip to Sunny Italy, 37-46
Touch, 169-173
"Turkey Hunt," poem, 418

United States, 251-270
Universal Mothers Unite, 209-214

Valentine Love, 73-79
Veteran's Day, 259-264
"Visit from St. Nicholas," poem, 452
Volunteers, 8

Washington, George, 105-109
Weddings, 233-237
Welcome Sweet Springtime
    General theme for May, 183-217
"Whether the Weather be Cold," poem, 99
Wheelchair dance, 53, 128, 411
World War One songs s.s., 264

Ye Olde Fashioned Piano Recital, 293-298
Yellow, 133-139
You and Me, 68-71
You Auto Remember Your Automobile, 345-350

Song Title Index

Key to abbreviations
m. - music (in text)
s.s. - song sheet (handout)
l. - song lyrics (in text)
v.a. - visual aid (handout)

Page numbers in italics denote handout /perforated pages

Whever possible, song titles are listed in the book exactly as they appear in *The Great Song Thesaurus* (Lax and Smith, 1984). However, some of the song titles listed below and used in the book are titles that have been adapted by the author to fit certain activities. Also, where a certain **line** in the song is the more appropriate reference for that weekly activitiy, that line or sub-title is put in parentheses in the text.

A, You're Adorable, l. 325
Ac-cent-tchu-ate the Positive, l. 120; s.s., *124*
America, s.s., *258*
America, the Beautiful, verses 2 and 3 s.s., *258;* verses 1 and 2 s.s., *416*
Angels We Have Heard on High, s.s., *451*
Aren't You Glad You're You? l., 153
Auld Lang Syne, l., 470; s.s., *474*

Battle Hymn of the Republic, l., 164
Best Things in Life Are Free, The, s.s., *190*
Bill Grogan's Goat, l., 305-306
Bless This House, s.s., *107, 424*
Bye Bye Blues, l., 116
By the Beautiful Sea, s.s., *42*

Columbia, the Gem of the Ocean, *see also under* Three Cheers for the Red, White and Blue, 215; s.s., *250, 284*
Coming Round the Mountain, m., 457
Count Your Blessings, s.s., *423*
Country Gardens, l., 198, 205; m., 206

Dear Hearts and Gentle People, s.s., *276*
Deck the Halls, l., 385-386, 391, 437
Do-Re-Mi, l. 293-294
Drink to Me Only with Thine Eyes, s.s, *168*
Dry Bones, l. 379-380

Enjoy Yourself, It's Later Than You Think, l., 121

Father, m., 212;
Five Foot Two, Eyes of Blue, s.s., *338*
For Health and Strength, l., 360, 411, 417; m., 364
For He's a Jolly Good Fellow, s.s., *110*
Funiculi, Funicula, *v.a.* large print responses, 43-36; l., 37-38

Garden Song, m., 194
Gesundheit, l., 47, 367; m., 51
Give Me That Old Time Religion, l., 339
Golden Rule, l., 327
Gonna Lay Down My Blues Awhile, l., 115
Goodbye Children, l., 307
Goodbye Flappers, l., 334
Goodbye Old Year, l., 469

Goodbye Sportsfans, l., 241
Good Morning To You, m. 61
Good Morning Springtime, l., 203

Halloween song, 385-387, 391-393
Hail, Hail the Gang's All Here, l., 99, 186, 333
Hail to the Chiefs, m,. 108
Hatikvah, s.s., *464*
Happy Birthday, m., 61
Happy Farmer, m., 194
Happy Springtime, l., 186
Hello Ladies, l., 81
Hello Gentlemen, l., 87
Hello! Ma Baby, s.s., *356*
Hello Marchers, l., 182
Here We Go Round the Mulberry Bush, l., 209, 320
He's Got the Whole World in His Hands, l., 81, 87, 271, 339
Hokey-Pokey, l., 157-357

I am Thankful, l., 413
I Feel the Christmas Spirit, l., 455, m. 457
I Feel Wonderful, l., 362; m., 364
I (We) Have Such a Wonderful Memory, l., 120, 239-240
I Love Coffee, l., 157; m., 160
I Wish You...., l., 387, 393, 400, 405, 438, 443, 445, 451
Ich bin der Musikant, l., 47-48, 425-426; m., 51
If You're Happy and You Know It, l., 141, 222, 229, 320; m., 322
I'm Wild About Horns on Automobiles, l., 346
In My Merry Oldsmobile, s.s., *350*
In the Garden, s.s., *196*
In the Good Old Summer Time, l., 311; s.s., *244, 292*
It Isn't Any Trouble Just to S-M-I-L-E, l., 94
It's a Good Time to Get Acquainted, l., 265
It's a Long Way to Tipperary, s.s., *264*
It's Love That Makes the World Go 'Round, l., 71, 71, 159, 233; m., 70
I've Got Music in My Hands, l., 74, 152, 367, 374, 381, 425; m., 75
I Want a Girl—Just Like the Girl That Married Dear Old Dad, s.s., *238*

Peace Like a River, l., 456; m., 458

I Love You Truly, s.s., *72*
I've Got That Joy, l., 119

K-K-K-Katy, s.s., *264*

La Cucaracha, l., 53
Last Night on the Back Porch—I Loved Her Most of All, l.,
    289
Let's All Do a Little Waving, l., 437, 449
Let's All Sing Like the Birdies Sing, w,. 121, 199; m., 200
Little Sir Echo, l., 114-115, 254
Look for the Silver Lining, l., 100; s.s., *118*
Love is Something, l., 94
Love's Old Sweet Song, s.s., *78*

Make New Friends , l., 59, 68, 292, 299, 469
More We Get Together, The, l., 49, 175, 417
M-O-T-H-E-R, l., 210; m., 212; s.s., *214*
Music Alone Shall Live, l., 428; m. 428
Must Be Santa, l., 437-438; m. 440
My Hand on My Head, l., 169; m., 172
My Wild Irish Rose, s.s., *64*

O Christmas Tree, l., 443, s.s., *52, 442*
O Tannenbaum, l., 443; s.s., *52, 442*
Oh Where, Oh Where Has My Little Dog Gone? s.s., *310*
Oh You Beautiful Doll, s.s., *304*
Old Abe Lincoln, l., 107
On Top of Spaghetti, l., 158
Once I Had a Pumpkin, l., 386
Open Up Your Heart, l., 133-134; s.s., *138*
Over the River and Through the Woods, s.s., *422*
Over There, s.s., *264*

Pack up Your Trouble, l., 93; s.s., *264*
Peg o' My Heart, s.s., *378*
Playmates, l., 299
Praise to the Ladies, l., 209
Put on Your Old Grey Bonnet, s.s, *174*

Reach Out and Touch, l., 169, 369; m., 172
Ring, Ring, Ring the Bells, l., 438, 450
Robin Was It's Name, l., 197
Rock of Ages, l., 462

Sailing, s.s., *36*
School Days, s.s., *330*
See the USA In Your Chevrolet, m., 348
Shalom, l., 341
Shine on Harvest Moon, s.s., *404*
Silent Night, s.s., *460*
Silver Bells, l., 450
Sippin' Cider Through a Straw, l., 361-362
Smile a While, l., 93, 163, 367
Smiles, s.s., *98*
So Long Ladies, l., 83
So Long Gentlemen, l., 89
Steven Got Even, l., 346
Stille Nacht, s.s., *460*
Still, Still, Still, l., 456; m., 458
Styles up to the Ankle, l., 333
Sweet Adeline, l., 204
Swing Low Sweet Chariot, m., 339

Ta-Ra-Ra-Boom-De-Ay, s.s., *390*
Tea for Two, l., 69
Thank God for the Sunshine, l., 133, 191, 305
There are Many Flags, s.s., *250*
There's a Long, Long Trail, s.s., *264*
Three Cheers for the Red, White and Blue, l., 245, s.s.,
    250, 284
Till We Meet Again, l., 93, s.s., *264*
Tiny Bubbles, l., 33
Top of the Morning to You, l., 127
Turkey Dinner, l., 417
Turkey in the Straw, s.s., *202*
Twelve Days of Christmas, l., 450
Twelve Days of Halloween, l., 392

Ummmmm Good, l., 257

Vive La Compagnie, l., 379

Wave that Branch, l., 443
We're Old and We're Proud of It, l., 141, 154; m., 144
What Did Delaware? l., 266; m., 267; s.s., *270*
When Johnny Comes Marching Home Again, l., 89
When Irish Eyes are Smiling, s.s., *132*
Where are the _____? l., 148, 181-182, 186,
    227, 280
When the Roll is Called Up Yonder, s.s., *448*
Whistle While You Work, l., 321
World War One songs, s.s., *264*

Yes! We Have No Bananas, l., 159; s.s., *162*
You're a Grand Old Flag, l., 250, s.s., *218, 250*

Zum Gali, Gali, l., 340

PART FOUR

RESOURCES

Music Book Resource List

All American Song Book. Miami: Big 3 Publication CPP Belwin. 1984.
Amy Grant's Greatest Hits, Edited by J. Thompson. Milwaukee WI: Hal Leornard Pub. 1984.
Best Fake Book Ever. Milwaukee, WI: Hal Leonard. 1990.
Best of Irish Music. Ojai, CA: Creative Concerns, 1992.
Broadway Gold. Milwaukee, WI: Hal Leonard Pub. 1982
Children's Song Book. Pleasantville, NY: Readers Digest, 1988.
Collected Piano Works of Scott Joplin, Edited by V. Lawrence. New York: Public Library (This edition distributed by Belwin-Mills Publishing Corp.) 1972.
Country Western Song Book. Pleasantville, NY: Readers Digest, 1983.
Disney Collection of Songs. Milwaukee, WI: Leonard Pub., 1990.
Everybody's Favorite Songs. New York: Amsco Pub., 1933.
Family Song Book of Faith and Joy. Pleasantville, NY: Readers Digest, 1981.
Favorite Hawaiian Songs,. Milwaukee, WI: Hal Leonard, 1989.
Festival of Popular Songs. Pleasantville, NY: Readers Digest, 1977.
Fireside Book of Children's Songs. New York: Simon and Schuster, 1966.
Germania Album, A. Fassio & Edward Marcus. Milwaukee: Hal Leonard, 1934 (Reprint)
Golden Book of Favorite Songs, Schmitt, Hall, McCreary. Melville, NY: Belwin Mills, 1946.
Greatest Legal Fake Book of All Times. Secaucus, NJ: Warner Bros., 1985.
Greatest Songs of 1890-1920. Hialeah, FL: New Home Library Series, CPP Belwin. 1990.
Great Latin American Song Book. Katonah, NY: Ekay Music, 1985.
Great Music's Greatest Hits. Pleasantville, NY: Readers Digest 1982.
Irving Berlin's Best Song Collection. New York: Irving Berlin Music Corp. 1964.
Jewish Folk and Holiday Songs. Miami, FL: John Schaum. 1978 (Reprint).
Latin American Music. Milwaukee: John Schaum Pub., 1969.
Legal Fake Book. Miami: Warner Bros. Hanson House, 1979.
Legion Airs Songs of "Over There" and "Over Here." Frank Peat and L. Smith. New York: Leo Feist Inc., 1932.
Legit Fake Book, Edited by R. Wolfe. Miami FL: CPP Belwin, 1990.
Masterpieces of Piano Music. New York: Fischer, 1918.
Merry Christmas Song Book. Pleasantville, NY: Readers Digest, 1981 edition and 1987.
Mitch Miller Community Song Book, G. Freedman. New York: Remick Corp, 1962.
New Oxford Book of English Verse. Edited by H. Gardner. New York: Oxford University Press. 1972.
100 Hit Songs from Broadway's Greatest Musicals New York: M.F. Productions, Inc. 1974.
One Thousand and One Jumbo (Fake Book with words and music). Las Vegas: TVegas Songs Inc. 1985.
Popular Songs Live Forever. Pleasantville, NY: Readers Digest, 1982.
Remembering the Fifties. Pleasantville, NY: Readers Digest, 1992.
Selections from the Messiah. Edited by David Jessie. Secaucus, NJ: WB Music. 1986.
Sigmund Spaeth's Song Session Community Song Book . Arr. Don Wilson. Secaucus, NJ: Warner Bros. 1958.
Sing Together 3rd Edition. Girl Scouts of the USA. New York: Girl Scout Inc. 1973.
Sixty Progressive Piano Pieces. New York: G. Shirmer, 1938.
Song Session Community Song Book. D. Wilson. Secaucus, NJ: Warner Bros., 1953.
Songs for Swinging Housemothers. Frank Lynn. San Francisco: Chandler Pub. Co. 1961.
Songs of the Gay Nineties, Bill Hardey. New York: Robbins Music Corp., 1942.
Songs of the 1950s, Milwaukee, WI: Hal Leonard. 1988.
Songs We Sing, Edited by H. Coppersmith. Philadelphia, PA: Jewish Publication Society of America, 1950.
Sunny Italy's Folk Songs and Dances, Milwaukee, WI: John Schaum Pub. 1983.
The Original, Legal Musicians Fake Book, Miami, FL: Hansen House. 1980.
Treasury of Best Loved Songs, Pleasantville, NJ: Readers Digest, 1981.
Treasury of Grand Opera, Edited by Henry Simon. New York: Simon and Shuster, 1946.
Tune Book Songs, Yohann Anderson. San Anselmo, CA: Songs and Creations, 1982.
T.V. Theme Song Sing-Along, Song Book. J. Javna. New York: St. Martin's Press, 1984.
Ultimate Fake Book, Milwaukee: Hal Leonard Pub. 1981.
Wee Sing and Play Musical Games. Los Angeles: Price, Stern, Sloan, 1986.
Wee Sing America. Los Angeles: Price, Stern, Sloan, 1988.
Wee Sing Around the Campfire. Los Angeles: Price, Stern, Sloan, 1984.
Wee Sing Bible Songs. Los Angeles: Price, Stern, Sloan, 1986.
Wee Sing Children's Songs. Los Angeles: Price, Stern, Sloan, 1986.
Wee Sing for Christmas. Los Angeles: Price, Stern, Sloan, 1986.
Wee Sing Silly Songs. Los Angeles: Price, Stern, Sloan, 1984.
Wee Sing for Christmas. Los Angeles: Price, Stern, Sloan, 1986.
Wings of Song. Unity Village, MO: Unity School of Christianity, 1984.

Book Resource List

American Music Conference: *Review of US Music Industry*. Carlsbad, CA: Music USA Publications. 1991.

American Treasury 1955. New York: Harper. 1955.

Ashworth, E. 1982. *Let's Talk*. Berkeley, CA: L'Anciana Press.

Atlas of the United States 1986. New York: Macmillan.

Bailey, S. 1982. *Big Book of Baby Names*. Tuscon, AZ: HP Books.

Bauer, C. 1985. *Celebrations*. Bronx, NY: Wilson Co.

Berlin, E. 1980. *Ragtime*. Berkeley, CA: University of California Press.

Bitcon, C. 1976. *Alike and Different*. Santa Ana, CA: Rasha Press.

Blesh, R. and H. Janis. 1971. *They All Played Ragtime*. New York: Oak Publications.

Boehn, Max von. 1972. *Dolls*. New York: Dover Publications.

Bright, R. 1981. *Practical Planning in Music Therapy for the Aged*. Lynbrook, NY: Musicgraphics.

_____1991. *Music in Geriatric Care: A Second Look*. Wahroonga, New South Wales, Australia: Music Therapy Enterprises.

Butler, R. 1975. *Why Survive? Being Old in America*. New York: Harper and Row.

_____ and M. Lewis. 1982. *Aging and Mental Health*. St. Louis, MP: Moscy Co.

Chases Annual Events. 1992 and 1993. Chicago: Contemporary Books.

Cheil, K. 1972. *The Complete Book of Hanukkah*. (sic) New York: Friendly House Publishers.

Ciolfi M., Dearling, Z. A., Summers, D., and L.A. Wasserman. 1988. *Sense Up*. St. Louis, MO: Jewish Center for the Aged.

Comfort, A. 1976. *A Good Age*. New York: Crown Publishers.

Complete Words of James Whitcomb Riley 1937. New York: Grosset and Dunlap.

Coni, N., W. Davison, and S. Webster. 1984. *Ageing, (sic.)The Facts*. New York: Oxford Press.

Cosby, W. and A. Poussant. 1987. *Time Flies*. New York: Doubleday.

Dictionary of Musical Quotations. 1985. New York: Shirmer/Macmillan.

Downs, H. 1975. *30 Dirty Lies about Old*. Niles, IL: Argos.

Erb. R. 1968. *Common Sense of Smell*. Los Angeles, CA: World Pub.

Edwards, T. 1936. *New Dictionary of Thoughts*. New York: Standard Book Co.

Encyclopedia Americana 1990. Danbury, Conn: Grolier Inc.

Encyclopedia of Science and Technology 1992. New York: McGraw Hill.

Faires, D. 1987. *Older is Beautiful, Too*. Hazelwood, MO: Shalom Publications.

Favorite Poems Old and New. 1957. Edited by Helen Ferris. Garden City, NY: Doubleday.

Ferguson, M. 1980. *The Acquarian Conspiracy*. Los Angeles: Tarcher.

Gibran, Kahlil. 1968. *The Prophet*. New York: Alfred Knopf.

Girl Scout Handbook, (1933) (Revised 1967). New York: Girl Scout Inc.

Gaston, D.T. 1968. *Music in Therapy*. New York: Macmillan.

Hendricks, J. 1982. *Aging in Mass Society*. Cambridge, MA: Winthrop Publications.

Hodges, D. 1980. *Handbook of Music Psychology*. Washington, DC: National Association of Music Therapy.

Information Please Almanac, 1992. Boston: Houghton Mifflin.

Karras, B. 1988. *With a Smile and a Song*. Mt. Airy, MD: Eldersong Publications.

_____. 1985. *Down Memory Lane*. Mt. Airy, MD: Eldersong Publications.

Kolatch, A. 1986. *Name Dictionary*. Flushing, NY: Jonathan David.

Lansky, B. and V. Lansky 1984. *Best Baby Name Book*. Wayzata, MN: Meadowbank Press.

Lax, R. and F. Smith 1984. *The Great Song Thesaurus*. New York: Oxford University Press.

McCann, R. 1932. *Complete Cheerful Cherub*. New York: Covici Friede.

Myers, R. 1972. *Celebrations*. Garden City, NY: DoubleDay.

Neely, M.E. Jr. 1982. *Abraham Lincoln Encyclopedia*. New York: McGraw Hill.

New Oxford Book of English Verse, 1972. Edited by H. Gardner. New York: Oxford University Press.

One Hundred and One Famous Poems, 1958. Edited by Roy J. Cook. Chicago, IL: Contemporary Books.

Older is Beautiful, Too, 1987. Hazelwood, MO: Shalom Publications.[1]

Porcino, Dr. Jane. 1984. *Growing Older, Getting Better*. Reading, Mass: Addison-Wesley Pub.

Read, H. 1977. *Morning Chores and Other Times Remembered*. Champaign, IL: University of Illinois Press.

Rosenkrantz, L. and P. Satran. 1988. *Beyond Jennifer and Jason*. New York: St. Martin's Press.

Rupp, R. 1987. *Blue Corn and Square Tomatoes*. Pownal, VT: Garden Way Publishing (Storey Communications).

Safire, W. and L. Safir. 1982. *Good Advice*. New York: New York Times Books.

Sandell, S.L. and D.R. Johnson. 1987. *Waiting at the Gate: Creativity and Hope in the Nursing Home*. New York: Haworth Press.

Saul, S. 1974. *Aging*. New York: Wiley and Sons.

Schafer, W. and J. Riedel 1974. *The Art of Ragtime*. Baton Rouge: Louisiana State University Press.

Shullian, D and M. Schoen. 1948. *Music and Medicine*. New York: Henry Schuman, Inc.

---

[1] Songs from this publication used by permission of Shalom Publications, 7225 Berkridge, Hazelwood, MO 63042.

Siegel, B. 1988. *Love, Medicine and Miracles.* New York: Harper and Row.
Smith, L. 1978. *The Mother Book.* New York: Doubleday.
Stewart, G. 1979. *American Given Names.* New York: Oxford University Press.
Taylor, T. 1972. *Book of American Presidents.* Salem, MA: Arno Press, Ayer Co.
Train, J. 1977. *Remarkable Names of Real People.* New York: Clarkson Potter Pub. distr. by Crown.
Treasury of the Familiar. 1950. Edited by R. Woods. New York: Macmillan.
Wenrick, N. 1972. *So Much More Than a Singalong.* Long Beach CA: Therapeutical Arts Materials.
Whitfield, P. 1984. *Hearing, Taste and Smell.* Tarrington, NY: Torstar Press.
World Book Encyclopedia 1991. Chicago, IL: World Book Inc.
World Almanac, 1991 and 1992. NY: Scripps Howard.

Recommended Geriatric Resources

The following are available from MMB Music, Inc.
MMB HORIZON SERIES
PO Box 32410
10370 Page Industrial Blvd.
St. Louis, MO 63132.

Accent on Rhythm, Donna Douglass, RMT-BC
Music Therapy and the Dementias, Ruth Bright, CMT
Guided Imagery and Music, Lisa Summer, RMT-BC
Risk It. . . . Express, Carol Bitcon, RMT-BC